Embedded Linux Development Using Yocto Project Cookbook
Second Edition

Practical recipes to help you leverage the power of Yocto to build exciting Linux-based systems

Alex González

BIRMINGHAM - MUMBAI

Embedded Linux Development Using Yocto Project Cookbook
Second Edition

Commissioning Editor: Gebin George
Acquisition Editor: Prachi Bisht
Content Development Editor: Dattatraya More
Technical Editor: Jovita Alva
Copy Editor: Safis Editing
Project Coordinator: Shweta H Birwatkar
Proofreader: Safis Editing
Indexer: Francy Puthiry
Graphics: Tania Dutta
Production Coordinator: Arvindkumar Gupta

First published: March 2015
Second edition: January 2018

Production reference: 1240118

Published by Packt Publishing Ltd.
Livery Place
35 Livery Street
Birmingham
B3 2PB, UK.

ISBN 978-1-78839-921-0

www.packtpub.com

I dedicate this second edition to the loving memory of my mum whose example makes me constantly challenge myself.

`mapt.io`

Mapt is an online digital library that gives you full access to over 5,000 books and videos, as well as industry leading tools to help you plan your personal development and advance your career. For more information, please visit our website.

Why subscribe?

- Spend less time learning and more time coding with practical eBooks and Videos from over 4,000 industry professionals
- Improve your learning with Skill Plans built especially for you
- Get a free eBook or video every month
- Mapt is fully searchable
- Copy and paste, print, and bookmark content

PacktPub.com

Did you know that Packt offers eBook versions of every book published, with PDF and ePub files available? You can upgrade to the eBook version at `www.PacktPub.com` and as a print book customer, you are entitled to a discount on the eBook copy. Get in touch with us at `service@packtpub.com` for more details.

At `www.PacktPub.com`, you can also read a collection of free technical articles, sign up for a range of free newsletters, and receive exclusive discounts and offers on Packt books and eBooks.

Foreword

Adoption of Linux continues to grow year by year, with the majority of growth in the area of embedded systems. While it is possible to build an embedded Linux operating system from scratch, it is hard work and error prone. Thankfully, there is a better way—using the BitBake build tool, the OpenEmbedded Core metadata and the Poky distribution, which, together, make up the Yocto Project.

Since its inception in 2010, the Yocto Project has progressed to become the de facto build system for a wide range of appliances and devices running Linux. Now, with the advent of the connected world known as the Internet of Things, the Yocto Project is taking on a key role in creating the backbone operating systems for devices that we rely on every day. So, the Yocto Project does not stand still, it has to continually evolve to cater for current generations of hardware and to support the tools and applications used in modern connected devices.

However, as anyone who has dipped a toe into the Yocto Project pool will know, the water gets deep very quickly. The flexibility of the Yocto Project means that you need to be aware of many concepts if you are to make best use of the tool. I heartily recommend this book as your lifesaver! Alex's thorough understanding of the topic, coupled with a practical approach to problem solving, makes this an easy-to-read, essential companion that will help you not only to keep your head above water but to become a proficient swimmer.

This second edition of *Embedded Linux Development Using Yocto Project Cookbook* follows in the same style and technical content as the first, but has been refreshed and extended to describe the current versions of the Yocto Project. Alex's deep understanding of the Yocto Project conjoins with his practical knowledge of the subject to produce a practical guide to the Yocto Project. The cookbook style allows you to dip in and out as needed to find answers to particular problems. Alex always adds pointers to more detailed descriptions of the problems covered, so that, step by step, you can build up a thorough understanding of the underlying principles. As an educator, I am always looking for books to recommend to my students. This is at the top of my list when teaching people about the Yocto Project.

Chris Simmonds

Founder of 2net.co.uk, author and teacher

Contributors

About the author

Alex González is a software engineering supervisor at Digi International and product owner of the Digi Embedded Yocto distribution. He started working professionally with embedded systems in 1999 and the Linux kernel in 2004, designing products for voice and video over IP networks, and followed his interests into machine-to-machine (M2M) technologies and the Internet of Things. Born and raised in Bilbao, Spain, Alex has an electronic engineering degree from the University of the Basque Country and he received his MSc in communication systems from the University of Portsmouth.

I would like to thank the Yocto and OpenEmbedded communities, whose dedication keep the Yocto Project running, and the people involved with the Freescale BSP community layer, whose joint work is the basis for this book.

Also, the amazing people who work with me on a daily basis and from whom I am constantly learning, and especially to Javier Viguera for his efforts in thoroughly reviewing the contents of the book.

About the reviewer

Javier Viguera has been a Linux fan since the mid-1990s, when he managed to install Slackware at home to avoid fighting for a two hour slot in the university's computer lab.

With a master's degree in telecommunications engineering and a bachelor's degree in computer science, he is currently working at Digi International as an embedded software engineer.

Living in La Rioja, Spain, in his spare time Javier likes to see good classical movies. He is also a fan of airplanes and aviation.

I would like to thank the author Alex, for this opportunity. Also, and especially, my wife and daughter for supporting me during the review.

Packt is searching for authors like you

If you're interested in becoming an author for Packt, please visit authors.packtpub.com and apply today. We have worked with thousands of developers and tech professionals, just like you, to help them share their insight with the global tech community. You can make a general application, apply for a specific hot topic that we are recruiting an author for, or submit your own idea.

Table of Contents

Preface

A few years ago, embedded would have been a synonym for a small, resource-constrained, dedicated system. Nowadays, it's easy to find embedded systems with 1 GB or more of memory, plenty of storage, and dedicated hardware accelerators for things such as graphics, video, cryptography, and even high-end 64-bit multicore systems.

The embedded space is split between small microcontroller-based systems that are direct successors of the embedded systems from a few years back, and a new generation of embedded Linux-based systems which require a different set of tools, skills, and workflows to develop them.

Since the first edition of this book was published, the embedded Linux space has started to be influenced by young engineers with roots in the maker movement who are used to the rapid prototyping of products and ideas with Raspberry Pi-like hardware and PC-like distributions such as Debian, as well as the emergence of the Internet of Things as a disruptive force. This has brought the security of always-available, cloud-connected embedded devices to the front line, but has also blurred the line between professional embedded Linux systems and hobbyist products.

Still, professional embedded systems have a distinct set of requirements that are common to all of them:

- Industrial specifications, robustness, and reliability
- Dedicated optimized applications
- Security guarantees
- Remote and secure over-the-air updates
- Power management considerations
- Fast startup time
- Graphical user interfaces
- Some degree of real-time capabilities
- Long maintenance of line both for hardware and software, usually above 5 years.

When designing embedded products with the preceding requirements in mind, it is clear that educational hardware and desktop-oriented distributions are never going to be able to provide the level of control, configurability, and flexibility needed to design a professional embedded product.

This is why the Yocto Project remains the chosen embedded Linux builder for professional systems. It's flexibility and scalability allows it to build resource-constrained low-end to high-end embedded Linux products and adapt software accordingly.

In this new edition, the content has been completely reviewed and updated to the Yocto Project 2.4 release, and new content has been added to address some of the changes and trends that have appeared since the first edition was published.

Who this book is for

This book is the ideal way for embedded developers learning about embedded Linux and the Yocto project to become proficient and broaden their knowledge with examples that are immediately applicable to embedded developments.

Experienced embedded Yocto developers will find new insights into working methodologies and ARM-specific development competence.

What this book covers

Chapter 1, *The Build System*, describes and uses the Poky build system and extends it to the Freescale BSP Community layer. It also describes common build system configurations and features to optimize the build of target images, including the use of Toaster and Docker.

Chapter 2, *The BSP Layer*, guides the reader through the customization of the BSP for their own product. It then explains how to configure, modify, build, and debug the U-Boot boot loader, Linux kernel, and its device tree.

Chapter 3, *The Software Layer*, describes the process of creating a new software layer to hold new applications, services, or modifications to existing packages; explains size and security optimization methodologies for both the Linux kernel and the root filesystem; and discusses a release process for license compliance.

Chapter 4, *Application Development*, starts by introducing both the standard and extensible SDKs, and deals with application development in detail, including different graphical backends and development environments such as Eclipse and Qt Creator, and recipe creation for different programming languages.

Chapter 5, *Debugging, Tracing and Profiling*, discusses debugging tools and techniques, and explores the tracing functionalities offered by the Linux kernel along with some of the user space tracing and profiling tools that make use of them.

To get the most out of this book

This books assumes some basic working knowledge of GNU/Linux systems and applications such as the bash shell and derivatives, as well as standard tools such as grep, patch, and diff. The examples have been tested with an Ubuntu 16.04 LTS system, but any Linux distribution supported by the Yocto project can be used.

The book is structured to follow the usual development workflow of an embedded Linux product, but chapters, or even individual recipes, can be read independently.

Recipes take a practical, hands-on approach using an NXP i.MX6-based system, the Wandboard Quad, as base hardware. However, any other i.MX-based hardware can be used to follow the examples.

Download the example code files

You can download the example code files for this book from your account at www.packtpub.com. If you purchased this book elsewhere, you can visit www.packtpub.com/support and register to have the files emailed directly to you.

You can download the code files by following these steps:

1. Log in or register at www.packtpub.com.
2. Select the **SUPPORT** tab.
3. Click on **Code Downloads & Errata**.
4. Enter the name of the book in the **Search** box and follow the onscreen instructions.

Once the file is downloaded, please make sure that you unzip or extract the folder using the latest version of:

- WinRAR/7-Zip for Windows
- Zipeg/iZip/UnRarX for Mac
- 7-Zip/PeaZip for Linux

The code bundle for the book is also hosted on GitHub at https://github.com/PacktPublishing/Embedded-Linux-Development-Using-Yocto-Project-Cookbook-Second-Edition. We also have other code bundles from our rich catalog of books and videos available at https://github.com/PacktPublishing/. Check them out!

Download the color images

We also provide a PDF file that has color images of the screenshots/diagrams used in this book. You can download it here:
http://www.packtpub.com/sites/default/files/downloads/EmbeddedLinuxDevelopmentU singYoctoProjectCookbookSecondEdition_ColorImages.pdf.

Conventions used

There are a number of text conventions used throughout this book.

CodeInText: Indicates code words in text, database table names, folder names, filenames, file extensions, pathnames, dummy URLs, user input, and Twitter handles. Here is an example: "In this case, both imx6q.dtsi and ;imx6qdl-wandboard-revd1.dtsi are overlaid with the contents of imx6qp-wandboard-revd1.dts."

A block of code is set as follows:

```
#include "imx6q-wandboard-revd1.dts"
#include "imx6qp.dtsi"
/ {
        model = "Wandboard i.MX6QuadPlus rev.D1";
};
```

When we wish to draw your attention to a particular part of a code block, the relevant lines or items are set in bold:

```
# Allow override of WANDBOARD_GITHUB_MIRROR to make use of
# local repository easier
WANDBOARD_GITHUB_MIRROR ?= "git://github.com/wandboard-org/linux.git"
```

Any command-line input or output is written as follows:

```
$ cd /opt/yocto/fsl-community-bsp/wandboard/tmp/deploy/sdk/
$ ./poky-glibc-x86_64-core-image-minimal-cortexa9hf-neon-toolchain-2.4.sh
```

Bold: Indicates a new term, an important word, or words that you see onscreen. For example, words in menus or dialog boxes appear in the text like this. Here is an example: "Build the project by going to **Project | Build Project**."

Warnings or important notes appear like this.

Tips and tricks appear like this.

Get in touch

Feedback from our readers is always welcome.

General feedback: Email `feedback@packtpub.com` and mention the book title in the subject of your message. If you have questions about any aspect of this book, please email us at `questions@packtpub.com`.

Errata: Although we have taken every care to ensure the accuracy of our content, mistakes do happen. If you have found a mistake in this book, we would be grateful if you would report this to us. Please visit `www.packtpub.com/submit-errata`, selecting your book, clicking on the Errata Submission Form link, and entering the details.

Piracy: If you come across any illegal copies of our works in any form on the Internet, we would be grateful if you would provide us with the location address or website name. Please contact us at `copyright@packtpub.com` with a link to the material.

If you are interested in becoming an author: If there is a topic that you have expertise in and you are interested in either writing or contributing to a book, please visit `authors.packtpub.com`.

Reviews

Please leave a review. Once you have read and used this book, why not leave a review on the site that you purchased it from? Potential readers can then see and use your unbiased opinion to make purchase decisions, we at Packt can understand what you think about our products, and our authors can see your feedback on their book. Thank you!

For more information about Packt, please visit `packtpub.com`.

1
The Build System

In this chapter, we will cover the following recipes:

- Setting up the host system
- Installing Poky
- Creating a build directory
- Building your first image
- Explaining the NXP Yocto ecosystem
- Installing support for NXP hardware
- Building Wandboard images
- Using the Toaster web interface
- Running a Toaster Docker container
- Configuring network booting for a development setup
- Using Docker as a Yocto build system container
- Sharing downloads
- Sharing the shared state cache
- Setting up a package feed
- Using build history
- Working with build statistics
- Debugging the build system

Introduction

The Yocto Project (http://www.yoctoproject.org/) is an embedded Linux distribution builder that makes use of several other open source projects. In this book, the generic term *Yocto* refers to the Yocto Project.

A Linux distribution is a collection of software packages and policies, and there are hundreds of Linux distributions available. Most of these are not designed for embedded systems and they lack the flexibility needed to accomplish target footprint sizes and functionality tweaks, as well as not catering well for resource constrained systems.

The Yocto Project, in contrast, is not a distribution per se; it allows you to create a Linux distribution designed for your particular embedded system. The Yocto Project provides a reference distribution for embedded Linux, called **Poky**.

The Yocto Project has the **BitBake** and **OpenEmbedded-Core** (**OE-Core**) projects at its base. Together they form the Yocto build system which builds the components needed for an embedded Linux product, namely:

- A bootloader image
- A Linux kernel image
- A root filesystem image
- Toolchains and **software development kits** (**SDKs**) for application development

With these, the Yocto Project covers the needs of both system and application developers. When the Yocto Project is used as an integration environment for bootloaders, the Linux kernel, and user space applications, we refer to it as system development.

For application development, the Yocto Project builds SDKs that enable the development of applications independently of the Yocto build system.

The Yocto Project makes a new release every 6 months. The latest release at the time of this writing is Yocto 2.4 Rocko, and all the examples in this book refer to the 2.4 release.

A Yocto release comprises the following components:

- Poky, the reference build system and distribution
- **Board Support Packages** (**BSPs**) with the recipes needed to support different architectures and boards
- Build Appliance, a virtual machine image ready to use Yocto
- Standard and extensible SDKs for the host system
- Eclipse plugins

And for the different supported platforms:

- Prebuilt toolchains
- Prebuilt images

The Yocto 2.4 release is available to download from
`http://downloads.yoctoproject.org/releases/yocto/yocto-2.4/`.

Setting up the host system

This recipe will explain how to set up a host Linux system to use the Yocto Project.

Getting ready

The recommended way to develop an embedded Linux system is using a native Linux workstation. Development work using virtual machines, such as the Build Appliance, is discouraged, although they may be used for demo and test purposes.

Docker containers are increasingly used as they provide a maintainable way to build the same version of Yocto over the course of several years, which is a common need for embedded systems with long product lifetimes. We will cover using Docker as a Yocto build system in the *Using Docker as a Yocto build system container* recipe in this same chapter.

Yocto builds all the components mentioned before from scratch, including the cross-compilation toolchain and the native tools it needs, so the Yocto build process is demanding in terms of processing power and both hard drive space and I/O.

Although Yocto will work fine on machines with lower specifications, for professional developers' workstations, it is recommended to use **symmetric multiprocessing** (**SMP**) systems with 8 GB or more system memory and a high capacity, fast hard drive, and **solid state drives** (**SSD**) if possible. Due to different bottlenecks in the build process, there does not seem to be much improvement above eight CPUs or around 16 GB RAM.

The first build will also download all the sources from the internet, so a fast internet connection is also recommended.

How to do it...

Yocto supports several Linux host distributions, and each Yocto release will document a list of the supported ones. Although the use of a supported Linux distribution is strongly advised, Yocto is able to run on any Linux system if it has the following dependencies:

- Git 1.8.3.1 or greater
- Tar 1.27 or greater
- Python 3.4.0 or greater

Yocto also provides a way to install the correct version of these tools by either downloading a buildtools-tarball or building one on a supported machine. This allows virtually any Linux distribution to be able to run Yocto, and also makes sure that it will be possible to replicate your Yocto build system in the future. The Yocto Project build system also isolates itself from the host distribution's C library, which makes it possible to share build caches between different distributions and also helps in future-proofing the build system. This is important for embedded products with long-term availability requirements.

This book will use the Ubuntu 16.04 **Long-Term Stable** (**LTS**) Linux distribution for all examples. Instructions to install on other Linux distributions can be found in the *Supported Linux Distributions* section of the *Yocto Project Reference Manual*, but the examples will only be tested with Ubuntu 16.04 LTS.

To make sure you have the required package dependencies installed for Yocto and to follow the examples in the book, run the following command from your shell:

```
$ sudo apt-get install gawk wget git-core diffstat unzip texinfo gcc-
multilib build-essential chrpath socat libsdl1.2-dev xterm bmap-tools make
xsltproc docbook-utils fop dblatex xmlto cpio python python3 python3-pip
python3-pexpect xz-utils debianutils iputils-ping python-git bmap-tools
python3-git curl parted dosfstools mtools gnupg autoconf automake libtool
libglib2.0-dev python-gtk2  bsdmainutils  screen libstdc++-5-dev libx11-dev
```

Downloading the example code
You can download the example code files for all Packt books you have purchased from your account at `http://www.packtpub.com`. If you purchased this book elsewhere, you can visit `http://www.packtpub.com/support` and register to have the files emailed directly to you.
The example code in the book can be accessed through several GitHub repositories at `https://github.com/yoctocookbook2ndedition`. Follow the instructions on GitHub to obtain a copy of the source in your computer.

You will also need to configure the Git revision control software as follows:

```
$ git config --global user.email "your.email.address@somewhere.com"
$ git config --global user.name "Your Name"
```

How it works...

The preceding command uses `apt-get`, the **Advanced Packaging Tool** (**APT**) command-line tool. It is a frontend of the `dpkg` package manager that is included in the Ubuntu distribution. It will install all the required packages and their dependencies to support all the features of the Yocto Project as well as the examples in this book.

Git is a distributed source control versioning system under the **General Public License** v2 (**GNU**) originally developed by Linus Torvalds for the development of the Linux kernel. Since then, it has become the standard for many open source projects. Git will be the tool of choice for source version control used in this book.

There's more...

If build times are an important factor for you, there are certain steps you can take when preparing your disks to optimize them even further:

- Place the build directories on their own disk partition or a fast external solid state drive.
- Use the ext4 filesystem but configure it not to use journalism on your Yocto-dedicated partitions. Be aware that power losses may corrupt your build data.
- Mount the filesystem in such a way that read times are not written/recorded on file reads, disable write barriers, and delay committing filesystem changes with the following mount options:

  ```
  noatime,barrier=0,commit=6000
  ```

These changes reduce the data integrity safeguards, but with the separation of the build directories to their own disk, failures would only affect temporary build data, which can be erased and regenerated.

See also

- The complete Yocto Project installation instructions for Ubuntu and other supported distributions can be found in the *Yocto Project Reference Manual* at `http://www.yoctoproject.org/docs/2.4/ref-manual/ref-manual.html`

- Git documentation and other reference material can be found at `https://git-scm.com/documentation`

Installing Poky

This recipe will explain how to set up your host Linux system with Poky, the Yocto Project reference system.

Getting ready

Poky uses the OpenEmbedded build system and, as such, uses the BitBake tool, a task scheduler written in Python which is forked from Gentoo's Portage tool. You can think of BitBake as the make utility in Yocto. It will parse the configuration and recipe metadata, schedule a task list, and run through it.

BitBake is also the command-line interface to Yocto.

Poky and BitBake are two of the open source projects used by Yocto:

- The **Poky project** is maintained by the Yocto community. You can download Poky from its Git repository at `http://git.yoctoproject.org/cgit/cgit.cgi/poky/`.
    - Development discussions can be followed and contributed to by visiting the development mailing list at `https://lists.yoctoproject.org/listinfo/poky`.
    - Poky development takes place in the master branch. Before merging submitted patches into the master, maintainers test them in the master-next branch.
    - Stable Yocto releases have their own branch. Yocto 2.4 is maintained in the `rocko` branch, and Yocto releases are tagged in that branch.

- BitBake, on the other hand, is maintained by both the Yocto and OpenEmbedded communities, as the tool is used by both. BitBake can be downloaded from its Git repository at `http://git.openembedded.org/bitbake/`.
    - Development discussions can be followed and contributed to by visiting the development mailing list at `http://lists.openembedded.org/mailman/listinfo/bitbake-dev el`.
    - Bitbake also uses master and master-next in the same way, but then creates a new branch per release, for example 1.32, with tags going into the corresponding release branch.

The Poky distribution only supports virtualized QEMU machines for the following architectures:

- ARM (qemuarm, qemuarm64)
- x86 (qemux86)
- x86-64 (qemux86-64)
- PowerPC (qemuppc)
- MIPS (qemumips, qemumips64)

Apart from these, it also supports some reference hardware BSPs, representative of the architectures just listed. These are:

- Texas Instruments BeagleBone (beaglebone)
- Freescale MPC8315E-RDB (mpc8315e-rdb)
- Intel x86-based PCs and devices (genericx86 and genericx86-64)
- Ubiquiti Networks EdgeRouter Lite (edgerouter)

To develop on different hardware, you will need to complement Poky with hardware-specific Yocto layers. This will be covered later on.

How to do it...

The Poky project incorporates a stable BitBake release, so to get started with Yocto, we only need to install Poky in our Linux host system.

Note that you can also install BitBake independently through your distribution's package management system. This is not recommended and can be a source of problems, as BitBake needs to be compatible with the metadata used in Yocto. If you have installed BitBake from your distribution, please remove it.

The current Yocto release is 2.4, or Rocko, so we will install that into our host system. We will use the /opt/yocto folder as the installation path:

```
$ sudo install -o $(id -u) -g $(id -g) -d /opt/yocto
$ cd /opt/yocto
$ git clone --branch rocko git://git.yoctoproject.org/poky
```

How it works...

The previous instructions use Git (the source code management system command-line tool) to clone the Poky repository, which includes BitBake, into a new poky directory under /opt/yocto, and point it to the rocko stable branch.

There's more...

Poky contains three metadata directories, meta, meta-poky, and meta-yocto-bsp, as well as a template metadata layer, meta-skeleton, which can be used as a base for new layers. Poky's three metadata directories are explained here:

- meta: This directory contains the OpenEmbedded-core metadata, which supports the ARM, ARM64, x86, x86-64, PowerPC, MIPS, and MIPS64 architectures and the QEMU emulated hardware. You can download it from its Git repository at http://git.openembedded.org/openembedded-core/.

  Development discussions can be followed and contributed to by visiting the development mailing list at http://lists.openembedded.org/mailman/listinfo/openembedded-core.

- meta-poky: This contains Poky's distribution-specific metadata.

- meta-yocto-bsp: This contains metadata for the reference hardware boards.

See also

- More information about OpenEmbedded, the build framework for embedded Linux used by the Yocto Project, can be found at http://www.openembedded.org
- The official Yocto Project documentation can be accessed at http://www.yoctoproject.org/docs/2.4/mega-manual/mega-manual.html

Creating a build directory

Before building your first Yocto image, we need to create a build directory for it.

The build process, on a host system as outlined before, can take up to 1 hour and needs around 20 GB of hard drive space for a console-only image. A graphical image, such as core-image-sato, can take up to 4 hours for the build process and occupy around 50 GB of space.

How to do it...

The first thing we need to do is create a build directory for our project, where the build output will be generated. Sometimes, the build directory may be referred to as the project directory, but build directory is the appropriate Yocto term.

There is no right way to structure the build directories when you have multiple projects, but a good practice is to have one build directory per architecture or machine type. They can all share a common downloads folder, and even a shared state cache (this will be covered later on), so keeping them separate won't affect the build performance, but it will allow you to develop on multiple projects simultaneously.

To create a build directory, we use the oe-init-build-env script provided by Poky. The script needs to be sourced into your current shell, and it will set up your environment to use the OpenEmbedded/Yocto build system, including adding the BitBake utility to your path.

You can specify a build directory to use or it will use build by default. We will use qemuarm for this example:

```
$ cd /opt/yocto/poky
$ source oe-init-build-env qemuarm
```

The script will change to the specified directory.

As `oe-init-build-env` only configures the current shell, you will need to source it on every new shell. But, if you point the script to an existing build directory, it will set up your environment but won't change any of your existing configurations.

BitBake is designed with a client/server abstraction, so we can also start a persistent server and connect a client to it. To instruct a BitBake server to stay resident, configure a timeout in seconds in your build directory's `conf/local.conf` configuration file as follows:

```
BB_SERVER_TIMEOUT = "n"
```

With n being the time in seconds for BitBake to stay resident.

With this setup, loading cache and configuration information each time is avoided, which saves some overhead.

How it works...

The `oe-init-build-env` script calls `scripts/oe-setup-builddir` script inside the `Poky` directory to create the build directory.

On creation, the `qemuarm` build directory contains a `conf` directory with the following three files:

- `bblayers.conf`: This file lists the metadata layers to be considered for this project.
- `local.conf`: This file contains the project-specific configuration variables. You can set common configuration variables to different projects with a `site.conf` file, but this is not created by default. Similarly, there is also an `auto.conf` file which is used by autobuilders. BitBake will first read `site.conf`, then `auto.conf`, and finally `local.conf`.
- `templateconf.cfg`: This file contains the directory that includes the template configuration files used to create the project. By default it uses the one pointed to by the `templateconf` file in your Poky installation directory, which is `meta-poky/conf` by default.

To start a build from scratch, that's all the build directory needs. Erasing everything apart from these files will recreate your build from scratch, as shown here:
```
$ cd /opt/yocto/poky/qemuarm
$ rm -Rf tmp sstate-cache
```

There's more...

You can specify different template configuration files to use when you create your build directory using the TEMPLATECONF variable, for example:

```
$ TEMPLATECONF=meta-custom/config source oe-init-build-env <build-dir>
```

The TEMPLATECONF variable needs to refer to a directory containing templates for both local.conf and bblayer.conf, but named local.conf.sample and bblayers.conf.sample.

For our purposes, we can use the unmodified default project configuration files.

Building your first image

Before building our first image, we need to decide what type of image we want to build. This recipe will introduce some of the available Yocto images and provide instructions to build a simple image.

Getting ready

Poky contains a set of default target images. You can list them by executing the following commands:

```
$ cd /opt/yocto/poky
$ ls meta*/recipes*/images/*.bb
```

A full description of the different images can be found in the *Yocto Project Reference Manual*, on Chapter 13, *Images*. Typically, these default images are used as a base and customized for your own project needs. The most frequently used base default images are:

- core-image-minimal: This is the smallest BusyBox, sysvinit, and udev-based console-only image
- core-image-full-cmdline: This is the BusyBox-based console-only image with full hardware support and a more complete Linux system, including Bash
- core-image-lsb: This is a console-only image that is based on **Linux Standard Base (LSB)** compliance
- core-image-x11: This is the basic X11 Windows-system-based image with a graphical terminal

- `core-image-sato`: This is the X11 Window-system-based image with a SATO theme and a GNOME mobile desktop environment
- `core-image-weston`: This is a Wayland protocol and Weston reference compositor-based image

You will also find images with the following suffixes:

- `dev`: This image is suitable for development work, as it contains headers and libraries
- `sdk`: This image includes a complete SDK that can be used for development on the target
- `initramfs`: This is an image that can be used for a RAM-based root filesystem, which can optionally be embedded with the Linux kernel

How to do it...

1. To build an image, we need to configure the machine we are building it for and pass its name to BitBake. For example, for the `qemuarm` machine, we would run the following:

```
$ cd /opt/yocto/poky/
$ source /opt/yocto/poky/oe-init-build-env qemuarm
$ MACHINE=qemuarm bitbake core-image-minimal
```

2. Or we could export the `MACHINE` variable to the current shell environment before sourcing the `oe-init-build-env` script with the following:

```
$ export MACHINE=qemuarm
```

3. On an already configured project, we could also edit the `conf/local.conf` configuration file to change the default machine to `qemuarm`:

```
- #MACHINE ?= "qemuarm"
+ MACHINE ?= "qemuarm"
```

4. Then, after setting up the environment, we execute the following:

```
$ bitbake core-image-minimal
```

With the preceding steps, BitBake will launch the build process for the specified target image.

How it works...

When you pass a target recipe to BitBake, it first parses the following configuration files in order:

- `conf/bblayers.conf`: This file is parsed to find all the configured layers
- `conf/layer.conf`: This file is parsed on each configured layer
- `meta/conf/bitbake.conf`: This file is parsed for its own configuration
- `conf/local.conf`: This file is used for any other configuration the user may have for the current build
- `conf/machine/<machine>.conf`: This file is the machine configuration; in our case, this is `qemuarm.conf`
- `conf/distro/<distro>.conf`: This file is the distribution policy; by default, this is the `poky.conf` file

  There are also some other distribution variants included with Poky:

  - `poky-bleeding`: Extension to the Poky default distribution that includes the most up-to-date versions of packages
  - `poky-lsb`: LSB compliance extension to Poky
  - `poky-tiny`: Oriented to create headless systems with the smallest Linux kernel and BusyBox read-only or RAM-based root filesystems, using the `musl` C library

And then, BitBake parses the target recipe that has been provided and its dependencies. The outcome is a set of interdependent tasks that BitBake will then execute in order.

A depiction of the BitBake build process is shown in the following diagram:

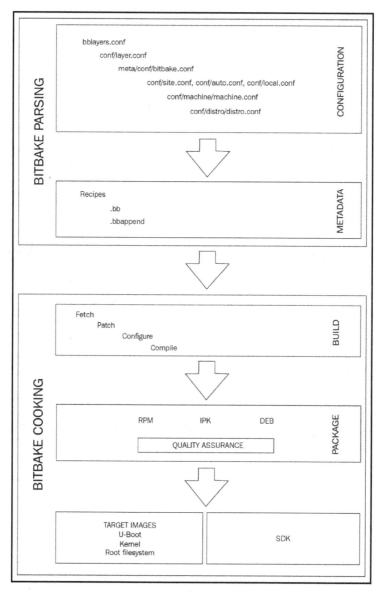

BitBake build process

There's more...

Most developers won't be interested in keeping the whole build output for every package, so it is recommended to configure your project to remove it with the following configuration in your `conf/local.conf` file:

```
INHERIT += "rm_work"
```

But at the same time, configuring it for all packages means that you won't be able to develop or debug them.

You can add a list of packages to exclude from cleaning by adding them to the `RM_WORK_EXCLUDE` variable. For example, if you are going to do BSP work, a good setting might be:

```
RM_WORK_EXCLUDE += "linux-wandboard u-boot-fslc"
```

Remember that you can use a custom template `local.conf.sample` configuration file in your own layer to keep these configurations and apply them for all projects so that they can be shared across all developers.

On a normal build, the `-dbg` packages that include debug symbols are not needed. To avoid creating `-dbg` packages, do this:

```
INHIBIT_PACKAGE_DEBUG_SPLIT = "1"
```

Once the build finishes, you can find the output images in the `tmp/deploy/images/qemuarm` directory inside your build directory.

You can test run your images on the QEMU emulator by executing this:

```
$ runqemu qemuarm core-image-minimal
```

The `runqemu` script included in Poky's `scripts` directory is a launch wrapper around the QEMU machine emulator to simplify its usage.

The Yocto Project also has a set of precompiled images for supported hardware platforms that can be downloaded from `http://downloads.yoctoproject.org/releases/yocto/yocto-2.4/machines/`.

Explaining the NXP Yocto ecosystem

As we saw, Poky metadata starts with the `meta`, `meta-poky`, and `meta-yocto-bsp` layers, and it can be expanded by using more layers.

An index of the available OpenEmbedded layers that are compatible with the Yocto Project is maintained at `http://layers.openembedded.org/`.

An embedded product's development usually starts with hardware evaluation using a manufacturer's reference board design. Unless you are working with one of the reference boards already supported by Poky, you will need to extend Poky to support your hardware by adding extra BSP layers.

Getting ready

The first thing to do is to select which base hardware your design is going to be based on. We will use a board that is based on a NXP i.MX6 **System on Chip** (**SoC**) as a starting point for our embedded product design.

This recipe gives an overview of the support for NXP hardware in the Yocto Project.

How to do it...

The SoC manufacturer (in this case, NXP) has a range of reference design boards for purchase, as well as official Yocto-based software releases. Similarly, other manufacturers that use NXP's SoCs offer reference design boards and their own Yocto-based BSP layers and even distributions.

Selecting the appropriate hardware to base your design on is one of the most important design decisions for an embedded product. Depending on your product needs, you will decide to either:

- Use a production-ready board, like a **single-board computer** (**SBC**)
- Use a **System-on-Module** (**SoM**) and build your custom carrier board around it
- Use NXP's SoC directly and design your own board

Most of the time, a production-ready board will not match the specific requirements of a professional embedded system, and the process of designing a complete carrier board using NXP's SoC would be too time consuming. So, using an appropriate module that already solves the most technically challenging design aspects is a common choice.

Some of the characteristics that are important to consider are:

- Industrial temperature ranges
- Power management
- Long-term availability
- Pre-certified wireless and Bluetooth (if applicable)

The Yocto community that support NXP-based boards is called the FSL community BSP and their main layers are called `meta-freescale` and `meta-freescale-3rdparty`. The Freescale brand was acquired by NXP with the purchase of Freescale. The selection of boards that are supported on `meta-freescale` is limited to NXP reference designs, which would be the starting point if you are considering designing your own carrier board around NXP's SoC. Boards from other vendors are maintained on the `meta-freescale-3rdparty` layer.

There are other embedded manufacturers that use `meta-freescale`, but they have not integrated their boards in the `meta-freescale-3rdparty` community layer. These manufacturers keep their own BSP layers, which depend on `meta-freescale`, with specific support for their hardware. An example of this is Digi International and its ConnectCore product range, with the Yocto layers available at `https://github.com/digi-embedded/meta-digi`. There is also a Yocto-based distribution available called Digi Embedded Yocto.

How it works...

To understand NXP's Yocto ecosystem, we need to start with the FSL community BSP, comprising the `meta-freescale` layer with support for NXP's reference boards, and its companion, `meta-freescale-3rdparty`, with support for boards from other vendors, and its differences with the official NXP Yocto BSP releases that NXP offers for their reference designs.

There are some key differences between the community and NXP Yocto releases:

- NXP releases are developed internally by NXP without community involvement and are used for BSP validation on NXP reference boards.
- NXP releases go through an internal QA and validation test process, and they are maintained by NXP support.
- NXP releases for a specific platform reach a maturity point, after which they are no longer worked on. At this point, all the development work has been integrated into the community layer and the platforms are further maintained by the FSL BSP community.
- NXP Yocto releases are not Yocto compatible, while the community release is.

NXP's engineering works very closely with the FSL BSP community to make sure that all development in their official releases is integrated in the community layer in a reliable and quick manner.

The FSL BSP community is also very responsive and active, so problems can usually be worked on with them to benefit all parts.

There's more...

The FSL community BSP extends Poky with the following layers:

- `meta-freescale`: This is the community layer that supports NXP reference designs. It has a dependency on OpenEmbedded-Core. Machines in this layer will be maintained even after NXP stops active development on them. You can download `meta-freescale` from its Git repository at http://git.yoctoproject.org/cgit/cgit.cgi/meta-freescale/.

  Development discussions can be followed and contributed to by visiting the development mailing list at https://lists.yoctoproject.org/listinfo/meta-freescale.

The `meta-freescale` layer provides both the i.MX6 Linux kernel and the U-Boot source either from NXP's or from FSL community BSP maintained repositories using the following links:

- **NXP's Linux kernel Git repository**:
  `http://git.freescale.com/git/cgit.cgi/imx/linux-imx.git/`
- **FSL community Linux kernel Git
  repository**: `https://github.com/Freescale/linux-fslc.git`
- **NXP's U-Boot Git repository**:
  `http://git.freescale.com/git/cgit.cgi/imx/uboot-imx.git/`
- **FSL community U-Boot Git
  repository**: `https://github.com/Freescale/u-boot-fslc.git`

Other Linux kernel and U-Boot versions are available, but keeping the manufacturer's supported version is recommended.

The `meta-freescale` layer includes NXP's proprietary binaries to enable some hardware features—most notably its hardware graphics, multimedia, and encryption capabilities. To make use of these capabilities, the end user needs to accept the NXP **End-User License Agreement** (**EULA**), which is included in the `meta-freescale` layer.

- `meta-freescale-3rdparty`: This layer adds support for other community-maintained boards, for example, the Wandboard. To download the layer's content, you may visit
  `https://github.com/Freescale/meta-freescale-3rdparty/`.

- `meta-freescale-distro`: This layer adds a metadata layer for demonstration target images. To download the layer's content, you may visit
  `https://github.com/Freescale/meta-freescale-distro`.

This layer adds two different sets of distributions, one maintained by the FSL BSP community (`fslc-` distributions) and one maintained by NXP (`fsl-` distributions). They are a superset of Poky that allows you to easily choose the graphical backend to use between:

- framebuffer
- x11
- Wayland
- XWayland

We will learn more about the different graphical backends in `Chapter 4,` *Application Development.*

NXP uses another layer on top of the layers previously mentioned for their official software releases:

- `meta-fsl-bsp-release`: This is an NXP-maintained layer that is used in the official NXP software releases. It contains modifications to both `meta-freescale` and `meta-freescale-distro`. It is not part of the community release but can be accessed at
`http://git.freescale.com/git/cgit.cgi/imx/meta-fsl-bsp-release.git/`.

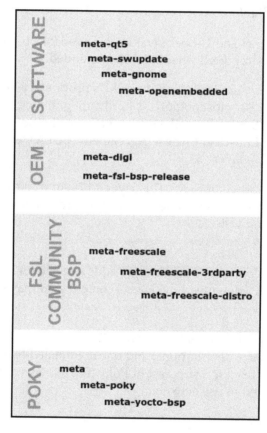

NXP-based platforms extended layers hierarchy

See also

- For more information, refer to the FSL community BSP web page available at `http://freescale.github.io/`

- NXP's official support community can be accessed at `https://community.nxp.com/`

Installing support for NXP hardware

In this recipe, we will install the FSL community BSP Yocto release that adds support for NXP hardware to our Yocto installation.

Getting ready

With so many layers, manually cloning each of them and adding them to your project's `conf/bblayers.conf` file is cumbersome. The community uses the repo tool developed by Google for their community Android to simplify the installation of Yocto.

To install repo in your host system, type in the following commands:

```
$ mkdir -p ${HOME}/bin/
$ curl https://storage.googleapis.com/git-repo-downloads/repo >
  ${HOME}/bin/repo
$ chmod a+x ${HOME}/bin/repo
```

The repo tool is a Python utility that parses an XML file, called `manifest`, with a list of Git repositories. The repo tool is then used to manage those repositories as a whole.

How to do it...

For an example, we will use repo to download all the repositories listed in the previous recipe to our host system. For that, we will point it to the FSL community BSP `manifest` for the Rocko release:

```
<?xml version="1.0" encoding="UTF-8"?>
<manifest>

  <default sync-j="4" revision="master"/>
```

```
    <remote fetch="https://git.yoctoproject.org/git" name="yocto"/>
    <remote fetch="https://github.com/Freescale" name="freescale"/>
    <remote fetch="https://github.com/openembedded" name="oe"/>

    <project remote="yocto" revision="rocko" name="poky"
path="sources/poky"/>
    <project remote="yocto" revision="rocko" name="meta-freescale"
path="sources/meta-freescale"/>

    <project remote="oe" revision="rocko" name="meta-openembedded"
path="sources/meta-openembedded"/>

    <project remote="freescale" revision="rocko" name="fsl-community-bsp-
base" path="sources/base">
       <linkfile dest="README" src="README"/>
       <linkfile dest="setup-environment" src="setup-environment"/>
    </project>

    <project remote="freescale" revision="rocko" name="meta-
freescale-3rdparty" path="sources/meta-freescale-3rdparty"/>
    <project remote="freescale" revision="rocko" name="meta-freescale-distro"
path="sources/meta-freescale-distro"/>
    <project remote="freescale" revision="rocko" name="Documentation"
path="sources/Documentation"/>

</manifest>
```

The `manifest` file shows all the installation paths and repository sources for the different components that are going to be installed.

How it works...

The `manifest` file is a list of the different layers that are needed for the FSL community BSP release. We can now use `repo` to install it. Run the following:

```
$ mkdir /opt/yocto/fsl-community-bsp
$ cd /opt/yocto/fsl-community-bsp
$ repo init -u https://github.com/Freescale/fsl-community-bsp-platform -b
rocko
$ repo sync
```

You can optionally pass a `-jN` argument to sync if you have a multicore machine for multithreaded operations; for example, you could pass `repo sync -j8` in an eight-core host system.

There's more...

To list the hardware boards supported by the different layers, we may run:

```
$ ls sources/meta-freescale*/conf/machine/*.conf
```

And to list the newly introduced target images, use the following:

```
$ ls sources/meta-freescale*/recipes*/images/*.bb
```

The FSL community BSP release introduces the following new target images:

- `fsl-image-mfgtool-initramfs`: This is a small, RAM-based initramfs image used with the NXP manufacturing tool
- `fsl-image-multimedia`: This is a console-only image that includes the `gstreamer` multimedia framework over the framebuffer
- `fsl-image-multimedia-full`: This is an extension of `fsl-image-multimedia`, that extends the `gstreamer` multimedia framework to include all available plugins
- `fsl-image-machine-test`: This is an extension of `fsl-image-multimedia-full` for testing and benchmarking

The release includes a `sources/Documentation` repository with buildable documentation. To build, we first need to install some host tools as follows:

```
$ sudo apt-get install libfreetype6-dev libjpeg8-dev python3-dev python3-pip python3-sphinx texlive-fonts-recommended texlive-latex-extra zlib1g-dev fonts-liberation
$ sudo pip3 install reportlab sphinxcontrib-blockdiag
```

And then we can build the different documents by entering its sub-directory, and build an HTML document with:

```
$ make singlehtml
```

Or a PDF version with:

```
$ make latexpdf
```

For example, to build the release notes in both HTML and PDF versions we do:

```
$ cd /opt/yocto/fsl-community-bsp/sources/Documentation/release-notes
$ make latexpdf singlehtml
```

The documents can be found inside the `build/latex` and `build/singlehtml` directories.

See also

- Instructions to use the repo tool, including using repo with proxy servers, can be found in the Android documentation at `https://source.android.com/setup/downloading`
- The FSL community BSP manifest can be accessed at `https://github.com/Freescale/fsl-community-bsp-platform/blob/rocko/default.xml`

Building Wandboard images

The Wandboard is an inexpensive NXP i.MX6-based board with broad community support. It is perfect for exploration and educational purposes, more feature rich than a Raspberry Pi, and much closer to professional high-end embedded systems.

Designed and sold by Technexion, a Taiwanese company, it comes in four flavors based around a SoM with different i.MX6 SoC variants, the solo, dual, quad, and quad plus, featuring one, two, or four cores.

Technexion made the schematics for both the board and the SoM available as PDF, which gave the board a taint of openness.

The Wandboard is still widely used, easy to purchase, and with a wide community, so we will use it as an example in the following chapters. However, any i.MX6-based board could be used to follow the book. The know-how will then be applicable to any embedded platform that uses the Yocto Project.

The Wandboard has been released in different revisions throughout its history: a0, b1, c1, and d1. The revision is printed on the PCB and it will become important as the software that runs in each revision differs.

The Wandboard features the following specification:

- 2 GB RAM
- Broadcom BCM4330 802.11n Wi-Fi
- Broadcom BCM4330 4.0 Bluetooth
- HDMI
- USB
- RS-232
- uSD

Revision D introduced a MMPF0100 PMIC, replaced the Ethernet PHY Atheros AR8031 with Atheros AR8035, and replaced the BCM4330 with a BCM4339 802.11ac Wi-Fi, among other minor changes.

It is a perfect multimedia enabled system with a Vivante 2D and 3D graphical processing unit, hardware graphics and video acceleration, and an SGTL5000 audio codec. The different i.MX6-based systems are widely used in industrial control and automation, home automation, automotive, avionics, and other industrial applications.

For production, professional OEMs and products are recommended, as they can offer the industrial quality and temperature ranges, component availability, support, and manufacturing guarantees that final products require.

How to do it...

Support for the Wandboard is included in the `meta-freescale-3rdparty` FSL community BSP layer. All of the Wandboard board variants are bundled in a single Yocto machine called `wandboard`.

To build an image for the `wandboard` machine for the Poky distribution, use the following commands:

```
$ cd /opt/yocto/fsl-community-bsp
$ MACHINE=wandboard DISTRO=poky source setup-environment wandboard
$ bitbake core-image-minimal
```

 The current version of the `setup-environment` script only works if the build directory is under the installation folder; in our case, `/opt/yocto/fsl-community-bsp`.

How it works...

The `setup-environment` script is a wrapper around the `oe-init-build-env` we used before. It will create a build directory, set up the `MACHINE` variable and `DISTRO` with the provided values, and prompt you to accept the NXP EULA as described earlier. Your `conf/local.conf` configuration file will be updated both with the specified machine and the `EULA` acceptance variable. To accept the license, the following line has been automatically added to the project's `conf/local.conf` configuration file:

```
ACCEPT_FSL_EULA = "1"
```

Remember that if you close your Terminal session, you will need to set up the environment again before being able to use BitBake. You can safely rerun the setup-environment script shown next, as it will not touch an existing `conf/local.conf` file:
```
$ cd /opt/yocto/fsl-community-bsp/
$ source setup-environment wandboard
```

The preceding BitBake command creates a `core-image-minimal-wandboard.wic.gz` file, that is, a compressed WIC file, inside the `tmp/deploy/images/wandboard` folder.

A WIC file is created by Yocto using the WIC tool and it is a partitioned image from Yocto build artifacts that can then be directly programmed.

This image can be programmed into a microSD card, inserted in the primary slot in the Wandboard CPU board (the one in the side of the i.MX6 SoM and under the heatsink), and booted using the following commands:

```
$ cd /opt/yocto/fsl-community-bsp/wandboard/tmp/deploy/images/wandboard/
$ sudo bmaptool copy --nobmap core-image-minimal-wandboard.wic.gz /dev/sdN
```

Here, `/dev/sdN` corresponds to the device node assigned to the microSD card in your host system.

If the bmaptool utility is missing from your system, you can install it with:
```
$ sudo apt-get install bmap-tools
```
bmaptool will refuse to program mounted devices and it will complain with:
```
bmaptool: ERROR: cannot open block device '/dev/sdN' in
exclusive mode: [Errno 16] Device or resource busy:
'/dev/sdN'
```
You will need to unmount the SD card if Ubuntu auto mounted it with:
```
$ sudo umount /dev/sdN
```
Here, N is a letter assigned by the Linux kernel. Check the `dmesg` to find out the device name.

The `--nobmap` option passed to bmaptool requires some explanation. bmaptool is a utility specialized in copying data to block devices, similar to the traditional `dd` command. However, it has some extra functionality that makes it a very convenient tool to use in embedded device development work:

- It is able to copy from compressed files, as we can see with the `wic.gz` file
- It is able to use a BMAP file to speed up the copying of sparse files

When data is stored in a filesystem, blocks of data are mapped to disk sectors using an on-disk index. When a block of data is not mapped to any disk sector, it's called a **hole**, and files with holes are called **sparse** files. A BMAP file provides a list of mapped areas as well as checksums for both the BMAP file itself and the mapped areas.

Using this BMAP file, bmaptool can significantly speed up the process of copying sparse files.

However, as we are not using a BMAP file, we pass the `--nobmap` file and use bmaptool for the convenience of using a compressed file. It also has other optimizations over `dd` that make it a better tool for the job.

See also

- You can find more information regarding the repo tool in Android's documentation at `https://source.android.com/setup/using-repo`
- The bmaptool documentation can be accessed at `https://source.tizen.org/documentation/reference/bmaptool`

More information about the different hardware mentioned in this section can be found at:

- Digi International's ConnectCore 6 SBC at `https://www.digi.com/products/embedded-systems/single-board-computers/connectcore-6-sbc`
- The Wandboard at `https://www.wandboard.org/`

Using the Toaster web interface

Toaster is a web application interface to the Yocto Project's build system built on the Django framework with a database backend to store and represent build data. It replaces the Hob user interface, which could be found on releases prior to Yocto 1.8. The welcome page is shown next:

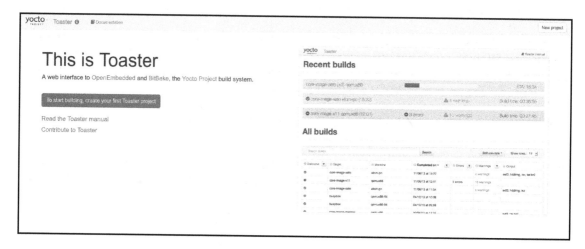

Welcome to Toaster

It allows you to perform the following actions:

- Configure local or remote builds
- Manage layers
- Set configuration variables
- Set build targets
- Start builds either from the command line (analysis mode) or the web UI (managed mode)
- Collect and represent build data
- Browse final images
- List installed packages
- See build variable values
- Explore recipes, packages, and task dependencies
- Examine build warnings, errors, and trace messages
- Provide build performance statistics
- Examine build tasks and use of shared state cache

Getting ready

In order to run the Toaster Django web application, your host machine needs to be set up as follows:

```
$ sudo apt-get install python3-pip
$ pip3 install --user -r /opt/yocto/poky/bitbake/toaster-requirements.txt
```

How to do it...

Toaster can be started with the following commands:

```
$ cd /opt/yocto/poky
$ source oe-init-build-env
$ source toaster start
```

`/opt/yocto/poky/bitbake/bin/toaster` is a shell script that will set up Toaster's environment, load the default configuration and database migrations, connect to the OpenEmbedded Layer Index, and download information about the metadata layers it has available for the current release, as well as starting the web server and the runbuilds poller process.

To access the web user interface, go to `http://127.0.0.1:8000`.

By default, Toaster binds to localhost on port `8000`, but this can be specified as follows:

```
$ source toaster start webport=<IP>:<PORT>
```

Administrator interface

The administrator interface can be accessed at `http://127.0.0.1:8000/admin`.

This administration interface can be used to configure Toaster itself, but it needs a superuser account to be created from the directory that contains the Toaster database:

```
$ cd /opt/yocto/poky/build
$ ../bitbake/lib/toaster/manage.py createsuperuser
```

Starting a build

Toaster can run two different types of builds:

1. You can manually start a build on the terminal and Toaster will monitor it. You can then use the Toaster web UI to explore the build results. The following image shows the command line builds page:

Toaster command line builds

2. You can also use the Toaster web interface to create a new project. This will be named `build-toaster-<project_id>` and will be created inside the `Poky` directory:

Toaster's create a new project wizard

You can use the `TOASTER_DIR` configuration variable to specify a different build directory for Toaster.

When creating a Toaster project, you can choose between two different types:

- **Local builds**: This uses the local Poky clone on your computer. Using this build type limits the build to the layers available on the Yocto Project, `openembedded-core`, `meta-poky`, and `meta-yocto-bsp`. Other layers would need to be manually imported using the **Import Layer** page.
- **Yocto Project builds**: When a Yocto Project release is chosen, Toaster fetches the source from the Yocto Project upstream Git repositories, and updates it every time you run a build. In this mode, compatible layers can be selected, including BSP layers that allow you to build for different machines. The Toaster project configuration page looks like the following:

Toaster's project configuration page

Customizing images with Toaster

After an image is built, Toaster offers the possibility to create a custom image based on that image's recipe where packages can easily be added/removed.

Building SDKs with Toaster

You can instruct Toaster to build both the standard and the extensible SDK by specifying the `populate_sdk` and `populate_sdk_ext` tasks to the target image. For example, to create SDKs for the `core-image-base` target image, you would use the following.

For the standard SDK:

```
core-image-base:populate_sdk
```

Or for the extensible SDK:

```
core-image-base:populate_sdk_ext
```

We will learn more about using SDKs on `Chapter 4`, *Application Development*.

How it works...

The version of Django that Toaster uses is specified on the `/opt/yocto/poky/bitbake/toaster-requirements.txt` file, for example:

```
Django>1.8,<1.9.9
```

Django and hence Toaster store data in a relational database. The backend configuration is done in the `/opt/yocto/poky/bitbake/lib/toaster/toastermain/settings.py` file as follows:

```
TOASTER_SQLITE_DEFAULT_DIR = os.environ.get('TOASTER_DIR')
DATABASES = {
    'default': {
        # Add 'postgresql_psycopg2', 'mysql', 'sqlite3' or 'oracle'.
        'ENGINE': 'django.db.backends.sqlite3',
        # DB name or full path to database file if using sqlite3.
        'NAME': "%s/toaster.sqlite" % TOASTER_SQLITE_DEFAULT_DIR,
        'USER': '',
        'PASSWORD': '',
        #'HOST': '127.0.0.1', # e.g. mysql server
        #'PORT': '3306', # e.g. mysql port
    }
}
```

By default, Toaster will create a `toaster.sqlite` database on the configured `TOASTER_DIR` path. For production servers, MySQL is the recommended backend.

Django has a built in object-relational mapper, Django ORM, which automates the transfer of data from the relational database to Python objects and allows database accesses in Python code. The initial state of the database is created from a set of fixtures (data dumps) under `/opt/yocto/poky/bitbake/lib/toaster/orm/fixtures`. Toaster fixtures are in XML format:

- `settings.xml`: This contains Toaster and BitBake variable settings. Some of these can be changed through the Toaster administrative interface.
- `poky.xml` and `oe-core.xml`: These are defaults for both the Poky and OE-core builds.
- `custom.xml`: This allows you to override data on any of the preceding fixtures with a custom configuration. XML, JSON, and YAML formats are all supported.

When Toaster is launched, these Django fixtures are used to populate its database with initial data.

Toaster has extended the Django `manage.py` command with some custom Toaster-specific options. The `manage.py` management script needs to be invoked from the `build` directory, which contains the Toaster database:

```
$ cd /opt/yocto/poky/build
$ /opt/yocto/poky/bitbake/lib/toaster/manage.py <command> [<command
option>]
```

The commands can be the following:

From `/opt/yocto/poky/bitbake/lib/toaster/toastermain/managements/commands/`:

- `buildlist`: This returns the current build list including their build IDs
- `buildelete <build_id>`: This deletes all build dates for the build specified by its build ID
- `checksocket`: This verifies that Toaster can bind to the provided IP address and port
- `perf`: This is a sanity check that measures performance by returning page loading times

From `/opt/yocto/poky/bitbake/lib/toaster/orm/managements/commands/`:

- `lsupdates`: This updates the local layer index cache

From
`/opt/yocto/poky/bitbake/lib/toaster/bldcontrol/managements/commands/`:

- `checksettings`: This verifies that the existing Toaster database settings are enough to start a build
- `runbuilds`: This launches scheduled builds

There's more...

Toaster enables you to set up a build server on a shared hosted/cloud environment that allows you to:

- Use it with multiple users
- Distribute it across several build hosts
- Handle heavy loads

Typically, when setting up Toaster on a shared hosted environment, the Apache web server and MySQL as a database backend are used.

Installation instructions for this type of production server can be found in the *Yocto Project's Toaster User Manual*. The installation can be spread across different hosts for load sharing.

Running a Toaster Docker container

Docker is a software technology that provides operating system level virtualization. Functionality-wise it can be compared with a virtual machine, except that it suffers less of a performance penalty. On Linux it uses the resource isolation features of the Linux kernel to provide abstraction and process isolation. It allows you to create containers that run on Docker and are independent of the operating system underneath.

There are Docker instances of the Toaster user interface available, which will be introduced in this recipe.

How to do it...

1. To install Docker on your Ubuntu 16.04 machine, add the GPG key for the official Docker repository to the system:

   ```
   $ curl -fsSL https://download.docker.com/linux/ubuntu/gpg | sudo
   apt-key add -
   ```

2. Then add the Docker repository to APT sources:

   ```
   $ sudo add-apt-repository "deb [arch=amd64]
   https://download.docker.com/linux/ubuntu $(lsb_release -cs) stable"
   ```

3. Next, update the package database with the Docker packages from the newly added repository:

   ```
   $ sudo apt-get update
   $ sudo apt-get install docker-ce
   ```

4. Add your user to the docker group:

   ```
   $ sudo usermod -aG docker ${USER}
   $ su - ${USER}
   ```

5. Finally, test run Docker by running the hello-world container:

   ```
   $ docker run hello-world
   ```

6. To run a docker-toaster instance, we will first create a directory in our host machine for the docker container to store the builds:

   ```
   $ mkdir /opt/yocto/docker-toaster
   ```

7. We can then instruct Docker to run the crops/toaster container and point its /workdir directory to the local directory we just created:

   ```
   $ docker run -it --rm -p 127.0.0.1:18000:8000 -v /opt/yocto/docker-
   toaster:/workdir crops/toaster
   ```

If you see the following error:

```
Refusing to use a gid of 0
Traceback (most recent call last):
  File "/usr/bin/usersetup.py", line 62, in <module>
    subprocess.check_call(cmd.split(), stdout=sys.stdout,
stderr=sys.stderr)
  File "/usr/lib/python2.7/subprocess.py", line 541, in
check_call
    raise CalledProcessError(retcode, cmd)
subprocess.CalledProcessError: Command '['sudo',
'restrict_groupadd.sh', '0', 'toasteruser']' returned non-
zero exit status 1
```

Make sure the `/opt/yocto/docker-toaster` directory was created before running Docker and is not owned by root. If you don't create it beforehand, Docker will do it with the root user and the setup will fail as above.

See `https://github.com/crops/poky-container/issues/20`.

Note that you can replace the `127.0.0.1` above with an IP address that is externally accessible if you are running Docker on a different machine.

8. You can now detach from the `docker` container with *Ctrl + P Ctrl + Q*. Check the container is still running with:

    `$ docker ps`

9. You can now access the Toaster web interface at `http://127.0.0.1:18000`.
10. The `docker` container can be stopped with the following command:

    `$ docker stop <container-id>`

See also

- Django documentation can be accessed at
  `https://docs.djangoproject.com/en/1.9/`
- The Django management command available at `toaster/manage.py` is
  documented as part of the Django documentation at
  `https://docs.djangoproject.com/en/1.9/ref/django-admin/`
- Docker specific documentation can be accessed at
  `https://docs.docker.com/engine/reference/commandline/dockerd/`
- The Toaster `docker` container home page is
  `https://github.com/crops/toaster-container`

Configuring network booting for a development setup

Most professional i.MX6 boards will have an internal flash memory, and that would be the recommended way to boot firmware. The Wandboard is not really a product meant for professional use, so it does not have one, booting from a microSD card instead. But neither the internal flash nor the microSD card are ideal for development work, as any system change would involve a reprogramming of the firmware image.

Getting ready

The ideal setup for development work is to use both **Trivial File Transfer Protocol** (**TFTP**) and **Network File System** (**NFS**) servers in your host system and to only store the U-Boot bootloader in either the internal flash or a microSD card. With this setup, the bootloader will fetch the Linux kernel from the TFTP server and the kernel will mount the root filesystem from the NFS server. Changes to either the kernel or the root filesystem are available without the need to reprogram. Only bootloader development work would need you to reprogram the physical media.

Installing a TFTP server

If you are not already running a TFTP server, follow the next steps to install and configure a TFTP server on your Ubuntu 16.04 host:

```
$ sudo apt-get install tftpd-hpa
```

The `tftpd-hpa` configuration file is installed in `/etc/default/tftpd-hpa`. By default, it uses `/var/lib/tftpboot` as the root TFTP folder. Change the folder permissions to make it accessible to all users using the following command:

```
$ sudo chmod 1777 /var/lib/tftpboot
```

Now copy the Linux kernel and device tree for the Wandboard Quad Plus from your build directory as follows:

```
$ cd /opt/yocto/fsl-community-bsp/wandboard/tmp/deploy/images/wandboard/
$ cp zImage-wandboard.bin zImage-imx6qp-wandboard-revd1.dtb
/var/lib/tftpboot
```

If you have a different hardware variant or revision of the Wandboard, you will need to use a different device tree, as shown next. The corresponding device trees for the Wandboard Quad are:

- **revision b1**: `zImage-imx6q-wandboard-revb1.dtb`
- **revision c1**: `zImage-imx6q-wandboard.dtb`
- **revision d1**: `zImage-imx6q-wandboard-revd1.dtb`

The corresponding device trees for the Wandboard solo/dual lite are:

- **revision b1**: `zImage-imx6dl-wandboard-revb1.dtb`
- **revision c1**: `zImage-imx6dl-wandboard.dtb`
- **revision d1**: `zImage-imx6dl-wandboard-revd1.dtb`

And the device tree for the Wandboard Quad Plus is:

- **revision d1**: `zImage-imx6qp-wandboard-revd1.dtb`

Installing an NFS server

If you are not already running an NFS server, follow the next steps to install and configure one on your Ubuntu 16.04 host:

```
$ sudo apt-get install nfs-kernel-server
```

We will use the /nfsroot directory as the root for the NFS server, so we will untar the target's root filesystem from our Yocto build directory in there.

By default, the Wandboard only builds WIC images. We will need to modify our build project to build a compressed copy of the target's root filesystem. For that, follow the next steps:

```
$ cd /opt/yocto/fsl-community-bsp/wandboard
```

Edit conf/local.conf and add the following:

```
IMAGE_FSTYPES = "wic.gz tar.bz2"
```

This will build a core-image-minimal-wandboard.tar.bz2 file that we can then uncompress under /nfsroot, as follows:

```
$ sudo mkdir /nfsroot
$ cd /nfsroot
$ sudo tar --numeric-owner -x -v -f /opt/yocto/fsl-community-
bsp/wandboard/tmp/deploy/images/wandboard/core-image-minimal-
wandboard.tar.bz2
```

The extraction of the root filesystem can also be done without superuser permissions by using the runqemu-extract-sdk script, which uses pseudo to correctly extract and set the permissions of the root filesystem, as follows:

```
$ cd /opt/yocto/fsl-community-bsp/wandboard
$ bitbake meta-ide-support
$ runqemu-extract-sdk tmp/deploy/images/wandboard/core-image-minimal-
wandboard.tar.bz2 /nfsroot/rootfs/
```

For this to work, the destination nfsroot directory needs to be writable by the current user.

Next, we will configure the NFS server to export the /nfsroot folder.

Add the following line to `/etc/exports`:

```
/nfsroot/ *(rw,no_root_squash,async,no_subtree_check)
```

We will then restart the NFS server for the configuration changes to take effect:

```
$ sudo service nfs-kernel-server restart
```

How to do it...

We now have the boot binaries and root filesystem ready for network booting, and we need to configure U-Boot to perform the network boot.

Boot the Wandboard and stop at the U-Boot prompt by pressing any key on the serial console. Make sure it has an Ethernet cable plugged in and connected to your local network. You should see the U-Boot banner and prompt as follows:

```
=>
U-Boot SPL 2017.09+fslc+ga6a15fedd1a5 (Oct 28 2017 - 13:55:35)
Trying to boot from MMC1


U-Boot 2017.09+fslc+ga6a15fedd1a5 (Oct 28 2017 - 13:55:35 +0200)

CPU:   Freescale i.MX6Q rev1.2 at 792 MHz
Reset cause: POR
I2C:   ready
DRAM:  2 GiB
Can't find PMIC:PFUZE100
MMC:   FSL_SDHC: 0, FSL_SDHC: 1
*** Warning - bad CRC, using default environment

auto-detected panel HDMI
Display: HDMI (1024x768)
In:    serial
Out:   serial
Err:   serial
Board: Wandboard rev C1
Net:   FEC [PRIME]
Hit any key to stop autoboot:  0
=> ▌
```

U-Boot banner

The Yocto 2.4 version of U-Boot for the Wandboard has introduced changes in the default environment so that there is less platform-specific customization made in the source. As such, previous versions used to have a default environment ready to perform a network boot just by setting a few environmental variables and running the `netboot` script.

The current U-Boot has instead replaced it with a network boot mechanism that looks for a U-Boot script called `extlinux.conf` on the configured TFTP server and executes it. In that way, platform-specific booting options are isolated into the boot script which is compiled with the U-Boot source.

The Yocto Project prepares an `extlinux.conf` boot script and copies it to the `deploy` directory along with the images. We can add kernel command line arguments to pass to the Linux kernel in this boot script by using the `UBOOT_EXTLINUX_KERNEL_ARGS` configuration variable. More details about customizing the `extlinux.conf` script is provided in `Chapter 2`, *The BSP Layer*.

However, for development purposes, it is more flexible to restore the previous network boot environment variables:

```
> env set netload 'tftpboot ${loadaddr} ${image};tftpboot ${fdt_addr}
${fdt_file}'
> env set netargs 'setenv bootargs console=${console} ${optargs}
root=/dev/nfs ip=${ipaddr} nfsroot=${serverip}:${nfsroot},v3,tcp'
> env set netboot 'echo Booting from net ...;run netargs;run netload;bootz
${loadaddr} - ${fdt_addr}'
```

The `netload` script loads the Linux kernel binary and the device tree blob into memory. The `netargs` script prepares the `bootargs` environmental variable to pass the correct kernel command line parameters for a network boot, and the `netboot` command executes the network boot by running `netargs` and using the `bootz` command.

Now we will prepare the rest of the environmental variables it needs:

1. Configure a static IP address with:

   ```
   > env set ipaddr <static_ip>
   ```

2. Configure the IP address of your host system, where the TFTP and NFS servers have been set up:

   ```
   > env set serverip <host_ip>
   ```

3. Configure the root filesystem mount:

   ```
   > env set nfsroot /nfsroot
   ```

4. Configure the Linux kernel and device tree filenames:

   ```
   > env set image zImage-wandboard.bin
   > env set fdt_file zImage-imx6qp-wandboard-revd1.dtb
   ```

5. Save the U-Boot environment to the microSD card:

> **env save**

6. Perform a network boot:

> **run netboot**

The Linux kernel and device tree will be fetched from the TFTP server, and the root filesystem will be mounted by the kernel from the NFS share.

You should be able to log in with the root user without a password prompt.

Once booted, we can find out the kernel command line arguments used to boot by doing:

```
$ cat /proc/cmdline
console=ttymxc0,115200 root=/dev/nfs ip=192.168.1.15
nfsroot=192.168.1.115:/nfsroot,v3,tcp
```

Using Docker as a Yocto build system container

Embedded systems often have a long product lifetime so software needs to be built with the same Yocto version over several years in a predictable way. Older versions of Yocto often have problems in running with state-of-the-art distributions.

To work around this, there are several alternatives:

- Keep a build machine with a fixed operating system. This is problematic as the machine also ages and it may suffer from hardware problems and need re-installation.
- Use a cloud machine with a fixed operating system. Not everyone has this type of infrastructure available and it usually has a price tag attached.
- Build in a virtual machine such as VMware or VirtualBox. This affects the build performance significantly.
- Use a Docker Yocto builder container. This has the advantage of providing the same isolation as the virtual machine but with a much better build performance.

We saw how to run a `docker` container in the *Using the Toaster web interface* recipe. Now we will see how to create our own Docker image to use as a Yocto builder.

Getting ready

Docker is able to build images automatically by reading instructions from a text file called a `Dockerfile`. Dockerfiles can be layered on top of each other, so to create a Docker Yocto builder image we would start by using a Ubuntu 16.04 Docker image or one of the other supported distributions, and sequentially configure the image.

An example `Dockerfile` for a Yocto builder follows:

```
FROM ubuntu:16.04
MAINTAINER Alex Gonzalez <alex@lindusembedded.com>
# Upgrade system and Yocto Proyect basic dependencies
RUN apt-get update && apt-get -y upgrade && apt-get -y install gawk wget
git-core diffstat unzip texinfo gcc-multilib build-essential chrpath socat
cpio python python3 python3-pip python3-pexpect xz-utils debianutils
iputils-ping libsdl1.2-dev xterm curl
# Set up locales
RUN apt-get -y install locales apt-utils sudo && dpkg-reconfigure locales
&& locale-gen en_US.UTF-8 && update-locale LC_ALL=en_US.UTF-8
LANG=en_US.UTF-8
ENV LANG en_US.utf8
# Clean up APT when done.
RUN apt-get clean && rm -rf /var/lib/apt/lists/* /tmp/* /var/tmp/*
# Replace dash with bash
RUN rm /bin/sh && ln -s bash /bin/sh
# User management
RUN groupadd -g 1000 build && useradd -u 1000 -g 1000 -ms /bin/bash build
&& usermod -a -G sudo build && usermod -a -G users build
# Install repo
RUN curl -o /usr/local/bin/repo
https://storage.googleapis.com/git-repo-downloads/repo && chmod a+x
/usr/local/bin/repo
# Run as build user from the installation path
ENV YOCTO_INSTALL_PATH "/opt/yocto"
RUN install -o 1000 -g 1000 -d $YOCTO_INSTALL_PATH
USER build
WORKDIR ${YOCTO_INSTALL_PATH}
# Set the Yocto release
ENV YOCTO_RELEASE "rocko"
# Install Poky
RUN git clone --branch ${YOCTO_RELEASE} git://git.yoctoproject.org/poky
# Install FSL community BSP
RUN mkdir -p ${YOCTO_INSTALL_PATH}/fsl-community-bsp && cd
${YOCTO_INSTALL_PATH}/fsl-community-bsp && repo init -u
https://github.com/Freescale/fsl-community-bsp-platform -b ${YOCTO_RELEASE}
&& repo sync
# Create a build directory for the FSL community BSP
```

```
RUN mkdir -p ${YOCTO_INSTALL_PATH}/fsl-community-bsp/build
# Make /home/build the working directory
WORKDIR /home/build
```

How to do it...

1. To build the container locally from the directory containing the Dockerfile, run the following command:

   ```
   $ docker build
   ```

2. However, there is no need to build it locally as the container is automatically built on the Docker registry:
   https://hub.docker.com/r/yoctocookbook2ndedition/docker-yocto-builder

   First create an empty folder owned by a user with the same uid and gid that the `build` user inside the container:

   ```
   $ sudo install -o 1000 -g 1000 -d /opt/yocto/docker-yocto-builder
   ```

   And change inside the new directory:

   ```
   $ cd /opt/yocto/docker-yocto-builder
   ```

   To run the container and map its `/home/build` folder to the current directory, type:

   ```
   $ docker run -it --rm -v $PWD:/home/build
   yoctocookbook2ndedition/docker-yocto-builder
   ```

   Where:

   - `-it` instructs Docker to keep `stdin` open even when the container is not attached and assign a `pseudo-tty` to the interactive shell
   - `--rm` instructs Docker to remove the container on exit
   - `-v` maps the host current directory as the `/home/build` container volume

3. We can now instruct the container to build a Poky project with:

```
build@container$ source /opt/yocto/poky/oe-init-build-env qemuarm
build@container$ MACHINE=qemuarm bitbake core-image-minimal
```

4. To build a FSL community BSP project, you need to map the /opt/yocto/fsl-community-bsp/build container directory with the current directory as the setup-environment script only works when the build directory is under the installation folder:

```
$ docker run -it --rm -v $PWD:/opt/yocto/fsl-community-bsp/build
yoctocookbook2ndedition/docker-yocto-builder
```

5. Then we can run the following command inside the container to create a new project and start a build:

```
build@container$ cd /opt/yocto/fsl-community-bsp/
build@container$ mkdir -p wandboard
build@container$ MACHINE=wandboard DISTRO=poky source setup-
environment build
build@container$ bitbake core-image-minimal
```

How it works...

Instructing Docker to start the image creation process with a Ubuntu 16.04 image is as easy as starting the Dockerfile with the following:

```
FROM ubuntu:16.04
```

To inherit a Docker image, you use the Dockerfile FROM syntax.

Other commands used in the Dockerfile are:

- RUN, which will run the specified command in a new layer and commit the result
- ENV, to set an environmental variable
- USER, which sets the username to use for RUN and CMD instructions following it
- WORKDIR, which sets the working directory for RUN and CMD instructions that follow it
- CMD, which provides the default executable for the container, in this case the Bash shell

The rest of the `Dockerfile` does the following:

- Updates Ubuntu 16.04 to the latest packages
- Installs Yocto dependencies
- Sets up the locale for the container
- Adds a new `build` user
- Installs both Poky and the FSL community BSP release

The image has Poky installed at `/opt/yocto/poky` and the FSL community BSP installed at `/opt/yocto/fsl-community-bsp`. When it starts, the default directory is `/home/build`.

The usual way to work with a `docker` container is to instruct it to run commands but store the output in the host filesystem.

In our case, we instruct the container to run BitBake for us, but we map the build directories to the host by doing the external volume mapping when the container is initialized. In that way, all the build output is stored on the host machine.

See also

- Docker documentation for the image builder can be found at `https://docs.docker.com/engine/reference/builder/`

Sharing downloads

You will usually work on several projects simultaneously, probably for different hardware platforms or different target images. In such cases, it is important to optimize the build times by sharing downloads.

Getting ready

The build system runs a search for downloaded sources in a number of places:

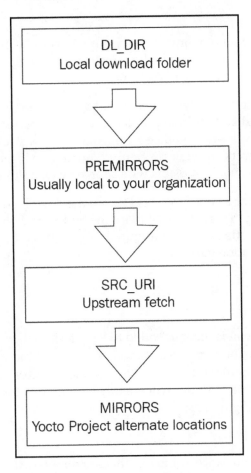

Source download hierarchy

- It tries the local `downloads` folder.
- It looks into the configured pre-mirrors, which are usually local to your organization.

- It then tries to fetch from the upstream source as configured in the package recipe.
- Finally, it checks the configured mirrors. Mirrors are public alternate locations for the source.

If a package source is not found in any of these four sources, the package build will fail with an error. Build warnings are also issued when upstream fetching fails and mirrors are tried, so that the upstream problem can be looked at.

The Yocto Project, including BSP layers such as `meta-freescale`, maintains a set of mirrors to isolate the build system from problems with the upstream servers. However, when adding external layers, you could be adding support for packages that are not in the Yocto Project's mirror servers, or other configured mirrors, so it is recommended that you keep a local pre-mirror to avoid problems with source availability.

The default Poky setting for a new project is to store the downloaded package sources on the current build directory. This is the first place the build system will run a search for source downloads. This setting can be configured in your project's `conf/local.conf` file with the `DL_DIR` configuration variable.

How to do it...

To optimize the build time, it is recommended to keep a shared `downloads` directory between all your projects. The `setup-environment` script of the `meta-freescale` layer changes the default `DL_DIR` to the `fsl-community-bsp` directory created by the repo tool. With this setup, the `downloads` folder will already be shared between all the projects in your host system. It is configured as:

```
DL_DIR ?= "${BSPDIR}/downloads/"
```

A more scalable setup (for instance, for teams that are remotely distributed) is to configure a pre-mirror. For example, add the following to your `conf/local.conf` file:

```
INHERIT += "own-mirrors"
SOURCE_MIRROR_URL = "http://example.com/my-source-mirror"
```

A usual setup is to have a build server serve its `downloads` directory. The build server can be configured to prepare tarballs of the `Git` directories to avoid having to perform Git operations from upstream servers. This setting in your `conf/local.conf` file will affect the build performance, but this is usually acceptable in a build server. Add the following:

```
BB_GENERATE_MIRROR_TARBALLS = "1"
```

An advantage of this setup is that the build server's `downloads` folder can also be backed up to guarantee source availability for your products in the future. This is especially important in embedded products with long-term availability requirements.

In order to test this setup, you may check to see whether a build is possible just by using the pre-mirrors with the following:

```
BB_FETCH_PREMIRRORONLY = "1"
```

This setting in your `conf/local.conf` file can also be distributed across the team with the `TEMPLATECONF` variable during the project's creation.

Sharing the shared state cache

The Yocto Project builds everything from source. When you create a new project, only the configuration files are created. The build process then compiles everything from scratch, including the cross-compilation toolchain and some native tools important for the build.

This process can take a long time, and the Yocto Project implements a shared state cache mechanism that is used for incremental builds with the aim to build only the strictly necessary components for a given change.

For this to work, the build system calculates a checksum of the given input data to a task. If the input data changes, the task needs to be rebuilt. In simplistic terms, the build process generates a run script for each task that can be checksummed and compared. It also keeps track of a task's output, so that it can be reused.

A package recipe can modify the shared state caching to a task, for example, to always force a rebuild by marking it as `nostamp`. A more in-depth explanation of the shared state cache mechanism can be found in the *Yocto Project Reference Manual* at `http://www.yoctoproject.org/docs/2.4/ref-manual/ref-manual.html`.

How to do it...

By default, the build system will use a shared state cache directory called `sstate-cache` on your build directory to store the cached data. This can be changed with the `SSTATE_DIR` configuration variable in your `conf/local.conf` file. The cached data is stored in directories named with the first two characters of the hash. Inside, the filenames contain the whole task checksum, so the cache validity can be ascertained just by looking at the filename. The build process set scene tasks will evaluate the cached data and use it to accelerate the build if valid.

When you want to start a build from a clean state, you need to remove both the `sstate-cache` directory and the `tmp` directory.

You can also instruct BitBake to ignore the shared state cache by using the `--no-setscene` argument when running it.

It's a good practice to keep backups of clean shared state caches (for example, from a build server), which can be used in case of shared state cache corruption.

There's more...

Sharing a shared state cache is possible; however, it needs to be approached with care. Not all changes are detected by the shared state cache implementation, and when this happens, some or all of the cache needs to be invalidated. This can cause problems when the state cache is being shared.

The recommendation in this case depends on the use case. Developers working on Yocto metadata should keep the shared state cache as default, separated per project.

However, validation and testing engineers, kernel and bootloader developers, and application developers would probably benefit from a well-maintained shared state cache.

To configure an NFS share drive to be shared among the development team to speed up the builds, you can add the following to your `conf/local.conf` configuration file:

```
SSTATE_MIRRORS ?= "\
    file://.* file:///nfs/local/mount/sstate/PATH"
```

To configure shared state cache sharing via HTTP, add the following to your conf/local.conf configuration file:

```
SSTATE_MIRRORS ?= "file://.*
http://example.com/some_path/sstate-cache/PATH"
```

The expression PATH in these examples will get substituted by the build system with a directory named with the hash's first two characters.

Setting up a package feed

An embedded system project seldom has the need to introduce changes to the Yocto build system. Most of the time and effort is spent in application development, followed by a lesser amount in system development, maybe kernel and bootloader work.

As such, a whole system rebuild is probably done very few times. A new project is usually built from a prebuilt shared state cache, and application development work only needs to be done to perform full or incremental builds of a handful of packages.

Once the packages are built, they need to be installed on the target system for testing. Emulated machines are fine for application development, but most hardware-dependent work needs to be done on embedded hardware.

Getting ready

An option is to manually copy the build binaries to the target's root filesystem, either copying it to the NFS share on the host system the target is mounting its root filesystem from (as explained in the *Configuring network booting for a development setup* recipe earlier) or using any other method such as SCP, FTP, or even a microSD card.

This method is also used by IDEs such as Eclipse when debugging an application you are working on, and by the devtool Yocto command-line tool which will be introduced later on. However, this method does not scale well when you need to install several packages and dependencies.

The next option would be to copy the packaged binaries (that is, the RPM, DEB, or IPK packages) to the target's filesystem and then use the target's package management system to install them. For this to work, your target's filesystem needs to be built with package management tools. Doing this is as easy as adding the `package-management` feature to your root filesystem; for example, you may add the following line to your project's `conf/local.conf` file:

```
EXTRA_IMAGE_FEATURES += "package-management"
```

The default package type in Yocto is RPM, and for an RPM package, you will copy it to the target and use the `rpm` or `dnf` utilities to install it. In Yocto 2.4, the default RPM package manager is **Dandified Yum** (**DNF**). It is the next generation version of the **Yellodog Updater Modified** (**YUM**) and licensed under the General Public License v2.

However, the most convenient way to do this is to convert your host system package's output directory into a package feed. For example, if you are using the default RPM package format, you may convert `tmp/deploy/rpm` in your build directory into a package feed that your target can use to update.

For this to work, you need to configure an HTTP server on your computer that serves the packages.

Versioning packages

You also need to make sure that the generated packages are correctly versioned, and that means updating the recipe revision, **PR**, with every change. It is possible to do this manually, but the recommended and compulsory way if you want to use package feeds is to use a PR server.

However, the PR server is not enabled by default. The packages generated without a PR server are consistent with each other but offer no update guarantees for a system that is already running.

The simplest PR server configuration is to run it locally on your host system. To do this, you add the following to your `conf/local.conf` file:

```
PRSERV_HOST = "localhost:0"
```

With this setup, update coherency is guaranteed for your feed.

If you want to share your feed with other developers, or you are configuring a build server or package server, you would run a single instance of the PR server by running the following command:

```
$ bitbake-prserv --host <server_ip> --port <port> --start
```

And you will update the project's build configuration to use the centralized PR server, editing `conf/local.conf` as follows:

```
PRSERV_HOST = "<server_ip>:<port>"
```

Also, if you are using a shared state cache as described before, all of the contributors to the shared state cache need to use the same PR server.

Once the feed's integrity is guaranteed, we need to configure an HTTP server to serve the feed.

How to do it...

We will use `lighttpd` for this example, as it is lightweight and easy to configure. Follow these steps:

1. Install the web server:

    ```
    $ sudo apt-get install lighttpd
    ```

2. By default, the document root specified in the `/etc/lighttpd/lighttpd.conf` configuration file is `/var/www/html`, so we only need a symlink to our package feed:

    ```
    $ sudo ln -s /opt/yocto/fsl-community-bsp/wandboard/tmp/deploy/rpm
    /var/www/html/rpm
    ```

3. Next, reload the configuration as follows:

    ```
    $ sudo service lighttpd reload
    ```

    For development, you can also launch a Python HTTP server from the feeds directory as follows:
    ```
    $ cd /opt/yocto/fsl-community-
    bsp/wandboard/tmp/deploy/rpm
    $ sudo python -m SimpleHTTPServer 80
    ```

4. Refresh the package index. This needs to be done manually to update the package feed after every build:

```
$ bitbake package-index
```

5. If you want to serve the packages from a different directory instead of directly from your build directory:

   1. You will need to copy the packages:

   ```
   $ rsync -r -u /opt/yocto/fsl-community-
   bsp/wandboard/tmp/deploy/rpm/* <new_dir>/
   ```

   2. Then add the corresponding metadata to the repositories. For that, you will need to install the createrepo tool:

   ```
   $ sudo apt-get install createrepo
   ```

   3. And direct it to the new `feed` directory:

   ```
   $ createrepo <new_dir>
   ```

   The createrepo tool will create XML-based metadata from the RPM packages:

You can also build and use the `createrepo-c` utility from your Yocto build system, a C implementation of createrepo, as follows:
```
$ bitbake createrepo-c-native -c addto_recipe_sysroot
$ oe-run-native createrepo-c-native createrepo_c
<new_dir>
```

Then we need to configure our target filesystem with the new package feeds:

1. Log in to the target and create a new directory to contain the repository configuration:

```
$ mkdir -p /etc/yum.repos.d
```

The repository configuration files will have the following format:

```
[<repo name>]
name=<Repository description>
baseurl=<url://path/to/repo>
enabled=<0 (disable) or 1 (enabled)>
gpgcheck=<0 (disable signature check) or 1 (enabled)>
gpgkey=<url://path/to/gpg-file if gpgcheck is enabled>
```

The previously mentioned `baseurl` is the complete URL for the repositories, with a `http://`, `https://`, `ftp://`, or `file://` prefix.

An example repository configuration file is as follows:

```
$ vi /etc/yum.repos.d/yocto.repo
[yocto-rpm]
name=Yocto 2.4: rpm
baseurl=http://<server-ip>/rpm/
```

2. Once the setup is ready, we will be able to query and update packages from the target's root filesystem with the following:

```
# dnf --nogpgcheck makecache
# dnf --nogpgcheck search <package_name>
# dnf --nogpgcheck install <package_name>
```

By default, `dnf` is built to use sign package feeds so we need to either configure the preceding repository with:

```
gpgcheck=0
```

Or use the `--nogpgcheck` command line argument as shown previously.

3. To make this change persistent in the target's root filesystem, we can configure the package feeds at compilation time by using the `PACKAGE_FEED_*` variables in `conf/local.conf`, as follows:

```
PACKAGE_FEED_URIS = "http://<server_ip>/"
PACKAGE_FEED_BASE_PATHS = "rpm"
```

The package feed's base URL is composed as shown next:

```
${PACKAGE_FEED_URIS}/${PACKAGE_FEED_BASE_PATHS}/${PACKAGE_FEED_ARCH
S}.
```

By default, the package feed is prepared as a single repository so there is no need to use the `PACKAGE_FEED_ARCHS` variable.

The variables shown previously will configure the filesystem for any of the supported package formats.

There's more...

The Yocto build system can both generate signed packages and configure target images to use a signed package feed.

The build system will use the GNU privacy guard (GNUPG), an RFC 4880-compliant cryptographic software suite licensed under the GNU General Public License GPLv3.

Generating signed packages

To configure the project for RPM package signing, add the following to your `conf/local.conf` configuration file:

```
INHERIT += "sign_rpm"
```

For IPK package signing, do the following instead:

```
INHERIT += "sign_ipk"
```

You will then need to define the name of the GPG key to use for signing, and its passphrase:

```
RPM_GPG_NAME = "<key ID>"
RPM_GPG_PASSPHRASE = "<key passphrase>"
```

Or for the IPK package format:

```
IPK_GPG_NAME = "<key ID>"
IPK_GPG_PASSPHRASE_FILE = "<path/to/passphrase/file>"
```

See the *Creating a GNUPG key pair* next section in this same recipe to find the generated key ID.

The Yocto build system will locate the private GPG key in the host and use it to sign the generated packages.

The Yocto 2.4 release supports signing RPM and IPK packages, but not DEB packages.

Using signed package feeds

To enable your target image to use a signed package feed, you will need to add the following configuration to your `conf/local.conf` configuration file:

```
INHERIT += "sign_package_feed"
PACKAGE_FEED_GPG_NAME = "<key name>"
PACKAGE_FEED_GPG_PASSPHRASE_FILE = "<path/to/passphrase/file>"
```

The `<path/to/passphrase/file>` shown previously is the absolute path to a text file containing the passphrase.

The `dnf` package manager will use the configured public key to verify the authenticity of the package feed.

Creating a GNUPG key pair

In the *Setting up the host system* recipe in this same chapter, you installed the gnupg package in your host machine; if you didn't, you can do so now with:

```
$ sudo apt-get install gnupg
```

To generate a key, type the following command:

```
$ gpg --gen-key
```

Follow the instructions, keeping the default values. You may need to generate random data with mouse movements and disk activity.

You can check your key with:

```
$ gpg --list-keys
/home/alex/.gnupg/pubring.gpg
-----------------------------
pub     2048R/4EF0ECE0 2017-08-13
uid                     Alex Gonzalez <alex@lindusembedded.com>
sub     2048R/298446F3 2017-08-13
```

The GPG key ID in the previous example is 4EF0ECE0.

And export it with the following command:

```
$ gpg --output rpm-feed.gpg --export <id>
```

The ID may be the key ID or any part of the user ID, such as the email address. The exported public key may now be moved to its final destination, such as the package feed web server.

An example `conf/local.conf` configuration would be:

```
INHERIT += "sign_rpm"
RPM_GPG_NAME = "4EF0ECE0"
RPM_GPG_PASSPHRASE = "<very-secure-password>"
INHERIT += "sign_package_feed"
PACKAGE_FEED_GPG_NAME = "4EF0ECE0"
PACKAGE_FEED_GPG_PASSPHRASE_FILE = "/opt/yocto/passphrase.txt"
```

Remember to run the following after rebuilding the image so that the repository feed is signed:
```
$ bitbake package-index
```
If you are preparing a repository manually, you will have to sign it too.

Backing up your keys

You can move your key pair to a secure location with:

```
$ gpg --output rpm-feed.pub --armor --export <key id>
$ gpg --output rpm-feed.sec --armor --export-secret-key <key id>
```

Copy them securely to a new location and import them with:

```
$ gpg --import  rpm-feed.pub
$ gpg --allow-secret-key-import --import  rpm-feed.sec
```

See also

- More information and a user manual for the `dnf` utility can be found at
  `http://dnf.readthedocs.io/en/latest/index.html`
- The GNUPG documentation can be accessed at
  `https://www.gnupg.org/documentation/`

Using build history

When maintaining software for an embedded product, you need a way to know what has changed and how it is going to affect your product.

On a Yocto system, you may need to update a package revision (for instance, to fix a security vulnerability), and you need to make sure what the implications of this change are, for example, in terms of package dependencies and changes to the root filesystem.

Build history enables you to do just that, and we will explore it in this recipe.

How to do it...

To enable build history, add the following to your `conf/local.conf` file:

```
INHERIT += "buildhistory"
```

The preceding configuration enables information gathering, including dependency graphs.

To enable the storage of build history in a local Git repository add the following line to the `conf/local.conf` configuration file as well:

```
BUILDHISTORY_COMMIT = "1"
```

The Git repository location can be set by the `BUILDHISTORY_DIR` variable, which by default is set to a `buildhistory` directory on your build directory.

By default, `buildhistory` tracks changes to packages, images, and SDKs. This is configurable using the `BUILDHISTORY_FEATURES` variable. For example, to track only image changes, add the following to your `conf/local.conf`:

```
BUILDHISTORY_FEATURES = "image"
```

It can also track specific files and copy them to the `buildhistory` directory. By default, this includes only `/etc/passwd` and `/etc/groups`, but it can be used to track any important files, such as security certificates. The files need to be added with the `BUILDHISTORY_IMAGE_FILES` variable in your `conf/local.conf` file, as follows:

```
BUILDHISTORY_IMAGE_FILES += "/path/to/file"
```

Build history will slow down the build, increase the build size, and may also grow the Git directory to an unmanageable size. The recommendation is to enable it on a build server for software releases, or in specific cases, such as when updating production software.

How it works...

When enabled, it will keep a record of the changes to each package and image in the form of a Git repository in a way that can be explored and analyzed.

 Note that build history will only record changes to the build. If your project is already built, you will have to modify something or remove the `tmp` folder in order for build history to be generated.

The build configuration and metadata revision, as printed by Bitbake, is stored in the `build-id.txt` file.

For a package, build history records the following information:

- Package and recipe revision
- Dependencies
- Package size
- Files

For an image, it records the following information:

- Build configuration
- Dependency graphs
- A list of files that include ownership and permissions, as well as size and symlink information
- A list of installed packages

And for an SDK, it records the following information:

- SDK configuration
- A list of both host and target files, including ownership and permissions, as well as size and symlinks information
- Package-related information is only generated for the standard SDK, not for the extensible SDK. This includes:
    - Dependency graphs
    - A list of installed packages

For more details about using Yocto SDKs, please refer to the *Preparing an SDK* and *Using the extensible SDK* recipes in `Chapter 4`, *Application Development*.

Looking at build history

Inspecting the `Git` directory with build history can be done in several ways:

- Using Git tools such as `gitk` or `git log`
- Using the `buildhistory-diff` command-line tool, which displays the differences in a human-readable format
- Using a Django-1.8-based web interface

To install the Django web interface on a development machine, you first need to install some host dependencies:

```
$ sudo apt-get install python3-django
$ sudo apt-get install python-django-registration
```

 This will install Django 1.8 both for Python 2.7, and Python 3. The `buildhistory-web` interface will only currently work on Python 2.7 but the build history import script will need to run under Python 3 as that is what the Yocto 2.4 BitBake uses.

Now we can clone the web interface source and configure it:

```
$ cd /opt/yocto/fsl-community-bsp/sources
$ git clone git://git.yoctoproject.org/buildhistory-web
$ cd buildhistory-web/
```

Edit the `settings.py` file to change the path to the database engine:

```
DATABASES = {
    'default': {
        'ENGINE': 'django.db.backends.sqlite3',
        'NAME': '/opt/yocto/fsl-community-bsp/sources/buildhistory-
web/bhtest.db3',
        'USER': '',
        'PASSWORD': '',
        'HOST': '',
        'PORT': '',
    }
}
```

You then need to set up the Django application with:

```
$ python manage.py migrate
```

Next, import `buildhistory` as follows:

```
$ python3 warningmgr/import.py /opt/yocto/fsl-community-bsp/sources/poky/
/opt/yocto/fsl-community-bsp/wandboard/buildhistory/
```

The preceding command will need to be executed each time there is a new build.

And finally, start the web server on the localhost with:

```
$ python manage.py runserver
```

 To bind it to a different IP address and port you can do:
`$ python manage.py runserver <host>:<port>`
But you will need to configure your `settings.py` accordingly with:
`ALLOWED_HOSTS = [u'<host>']`

The following image shows the **Buildhistory** web interface home page:

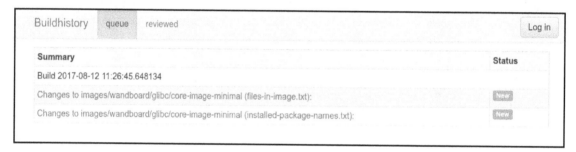

Buildhistory web interface

There's more...

To maintain build history, it's important to optimize it and prevent it from growing over time. Periodic backups of build history and clean-ups of older data are important to keep the build history repository at a manageable size.

Once the `buildhistory` directory has been backed up, the following process will trim it and keep only the most recent history:

1. Copy your repository to a temporary RAM filesystem (`tmpfs`) to speed things up. Check the output of the `df -h` command to see which directories are `tmpfs` filesystems and how much space they have available, and use one. For example, in Ubuntu 16.04, the `/run/` directory is available.

2. Copy build history to the /run directory as follows:

```
$ sudo mkdir /run/workspace
$ sudo chown ${USER} /run/workspace/
$ cp -r /opt/yocto/fsl-community-bsp/wandboard/buildhistory/
/run/workspace/
$ cd /run/workspace/buildhistory/
```

3. Add a graft point for a commit 1 month ago with no parents:

```
$ git rev-parse "HEAD@{1 month ago}" > .git/info/grafts
```

4. Make the graft point permanent:

```
$ git filter-branch
```

5. Clone a new repository to clean up the remaining Git objects:

```
$ git clone file://${tmpfs}/buildhistory buildhistory.new
```

6. Replace the old buildhistory directory with the new cleaned one:

```
$ rm -rf buildhistory
$ mv buildhistory.new /opt/yocto/fsl-community-
bsp/wandboard/buildhistory/
```

7. And finally, remove the workspace:

```
$ rm -rf /run/workspace/
```

Working with build statistics

The build system can collect build information per task and image. The data may be used to identify areas of optimization of build times and bottlenecks, especially when new recipes are added to the system. This recipe will explain how the build statistics work.

How to do it...

To enable the collection of statistics, your project needs to inherit the buildstats class by adding it to USER_CLASSES in your conf/local.conf file. By default, the fsl-community-bsp build project is configured to enable them:

```
USER_CLASSES ?= "buildstats"
```

You can configure the location of these statistics with the BUILDSTATS_BASE variable, and by default it is set to the buildstats folder in the tmp directory under the build directory (tmp/buildstats).

The buildstats folder contains a folder per image with the build stats under a timestamp folder. Under it will be a sub-directory per package in your built image, and a build_stats file that contains:

- Host system information
- Root filesystem location and size
- Build time
- Average CPU usage

How it works...

The accuracy of the data depends on the download directory, DL_DIR, and the shared state cache directory, SSTATE_DIR, existing on the same partition or volume, so you may need to configure them accordingly if you are planning to use the build data.

An example build-stats file looks like the following:

```
Host Info: Linux langabe 4.10.0-30-generic #34~16.04.1-Ubuntu SMP Wed Aug 2
02:13:56 UTC 2017 x86_64 x86_64
Build Started: 1502529685.16
Uncompressed Rootfs size: 93M   /opt/yocto/fsl-community-
bsp/wandboard/tmp/work/wandboard-poky-linux-gnueabi/core-image-minimal/1.0-
r0/rootfs
Elapsed time: 101.87 seconds
CPU usage: 47.8%
```

Inside each package, we have a list of tasks; for example, for `ncurses-6.0+20161126-r0`, we have the following tasks:

- do_compile
- do_fetch
- do_package
- do_package_write_rpm
- do_populate_lic
- do_rm_work
- do_configure
- do_install
- do_packagedata
- do_package_qa
- do_patch
- do_prepare_recipe_sysroot
- do_populate_sysroot
- do_unpack

Each one of them contains the following:

- Build time
- CPU usage
- Disk stats

The information is displayed as follows:

```
Event: TaskStarted
Started: 1502541082.15
ncurses-6.0+20161126-r0: do_compile
Elapsed time: 35.37 seconds
utime: 31
stime: 2
cutime: 7790
cstime: 1138
IO rchar: 778886123
IO read_bytes: 3354624
IO wchar: 79063307
IO cancelled_write_bytes: 1507328
IO syscr: 150688
IO write_bytes: 26726400
```

```
IO syscw: 31565
rusage ru_utime: 0.312
rusage ru_stime: 0.027999999999999997
rusage ru_maxrss: 78268
rusage ru_minflt: 5050
rusage ru_majflt: 0
rusage ru_inblock: 0
rusage ru_oublock: 1184
rusage ru_nvcsw: 705
rusage ru_nivcsw: 126
Child rusage ru_utime: 77.908
Child rusage ru_stime: 11.388
Child rusage ru_maxrss: 76284
Child rusage ru_minflt: 2995484
Child rusage ru_majflt: 0
Child rusage ru_inblock: 6552
Child rusage ru_oublock: 51016
Child rusage ru_nvcsw: 18280
Child rusage ru_nivcsw: 29984
Status: PASSED
Ended: 1502541117.52
```

The CPU usage is given with data extracted from `/proc/<pid>/stat` and given in units of clock ticks:

- `utime` is the amount of time the process has been scheduled in user mode
- `stime` is the amount of time it has been scheduled in kernel mode
- `cutime` is the time the process's children were scheduled in user mode
- `cstime` is the time they were scheduled in kernel mode

And the following is also available from the resource usage information provided from `getrusage()`, representing the resource usage of the calling process, including all threads, as well as the children and their descendants:

- `ru_utime` is the user CPU time used in seconds
- `ru_stime` is the system CPU time used in seconds
- `ru_maxrss` is the maximum resident set size in KB
- `ru_minflt` is the number of page faults without I/O activity
- `ru_majflt` is the number of page faults with required I/O activity
- `ru_inblock` is the count of filesystem inputs

- `ru_oublock` is the count of filesystem outputs
- `ru_nvcsw` is the count of times a process yielded voluntarily
- `ru_nivcsw` is the count of times a process was forced to yield

Finally, the disk access statistics are provided from `/proc/<pid>/io` as follows:

- `rchar` is the number of bytes read from storage
- `wchar` is the number of bytes written to disk
- `syscr` is the estimated number of read I/O operations
- `syscw` is the estimated number of write I/O operations
- `read_bytes` is the number of bytes read from storage (estimate-accurate for block-backed filesystems)
- `write_bytes` is the estimated number of bytes written to the storage layer
- `cancelled_write_bytes` is the number of bytes written that did not happen, by truncating page cache

There's more...

You can also obtain a graphical representation of the data using the `pybootchartgui.py` tool included in the Poky source. From your project's build folder, you can execute the following command to obtain a `bootchart.png` graphic in `/tmp`:

```
$ cd /optyocto/fsl-community-bsp/wandboard/
$ /opt/yocto/fsl-community-
bsp/sources/poky/scripts/pybootchartgui/pybootchartgui.py
    tmp/buildstats/ -o /tmp
```

An example graphic is shown next:

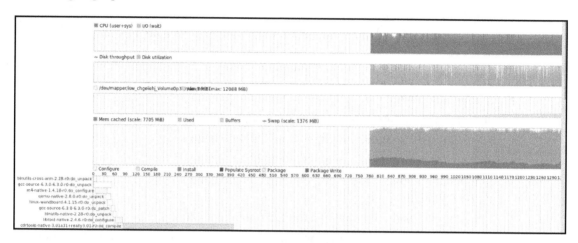

Graphical build statistics documentation

See also

- Refer to the Linux kernel documentation for more details regarding the data obtained through the proc filesystem: `https://git.kernel.org/pub/scm/linux/kernel/git/torvalds/linux.git/tree/Documentation/filesystems/proc.txt`

Debugging the build system

In the last recipe of this chapter, we will explore the different methods available to debug problems with the build system and its metadata.

Getting ready

Let's first introduce some of the usual use cases for a debugging session.

Finding recipes

A good way to check whether a specific package is supported in your current layers is to search for it as follows:

```
$ cd /opt/yocto/fsl-community-bsp/sources
$ find -name "*busybox*"
```

This will recursively search all layers for the BusyBox pattern. You can limit the search to recipes and append files by executing:

```
$ find -name "*busybox*.bb*"
```

Yocto includes a `bitbake-layers` command-line utility that can also be used to search for specific recipes on the configured layers, with the preferred version appearing first:

```
$ bitbake-layers show-recipes "<package_name>"
```

Here, <package_name> also supports wildcards.

For example:

```
$ bitbake-layers show-recipes gdb*
=== Matching recipes: ===
gdb:
  meta                   7.12.1
gdb-cross-arm:
  meta                   7.12.1
gdb-cross-canadian-arm:
  meta                   7.12.1
gdbm:
  meta                   1.12
```

To use `bitbake-layers`, the environment script must have been sourced first.

Finally, the devtool command-line utility can also be used to search the dependency cache with a regular expression. It will search on recipe or package names but also description and install files, so it is better suited in the context of developing recipes metadata:

```
$ devtool search <regular expression>
```

To use devtool, the environment needs to be previously set up, and the shared state cache populated:

```
$ cd /opt/yocto/fsl-community-bsp
$ source setup-environment wandboard
$ bitbake <target-image>
$ devtool search gdb
Loaded 2323 entries from dependency cache.
perl                   Perl scripting language
shared-mime-info       Shared MIME type database and specification
bash-completion        Programmable Completion for Bash 4
glib-2.0               A general-purpose utility library
python                 The Python Programming Language
gdbm                   Key/value database library with extensible hashing
gcc-runtime            Runtime libraries from GCC
```

Dumping BitBake's environment

When developing or debugging package or image recipes, it is very common to ask BitBake to list its environment both globally and for a specific target, be it a package or image.

To dump the global environment and `grep` for a variable of interest (for example, DISTRO_FEATURES), use the following command:

```
$ bitbake -e | grep -w DISTRO_FEATURES
```

Optionally, to locate the source directory for a specific package recipe such as BusyBox, use the following command:

```
$ bitbake -e busybox | grep ^S=
```

You could also execute the following command to locate the working directory for a package or image recipe:

```
$ bitbake -e <target> | grep ^WORKDIR=
```

Using the development shell

BitBake offers the `devshell` and `devpyshell` tasks to help developers. They are executed with the following commands:

```
$ bitbake -c devshell <target>
```

And:

```
$ bitbake -c devpyshell <target>
```

They will unpack and patch the source, and open a new Terminal (they will autodetect your Terminal type or it can be set with `OE_TERMINAL`) in the target source directory, which has the environment correctly set up. They run with the `nostamp` flag so up-to-date tasks will be rerun.

The `devpyshell` command will additionally set up the Python environment including Python objects and code such as the datastore d object.

 While in a graphical environment, `devshell` and `devpyshell` will open a new Terminal or console window, but if we are working on a non-graphical environment, such as Telnet or SSH, you may need to specify `screen` as your Terminal in your `conf/local.conf` configuration file as follows:
`OE_TERMINAL = "screen"`

Inside the `devshell`, you can run development commands such as `configure` and `make` or invoke the cross-compiler directly (use the `$CC` environment variable, which has been set up already). You can also run BitBake tasks inside `devshell` by calling the `${WORKDIR}/temp/run*` script directly. This has the same result as invoking BitBake externally to `devshell` for that task.

Inside the `devpyshell` Python interpreter, you can call functions, such as `d.setVar()` and `d.getVar()`, or any Python code, such as `bb.build.exec_fun()`.

How to do it...

The starting point for debugging a package build error is the BitBake error message printed on the build process. This will usually point us to the task that failed to build.

1. To list all the tasks available for a given recipe, with descriptions, we execute the following:

   ```
   $ bitbake -c listtasks <target>
   ```

2. If you need to recreate the error, you can force a build with the following:

   ```
   $ bitbake -f <target>
   ```

3. Or you can ask BitBake to force-run only a specific task using the following command:

   ```
   $ bitbake -c compile -f <target>
   ```

 Forcing a task to run will taint the task and BitBake will show a warning. This is meant to inform that the build has been modified. You can remove the warnings by cleaning the work directory with the -c clean argument.

Task log and run files

To debug the build errors, BitBake creates two types of useful files per shell task and stores them in a temp folder in the working directory. Taking BusyBox as an example, we would look into:

```
/opt/yocto/fsl-community-bsp/wandboard/tmp/work/cortexa9hf-neon-poky-linux-
gnueabi/busybox/1.24.1-r0/temp
```

And find a list of log* and run* files. The filename format is:

```
log.do_<task>.<pid> and run.do_<task>.<pid>.
```

But luckily, we also have symbolic links without the <pid> part that link to the latest version.

The `log` files will contain the output of the task, and that is usually the only information we need to debug the problem. The `run` file contains the actual code executed by BitBake to generate the log mentioned before. This is only needed when debugging complex build issues.

Python tasks, on the other hand, do not currently write files as described previously, although it is planned to do so in the future. Python tasks execute internally and log information to the Terminal.

> If using the `rm_work` class, the package name needs to be added to the `RM_WORK_EXCLUDE` variable for the task log and run files to be accessible.

Adding logging to recipes

BitBake recipes accept either Bash or Python code. Python logging is done through the `bb` class and uses the standard logging Python library module. It has the following components:

- `bb.plain`: This uses `logger.plain`. It can be used for debugging, but should not be committed to the source.
- `bb.note`: This uses `logger.info`.
- `bb.warn`: This uses `logger.warn`.
- `bb.error`: This uses `logger.error`.
- `bb.fatal`: This uses `logger.critical` and exits BitBake.
- `bb.debug`: This should be passed a log level as the first argument and uses `logger.debug`.

To print debug output from Bash in our recipes, we need to use the `logging` class by executing:

```
inherit logging
```

The `logging` class is inherited by default by all recipes containing `base.bbclass`, so we don't usually have to inherit it explicitly. We will then have access to the following Bash functions:

- `bbplain`: This function outputs literally what's passed in. It can be used in debugging but should not be committed to a recipe source.
- `bbnote`: This function prints with the `NOTE` prefix.
- `bbwarn`: This prints a non-fatal warning with the `WARNING` prefix.
- `bberror`: This prints a non-fatal error with the `ERROR` prefix.
- `bbfatal`: This function halts the build and prints an error message as with `bberror`.
- `bbdebug`: This function prints debug messages with the log level passed as the first argument. It is used with the following format:

```
bbdebug [123] "message"
```

The Bash functions mentioned here do not log to the console but only to the `log` files.

Looking at dependencies

You can ask BitBake to print the current and provided versions of packages with the following command:

```
$ bitbake --show-versions
```

Another common debugging task is the removal of unwanted dependencies.

To see an overview of pulled-in dependencies, you can use BitBake's verbose output by running this:

```
$ bitbake -v <target>
```

To analyze what dependencies are pulled in by a package, we can ask BitBake to create DOT files that describe these dependencies by running the following command:

```
$ bitbake -g <target>
```

The DOT format is a text description language for graphics that is understood by the **GraphViz** open source package and all the utilities that use it. DOT files can be visualized or further processed.

You can omit dependencies from the graph to produce more readable output. For example, to omit dependencies from `glibc`, you would run the following command:

```
$ bitbake -g <target> -I glibc
```

Once the preceding commands have been run, we get the following files in the current directory:

- `pn-buildlist`: This file shows the list of packages that would be built by the given target
- `recipes-depends.dot`: This file shows the dependencies between recipes
- `task-depends.dot`: This file shows the dependencies between tasks

To convert the `.dot` files to postscript files (`.ps`), you may execute:

```
$ dot -Tps filename.dot -o outfile.ps
```

However, the most useful way to display dependency data is to ask BitBake to display it graphically with the dependency explorer, as follows:

```
$ bitbake -g -u taskexp <target>
```

The result may be seen in the following screenshot:

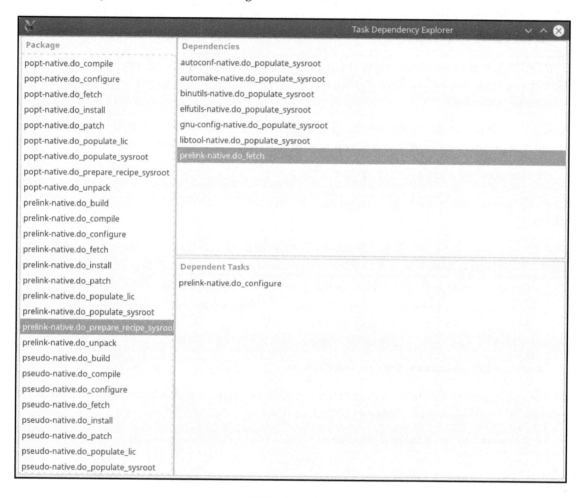

Task dependency explorer

Debugging dependencies

On rare occasions, you may find yourself debugging a task dependency problem, for example, if BitBake misses a task dependency.

In the `tmp/stamps` sub-directory inside the build directory, you can find two file types that are helpful when debugging dependency problems:

- `sigdata`, a Python database of all the metadata that is used to calculate the task's input checksum
- `siginfo`, which is the same but for shared state cache accelerated recipes

You can use `bitbake-dumpsig` on both of these file types to dump the variable dependencies for the task, variable values, as well as a list of variables never included in any checksum.

When trying to compare two versions of a given task, `bitbake-diffsig` can be used to dump the differences between two `sigdata` or `siginfo` revisions.

Debugging BitBake

It is not common to have to debug BitBake itself, but you may find a bug in BitBake and want to explore it by yourself before reporting it to the BitBake community. For such cases, you can ask BitBake to output the debug information at three different levels with the `-D` flag. To display all the debug information, run the following command:

```
$ bitbake -DDD <target>
```

Error reporting tool

Sometimes, you will find a build error on a Yocto recipe that you have not modified. The first place to check for errors is the community itself, but before launching your mail client, head to `http://errors.yoctoproject.org`. The welcome page is displayed as follows:

Error reporting web interface

This is a central database of mostly autobuilder, but also user-reported, errors. Here, you may check whether someone else is experiencing the same problem.

You can submit your own build failure to the database to help the community debug the problem. To do so, you may use the `report-error` class. Add the following to your `conf/local.conf` file:

```
INHERIT += "report-error"
```

By default, the error information is stored under `tmp/log/error-report` under the build directory, but you can set a specific location with the `ERR_REPORT_DIR` variable.

When the error reporting tool is activated, a build error will be captured in a file in the `error-report` folder. The build output will also print a command to send the error log to the server:

```
$ send-error-report ${LOG_DIR}/error-report/error-report_${TSTAMP}
```

When this command is executed, it will report back with a link to the upstream error.

You can set up a local error server, and use that instead by passing a server argument. The error server code is a Django web application and setting up details can be found at `http://git.yoctoproject.org/cgit/cgit.cgi/error-report-web/tree/README`.

2

The BSP Layer

In this chapter, we will cover the following recipes:

- Creating a custom BSP layer
- Adding a custom kernel and bootloader
- Building the U-Boot bootloader
- Describing Linux's build system
- Configuring the Linux kernel
- Building the Linux kernel
- Building external kernel modules
- Debugging the Linux kernel and modules
- Debugging the Linux kernel booting process
- Using the kernel tracing system
- Managing the device tree
- Debugging device tree issues

Introduction

In the previous chapter, we became comfortable with the build system and the reference hardware we are using. We built images, ran them, and learned how to customize and optimize our build system.

Now we have our build environment ready with the Yocto Project, it's time to think about beginning development work on our embedded Linux project.

Most embedded Linux projects require both custom hardware and software. An early task in the development process is to test different hardware reference boards and select one to base our design on. As we saw in the *Building Wandboard images* recipe in Chapter 1, *The Build System*, for this book we have chosen the Wandboard, an NXP i.MX6-based platform, as it is an affordable and open board, which makes it perfect for our needs.

The Wandboard uses a SoM that is then mounted into a carrier board and sold as a single-board computer. As the schematics are open, the SoM could be used with a different carrier board design for a much more specific product.

This chapter will introduce us to system development with a focus on the BSP layer. It will explain how to create a BSP layer to contain those hardware-specific changes, as well as show how to work with the U-Boot bootloader and the Linux kernel, components which are likely to take most of the system customization work.

Creating a custom BSP layer

The changes needed to support a new hardware platform, or machine, are kept on a separate Yocto layer, called a BSP layer. This separation is best for future updates and patches to the system. A BSP layer can support any number of new machines and any new software feature that is linked to the hardware itself.

How to do it...

By convention, Yocto layer names start with meta, short for metadata. A BSP layer may then add a bsp keyword, and finally a unique name. We will call our layer meta-bsp-custom.

There are several ways to create a new layer:

- Manually, once you know what is required
- By copying the meta-skeleton layer included in Poky
- By using the yocto-layer command-line tool

You can have a look at the `meta-skeleton` layer in Poky and see that it includes the following elements:

- A `layer.conf` file, where the layer configuration variables are set
- A `COPYING.MIT` license file
- Several directories named with the `recipes-` prefix with example recipes for BusyBox, the Linux kernel and an example module, an example service recipe, an example user management recipe, and a multilib example.

How it works...

We will cover some of the use cases that appear in the available examples in the next few book recipes, so for our needs, we will use the `yocto-layer` tool, which allows us to create a minimal layer.

Open a new Terminal and change to the `fsl-community-bsp` directory. Then set up the environment as follows:

```
$ source setup-environment wandboard
```

 Note that once the build directory has been created, the `MACHINE` and `DISTRO` variables have already been configured in the `conf/local.conf` file and can be omitted from the command line.

Change to the `sources` directory and run the following command:

```
$ yocto-layer create bsp-custom
```

Note that the `yocto-layer` tool will add the `meta` prefix to your layer, so you don't need to. It will prompt a few questions:

- The layer priority, which is used to decide the layer precedence in cases where the same recipe (with the same name) exists in several layers simultaneously. It is also used to decide in what order `bbappends` are applied if several layers append the same recipe. Leave the default value of 6. This will be stored in the layer's `conf/layer.conf` file as `BBFILE_PRIORITY`.
- Whether to create example recipes and append files. Let's leave the default `no` for the time being.

Our new layer has the following structure:

```
meta-bsp-custom/
    conf/layer.conf
    COPYING.MIT
    README
```

There's more...

The first thing to do is to add this new layer to your project's `conf/bblayer.conf` file. It is a good idea to add it to your template `conf` directory's `bblayers.conf.sample` file too, so that it is correctly appended when creating new projects. The highlighted line in the following code shows the addition of the layer to the `conf/bblayers.conf` file:

```
LCONF_VERSION = "7"
BBPATH = "${TOPDIR}"
BSPDIR := "${@os.path.abspath(os.path.dirname(d.getVar('FILE', True)) +
'/../..')}"
BBFILES ?= ""
BBLAYERS = " \
  ${BSPDIR}/sources/poky/meta \
  ${BSPDIR}/sources/poky/meta-poky \
  ${BSPDIR}/sources/meta-openembedded/meta-oe \
  ${BSPDIR}/sources/meta-openembedded/meta-multimedia \
  ${BSPDIR}/sources/meta-freescale \
  ${BSPDIR}/sources/meta-freescale-3rdparty \
  ${BSPDIR}/sources/meta-freescale-distro \
  ${BSPDIR}/sources/meta-bsp-custom \
  "
```

Now, BitBake will parse the `bblayers.conf` file and find the `conf/layer.conf` file from your layer. In it, we find the following line:

```
BBFILES += "${LAYERDIR}/recipes-*/*/*.bb \
            ${LAYERDIR}/recipes-*/*/*.bbappend"
```

It tells BitBake which directories to parse for recipes and append files. You need to make sure your directory and file hierarchy in this new layer matches the given pattern, or you will need to modify it.

BitBake will also find the following:

```
BBPATH .= ":${LAYERDIR}"
```

The `BBPATH` variable is used to locate the `bbclass` files and the configuration and files included with the `include` and `require` directives. The search finishes with the first match, so it is best to keep filenames unique.

Some other variables we might consider defining in our `conf/layer.conf` file are the following:

```
LAYERDEPENDS_bsp-custom = "freescale"
LAYERVERSION_bsp-custom = "1"
```

The `LAYERDEPENDS` literal is a space-separated list of other layers your layer depends on, and the `LAYERVERSION` literal specifies the version of your layer in case other layers want to add a dependency to a specific version.

The `COPYING.MIT` file specifies the license for the metadata contained in the layer. The Yocto Project is licensed under the MIT license, a permissive free software license compatible with the **General Public License** (**GPL**) and other licenses. This license applies only to the metadata, as every package included in your build will have its own license.

The `README` file will need to be modified for your specific layer. It is usual to describe the layer and provide any other layer dependencies and usage instructions.

Adding a new machine

When customizing your BSP, it is usually a good idea to introduce a new machine for your hardware. These are kept under the `conf/machine` directory in your BSP layer. The usual thing to do is to base it on the reference design. For example, the Wandboard has its machine configuration defined at `meta-freescale-3rdparty/conf/machine/wandboard.conf`. Let's take a look at it.

The machine configuration file starts with the following:

```
MACHINEOVERRIDES =. "mx6:mx6dl:mx6q:"
```

This prepends (=.) the attached overrides to the already defined ones. These are used to qualify variables in recipes so that they apply only to a specific machine type. For example, the following will apply to all i.MX6-based machines:

```
VARIABLE_append_mx6 = ""
```

However, the following will only apply to i.MX6 quad variants:

```
VARIABLE_append_mx6q = ""
```

Next, we have a couple of `include` files, which we will look into later on:

```
include conf/machine/include/imx-base.inc
include conf/machine/include/tune-cortexa9.inc
```

The following related variables are for U-Boot, the machine bootloader:

```
UBOOT_MAKE_TARGET = ""
UBOOT_SUFFIX = "img"
SPL_BINARY = "SPL"
UBOOT_MACHINE = "wandboard_config"
```

These are all variables that configure the U-Boot build process. They do the following:

- Set the default make target to empty so the default is used
- Specify a suffix for the U-Boot image
- Specify the name for the **Secondary Program Loader** (**SPL**), which is also built as part of U-Boot. This is a small executable loaded into SRAM which initializes the main memory and loads the main U-boot binary
- Define the name for the U-Boot Wandboard configuration target, used in the U-Boot compilation task

They then go to override some of the default `UBOOT_EXTLINUX` variables that are used for the Generic Distribution Configuration mechanism, a framework to remove the machine-specific environment configuration from the U-Boot source and move it to U-Boot scripts that are downloaded at runtime:

```
UBOOT_EXTLINUX = "1"
UBOOT_EXTLINUX_ROOT = "root=PARTUUID=${uuid}"
```

The previous variables instruct Yocto to build the default `extlinux.conf` configuration script for the machine and add the specified `root` kernel command-line argument to it. The `uuid` variable is replaced by a real value when the WIC image is generated.

The default U-Boot environment for the Wandboard configures variables in the U-Boot environment that are used to boot. For example, the `mmc_boot` variable calls the `scan_dev_for_boot_partition` script which loops through the partitions looking for one with a bootable flag. It then looks for an `extlinux.conf` file in that partition and executes it to boot.

The `uboot-extlinux-config` class generates this `extlinux.conf` file, and its contents can be modified by the different `UBOOT_EXTLINUX_*` variables. Some of the most used, apart from the `UBOOT_EXTLINUX_ROOT` we just saw, are as follows:

- `UBOOT_EXTLINUX_CONSOLE`, to set the default kernel command-line console argument. By default, this is set to the following:

  ```
  UBOOT_EXTLINUX_CONSOLE ??= "console=${console}"
  ```

- `UBOOT_EXTLINUX_KERNEL_IMAGE`, the kernel image name, which by default is the following:

  ```
  UBOOT_EXTLINUX_KERNEL_IMAGE ??= "../${KERNEL_IMAGETYPE}"
  ```

- `UBOOT_EXTLINUX_KERNEL_ARGS`, additional kernel command-line arguments, which by default are the following:

  ```
  UBOOT_EXTLINUX_KERNEL_ARGS ??= "rootwait rw"
  ```

- `UBOOT_EXTLINUX_FDT` to specify the device tree file and `UBOOT_EXTLINUX_FDTDIR` to specify the device tree directory. By default, these are set as the following:

  ```
  UBOOT_EXTLINUX_FDT ??= ""
  UBOOT_EXTLINUX_FDTDIR ??= "../"
  ```

Then it specifies the Linux kernel build process configuration:

```
WANDBOARD_DEFAULT_KERNEL = "linux-wandboard"
PREFERRED_PROVIDER_virtual/kernel ?= "${WANDBOARD_DEFAULT_KERNEL}"
```

The previous variables define the default Kernel recipe name to use as well as setting the `virtual/kernel` default provider to it. Virtual packages like this are used when a feature or element is provided by more than one recipe. It allows us to choose which of all those recipes will finally be used. Virtual packages will be further explained in the *Selecting a specific package version and provider* recipe in `Chapter 3`, *The Software Layer*.

Then the kernel device trees to build are specified:

```
KERNEL_DEVICETREE = " \
    imx6dl-wandboard.dtb \
    imx6dl-wandboard-revb1.dtb \
    imx6dl-wandboard-revd1.dtb \
    imx6q-wandboard.dtb \
    imx6q-wandboard-revb1.dtb \
```

```
            imx6q-wandboard-revd1.dtb \
            imx6qp-wandboard-revd1.dtb \
    "
```

The different device trees correspond to different Wandboard variants (solo/dual lite, quad, or quad plus) and the board revision (b1, c1, or d1).

The name of the kernel image is also specified:

```
    KERNEL_IMAGETYPE = "zImage"
```

The file follows with a set of extra machine features:

```
    MACHINE_FEATURES += "bluetooth pci wifi touchscreen"
```

And then there is a list of packages that are not essential to boot the machine so the build will not fail without them, but are needed for a fully featured image, in this case Wi-Fi and Bluetooth configuration support:

```
    MACHINE_EXTRA_RRECOMMENDS += " \
      bcm4329-nvram-config \
      bcm4330-nvram-config \
    "
```

Next, it adds a list of packages that are essential for the machine to boot so they will be added as dependencies for all target images. These include the kernel, device tree, and U-Boot packages:

```
    MACHINE_ESSENTIAL_EXTRA_RDEPENDS += " \
        kernel-image \
        kernel-devicetree \
        u-boot-fslc \
    "
```

Then there is WIC-specific configuration needed to build the final partitioned images using the WIC tool:

```
    WKS_FILES ?= "imx-uboot-spl.wks"
```

It defines the WIC kickstart (**WKS**) file to use with the WIC image creation tool.

Finally, it defines the default console settings for the image, including baud rate and port:

```
    SERIAL_CONSOLE = "115200 ttymxc0"
```

A machine based on the Wandboard could define its own machine configuration file, `wandboard-custom.conf`, as follows:

```
require conf/machine/wandboard.conf
UBOOT_MACHINE = "wandboard-custom_defconfig"
KERNEL_DEVICETREE = "imx6qp-wandboard-custom-revd1.dtb"
```

The configuration file starts by including the original Wandboard's machine configuration. Usually, files that are designed to be included in others have the `.inc` extension, but any file type can be used. An alternative would be to copy and modify the original file, but including the file directly updates it along with the `meta-freescale-3rdparty` layer.

As the `wandboard.conf` file now resides on a different layer, in order for BitBake to find it, we need to specify the full path from the `BBPATH` variable in the corresponding layer.

It then overrides both the U-Boot configuration, assuming we need to use a custom configuration, which is seldom needed, and the device tree name, which is usually customized.

Adding a custom device tree to the Linux kernel

To add this device tree file to the Linux kernel, we need to add the device tree file to the `arch/arm/boot/dts` directory under the Linux kernel source, and a new default configuration under `/arch/arm/configs/`, initially both just copied from the reference board, and also modify the Linux build system's `arch/arm/boot/dts/Makefile` file to build it as follows:

```
dtb-$(CONFIG_SOC_IMX6Q) += \
+ imx6qp-wandboard-custom-revd1.dtb \
```

This code uses diff formatting, where the lines with a minus prefix are removed, the ones with a plus sign are added, and the ones without a prefix are left as reference.

Once the patch is prepared, it can be added to the `meta-bsp-custom/recipes-kernel/linux/linux-wandboard-4.1-2.0.x/` directory, as specified in the `FILESEXTRAPATHS` variable, and the Linux kernel recipe appended adding a `meta-bsp-custom/recipes-kernel/linux/linux-wandboard_4.1-2.0.x.bbappend` file with the following content:

```
FILESEXTRAPATHS_prepend := "${THISDIR}/${BP}:"
SRC_URI_append = " file://0001-01_02-Add-a-custom-device-tree-and-
configuration.patch"
COMPATIBLE_MACHINE = "(wandboard|wandboard-custom)"
```

The FILESEXTRAPATHS variable is used to extend BitBake's search path to include the directory with our patch, and using the := BitBake operator expands the variable's contents on definition instead of waiting until it is actually used.

It then adds the patch to the SRC_URI variable so that it is applied when building. Files added to the SRC_URI variable that end in the patch or diff prefixes will be applied in the order they are found. You can also force a file to be treated as patch by specifying an apply=yes property to it in SRC_URI.

Finally, it extends the COMPATIBLE_MACHINE variable to include both the wandboard and wandboard-custom machine, which means the recipe is not skipped when building for both machines.

A complete example patch that adds a custom device tree to the Linux kernel can be found in the source code that accompanies the book.

Adding a custom U-Boot machine

In the same way, the U-Boot source may be patched to add a new custom machine. Bootloader modifications are not as likely to be needed as kernel modifications though, and most custom platforms will leave the bootloader unchanged. The patch would be added to the meta-bsp-custom/recipes-bsp/u-boot/u-boot-fslc/ directory and the U-Boot recipe appended with a meta-bsp-custom/recipes-bsp/u-boot/u-boot-fslc_%.bbappend file with the following content:

```
FILESEXTRAPATHS_prepend := "${THISDIR}/${BPN}:"
SRC_URI_append = " file://0001-02_01-Add-a-custom-wandboard-custom-
machine.patch"
COMPATIBLE_MACHINE = "(wandboard|wandboard-custom)"
```

The percentage sign in u-boot-fslc_%.bbappend matches all versions of the recipe.

The changes needed to add a new machine to U-Boot are as follows:

1. Add a new board/wandboard-custom directory copied from the Wandboard reference board with the following content:

    - A Kconfig file
    - MAINTAINERS and README files

- A `Makefile`
- Copies of the `spl.c` (unchanged from the reference `spl.c`) and `wandboard-custom.c` (renamed from the reference `wandboard.c`) files

2. Add a new machine configuration file as the `configs/wandboard-custom_defconfig` file.

The configuration file needs to be already configured for the new `wandboard-custom` target platform.

3. Add a new machine include file under the `include/configs/wandboard-custom.h` include file (copied from the reference `wandboard.h` file)

An example patch that adds a custom machine to U-Boot can be found in the source code that accompanies the book.

Adding a custom formfactor file

Custom platforms can also define their own `formfactor` file with information that the build system cannot obtain from other sources, such as defining whether a touchscreen is available or defining the screen orientation. These are defined in the `recipes-bsp/formfactor/` directory in our `meta-bsp-custom` layer.

To specify, for example, that our new machine contains a touchscreen, we could define a `meta-bsp-custom/recipes-bsp/formfactor/formfactor_0.0.bbappend` file to include a `formfactor` file as follows:

```
FILESEXTRAPATHS_prepend := "${THISDIR}/${BPN}:"
```

And the machine-specific `meta-bsp-custom/recipes-bsp/formfactor/formfactor/wandboard-custom/machconfig` file would be as follows:

```
HAVE_TOUCHSCREEN=1
```

An example patch that adds this custom `formfactor` can be found in the source code that accompanies the book.

Build your custom machine

Now we are ready to create a new project and build for our new machine. Do the following to create a new project for the `wandboard-custom` machine:

```
$ cd /opt/yocto/fsl-community-bsp/
$ MACHINE=wandboard-custom DISTRO=poky source setup-environment wandboard-custom
```

Unless you have added the `meta-bsp-custom` layer to your template conf directory's `bblayers.conf.sample` file, you will need to add it to the new project's `conf/bblayer.conf` file. You can do that with:

```
$ bitbake-layers add-layer /opt/yocto/fsl-community-bsp/sources/meta-bsp-custom/
```

Then you can build the project with:

```
$ bitbake core-image-minimal
```

See also

- For a reference guide to the BitBake syntax, refer to the Yocto Project's *Bitbake User Manual*
- The example source is also available on the following GitHub repository: https://github.com/yoctocookbook2ndedition/meta-bsp-custom

Adding a custom kernel and bootloader

The BSP that encapsulates the hardware modifications for a given platform is mostly located in the bootloader, usually U-Boot (Das U-Boot) for ARM devices, and the Linux kernel. Both U-Boot and the Linux kernel have upstream development trees, at `git.denx.de` and `kernel.org` respectively, but it is very common for manufacturers of embedded hardware to provide their own trees for both bootloader and kernel.

Development in U-Boot and the Linux kernel is usually done externally to Yocto, as they are easy and quicker to build using a cross-compilation toolchain, like the one provided by Yocto's SDK.

The development work is then integrated into Yocto in one of two ways:

- With patches added to the kernel and U-Boot `bbappend` files. This method will build the same source as the reference design board we are using as a base, and apply our changes over it. This is what we have seen in the previous recipe.
- Using a different Git repository, forked from the Linux kernel and U-Boot Git repositories being used by the reference design, and using a `bbappend` file to point the recipe to it. This way, we can directly commit the changes to the repository and the Yocto build system will build them.

Usually, a forked Git repository is only needed when the hardware changes are substantial and the work in the Linux kernel and bootloader is going to be extensive. The recommendation is to start with patches, and only use a forked repository when they become difficult to manage.

Getting ready

The first question when starting work on the Linux kernel and U-Boot modifications is how do you find which of the several available recipes are being used for your build?

Finding the Linux kernel source

To find the Linux kernel source, we might use several methods. As we know we are building for a Wandboard machine, the first thing to do is find a machine configuration file:

```
$ cd /opt/yocto/fsl-community-bsp/sources
$ find -name wandboard.conf
./meta-freescale-3rdparty/conf/machine/wandboard.conf
```

As we have seen before, this machine configuration file specifies the Linux kernel recipe to use:

```
WANDBOARD_DEFAULT_KERNEL = "linux-wandboard"
WANDBOARD_DEFAULT_KERNEL_use-mainline-bsp = "linux-fslc"
PREFERRED_PROVIDER_virtual/kernel ?= "${WANDBOARD_DEFAULT_KERNEL}"
```

Unless we have modified our `conf/local.conf` with a `use-mainline-bsp` override, which we haven't, the machine will use the `linux-wandboard` recipe.

We can then use the `bitbake-layers` command-line application to find the available `linux-wandboard` packages:

```
$ bitbake-layers show-recipes linux-wandboard
=== Matching recipes: ===
linux-wandboard:
  meta-freescale-3rdparty 4.1-2.0.x
```

So the `linux-wandboard` recipe used is contained in the `meta-freescale-3rdparty` layer and is using Linux kernel version `4.1-2.0.x`.

 The Yocto Project maintains its own Linux Git repositories that can be built with the Linux-Yocto family of recipes. These kernels can be managed by Yocto-specific kernel tools, and support features such as configuration fragments. Unfortunately, the FSL community BSP does not use Linux-Yocto style recipes to integrate the kernel sources for the Wandboard and, for the sake of clarity, they will not be covered in this book. Refer to the Yocto Project's *Kernel Development Manual* for details about Linux-Yocto style kernels.

We can check the actual output from our previous `core-image-minimal` build:

```
$ find tmp/work -type d -name "linux-wandboard"
tmp/work/wandboard-poky-linux-gnueabi/linux-wandboard
```

As the `linux-wanboard` directory exists in our `work` folder, we can be sure the recipe has been used.

We can, finally, also check what the available Linux recipes are with the following:

```
$ cd /opt/yocto/fsl-community-bsp/
$ source setup-environment wandboard
$ bitbake-layers show-recipes 'linux*'
```

Not all those kernels support the Wandboard machine completely, but the ones in the `meta-freescale*` layers all support NXP ARM machines, so they are useful for comparison.

Finding the U-Boot source

Going back to the machine configuration file, we now need to look into one of the `include` files we mentioned before:

```
include conf/machine/include/imx-base.inc
```

Inside that file, the U-Boot preferred provider is defined:

```
PREFERRED_PROVIDER_u-boot ??= "u-boot-fslc"
PREFERRED_PROVIDER_virtual/bootloader ??= "u-boot-fslc"
```

So `u-boot-fslc` is the U-Boot recipe we are looking for.

Using `bitbake-layers` as before, we can find its containing layer and version:

```
$ bitbake-layers show-recipes u-boot-fslc
=== Matching recipes: ===
u-boot-fslc:
  meta-freescale          v2017.11+gitAUTOINC+ca0c3f3fac
```

The Wandboard machine is using `u-boot-fslc` on its `v2017.11` version. As we can see, the package version defined in the recipe also contains the specific SHA-1 being built.

Developing using a Git repository fork

We will show how to append a recipe to use a forked repository to work from. We will use the Linux kernel as an example, but the concept works just as well for U-Boot or any other package, although the specifics will change.

We will fork or branch the repository used in the reference design and use it to specify a `SRC_URI` for the recipe.

How to do it...

For this example, I have forked the Linux Wandboard kernel repository to `https://github.com/yoctocookbook2ndedition/linux.git`. Refer to the GitHub or source control software documentation for instructions on how to fork a Git repository.

And my `recipes-kernel/linux/linux-wandboard_4.1-2.0.x.bbappend` file has the following changes:

```
FILESEXTRAPATHS_prepend := "${THISDIR}/${BP}:"
WANDBOARD_GITHUB_MIRROR = "git://github.
com/yoctocookbook2ndedition/linux.git"
SRCBRANCH = "4.1-2.0.x-imx-dev"
SRCREV = "${AUTOREV}"
COMPATIBLE_MACHINE = "(wandboard|wandboard-custom)"
```

Note how the URL needs to start with `git://`. This is so that BitBake can recognize it as a Git source.

By default, BitBake will use the Git protocol to fetch. Even though GitHub supports the Git protocol, it does not offer it in the clone options in the web page. Cloning with the Git protocol in GitHub is read-only and does not need authentication, which is a good default for a build system.

You can also instruct BitBake to fetch using the HTTPS protocol, which in GitHub is read/write and performs user authentication for writes, by overriding the whole SRC_URI variable in the following way:

```
FILESEXTRAPATHS_prepend := "${THISDIR}/${BPN}-${PV}:"
WANDBOARD_GITHUB_MIRROR =
"git://github.com/yoctocookbook2ndedition/linux.git"
SRCBRANCH = "4.1-2.0.x-imx-dev"
SRCREV = "${AUTOREV}"
SRC_URI = "${WANDBOARD_GITHUB_MIRROR};protocol=https;branch=$
{SRCBRANCH} \
file://defconfig \
```

Note that when overriding the whole SRC_URI, we have to remember to include all the variable contents from the original recipe.

Now we can build the Linux kernel and the source will be fetched from the forked repository.

How it works...

Let's have a look at the `linux-wandboard_4.1-2.0.x.bb` recipe:

```
include linux-wandboard.inc
DEPENDS += "lzop-native bc-native"
SRCBRANCH = "4.1-2.0.x-imx"
SRCREV = "0d698de42426a92e3ba47071f11960aeb91eb349"
COMPATIBLE_MACHINE = "(wandboard)"
```

The first interesting thing is the inclusion of `linux-wandboard.inc`, which we will look into later on.

Then it declares two package dependencies, `lzop-native` and `bc-native`. The `native` part tells us that these are used in the host system, so they are used during the Linux kernel build process. The `lzop` tool is used to create the CPIO compressed files needed in the `initramfs` system, which is a system that boots from a memory-based root filesystem, and `bc` was introduced to avoid a Perl kernel dependency when generating certain kernel files.

Then it sets the branch and revision, and finally it sets `COMPATIBLE_MACHINE` to `wandboard`. We will speak about machine compatibility in the *Adding new packages* recipe of `Chapter 3`, *The Software Layer*.

Let's now have a look at the `linux-wandboard.inc` include file:

```
SUMMARY = "Linux kernel for Wandboard"
LICENSE = "GPLv2"
LIC_FILES_CHKSUM = "file://COPYING;md5=d7810fab7487fb0aad327b76f1be7cd7"

require recipes-kernel/linux/linux-imx.inc

# Put a local version until we have a true SRCREV to point to
SCMVERSION ?= "y"

SRCBRANCH ??= "master"
LOCALVERSION ?= "-${SRCBRANCH}"

# Allow override of WANDBOARD_GITHUB_MIRROR to make use of
# local repository easier
WANDBOARD_GITHUB_MIRROR ?= "git://github.com/wandboard-org/linux.git"


# SRC_URI for wandboard kernel
SRC_URI = "${WANDBOARD_GITHUB_MIRROR};branch=${SRCBRANCH} \
           file://defconfig \
"
```

This is actually the file we were looking for. Initially, it specifies the license for the kernel source and points to it, sets a default branch and local version kernel string, and sets up the `SCR_URI` variable, which is the place the source code is fetched from.

It then offers the `WANDBOARD_GITHUB_MIRROR` variable, which we can modify in our `bbappend` file.

So the logical setup would be to create a GitHub account and fork the provided `wandboard-org` Linux repository.

Once the fork is in place, we need to modify the `WANDBOARD_GITHUB_MIRROR` variable. But as we saw before, the recipe configures a specific revision and branch. We want to develop here, so we want to change this to a new development branch we have created based in the original recipe's source revision as specified in the `SRCREV` variable. Let's call it `4.1-2.0.x-imx-dev` and set the revision to automatically fetch the newest point in the branch using the `AUTOREV` variable. We can then add the patch that introduces the new machine to the head of the branch.

Building the U-Boot bootloader

We have seen how to modify the Yocto build system to both modify a U-Boot or Linux kernel recipe by adding patches or by building from a modified Git repository. Now we will see how to modify and build the U-Boot source in order to introduce our changes.

Even though the Yocto Project is very flexible, it is best not to use the Yocto Project build system while developing the BSP. The U-Boot and Linux kernel binaries are separate artifacts and can be programmed individually, so it is faster and less error-prone to just build them using the standalone Yocto SDK and not the Yocto build system. This also abstracts BSP developers from the complexities of the Yocto build system.

This may not apply to the Linux-Yocto kernel types, as in that case the Yocto Project provides specific tools to aid development.

Getting ready

We will use a Yocto toolchain to build the U-Boot source externally from the Yocto build system. The Yocto project has precompiled SDKs for both 32- and 64-bit hosts for the machines supported by Poky. You can download them from
`http://downloads.yoctoproject.org/releases/yocto/yocto-2.4/toolchain/`.

Unfortunately, since version 2.1, it does not offer a precompiled SDK for i.MX6-based machines.

Instead, let's build an SDK using our existing Yocto Project installation:

```
$ cd /opt/yocto/fsl-community-bsp
$ source setup-environment wandboard
$ bitbake core-image-minimal -c populate_sdk
```

We will learn more about Yocto's SDKs in `Chapter 4`, *Application Development*.

Execute the installation script from a new shell to avoid problems with the environment setup:

```
$ cd /opt/yocto/fsl-community-bsp/wandboard/tmp/deploy/sdk/
$ ./poky-glibc-x86_64-core-image-minimal-cortexa9hf-neon-toolchain-2.4.sh
```

Accept the default installation location. It is recommended not to change the default location to avoid relocation issues.

Now we need to download the U-Boot source:

1. Find the upstream Git repository:

   ```
   $ bitbake -e u-boot-fslc | grep ^SRC_URI=
   SRC_URI="git://github.com/Freescale/u-boot-
   fslc.git;branch=2017.11+fslc file://0001-02_01-Add-a-custom-
   wandboard-custom-machine.patch"
   ```

2. Clone U-Boot's source from its upstream repository:

   ```
   $ cd /opt/yocto/
   $ git clone git://github.com/Freescale/u-boot-fslc.git
   $ cd u-boot-fslc
   ```

The default branch should be `2017.11+fslc`, but if it's not, you can change it with the following:
```
$ git checkout -b 2017.11+fslc origin/2017.11+fslc.
```

How to do it...

Once we have the source locally available, we will build it using the Yocto SDK we have just built and installed:

1. Before setting up the environment, we will configure U-Boot for the Wandboard:

   ```
   $ make wandboard_config
   ```

2. To bring up a graphical configuration interface, we can do the following:

   ```
   $ make xconfig
   ```

This version of U-Boot is configured using the same Kconfig framework that is used by the Linux kernel. Unfortunately the kbuild configuration tools cannot be built once the Yocto build environment has been set up, so we do the configuration before sourcing the setup environmental script.

Note that we haven't yet used the environment setup script. This is because it's enough with the standard make package on the host to build the different configuration tools.

3. Now we set up the environment using the script provided with the SDK:

```
$ source /opt/poky/2.4/environment-setup-cortexa9hf-neon-poky-
linux-gnueabi
```

4. Next you can start the build with the following:

```
$ make -jN
```

You can optionally pass a -jN argument for multithreaded compilation. Here, N is the number of CPU cores.

Both the SPL image and u-boot.img, which we will program next, are now located on the current directory.

This version of U-Boot builds without problems. Previous versions would fail unless we adapted the default Yocto environment. If you hit build problems, take a quick look at the U-Boot recipe, which clears some flags before building:
```
$ unset LDFLAGS CFLAGS CPPFLAGS
```
And it also passes CC to the make utility in the EXTRA_OEMAKE flags as older U-Boot versions do not read it from the environment:
```
$ make CC="${CC}"
```

There's more...

Finally, we will reprogram the bootloader into the Wandboard's microSD card. We can do it either from the target or from your host computer.

From the host computer, we use dd to copy the new SPL image to an offset of 0x400, which is where the i.MX6 bootrom expects to find it:

```
$ sudo dd if=SPL of=/dev/sdN bs=1k seek=1 && sync
```

This writes with an offset of two blocks, which, given a 512-byte block size, is 0x400 (1,024) bytes.

Then, we will program the U-Boot binary. The SPL looks for it at the offset configured in the CONFIG_SYS_MMCSD_RAW_MODE_U_BOOT_SECTOR configuration variable, given in sectors. For the Wandboard, this is configured as 138 (0x8a) sectors, which with 512-byte sized sectors gives an offset of 69 KB. So we program the U-Boot image at that location with the following:

```
$ sudo dd if=u-boot.img of=/dev/sdN bs=1k seek=69 && sync
```

Be careful when running the dd command, as it could harm your machine. You need to be absolutely sure that the sdN device corresponds to your microSD card and not a drive on your development machine.

From the device itself, we can use U-Boot's mmc command as follows:

1. Load the SPL image to memory:

   ```
   > env set ipaddr <target_ip>
   > env set serverip <host_ip>
   > tftp ${loadaddr} SPL
   ```

   The hexadecimal file size of the TFTP transfer is kept in the filesize environment variable, which we will use later on.

2. Select the MMC device to operate on. You can use the mmc part to discover which is the correct device:

   ```
   > mmc dev 0
   > mmc part
    Partition Map for MMC device 0 -- Partition Type: DOS
    Part Start Sector Num Sectors UUID Type
    1 8192 596378 05465984-01 83
   ```

   We can see that partition 1 starts at sector 8192, leaving enough space to program both the SPL and U-Boot.

3. With a 512-byte block size, we calculate the number of blocks as follows:

```
> setexpr filesizeblks $filesize / 0x200
> setexpr filesizeblks $filesizeblks + 1
```

4. We then write to an offset of two blocks with the number of blocks occupied by our image:

```
> mmc write ${loadaddr} 0x2 ${filesizeblks}
```

5. Now load the U-Boot image to memory:

```
> tftp ${loadaddr} u-boot.img
```

6. And similarly, program it with an offset of 69 KB. Calculate the number of 512-byte blocks to fit the U-Boot image we just loaded:

```
> setexpr filesizeblks $filesize / 0x200
> setexpr filesizeblks $filesizeblks + 1
```

7. And then write to an offset of 69 blocks the number of blocks we have just calculated for our image:

```
> mmc write ${loadaddr} 0x8A ${filesizeblks}
```

8. We can then perform source code modifications and reprogramming iteratively until the change is finished and has been tested. We can then commit the changes to the local Git repository:

```
$ git add --all .
$ git commit -s -m "Well thought commit message"
```

9. Generate a patch into the U-Boot recipe patch directory as follows:

```
$ git format-patch -1 -o /opt/yocto/fsl-community-
bsp/sources/meta-bsp-custom/recipes-bsp/u-boot/u-boot-fslc-
v2017.11/
```

Finally, add the patch to the U-Boot recipe as explained before.

Describing Linux's build system

The Linux kernel is a monolithic kernel and, as such, shares the same address space. Although it has the ability to load modules at runtime, the kernel must contain all the symbols the module uses at compilation time. Once the module is loaded, it will share the kernel's address space too.

The kernel build system (kbuild), uses conditional compilation to decide which parts of the kernel are compiled. kbuild is independent of the Yocto build system.

In this recipe, we will explain how kbuild works.

How to do it...

The kernel kbuild system reads its configuration at build time from a `.config` text file in the kernel root directory. This is referred to as the kernel configuration file. It is a text file where each line contains a single configuration variable that starts with the `CONFIG_` prefix.

There are multiple ways to modify a kernel configuration file:

1. Manually editing the `.config` file, although this is not recommended.
2. Using one of the user interfaces the kernel offers (type the `make help` command for other options):

   - `menuconfig`: An ncurses menu-based interface (`make menuconfig`)
   - `xconfig`: A Qt-based interface (`make xconfig`)
   - `gconfig`: A GTK-based interface (`make gconfig`)

3. Automatically, via a build system such as Yocto.

 Note that to build and use these interfaces, your Linux host needs to have the appropriate dependencies.

4. Each machine also defines a default configuration in the kernel tree. For ARM platforms, these are stored in the `arch/arm/configs` directory. To configure an ARM kernel, that is, to produce a `.config` file from a default configuration, run the following:

```
$ make ARCH=arm <platform>_defconfig
```

For example, we can build a default configuration for NXP's i.MX6 processors by running the following:

```
$ make ARCH=arm imx_v6_v7_defconfig
```

By specifying the `ARCH=arm` configuration parameter, you instruct the kbuild system to look for the specified `defconfig` on the ARM configuration files directory. If you omit it, the kernel will default to the x86 configuration.

How it works...

kbuild uses `Makefile` and `Kconfig` files to build the kernel source. `Kconfig` files define configuration symbols and attributes, and `Makefile` files match configuration symbols to source files.

The kbuild system's options and targets can be seen by running the following:

```
$ make ARCH=arm help
```

There's more...

In recent kernels, a default configuration contains all the information needed to expand to a full configuration file. It is a minimal kernel configuration file where all dependencies are removed. To create a default configuration file from a current `.config` file, you run the following:

```
$ make ARCH=arm savedefconfig
```

This creates a `defconfig` file in the current `kernel` directory. This `make` target can be seen as the opposite of the `<platform>_defconfig` target explained before. The former creates a configuration file from a minimal configuration, and the latter expands the minimal configuration into a full configuration file.

Configuring the Linux kernel

The Linux kernel contains a set of default machine configurations. For ARM, these are under the `arch/arm/configs` directory on the Linux source. The Yocto Project, however, uses a copy of this configuration file inside the BSP layer metadata. This enables the use of different configuration files for different purposes.

In this recipe, we will see how to configure the Linux kernel and add the resulting configuration file to our BSP layer.

Getting ready

Before configuring the kernel, we need to provide a default configuration for our machine, which is the one the Yocto project uses to configure a kernel. When defining a new machine in your BSP layer, you need to provide a `defconfig` file.

The Wandboard's `defconfig` file is stored under `sources/meta-freescale-3rdparty/recipes-kernel/linux/linux-wandboard/defconfig`.

This will be the base `defconfig` file for our custom hardware, so we copy it to our BSP layer:

```
$ cd /opt/yocto/fsl-community-bsp/sources
$ mkdir -p meta-bsp-custom/recipes-kernel/linux/linux-wandboard-4.1-2.0.x/wandboard-custom/
$ cp meta-freescale-3rdparty/recipes-kernel/linux/linux-wandboard/defconfig meta-bsp-custom/recipes-kernel/linux/linux-wandboard-4.1-2.0.x/wandboard-custom/defconfig
```

We then add it to our kernel using `meta-bsp-custom/recipes-kernel/linux/linux-wandboard_4.1-2.0.x.bbappend` as follows:

```
FILESEXTRAPATHS_prepend := "${THISDIR}/${BP}:"
```

Note that the `defconfig` file is already part of the `SRC_URI` on the original recipe.

Kernel configuration changes to your platform can be made directly in this `defconfig` file.

How to do it...

Once we have a default configuration, we will want to make modifications to it. The recommended way to change the Linux kernel configuration is using the Linux kernel build system with a Yocto SDK:

1. First let's find the upstream Git repository by sourcing the environment setup script and using BitBake:

```
$ bitbake -e virtual/kernel | grep ^SRC_URI=
SRC_URI="git://github.com/wandboard-org/linux.git;branch=4.1-2.0.x-
imx          file://defconfig  file://0001-01_02-Add-a-custom-
device-tree-and-configuration.patch"
```

2. Clone the Linux kernel source from its upstream repository:

```
$ cd /opt/yocto/
$ git clone  https://github.com/wandboard-org/linux.git linux-
wandboard
$ cd linux-wandboard
```

 The git clone command shown previously replaces the git:// prefix with the https:// prefix that was specified via the protocol argument in the SRC_URI shown previously.

3. Next, check out the branch specified in the SRC_URI:

```
$ git checkout -b 4.1-2.0.x-imx origin/4.1-2.0.x-imx
```

4. Copy the configuration from the meta-bsp-custom layer to the kernel source:

```
$ cp /opt/yocto/fsl-community-bsp/sources/meta-bsp-custom/recipes-
kernel/linux/linux-wandboard-4.1-2.0.x/wandboard-custom/defconfig
arch/arm/configs/wandboard_defconfig
```

5. Then configure it with the default Wandboard configuration:

```
$ make ARCH=arm wandboard_defconfig
```

6. To bring out a graphical configuration tool to modify the configuration, run the following command:

```
$ make ARCH=arm xconfig
```

If you encounter compilation errors, attempt to run from a new Terminal that has not had the environment configured with the Yocto setup environment scripts.

Also, make sure you have installed all the dependencies listed in `Chapter 1`, *The Build System*.

7. A new window will open with the graphical configuration user interface:

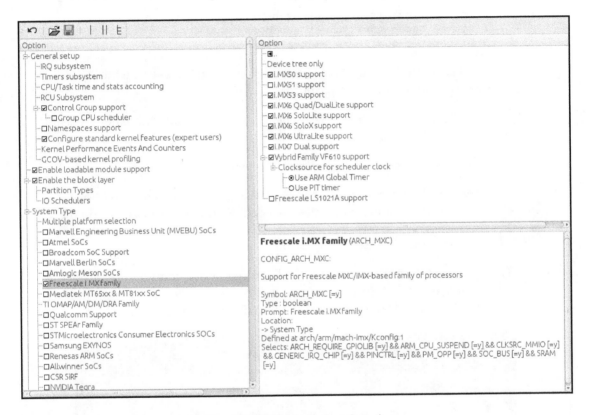

Linux kernel x11 graphical configuration

Note that we haven't used the environment setup script. This is because it's enough with the standard utilities on the host to build the different configuration tools.

8. When you save your changes, the `.config` file will be updated.

Using Yocto to configure the Linux kernel

The Yocto build system can also be used to configure the Linux kernel. This is useful for quick configuration changes while developing applications:

1. To create a `.config` file from the machine `defconfig` file, execute the following command:

```
$ cd /opt/yocto/fsl-community-bsp/
$ source setup-environment wandboard
$ bitbake -c configure virtual/kernel
```

   This will also run the `old config` kernel `make` target to validate the configuration against the Linux source.

2. We can then configure the Linux kernel from the BitBake command line using the following:

```
$ bitbake -c menuconfig virtual/kernel
```

In order to use the `menuconfig` interface you will need to have the `ncurses` development libraries installed. If you get build errors, do the following:

```
$ sudo apt-get install libncurses5-dev
```

The `menuconfig` user interface, as well as other kernel configuration user interfaces, has a search functionality that allows you to locate configuration variables by name. Have a look at the following screenshot:

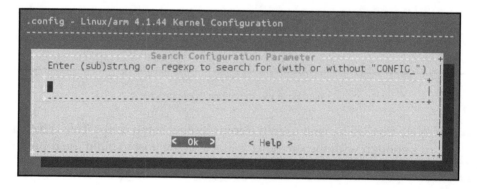

Linux kernel ncurses-based configuration interface search window

In the following chapters, we will mention specific kernel configuration variables, such as CONFIG_PRINTK, without specifying the whole path to the configuration variable. The search interface of the different UIs can be used to locate the configuration variable path.

3. When you save your changes, a new .config file is created in the kernel's build directory, which you can find using the following command:

```
$ bitbake -e virtual/kernel | grep ^B=B"/opt/yocto/fsl-community-
bsp/wandboard/tmp/work/wandboard-poky-linux-gnueabi/linux-
wandboard/4.1-2.0.x-r0/build"
```

 The ncurses-based menuconfig interface is the only one that can be invoked by BitBake.

There's more...

You can make your kernel changes permanent with the following steps:

1. Create a default configuration from your .config file from the kernel source directory and a clean environment (not configured with a Yocto setup environment script) by running the following:

```
$ cd /opt/yocto/fsl-community-bsp/wandboard/tmp/work/wandboard-
poky-linux-gnueabi/linux-wandboard/4.1-2.0.x-r0/build
$ make ARCH=arm savedefconfig
```

2. Copy the defconfig file from your kernel build directory to your kernel recipe's defconfig file as follows:

```
$ cp defconfig /opt/yocto/fsl-community-bsp/sources/meta-bsp-
custom/recipes-kernel/linux/linux-wandboard-4.1-2.0.x/wandboard-
custom
```

3. Alternatively, you can use BitBake from the build directory as follows:

```
$ bitbake -c savedefconfig virtual/kernel
```

This also creates a defconfig file in the Linux kernel's build directory, which needs to be copied to your recipe.

Building the Linux kernel

As was the case with U-Boot, Linux kernel development is quicker and less error-prone when using the Yocto SDK to build it. However, for smaller changes, the Yocto build system can also be used.

In this recipe, we will show you how to build and modify the Linux kernel source both with Yocto's SDK and the Yocto build system, and boot our target device with it.

How to do it...

We will use the Yocto Project's SDK already installed in your host:

1. Prepare the environment as follows:

   ```
   $ source /opt/poky/2.4/environment-setup-cortexa9hf-neon-poky-
   linux-gnueabi
   ```

2. Configure the kernel with the default machine configuration:

   ```
   $ cd /opt/yocto/linux-wandboard
   $ cp /opt/yocto/fsl-community-bsp/sources/meta-bsp-custom/recipes-
   kernel/linux/linux-wandboard-4.1-2.0.x/wandboard-custom/defconfig
   arch/arm/configs/wandboard_defconfig
   $ make wandboard_defconfig
   ```

3. Compile the kernel image, modules, and the device tree file with the following:

   ```
   $ make -jN
   ```

You can optionally pass a -jN argument to make to build multithreaded.

This will build the kernel's zImage, modules, and device tree files.

Older Yocto environment setup scripts set the LD variable to use gcc, but the Linux kernel uses LD instead. If your compilation is failing, try the following before running make:
```
$ unset LDFLAGS
```

4. To only build modules, you can run the following:

```
$ make modules
```

5. And to only build device tree files, you can run the following:

```
$ make dtbs
```

6. Copy the kernel image and device tree file to the TFTP root to test using network booting:

```
$ cp arch/arm/boot/zImage arch/arm/boot/dts/imx6qp-
wandboard-revd1.dtb /var/lib/tftpboot
```

Refer to the *Configuring network booting for a development setup* recipe in Chapter 1, *The Build System* for detailed network booting instructions.

Some other embedded Linux targets might need to compile a uImage if the U-Boot bootloader is not compiled with zImage booting support:

```
$ make LOADADDR=0x10800000 uImage
```

A kernel uImage is a kernel image that contains a header that is used by U-Boot when launching the kernel image that includes the kernel load address. It is generated by the kernel make system by invoking the mkimage tool. A zImage is a compressed self-extracting image that does not contain the kernel load address.

> The mkimage tool is part of the Yocto toolchain when built with the FSL community BSP. We will see how to build and install an SDK in the *Preparing and using an SDK* recipe in Chapter 4, *Application Development*. If it is not included in your toolchain, you can install the tool in your host using the following command:
> ```
> $ sudo apt-get install u-boot-tools
> ```

LOADADDR is the U-Boot entry point, the address where U-Boot will place the kernel in memory. It is defined in the meta-freescale/conf/machine/include/imx-base.inc file:

```
UBOOT_ENTRYPOINT_mx6  = "0x10008000"
```

Using Yocto to build the Linux kernel

When we have a small amount of changes or we don't own the source repository, we may be forced to work with patches and use the Yocto build system to build the Linux kernel.

A typical workflow when working on a modification would be as follows:

1. Start the kernel package compilation from scratch:

   ```
   $ cd /opt/yocto/fsl-community-bsp/
   $ source setup-environment wandboard
   $ bitbake -c cleanall virtual/kernel
   ```

   This will erase the build folder, shared state cache, and downloaded package source.

2. Configure the kernel as follows:

   ```
   $ bitbake -c configure virtual/kernel
   ```

   This will convert the machine defconfig file into a .config file and call oldconfig to validate the configuration with the kernel source.

3. You can optionally add your own configuration changes with the following:

   ```
   $ bitbake -c menuconfig virtual/kernel
   ```

4. Now, to modify the kernel source, start a development shell on the kernel:

   ```
   $ bitbake -c devshell virtual/kernel
   ```

   This spawns a new shell with the environment ready for kernel compilation. The new shell will change to the kernel build directory, which contains a local Git repository.

   We can then perform our modifications, including kernel configuration changes.

5. Go back to the Terminal with the sourced Yocto environment to compile the source without erasing our modifications as follows:

   ```
   $ bitbake -C compile virtual/kernel
   ```

   Note the capital C. This invokes the compile task but also all the tasks that follow it.

The kernel source is placed under the `tmp/work-shared/wandboard` folder. A `kernel-source` directory contains the checked-out source, and `kernel-build-artifacts` contains the build output, `defconfig` file, `map` file, and everything required to build external modules. The `work-shared` directory is used for packages that need to be kept outside of the shared state control.

The newly compiled kernel image is available under `tmp/deploy/images/wandboard`.

There's more...

Finally, we get to run the images in the target device. If working from a network-booted system, we would just copy the kernel image and the device tree file to the TFTP server root and boot the target with them using the following command:

```
$ cd tmp/deploy/images/wandboard/
$ cp zImage-wandboard.bin zImage-imx6qp-wandboard-revd1.dtb
/var/lib/tftpboot
```

Refer to the *Configuring network booting for a development setup* recipe in Chapter 1, *The Build System* for details.

Alternatively, the U-Boot bootloader can boot a Linux `zImage` kernel from memory with its corresponding device tree using the following syntax:

```
> bootz <kernel_addr> - <dtb_addr>
```

For example, after configuring U-Boot's network settings, we can fetch images from TFTP and boot Wandboard images as follows:

```
> tftp ${loadaddr} ${image}
> tftp ${fdt_addr} ${fdtfile}
> bootz ${loadaddr} - ${fdt_addr}
```

 For the kernel to correctly mount the root filesystem, we will need to pass the appropriate kernel command-line arguments in U-Boot's `bootargs` variable, for example, with the following:
```
> env set bootargs 'root=PARTUUID=<uuid> rootwait rw
console=ttymxc0,115200'
```

Here, `<uuid>` is replaced by the UUID of the root filesystem partition.

The command to boot a `uImage` Linux kernel image from memory would use `bootm` instead, as in the following:

```
> bootm <kernel_addr> - <dtb_addr>
```

If we were using an `initramdisk`, we would pass it as the second argument. Since we aren't, we use a dash instead.

Once the images are booted and tested, we can go back to the devshell and commit our change to the local Git repository:

```
$ git add --all .
$ git commit -s -m "Well thought commit message"
```

Finally, we generate a patch with our changes in the kernel recipe's patch directory:

```
$ git format-patch -1 -o /opt/yocto/fsl-community-
bsp/sources/meta-bsp-custom/recipes-kernel/linux/linux-wandboard-4.1-2.0.x
```

The `-1` argument to `format-patch` will just output the last commit as a patch. You may need to modify it if there are several patches you want to extract.

Now we can add the patch to the kernel recipe as previously described.

The Yocto build system can now be used to generate `wic.gz` images that can be programmed into the microSD card, as seen in the *Building Wandboard images* recipe in `Chapter 1`, *The Build System*.

Building external kernel modules

The Linux kernel has the ability to load modules at runtime that extend the kernel's functionality. Kernel modules share the kernel's address space and have to be linked against the kernel they are going to be loaded onto. Most device drivers in the Linux kernel can either be compiled into the kernel itself (built-in) or as loadable kernel modules that need to be placed in the root filesystem under the `/lib/modules` directory.

The recommended approach to develop and distribute a kernel module is to do it with the kernel source. A module in the kernel tree uses the kernel's kbuild system to build itself, so as long as it is selected as a module in the kernel configuration and the kernel has module support enabled, Yocto will build it.

However, it is not always possible to develop a module in the kernel. Common examples are hardware manufacturers that provide Linux drivers for a wide variety of kernel versions and have an internal development process separated from the kernel community. The internal development work is usually released first as an external out-of-tree module, although it is common for some or all of these internal developments to finish up in the mainstream kernel eventually. However, upstreaming is a slow process and hardware companies will therefore prefer to develop internally first.

It's worth remembering that the Linux kernel is covered under a GPLv2 license, so Linux kernel modules should be released with a compatible license. We will cover licenses in more detail in the following chapters.

Getting ready

To compile an external kernel module with Yocto, we first need to know how we would link the module source with the kernel itself. An external kernel module is also built using the kbuild system of the Linux kernel it is going to be linked against, so the first thing we need is a Makefile:

```
obj-m:= hello_world.o

SRC := $(shell pwd)
all:
        $(MAKE) -C $(KERNEL_SRC) M=$(SRC)

modules_install:
        $(MAKE) -C $(KERNEL_SRC) M=$(SRC) modules_install

clean:
        rm -f *.o *~ core .depend .*.cmd *.ko *.mod.c
        rm -f Module.markers Module.symvers modules.order
        rm -rf .tmp_versions Modules.symvers
```

The Makefile file just wraps the make command used to compile a module on a Linux system:

```
make -C $(KERNEL_SRC) M=$(SRC)
```

Here, `make` is instructed to build in the location of the kernel source, and the `M` argument tells kbuild it is building a module at the specified location.

And then we code the source of the module itself (`hello_world.c`):

```
/*
 * This program is free software; you can redistribute it and/or    modify
 * it under the terms of the GNU General Public License as    published by
 * the Free Software Foundation; either version 2 of the License,   or
 * (at your option) any later version.
 *
 * This program is distributed in the hope that it will be useful,
 * but WITHOUT ANY WARRANTY; without even the implied warranty of
 * MERCHANTABILITY or FITNESS FOR A PARTICULAR PURPOSE. See the
 * GNU General Public License for more details.
 *
 * You should have received a copy of the GNU General Public    License
 * along with this program. If not, see    <http://www.gnu.org/licenses/>.
 */

#include <linux/module.h>

static int hello_world_init(void)
{
        printk("Hello world\n");
        return 0;
}

static void hello_world_exit(void)
{
        printk("Bye world\n");
}
module_init(hello_world_init);
module_exit(hello_world_exit);

MODULE_LICENSE("GPL v2");
```

It's worth remembering that we need to compile against a kernel source that has already been built. Use the following steps for compilation:

1. We prepare the environment using the Yocto SDK environment setup script:

    ```
    $ source /opt/poky/2.4/environment-setup-cortexa9hf-neon-poky-
    linux-gnueabi
    ```

2. Next we build the module. We execute the following from the module source directory:

```
$ KERNEL_SRC=/opt/yocto/linux-wandboard make
```

The kernel source can also be made available as part of the SDK instead of having to clone it externally. This may be helpful for teams that use Yocto's SDK to develop out-of-tree modules. To include the kernel source in the SDK, we can add the following to the `conf/local.conf` configuration file:

```
TOOLCHAIN_TARGET_TASK_append = " kernel-devsrc"
```

We will still need to build the kernel sources before linking the module against it, or at least run the following on the kernel source:

```
$ make wandboard_defconfig
$ make modules_prepare
```

This will prepare the kernel source to build modules, but it will still not build a `Module.symvers` file. This is a file that contains all the kernel's exported symbols, including those in modules, as well as listing their CRCs if `CONFIG_MODVERSIONS` is defined in the kernel configuration. This file is used to check whether all the required symbols are defined.

How to do it...

Once we know how to compile the module externally, we are ready to prepare a Linux kernel module Yocto recipe for it:

1. We place the module source file and `Makefile` in `recipes-kernel/hello-world/files/` inside our `meta-bsp-custom` layer.
2. We then create a `recipes-kernel/hello-world/hello-world.bb` file with the following content:

```
# Copyright (C) 2017 Packt Publishing.

SUMMARY = "Simplest hello world kernel module."
LICENSE = "GPLv2"
LIC_FILES_CHKSUM =
"file://${COMMON_LICENSE_DIR}/GPL-2.0;md5=801f80980d171dd6425610833
a22dbe6"

inherit module
```

```
SRC_URI = " \
    file://hello_world.c \
    file://Makefile \
"

S = "${WORKDIR}"
COMPATIBLE_MACHINE = "(wandboard)"
```

The recipe defines the source directory and the two module files after inheriting the `module` class, which takes care of everything. The `KERNEL_SRC` argument in our `Makefile` is set by the `module` class to `STAGING_KERNEL_DIR`, the location where the `kernel` class places the Linux kernel headers needed for external module compilation.

3. We build it with the following command:

   $ bitbake hello-world

   The resulting module is called `hello_world.ko`.

There's more...

The previous instructions will build the module but will not install it in the root filesystem. For that, we need to add a dependency to the root filesystem. This is usually done in machine configuration files using `MACHINE_ESSENTIAL_*` (for modules that are needed to boot) or `MACHINE_EXTRA_*` (if they are not essential for boot but needed otherwise) variables.

The dependencies that are essential to boot are the following:

- `MACHINE_ESSENTIAL_EXTRA_RDEPENDS`: The build will fail if they can't be found
- `MACHINE_ESSENTIAL_EXTRA_RRECOMMENDS`: The build will not fail if they can't be found

The dependencies that are not essential to boot are the following:

- `MACHINE_EXTRA_RDEPENDS`: The build will fail if they can't be found
- `MACHINE_EXTRA_RRECOMMENDS`: The build will not fail if they can't be found

Module auto-loading

The `KERNEL_MODULE_AUTOLOAD` variable is used to list all kernel modules that need to be loaded automatically at boot. Modules that need load time arguments can be passed modprobe syntax by listing them in the `KERNEL_MODULE_PROBECONF` variable too, and the syntax provided as `module_conf_<module-name>` lines.

For example, to auto-load the Ethernet gadget driver at boot we could add the following to our kernel recipe:

```
KERNEL_MODULE_AUTOLOAD += "g_ether"
KERNEL_MODULE_PROBECONF += "g_ether"
module_conf_g_ether = "options g_ether iProduct=Wandboard
iManufacturer=Technexion"
```

See also

- Further information about Linux kernel module compilation can be found in the Linux kernel documentation folder under `Documentation/kbuild/modules.txt`

Debugging the Linux kernel and modules

We will highlight some of the most common methods employed by kernel developers to debug kernel issues.

How to do it...

Above all, debugging the Linux kernel remains a manual process, and the most important developer tool is the ability to print debug messages.

The kernel uses the `printk` function, which is very similar syntactically to the `printf` function call from standard C libraries, with the addition of an optional log level. The allowed formats are documented in the kernel source under `Documentation/printk-formats.txt`.

The `printk` functionality needs to be compiled into the kernel with the `CONFIG_PRINTK` configuration variable. You can also configure the Linux kernel to prepend a precise timestamp to every message with the `CONFIG_PRINTK_TIME` configuration variable, or even better, with the `printk.time` kernel command-line argument or through the `sysfs` under `/sys/module/printk/parameters`.

 The `sysfs` is a pseudo filesystem where the Linux kernel exposes device information to user space.

Usually, all kernels contain `printk` support, and the Wandboard kernel does too, although it is commonly removed on production kernels for small embedded systems.

The `printk` function can be used in any context: interrupt, **non-maskable interrupt** (**NMI**), or scheduler. Note that using it inside interrupt context is not recommended.

A useful debug statement to be used during development could be the following:

```
printk(KERN_INFO "[%s:%d] %pf -> var1: %d var2: %d\n",
    __FUNCTION__, __LINE__, __builtin_return_address(0), var1,
    var2);
```

The first thing to note is that there is no comma between the log-level macro and the print format. We then print the function and line where the debug statement is placed and then the parent function. Finally, we print the variables we are actually interested in.

How it works...

The available log levels in `printk` are presented in the following table:

Type	Symbol	Description
Emergency	KERN_EMERG	System is unstable and about to crash
Alert	KERN_ALERT	Immediate action is needed
Critical	KERN_CRIT	Critical software or hardware failure
Error	KERN_ERR	Error condition
Warning	KERN_WARNING	Nothing serious, but might indicate a problem
Notice	KERN_NOTICE	Nothing serious, but user should take note

Information	KERN_INFO	System information
Debug	KERN_DEBUG	Debug messages

If no log level is specified, the default log message as configured in the kernel configuration is used. By default, this is KERN_WARNING.

All printk statements go to the kernel log buffer, which may wrap around, except debug statements, which only appear if the DEBUG symbol is defined, or if the debug command-line argument is passed to the kernel. We will see how to enable dynamic kernel debug messages soon. The printk log buffer must be a power of two, and its size should be set in the CONFIG_LOG_BUF_SHIFT kernel configuration variable. You may modify it with the log_buf_len kernel command-line parameter.

We print the kernel log buffer with the dmesg command. Also, a Yocto user space will have a kernel log daemon running that will log kernel messages to disk under /var/log/messages.

Messages above the current console log level will also appear on the console immediately. The ignore_loglevel kernel command-line argument, also available under /sys/module/printk/parameters, may be used to print all kernel messages to the console independently of the log level.

You can also change the log level at runtime via the proc filesystem. The /proc/sys/kernel/printk file contains the current, default, minimum, and boot time default log levels. To change the current log level to the maximum, execute on the target's shell:

```
$ echo 8 > /proc/sys/kernel/printk
```

You can also set the console log level with the dmesg tool as follows:

```
$ dmesg -n 8
```

To make the change persistent, you can pass a loglevel command-line argument to the kernel, or on some Yocto root filesystem images, you could also use a /etc/sysctl.conf file (available through the procps package).

There's more...

Linux drivers do not use the `printk` function directly. They use, in order of preference, subsystem-specific messages (such as `netdev` or `v4l`) or the `dev_*` and `pr_*` family of functions. The latter are described in the following table:

Device message	Generic message	Printk symbol
dev_emerg	pr_emerg	KERN_EMERG
dev_alert	pr_alert	KERN_ALERT
dev_crit	pr_crit	KERN_CRIT
dev_err	pr_err	KERN_ERR
dev_warn	pr_warn	KERN_WARNING
dev_notice	pr_notice	KERN_NOTICE
dev_info	pr_info	KERN_INFO
dev_dbg	pr_debug	KERN_DEBUG

To enable the debug messages within a driver, you may do either of the following:

- Define DEBUG in a macro before any other header file in your driver source, as follows:

      #define DEBUG

  Of course, the kernel needs to be recompiled and reprogrammed for the `define` above to take effect.

- Use the dynamic debug kernel feature, which allows to control debug statements at runtime. You can then enable/disable all `dev_dbg` and `pr_debug` debug messages with granularity through `debugfs`.

Using dynamic debug

To use the dynamic debug functionality in the Linux kernel, follow these steps:

1. Make sure your kernel is compiled with dynamic debugging (CONFIG_DYNAMIC_DEBUG).

2. Mount the debug filesystem if it hasn't already been mounted:

```
$ mount -t debugfs nodev /sys/kernel/debug
```

3. Configure the debug through the `dynamic_debug/control` folder. It accepts a whitespace-separated sequence of words:

   - `func <function name>`
   - `file <filename>`
   - `module <module name>`
   - `format <pattern>`
   - `line <line or line range>`
   - `+ <flag>`: This adds the specified flag
   - `- <flag>`: This removes the specified flag
   - `= <flag>`: This sets the specified flag

The flags are defined as follows:

   - `f`: This flag includes the function name in the message
   - `l`: This flag includes the line number in the message
   - `m`: This flag includes the module name in the message
   - `p`: This flag enables the debug message
   - `t`: This flag includes the thread ID in non-interrupt context messages

By default, all debug messages are disabled. The `control` file contains all the available debug points and, by default, they have no flags enabled (marked as =_).

To enable all debug statements in a file, type the following:

```
$ echo -n 'file <filename> +p' >
/sys/kernel/debug/dynamic_debug/control
```

Or to just enable a specific debug statement, type the following:

```
$ echo -n 'file <filename> line nnnn +p' >
/sys/kernel/debug/dynamic_debug/control
```

4. To list all enabled debug statements, use the following command:

```
$ awk '$3 != "=_"' /sys/kernel/debug/dynamic_debug/control
```

To make the debug changes persistent, we can pass `dyndbg="<query>"` or `module.dyndbg="<query>"` for modules to the kernel in the command-line arguments.

Note that the query string needs to be passed surrounded by quotes so that it is correctly parsed. You can concatenate more than one query in the command-line argument by using a semicolon to separate them, for example:

```
dyndbg=\"file mxc_v4l2_capture.c +pfl; file ipu_bg_overlay_sdc.c +pfl\"
```

If, for example, we are using the `bootargs` U-Boot argument to pass kernel command-line arguments, we would do the following:

```
> env set bootargs 'dyndbg=\\"file one.c +pfl\; file two.c +pfl\; file
three.c +pfl\; file four.c +pfl\\"'
```

Rate-limiting debug messages

There are rate-limiting and one-shot extensions to the `dev_*`, `pr_*`, and `printk` family of functions:

- `printk_ratelimited()`, `pr_*_ratelimited()`, and `dev_*_ratelimited()` print no more than 10 times in a 5 * HZ interval
- `printk_once()`, `pr_*_once()`, and `dev_*_once()` will print only once

And you also have utility functions to dump a buffer in hexadecimal, for example, `print_hex_dump_bytes()`.

See also

- The dynamic debug is documented in the Linux kernel source under `Documentation/dynamic-debug-howto.txt`

Debugging the Linux kernel booting process

We have seen the most general techniques for debugging the Linux kernel. However, some special scenarios require the use of different methods. One of the most common scenarios in embedded Linux development is the debugging of the booting process. This recipe will explain some of the techniques used to debug the kernel's booting process.

How to do it...

A kernel crashing on boot usually provides no output whatsoever on the console. As daunting as that may seem, there are techniques we can use to extract debug information. Early crashes usually happen before the serial console has been initialized, so even if there were log messages, we would not see them. The first thing we will show is how to enable early log messages that do not need the serial driver.

In case that is not enough, we will also show techniques to access the log buffer in memory.

How it works...

Debugging booting problems have two distinctive phases: before and after the serial console is initialized. After the serial is initialized and we can see serial output from the kernel, debugging can use the techniques described earlier.

Before the serial is initialized, however, there is basic **UART** support in ARM kernels that allows you to use the serial from early boot. This support is compiled in with the CONFIG_DEBUG_LL configuration variable.

This adds support for a debug-only series of assembly functions that allow you to output data to a UART. The low-level support is platform-specific, and for the i.MX6 it can be found under arch/arm/include/debug/imx.S. The code allows for this low-level UART to be configured through the CONFIG_DEBUG_IMX_UART_PORT configuration variable.

We can use this support directly by using the printascii function as follows:

```
extern void printascii(const char *);
printascii("Literal string\n");
```

However, it is preferable to use the early_print function, which makes use of the function explained previously and accepts formatted input in printf style, for example:

```
early_print("%08x\t%s\n", p->nr, p->name);
```

Dumping the kernel's printk buffer from the bootloader

Another useful technique to debug Linux kernel crashes at boot is to analyze the kernel log after the crash. This is only possible if the RAM memory is persistent across reboots and does not get initialized by the bootloader.

As U-Boot keeps the memory intact, we can use this method to peek at the kernel login memory in search of clues.

Looking at the kernel source, we can see how the log ring buffer is set up in `kernel/printk/printk.c` and also note that it is stored in `__log_buf`:

1. To find the location of the kernel buffer, we will use the `System.map` file created by the Linux build process, which maps symbols with virtual addresses using the following command:

   ```
   $ grep __log_buf System.map
   80c37864 b __log_buf
   ```

2. To convert the virtual address to a physical address, we look at how `__virt_to_phys()` is defined for ARM:

   ```
   x - PAGE_OFFSET + PHYS_OFFSET
   ```

3. The `PAGE_OFFSET` variable is defined in the kernel configuration as follows:

   ```
   config PAGE_OFFSET
           hex
           default 0x40000000 if VMSPLIT_1G
           default 0x80000000 if VMSPLIT_2G
           default 0xC0000000
   ```

   Some ARM platforms, such as the i.MX6, will dynamically patch the `__virt_to_phys()` translation at runtime, so `PHYS_OFFSET` will depend on where the kernel is loaded into memory. As this can vary, the calculation we just saw is platform-specific.

   For the Wandboard, the physical address for `0x80c37864` is `0x10c37864`.

4. We can then force a reboot using a magic SysRq key, which needs to be enabled in the kernel configuration with `CONFIG_MAGIC_SYSRQ`, but is enabled in the Wandboard by default:

   ```
   $ echo b > /proc/sysrq-trigger
   ```

7. We then dump that memory address from U-Boot as follows:

   ```
   => md.1  0x10c37864
   10c37864: 00000000 00000000 00210034 c6000000    ........4.!.....
   10c37874: 746f6f42 20676e69 756e694c 6e6f2078    Booting Linux on
   10c37884: 79687020 61636973 5043206c 78302055    physical CPU 0x
   ```

```
10c37894:  00000030 00000000 00000000 009300a4    0...............
10c378a4:  a6000000 756e694c 65762078 6f697372    ....Linux versio
10c378b4:  2e34206e 35312e31 3433312d 2d393930    n 4.1.15-134099-
10c378c4:  35616667 30623765 35393866 69642d62    gfa5e7b0f895b-di
10c378d4:  20797274 656c6128 6f6c4078 696c2d67    rty (alex@log-li
10c378e4:  2d78756e 612d7068 7a6e6f67 20296c61    nux-hp-agonzal)
10c378f4:  63636728 72657620 6e6f6973 312e3720    (gcc version 7.1
10c37904:  2820302e 29434347 23202920 4d532031    .0 (GCC) ) #1 SM
10c37914:  52502050 504d4545 72462054 75412069    P PREEMPT Fri Au
10c37924:  35322067 3a393120 313a3535 45432030    g 25 19:55:10 CE
10c37934:  32205453 00373130 00000000 00000000    ST 2017.........
10c37944:  00400050 c6000000 3a555043 4d524120    P.@.....CPU: ARM
10c37954:  50203776 65636f72 726f7373 31345b20    v7 Processor [41
```

There's more...

Another method is to store the kernel log messages and kernel panics or oops into persistent storage. The Linux kernel's persistent store support (CONFIG_PSTORE) allows you to log in to the persistent memory kept across reboots.

To log panic and oops messages into persistent memory, we need to configure the kernel with the CONFIG_PSTORE_RAM configuration variable, and to log kernel messages, we need to configure the kernel with CONFIG_PSTORE_CONSOLE.

We then need to configure the location of the persistent storage on an unused memory location, but keep the last 1 MB of memory free:

1. For example, we could pass the following kernel command-line arguments to reserve a 128 KB region starting at 0x30000000:

   ```
   ramoops.mem_address=0x30000000 ramoops.mem_size=0x200000
   ```

2. We would then mount the persistent storage by adding it to /etc/fstab so that it is available on the next boot as well:

   ```
   /etc/fstab:
   pstore  /pstore  pstore  defaults  0  0
   ```

3. We then mount it as follows:

   ```
   # mkdir /pstore
   # mount /pstore
   ```

4. Next, we force a reboot with the magic SysRq key:

```
# echo b > /proc/sysrq-trigger
```

5. On reboot, we will see a file inside /pstore:

```
-r--r--r--  1 root root 4084 Sep 16 16:24 console-ramoops
```

6. This will have contents such as the following:

```
SysRq : Resetting
CPU3: stopping
CPU: 3 PID: 0 Comm: swapper/3 Not tainted 3.14.0-rc4-1.0.0-
wandboard-37774-g1eae
[<80014a30>] (unwind_backtrace) from [<800116cc>]
(show_stack+0x10/0x14)
[<800116cc>] (show_stack) from [<806091f4>] (dump_stack+0x7c/0xbc)
[<806091f4>] (dump_stack) from [<80013990>]
(handle_IPI+0x144/0x158)
[<80013990>] (handle_IPI) from [<800085c4>]
(gic_handle_irq+0x58/0x5c)
[<800085c4>] (gic_handle_irq) from [<80012200>]
(__irq_svc+0x40/0x70)
Exception stack(0xee4c1f50 to 0xee4c1f98)
```

7. We should move it out of /pstore or remove it completely so that it doesn't occupy memory.

Using the kernel function tracing system

Recent versions of the Linux kernel contain a set of tracers that, by instrumenting the kernel, allow you to analyze different areas such as the following:

- Interrupt latency
- Preemption latency
- Scheduling latency
- Process context switches
- Event tracing
- Syscalls
- Maximum stack

- Block layer
- Functions

The tracers have no performance overhead when not enabled.

Getting ready

The tracing system can be used in a wide variety of debugging scenarios, but one of the most common tracers used is the function tracer. It instruments every kernel function with an NOP call that is replaced and used to trace the kernel functions when a trace point is enabled.

To enable the function tracer in the kernel, use the CONFIG_FUNCTION_TRACER and CONFIG_FUNCTION_GRAPH_TRACER configuration variables.

The kernel tracing system is controlled via a tracing file in the debug filesystem, which is mounted by default on Yocto's default images. If not, you can mount it with the following:

```
$ mount -t debugfs nodev /sys/kernel/debug
```

We can list the available tracers in our kernel by executing the following:

```
$ cat /sys/kernel/debug/tracing/available_tracers
function_graph function nop
```

How to do it...

1. You can enable a tracer by echoing its name to the current_tracer file. No tracers are enabled by default:

    ```
    $ cat /sys/kernel/debug/tracing/current_tracer
    nop
    ```

2. You can disable all tracers by executing the following command:

    ```
    $ echo -n nop > /sys/kernel/debug/tracing/current_tracer
    ```

     We use echo -n to avoid the trailing newline when echoing to files in sysfs.

3. To enable the function tracer, you would execute:

```
$ echo -n function > /sys/kernel/debug/tracing/current_tracer
```

4. A prettier graph can be obtained by using the `function_graph` tracer as follows:

```
$ echo -n function_graph  >
/sys/kernel/debug/tracing/current_tracer
```

How it works...

Once we know how to enable tracing, let's explore how to make use of it:

1. You can look at the captured trace in human-readable format via the `trace` and `trace_pipe` files, with the latter blocking on `read` and consuming the data.

2. The `function` tracer provides the following output:

```
$ cat /sys/kernel/debug/tracing/trace_pipe
sh-394 [003] ...1 46.205203: mutex_unlock <-
tracing_set_tracer
sh-394 [003] ...1 46.205215: __fsnotify_parent <-
vfs_write
sh-394 [003] ...1 46.205218: fsnotify <-vfs_write
sh-394 [003] ...1 46.205220: __srcu_read_lock <-
fsnotify
sh-394 [003] ...1 46.205223: preempt_count_add <-
__srcu_read_lock
sh-394 [003] ...2 46.205226: preempt_count_sub <-
__srcu_read_lock
sh-394 [003] ...1 46.205229: __srcu_read_unlock <-
fsnotify
sh-394 [003] ...1 46.205232: __sb_end_write <-
vfs_write
sh-394 [003] ...1 46.205235: preempt_count_add <-
__percpu_counter_add
sh-394 [003] ...2 46.205238: preempt_count_sub <-
__percpu_counter_add
sh-394 [003] d..1 46.205247: gic_handle_irq <-
__irq_usr
<idle>-0 [002] d..2 46.205247: ktime_get <-
cpuidle_enter_state
```

The format for the function tracer output is as follows:

```
task-PID [cpu-nr] irqs-off need-resched hard/softirq preempt-depth
delay-timestamp function
```

4. The graphical function tracer output is as follows:

```
$ cat /sys/kernel/debug/tracing/trace_pipe
3)    ==========> |
3)                | gic_handle_irq() {
2)    ==========> |
2)                | gic_handle_irq() {
3)    0.637 us    |   irq_find_mapping();
2)    0.712 us    |   irq_find_mapping();
3)                |   handle_IRQ() {
2)                |   handle_IRQ() {
3)                |     irq_enter() {
2)                |     irq_enter() {
3)    0.652 us    |       rcu_irq_enter();
2)    0.666 us    |       rcu_irq_enter();
3)    0.591 us    |       preempt_count_add();
2)    0.606 us    |       preempt_count_add();
```

The format for the graphical function tracer output is as follows:

```
cpu-nr) timestamp | functions
```

There's more...

The kernel tracing system allows us to insert traces in the code by using the `trace_printk` function call. It has the same syntax as `printk` and can be used in the same scenarios, interrupts, NMI, or scheduler contexts.

Its advantage is that, as it prints to the tracing buffer in memory and not to the console, it has much lower delays than `printk`, so it is useful to debug scenarios where `printk` is affecting the system's behavior, for example, when masking a timing bug.

Tracing is enabled once a tracer is configured, but whether the trace writes to the ring buffer or not can be controlled:

1. To disable writing to the buffer, use the following command:

```
$ echo 0 > /sys/kernel/debug/tracing/tracing_on
```

2. And to re-enable it, use the following command:

```
$ echo 1 > /sys/kernel/debug/tracing/tracing_on
```

You can also enable and disable tracing from kernel space by using the `tracing_on` and `tracing_off` functions.

Inserted traces will appear in any tracer, including the `function` tracer, in which case it will appear as a comment.

Filtering function traces

You can get finer granularity in the functions being traced by using the dynamic tracer, which can be enabled with the `CONFIG_DYNAMIC_FTRACE` configuration variable. This is enabled with the tracing functionality by default. This adds two more files, `set_ftrace_filter` and `set_ftrace_notrace`. Adding functions to `set_ftrace_filter` will trace only those functions, and adding them to `set_ftrace_notrace` will not trace them, even if they are also added to `set_ftrace_filter`.

The set of available function names that can be filtered may be obtained by executing the following command:

```
$ cat /sys/kernel/debug/tracing/available_filter_functions
```

Functions can be added with the following command:

```
$ echo -n <function_name> >>
/sys/kernel/debug/tracing/set_ftrace_filter
```

Note that we use the concatenation operator (>>) so that the new function is appended to the existing ones.

Functions can also be removed with the following:

```
$ echo -n '!<function>' >>  /sys/kernel/debug/tracing/set_ftrace_filter
```

To remove all functions, just echo a blank line into the file:

```
$ echo > /sys/kernel/debug/tracing/set_ftrace_filter
```

There is a special syntax that adds extra flexibility to the filtering:

```
<function>:<command>:[<parameter>]
```

Let's explain each of the components individually:

- `function`: This specifies the function name. Wildcards are allowed.
- `command`: This has the following attributes:

    - `mod`: This enables the given function name only in the module specified in the parameter `command`
    - `traceon/traceoff`: This enables or disables tracing when the specified function is hit the number of times given in the parameter, or always if no parameter is given
    - `dump`: This dumps the contents of the tracing buffer when the given function is hit

Here are some examples:

```
$ echo -n 'ipu_*:mod:ipu' >
  /sys/kernel/debug/tracing/set_ftrace_filter
$ echo -n 'suspend_enter:dump' >
  /sys/kernel/debug/tracing/set_ftrace_filter
$ echo -n 'suspend_enter:traceon' >
  /sys/kernel/debug/tracing/set_ftrace_filter
```

Enabling trace options

Traces have a set of options that can be individually enabled in the `/sys/kernel/debug/tracing/options` directory. Some of the most useful options include the following:

- `print-parent`: This option displays the caller function too
- `trace_printk`: This option disables `trace_printk` writing

Using the function tracer on oops

Another alternative to log the kernel messages on oops or panic is to configure the function tracer to dump its buffer contents to the console so that the events leading up to the crash can be analyzed. Use the following command:

```
$ echo 1 > /proc/sys/kernel/ftrace_dump_on_oops
```

The `sysrq-z` combination will also dump the contents of the tracing buffer to the console, as does calling `ftrace_dump()` from the kernel code.

Getting a stack trace for a given function

The tracing code can create a backtrace for every function called. However, this is a dangerous feature and should only be used with a filtered selection of functions. Have a look at the following commands:

```
$ echo -n <function_name> > /sys/kernel/debug/tracing/set_ftrace_filter
$ echo -n function > /sys/kernel/debug/tracing/current_tracer
$ echo 1 > /sys/kernel/debug/tracing/options/func_stack_trace
$ cat /sys/kernel/debug/tracing/trace
$ echo 0 > /sys/kernel/debug/tracing/options/func_stack_trace
$ echo > /sys/kernel/debug/tracing/set_ftrace_filter
```

Configuring the function tracer at boot

The function tracer can be configured in the kernel command-line arguments and started as early as possible in the boot process. For example, to configure the graphic function tracer and filter some functions, we would pass the following arguments from the U-Boot bootloader to the kernel:

```
ftrace=function_graph ftrace_filter=mxc_hdmi*,fb_show*
```

See also

- More details can be found in the kernel source documentation folder at `Documentation/trace/ftrace.txt`

Managing the device tree

The device tree is a data structure that is passed to the Linux kernel to describe the physical devices in a system.

In this recipe, we will explain how to work with device trees.

Getting ready

Devices that cannot be discovered by the CPU are handled by the platform devices API on the Linux kernel. The device tree replaces the legacy platform data where hardware characteristics were hardcoded in the kernel source so that platform devices can be instantiated. Before device trees came into use, the bootloader (for example, U-Boot) had to tell the kernel what machine type it was booting. Moreover, it had to pass other information such as memory size and location, kernel command-line, and more.

The device tree was first used by the PowerPC architecture and was adopted later on by ARM and all others, except x86. It was defined by the Open Firmware specification, which defined the flattened device tree format in **Power.org Standard for Embedded Power Architecture Platform Requirements (ePAPR)**, which describes an interface between a boot program and a client.

Platform customization changes will usually happen in the device tree without the need to modify the kernel source.

How to do it...

A device tree is defined in a human-readable device tree syntax (`.dts`) text file. Every board has one or several DTS files that correspond to different hardware configurations.

These DTS files are compiled into **Device Tree Binary (DTB)** blobs, which have the following properties:

- They are relocatable, so pointers are never used internally
- They allow for dynamic node insertion and removal
- They are small in size

Device tree blobs can either be attached to the kernel binary (for legacy compatibility) or, as is more commonly done, passed to the kernel by a bootloader such as U-Boot.

To compile them, we use a **Device Tree Compiler** (**DTC**), which is included in the following:

- The kernel source inside `scripts/dtc` and is compiled along with the kernel itself
- The host sysroot in the Yocto SDK
- Or you could alternatively install it as part of your distribution

It is recommended to use the DTC compiler included in the kernel tree or the Yocto SDK.

Device trees can be compiled independently or with the Linux kernel kbuild system, as we saw previously. However, when compiling independently, modern device trees will need to be preprocessed by the C preprocessor first.

It's important to note that the DTC currently performs syntax checking but no binding checking, so invalid DTS files may be compiled, and the resulting DTB file may result in a non-booting kernel. Invalid DTB files usually hang the Linux kernel very early on so there will be no serial output.

The bootloader might also modify the device tree before passing it to the kernel.

How it works...

The DTS file for the Wandboard variant is under `arch/arm/boot/dts/imx6qp-wandboard-revd1.dts` and looks as follows:

```
#include "imx6q-wandboard-revd1.dts"
#include "imx6qp.dtsi"
/ {
        model = "Wandboard i.MX6QuadPlus rev.D1";
};
```

With `imx6q-wandboard-revd1.dts` being:

```
#include <dt-bindings/interrupt-controller/irq.h>
#include "imx6q.dtsi"
#include "imx6qdl-wandboard-revd1.dtsi"
/ {
        model = "Wandboard i.MX6Quad rev.D1";
        compatible = "fsl,imx6q-wandboard", "fsl,imx6q";
};
```

What we see here is a device tree root node that has no parents. The rest of the nodes will have a parent. The structure of a node can be represented as follows:

```
node@0{
    an-empty-property;
    a-string-property = "a string";
    a-string-list-property = "first string", "second string";
    a-cell-property = <1>;
    a-cell-property = <0x1 0x2>;
    a-byte-data-property = [0x1 0x2 0x3 0x4];
    a-phandle-property = <&node1>;
}
```

The node properties can have the following characteristics:

- Be empty
- Contain one or more strings
- Contain one or more unsigned 32-bit numbers, called **cells**
- Contain a binary byte stream
- Be a reference to another node, called a **phandle**

The device tree is initially parsed by the C preprocessor and it can include other DTS files. These `include` files have the same syntax and are usually appended with the `dtsi` suffix. File inclusion can also be performed with the device tree `/include/` operator, although `#include` is recommended, and they should not be mixed. In this case, both `imx6q.dtsi` and `imx6qdl-wandboard-revd1.dtsi` are overlaid with the contents of `imx6qp-wandboard-revd1.dts`.

Device tree nodes are documented in bindings contained in the `Documentation/devicetree/bindings/` directory of the kernel source. New nodes must include the corresponding bindings, and these must be reviewed and accepted by the device tree maintainers. Theoretically, all bindings need to be maintained, although it is likely this will be relaxed in the future.

The compatible property

The most important property in a device tree node is the compatible property. In the root node, it defines the machine types the device tree is compatible with. The DTS file we just saw is compatible in order of precedence with the `fsl,imx6q-wandboard` and `fsl,imx6q` machine types.

On a non-root node, it will define the driver match for the device tree node, binding a device with the driver. For example, a platform driver that binds with a node that defines a property that is compatible with `fsl,imx6q-tempmon` would contain the following excerpt:

```
static const struct of_device_id of_imx_thermal_match[] = {
    { .compatible = "fsl,imx6q-tempmon", },
    { /* end */ }
};
MODULE_DEVICE_TABLE(of, of_imx_thermal_match);

static struct platform_driver imx_thermal = {
    .driver = {
        .name    = "imx_thermal",
        .owner   = THIS_MODULE,
        .of_match_table = of_imx_thermal_match,
    },
    .probe    = imx_thermal_probe,
    .remove   = imx_thermal_remove,
};
module_platform_driver(imx_thermal);
```

The Wandboard device tree file

Usually, the first DTSI file to be included is `skeleton.dtsi`, which is the minimum device tree needed to boot, once a compatible property is added:

```
/ {
    #address-cells = <1>;
    #size-cells = <1>;
    chosen { };
    aliases { };
    memory { device_type = "memory"; reg = <0 0>; };
};
```

Here are the other common top nodes:

- `chosen`: This node defines fixed parameters set at boot, such as the Linux kernel command line or the `initramfs` memory location. It replaces the information traditionally passed in ARM tags (`ATAGS`).
- `memory`: This node is used to define the location and size of RAM. This is usually filled in by the bootloader.
- `aliases`: This defines shortcuts to other nodes.
- `address-cells` and `size-cells`: These are used for memory addressability and will be discussed later on.

A summary representation of the `imx6qp-wandboard-revd1.dts` file, showing only some selected buses and devices, follows:

```
#include "skeleton.dtsi"

/ {
    model = "Wandboard Quad Plus based on Freescale i.MX6 Quad Plus";
    compatible = "fsl,imx6q-wandboard", "fsl,imx6q";

    memory {};

    aliases {};

    intc: interrupt-controller@00a01000 {};

    clocks {};

    soc {
        compatible = "simple-bus";

        dma_apbh: dma-apbh@00110000 {};

        timer@00a00600 {};

        L2: l2-cache@00a02000 {};

        pcie: pcie@0x01000000 {};

        aips-bus@02000000 { /* AIPS1 */
            compatible = "fsl,aips-bus", "simple-bus";

            spba-bus@02000000 {
                compatible = "fsl,spba-bus", "simple-bus";
            };
```

```
                ecspi1: ecspi@02008000 {
                    compatible = "fsl,imx6q-ecspi", "fsl,imx51-ecspi";
                };
            };

            aips-bus@02100000 {
                compatible = "fsl,aips-bus", "simple-bus";
            };
        };
    };
```

In this pseudo-code DTS, we can find several nodes defining SoC buses and several other nodes defining onboard devices.

Defining buses and memory-addressable devices

Buses are typically defined by the `compatible` property or the `simple-bus` property (to define a memory-mapped bus with no specific driver binding), or both. The `simple-bus` property is needed so that child nodes to the bus are registered as platform devices.

For example, the `soc` node is defined as follows:

```
soc {
    compatible = "simple-bus";
    #address-cells = <1>;
    #size-cells = <1>;
    ranges;

    aips-bus@02000000 { /* AIPS1 */
        compatible = "fsl,aips-bus", "simple-bus";
        reg = <0x02000000 0x100000>;
    }
}
```

The properties on the `soc` node are used to specify the memory addressability of the child nodes:

- `address-cells`: This property indicates how many base address cells are needed in the `reg` property.
- `size-cells`: This property indicates how many size cells are needed in the `reg` property.
- `ranges`: This one describes an address translation between parent and child buses. In here, there is no translation and parent and child addressing are identical.

In this case, any child of `soc` needs to define its memory addressing with a `reg` property that contains one cell for the address and one cell for the size. The `aips-bus` node does that with the following property:

```
reg = <0x02000000 0x100000>;
```

There's more...

When the device tree binary blob is loaded in memory by the Linux kernel, it is expanded into a flattened device tree that is accessed by offset. The `fdt_*` kernel functions are used to access the flattened device tree. This `fdt` is then parsed and transformed into a tree memory structure that can be efficiently accessed with the `of_*` family of functions (the prefix comes from Open Firmware).

Modifying and compiling the device tree in Yocto

The following steps will guide you to modify and compile the device tree:

1. To modify the device tree in the Yocto build system, we execute the following set of commands:

   ```
   $ cd /opt/yocto/fsl-community-bsp/
   $ source setup-environment wandboard
   $ bitbake -c devshell virtual/kernel
   ```

2. We then edit `arch/arm/boot/dts/imx6qp-wandboard-revd1.dts` and compile the changes with the following:

   ```
   $ make dtbs
   ```

3. If we want to create a device tree with extra space, let's say 1,024 bytes (for example, to add nodes dynamically as explained in the next recipe), we need to specify it with a DTC flag as follows:

   ```
   $ DTC_FLAGS="-p 1024" make dtbs
   ```

4. To deploy it, we exit the devshell and build the kernel from the project's build directory:

   ```
   $ bitbake -c deploy -f virtual/kernel
   ```

See also

- More information regarding device trees can be found at
  `http://www.devicetree.org`

Debugging device tree issues

This recipe will show some techniques to debug common problems with the device tree.

How to do it...

As mentioned before, problems with the syntax of device tree files usually result in the kernel crashing early in the boot process. Other types of problems are more subtle and usually appear once a driver is making use of the information provided by the device tree. For both types of problems, it is helpful to be able to look not only at the device tree syntax file, but also at the device tree blob, as it is read by both U-Boot and the Linux kernel. It may also be helpful to modify the device tree on the fly using the tools that U-Boot offers.

How it works...

Let's see how to access the device tree at runtime, both from a running U-Boot and Linux.

Looking at the device tree from U-Boot

The U-Boot bootloader offers the `fdt` command to interact with a device tree blob. In the Wandboard's default environment, there are two variables related to the device tree:

- `fdtfile`: This variable contains the name of the device tree file used
- `fdt_addr`: This variable contains the location in memory to load the device tree

To fetch the Wandboard's device tree from the TFTP server location and place it in memory, we use the following command:

```
> tftp ${fdt_addr} ${fdtfile}
```

Once we have the device tree blob in memory, we tell U-Boot where it is located:

```
> fdt addr ${fdt_addr}
```

And then we can inspect nodes from the device tree using the full path to them from the root node. To inspect the selected levels, we use the `list` command, and to print complete subtrees, we use the `print` command:

```
> fdt list /cpus
cpus {
        #address-cells = <0x00000001>;
        #size-cells = <0x00000000>;
        cpu@0 {
        };
        cpu@1 {
        };
        cpu@2 {
        };
        cpu@3 {
        };
};
> fdt print /cpus
cpus {
        #address-cells = <0x00000001>;
        #size-cells = <0x00000000>;
        cpu@0 {
                compatible = "arm,cortex-a9";
                device_type = "cpu";
                reg = <0x00000000>;
                next-level-cache = <0x0000002c>;
                operating-points = <0x00124f80 0x00137478 0x000f32a0
0x001312d0 0x000d0020 0x001312d0 0x000c15c0 0x0011edd8 0x00060ae0
0x000ee098>;
                fsl,soc-operating-points = <0x00124f80 0x00137478
0x000f32a0 0x001312d0 0x000d0020 0x001312d0 0x000c15c0 0x0011edd8 0x0
0060ae0 0x0011edd8>;
                clock-latency = <0x0000ee6c>;
                clocks = <0x00000003 0x00000068 0x00000003 0x00000006
0x00000003 0x00000010 0x00000003 0x00000011 0x00000003 0x000000aa
 0x00000003 0x000000e7 0x00000003 0x000000ee 0x00000003 0x000000e0>;
                clock-names = "arm", "pll2_pfd2_396m", "step", "pll1_sw",
"pll1_sys", "pll1", "pll1_bypass", "pll1_bypass_src";
                arm-supply = <0x0000002d>;
                pu-supply = &lt;0x00000014>;
                soc-supply = <0x0000002e>;
        };
    ...
```

U-Boot can also attach new nodes to the tree, assuming there is extra space in the device tree (refer to the *Managing the device tree* recipe for instructions on how to create a device tree with extra space):

```
> fdt mknode / new-node
> fdt list /new-node
new-node {
};
```

It can also create or remove properties:

```
> fdt set /new-node testprop testvalue
> fdt print /new-node
new-node {
        testprop = "testvalue";
};
> fdt rm /new-node testprop
> fdt print /new-node
new-node {
};
```

For example, it can be useful to modify the kernel command line through the `chosen` node.

Looking at the device tree from the Linux kernel

Once the Linux kernel is booted, it exposes the device tree in `/proc/device-tree` as follows:

```
# ls /proc/device-tree/cpus/
#address-cells  #size-cells    cpu@0           cpu@1           cpu@2
cpu@3           name
```

The Software Layer

3

In this chapter, we will cover the following recipes:

- Exploring an image's contents
- Adding a new software layer
- Selecting a specific package version and provider
- Adding supported packages
- Adding new packages
- Adding data, scripts, or configuration files
- Managing users and groups
- Using the sysvinit initialization system
- Using the systemd initialization system
- Installing package installation scripts
- Reducing the Linux kernel image size
- Reducing the root filesystem image size
- Memory-based root filesystems
- Securing the root filesystem
- Releasing software
- Analyzing your system for compliance
- Working with open source and proprietary code

Introduction

With hardware-specific changes on their way, the next step is customizing the target root filesystem, the software that runs under the Linux kernel, also called the Linux user space.

The usual approach to this is to start with one of the available core images and both optimize and customize it as per the needs of your embedded project. Usually, the images chosen as a starting point are either `core-image-base` for a headless system, or `core-image-sato` for a graphical system, but any of them will do.

This chapter will show you how to add a software layer to contain those changes, and will explain some of the common customizations made, such as size optimization. It will also show you how to add new packages to your root filesystem, including licensing considerations.

Exploring an image's contents

We have already seen how to use the build history feature to obtain a list of packages and files included in our image. In this recipe, we will explain how the root filesystem is built so that we are able to track its components.

Getting ready

When packages are built, they are placed inside the working directory of your project, usually `tmp/work`, and classified according to their architecture. For example, on a `wandboard` build, we find the following directories:

- `all-poky-linux`: This is used for architecture-independent packages
- `cortexa9hf-neon-poky-linux-gnueabi`: This is used for `cortexa9`, hard floating point packages
- `cortexa9hf-neon-mx6qdl-poky-linux-gnueabi`: This is used for `cortexa9`, hard floating point packages that are specific to the i.MX6 architecture
- `wandboard-poky-linux-gnueabi`: This is used for machine-specific packages, in this case `wandboard`

- `x86_64-linux`: This is used for the packages that form the host `sysroot`
- `x86_64-nativesdk-pokysdk-linux`: This is used for host packages that are to be included in the SDK, for example, development tools that are built by Yocto but are to be used in the native host

BitBake will build all the packages included in its dependency list inside its own directory.

How to do it...

To find the build directory for a given package, we can execute the following command:

```
$ bitbake -e <package> | grep ^WORKDIR=
```

Inside the build directory, we find some subdirectories (assuming `rm_work` is not used) that the build system uses in the packaging task. These subdirectories include the following:

- `deploy-rpms`: This is the directory where the final packages are stored when using the default RPM package format. We look here for individual packages that can be locally copied to a target and installed. These packages are copied to the `tmp/deploy` directory and are also used when Yocto builds the root filesystem image.
- `image`: This is the default destination directory where the `do_install` task installs components. It can be modified by the recipe with the `D` configuration variable.
- `package`: This one contains the actual package contents, which may be different from the contents of the previous image directory.
- `packages-split`: This is where the contents are categorized in subdirectories named after their final packages. Recipes can split the package contents into several final packages, as specified by the `PACKAGES` variable. Some usual packages besides the default package name are:
    - `dbg`: This installs components used in debugging
    - `dev`: This installs components used in development, such as headers and libraries
    - `staticdev`: This installs libraries and headers used in static compilation
    - `doc`: This is where the documentation is placed
    - `locale`: This installs localization components

The components to be installed in each package are selected using the `FILES` variable. For example, to add to the default package, you could add the following variable to your recipe:

```
FILES_${PN} += "${bindir}/file.bin"
```

And to add to the development package, you could use the following:

```
FILES_${PN}-dev += "${libdir}/lib.so"
```

The `libdir` and `bindir` variables are defined on the BitBake configuration file in Poky, `meta/conf/bitbake.conf`, along with other helpful path helper variables.

How it works...

Once the Yocto build system has built all the individual packages in its dependency list, it runs the `do_rootfs` task, which populates the sysroot and builds the root filesystem before creating the final package images. You can find the location of the root filesystem by executing:

```
$ bitbake -e core-image-minimal | grep ^IMAGE_ROOTFS=
```

 Note that the `IMAGE_ROOTFS` variable is not configurable and should not be changed.

The contents of this directory will later be prepared into an image according to what image types are configured in the `IMAGE_FSTYPES` configuration variable. If something has been installed in this directory, it will then be installed in the final image.

Adding a new software layer

Root filesystem customization involves adding or modifying content to the base image. Metadata for this content goes into one or more software layers, depending on the amount of customization needed.

A typical embedded project will have just one software layer containing all non-hardware-specific customizations. But it is also possible to have extra layers for graphical frameworks or system-wide elements.

Getting ready

Before starting work on a new layer, it is a good practice to check whether someone else provides a similar layer. Also, if you are trying to integrate an open source project, check whether a layer with it already exists. There is an index of available layers at `http://layers.openembedded.org/`.

How to do it...

A new software layer can be created in the same way we did for a BSP layer in the previous chapter. We can, for example, create a new `meta-custom` layer using the `yocto-layer` command as we learned in the *Creating a custom BSP layer* recipe in `Chapter 2`, *The BSP Layer*. From the `sources` directory, execute the following command:

```
$ yocto-layer create custom
```

As already mentioned, the `yocto-layer` tool will add the `meta` prefix to the layer.

Don't forget to add the layer to your project's `conf/bblayers.conf` file and to your template's `conf` directory to make it available for all new projects.

The default `conf/layer.conf` configuration file is as follows:

```
# We have a conf and classes directory, add to BBPATH
BBPATH .= ":${LAYERDIR}"

# We have recipes-* directories, add to BBFILES
BBFILES += "${LAYERDIR}/recipes-*/*/*.bb \
        ${LAYERDIR}/recipes-*/*/*.bbappend"

BBFILE_COLLECTIONS += "custom"
BBFILE_PATTERN_custom = "^${LAYERDIR}/"
BBFILE_PRIORITY_custom = "6"
```

We discussed all the relevant variables in this snippet in the *Creating a custom BSP layer* recipe in `Chapter 2`, *The BSP Layer*.

How it works...

When adding content to a new software layer, we need to keep in mind that our layer needs to play well with other layers in the Yocto project. To this end, when customizing recipes, we will always use append files, and will only override existing recipes if we are completely sure there is no way to add the customization required through an append file.

To help us manage the content across several layers, we can use the following `bitbake-layers` command-line utilities:

- `$ bitbake-layers show-layers`: This will display the configured layers as BitBake sees them. It is helpful to detect errors on your `conf/bblayer.conf` file.

- `$ bitbake-layers show-recipes`: This command will display all the available recipes and the layers that provide them. It can be used to verify that BitBake is seeing your newly created recipe. If it does not appear, verify that the filesystem hierarchy corresponds to the one defined in your layer's `BBFILES` variable in `conf/layer.conf`.

- `$ bitbake-layers show-overlayed`: This command will show all the recipes that are overlayed by another recipe with the same name but in a higher priority layer. It helps detect recipe clashes.

- `$ bitbake-layers show-appends`: This command will list all available append files and the `recipe` files they apply to. It can be used to verify that BitBake is seeing your append files. Also, as before with recipes, if they don't appear, you will need to check the filesystem hierarchy and your layer's `BBFILES` variable.

- `$ bitbake-layers flatten <output_dir>`: This command will create a directory with the contents of all configured layers, without overlayed recipes and with all the append files applied. This is how BitBake will see the metadata. This flattened directory is useful to discover conflicts with your layer's metadata.

- `$ bitbake-layers show-cross-depends`: This command will show all recipe dependencies across layers, for example recipes with the `INHERIT`, `RRECOMMENDS`, `DEPENDS`, or `RDEPENDS` variables to recipes from a different layer.

The `bitbake-layers` command can also be used to add and remove layers to the `conf/bblayers.conf` file:

- `$ bitbake-layers add-layer </path/to/layer>`: This command will add the specified layer path to the BBLAYERS variable in your project's `conf/bblayers.conf`
- `$ bitbake-layers remove-layer </path/to/layer>`: This command will remove the specified layer path from the BBLAYERS variable in your project's `conf/bblayers.conf`

It can also use the OpenEmbedded Layer Index mentioned previously to automatically fetch and add the layer and its dependencies to your project:

```
$ bitbake-layers layerindex-fetch <layer name>
```

Or to just list the layer dependencies from the index:

```
$ bitbake-layers layerindex-show-depends <layer name>
```

The new layer will be placed inside the `poky` layer.

There's more...

We will sometimes add customizations that are specific to one board or machine. These are not always hardware-related, so they could be found both in a BSP or software layer.

When doing so, we will try to keep our customizations as specific as possible. One typical example is customizing for a specific machine or machine family. If you need to add a patch for the `wandboard` machine, you would use the following line of code:

```
SRC_URI_append_wandboard = " file://mypatch.patch"
```

And, if the patch is applicable to all i.MX6-based boards, you can use the following:

```
SRC_URI_append_mx6 = " file://mypatch.patch"
```

To be able to use machine family overrides, the machine configuration files need to include a MACHINEOVERRIDES variable, such as the one for the `wandboard` in the `meta-freescale-3rdparty` layer machine configuration file, as show here:

```
conf/machine/wandboard.conf:MACHINEOVERRIDES =. "mx6:mx6dl:mx6q:"
```

This is included as part of the default OVERRIDES variable as defined in
meta/conf/bitbake.conf in the poky layer:

```
OVERRIDES = "${TARGET_OS}:${TRANSLATED_TARGET_ARCH}:build-${BUILD_OS}:pn-
${PN}:${MACHINEOVERRIDES}:${DISTROOVERRIDES}:${CLASSOVERRIDE}:forcevariable
"
```

The override mechanism allows us to conditionally set variables as follows:

```
VARIABLE_override1_override2 = ""
```

Or we can use the _append, _prepend, and _remove syntax:

```
VARIABLE_append_override1_override2 = ""
VARIABLE_prepend_override1_override2 = ""
VARIABLE_remove_override1_override2 = ""
```

BitBake will search a predefined path, looking for files inside the package's working
directory, defined in the FILESPATH variable as a colon-separated list. Specifically:

```
${BPN}-${PV}/${DISTRO}
${BPN}/${DISTRO}
files/${DISTRO}

${BPN}-${PV}/${MACHINE}
${BPN}/${MACHINE}
files/${MACHINE}

${BPN}-${PV}/${MACHINEOVERRIDES}
${BPN}/${MACHINEOVERRIDES}
files/${MACHINEOVERRIDES}

${BPN}-${PV}/${TARGET_ARCH}
${BPN}/${TARGET_ARCH}
files/${TARGET_ARCH}

${BPN}-${PV}/
${BPN}/
files/
```

In the specific case of the wandboard, this translates to the following:

```
${BPN}-${PV}/poky
${BPN}/poky
files/poky
${BPN}-${PV}/wandboard
${BPN}/wandboard
files/wandboard
```

```
${BPN}-${PV}/mx6q
${BPN}/mx6q
files/mx6q
${BPN}-${PV}/mx6dl
${BPN}/mx6dl
files/mx6dl
${BPN}-${PV}/mx6
${BPN}/mx6
files/mx6
${BPN}-${PV}/armv7a
${BPN}/armv7a
files/armv7a
${BPN}-${PV}/arm
${BPN}/arm
files/arm
${BPN}-${PV}/
${BPN}/
files/
```

Here, BPN is the package name with prefixes and suffixes (such as nativesdk-, -native and others) removed, and PV is the package version.

It is best to place patches in the most specific of these, so wandboard, followed by mx6q or mx6dl, mx6, armv7a, arm, and finally the generic BPN-PV, BPN, and files directory.

Note that the search path refers to the location of the BitBake recipe, so append files need to always add the path when adding content. Our append files can add extra folders to this search path if needed by appending or prepending to the FILESEXTRAPATHS variable as follows:

```
FILESEXTRAPATHS_prepend := "${THISDIR}/folder:"
```

Note the immediate operator (:=) which expands THISDIR immediately, and the prepend, which places your added path before any other path so that your patches and files are found first in the search.
Also, we have seen the += and =+ style of operators in configuration files, but they should be avoided in recipe files and the append and prepend operators should be given preference, as seen in the example code explained previously, to avoid ordering issues.

Let's finish with a quick overview of the common BitBake syntax. The following assignments are evaluated first:

- = expand when used
- := expand when parsed
- ?= immediately expand when parsed if empty
- += immediately append when parsing with leading space
- .= immediately append when parsing without a space
- =+ immediately prepend when parsing with trailing space
- =. immediately prepend when parsing without a space

After BitBake evaluates the previous assignments, it will evaluate the _append and _prepend syntax. Finally, it will evaluate the ??= assignment, which is identical to ?= except for the parsing order.

With this explanation it is easier to understand that configuration files, which are parsed first by BitBake, make use of the _append and _prepend syntax so that the assignments are deferred and recipes and classes using weak symbols such as ?= have their defaults applied. If conf/local.conf, for example, used the =+ assignment, a recipe using ?= would not have the default applied.

See also

- Refer to the *Building your first image* recipe in Chapter 1, *The Build System* for a description of BitBake's file parsing order
- For a complete reference for BitBake's syntax, refer to Chapter 3, *Syntax and Operators* of the Yocto Project's *BitBake User Manual*

Selecting a specific package version and provider

Our layers can provide recipes for different versions of the same package. For example, the meta-freescale layer contains several different types of Linux kernel recipes:

- linux-imx: This corresponds to the NXP's i.MX BSP kernel source fetched from http://git.freescale.com/git/cgit.cgi/imx/linux-imx.git/

- `linux-fslc-imx`: This is a fork from NXP's i.MX BSP kernel tree with a stability release and community patches applied, fetched from `https://github.com/Freescale/linux-fslc`
- `linux-fslc`: This is a mainline Linux kernel fork with community patches, fetched from `https://github.com/Freescale/linux-fslc`
- `linux-qoriq`: This is a kernel with NXP's QorIQ PowerPC-based platform support fetched from `https://github.com/qoriq-open-source/linux.git`

As we mentioned before, all recipes provide the package name (for example, `linux-imx` or `linux-fslc`) by default, but all Linux recipes must also provide the `virtual/kernel` virtual package. The build system will resolve `virtual/kernel` to the most appropriate Linux recipe name, taking into account the requirements of the build, such as the machine it is building for.

And within those recipes, `linux-fslc`, for example, has both 4.9 and 4.14 recipe versions.

In this section, we will show you how to tell the Yocto build system which specific package and version to build.

How to do it...

To specify the exact package we want to build, the build system allows us to specify what provider and version to use.

How do we select which provider to use?

We can tell BitBake which recipe to use by using the `PREFERRED_PROVIDER` variable. To set a preferred provider for the `virtual/kernel` virtual package on our `wandboard` machine, we would add the following to its machine configuration file:

```
PREFERRED_PROVIDER_
virtual/kernel = "linux-fslc"
```

How do we select which version to use?

Within a specific provider, we can also tell BitBake which version to use with the
PREFERRED_VERSION variable. For example, to set a specific linux-fslc version for all
i.MX6-based machines, we would add the following to our conf/local.conf file:

```
PREFERRED_VERSION_linux-fslc_mx6 = "4.9"
```

The % wildcard is accepted to match any character, as we see here:

```
PREFERRED_VERSION_linux-fslc_mx6 = "4.9%"
```

This will match any 4.9.x kernel version.

It is, however, more common to see this type of configuration done in machine
configuration files, in which case we would not use the _mx6 append.

How do we select which version not to use?

We can use the DEFAULT_PREFERENCE variable set to -1 to specify that a version is not to
be used unless explicitly set by a PREFERRED_VERSION variable. This is commonly used in
development versions of packages:

```
DEFAULT_PREFERENCE = "-1"
```

Adding supported packages

It is common to want to add new packages to an image that already has an available recipe
in one of the included Yocto layers.

When the target image desired is very different from the supplied core images, it is
recommended to define a new image rather than to customize an existing one.

This recipe will show how to customize an existing image by adding supported packages to
it, but also to create a completely new image recipe if needed.

Getting ready

To discover whether a package we require is included in our configured layers, and what specific versions are supported, we can use `bitbake-layers` from our build directory as we saw previously:

```
$ bitbake-layers show-recipes htop
htop:
  meta-oe                 1.0.3
```

Alternatively, we can also use BitBake as follows:

```
$ bitbake -s | grep htop
htop                                           :1.0.3-r0
```

Or we can use the `find` Linux command in our `sources` directory:

```
$ find /opt/yocto/fsl-community-bsp/sources -type f -name "htop*.bb"
/opt/yocto/fsl-community-bsp/sources/meta-openembedded/meta-oe/recipes-
support/htop/htop_1.0.3.bb
```

Once we know what packages we want to include in our final images, let's see how we can add them to the image.

How to do it...

While developing, we will use our project's `conf/local.conf` file to add customizations. To add packages to all images, we can use the following line of code:

```
IMAGE_INSTALL_append = " htop"
```

Note that there is a space after the first quote to separate the new package from the existing ones, as the append operator does not add a space.

We could also limit the addition to a specific image with:

```
IMAGE_INSTALL_append_pn-core-image-minimal = " htop"
```

Another way to easily make customizations is by making use of **features**. A feature is a logical grouping of packages. For example, we could create a new feature called `debug-utils`, which will add a whole set of debugging utilities. We could define our feature in a configuration file or class as follows:

```
FEATURE_PACKAGES_debug-utils = "trace-cmd perf"
```

We could then add this feature to our image by adding an `EXTRA_IMAGE_FEATURES` variable to our `conf/local.conf` file as follows:

```
EXTRA_IMAGE_FEATURES += "debug-utils"
```

If you were to add it to an image recipe, you would use the `IMAGE_FEATURES` variable instead.

Usually, features get added as a `packagegroup` recipe instead of being listed as packages individually. Let's show how to define a `packagegroup` recipe in the `recipes-core/packagegroups/packagegroup-debug-utils.bb` file:

```
SUMMARY = "Debug applications packagegroup"

inherit packagegroup

RDEPENDS_${PN} = "\
    trace-cmd \
    perf \
"
```

And you would then add it to the `FEATURE_PACKAGES` variable as follows:

```
FEATURE_PACKAGES_debug-utils = "packagegroup-debug-utils"
```

We can use `packagegroups` to create more complex examples. Refer to the *Yocto Project Development Manual* at `http://www.yoctoproject.org/docs/2.4/dev-manual/dev-manual.html` for details.

How it works...

We can follow both a top-down and bottom-up approach to image customization. A top-down approach would start with either inheriting or appending one of the core images provided by Poky and configure them down, while the bottom-up approach would define a new image recipe from scratch and add features incrementally.

The smallest core image included in Poky is `core-image-minimal`, which is shown next:

```
IMAGE_INSTALL = "packagegroup-core-boot ${CORE_IMAGE_EXTRA_INSTALL}"
IMAGE_LINGUAS = " "
LICENSE = "MIT"
inherit core-image
IMAGE_ROOTFS_SIZE ?= "8192"
IMAGE_ROOTFS_EXTRA_SPACE_append = "${@bb.utils.contains("DISTRO_FEATURES",
"systemd", " + 4096", "" ,d)}"
```

The `IMAGE_LINGUAS` variable here is used to specify the set of locales to add to an image. By default, BitBake defines it as:

```
IMAGE_LINGUAS ?= "en-us en-gb"
```

Core images are designed to be customizable by adding features selectively based on the following variables:

- `MACHINE_FEATURES` is a list of features the hardware supports and it is usually configured in the machine configuration. The `core-image` class will add software features for the machine features specified.
- `DISTRO_FEATURES` is a list of software features the distribution supports used by packages for conditional compilation. For example, packages can have graphical support based on the x11 distro feature, or wireless support based on the Wi-Fi feature.
- `IMAGE_FEATURES` is a list of features to include in the image. Image features are defined in `packagegroups` that define sets of packages that provide specific functionality.
- `VIRTUAL-RUNTIME` is a variable used to select between packages that offer the same functionality, for example the `sysvinit` and `systemd` init systems.

We could, for example, start with `core-image-minimal.bb` and customize it by adding the following `meta-custom/recipes-core/images/custom-image.bb` image file:

```
require recipes-core/images/core-image-minimal.bb
IMAGE_FEATURES += "ssh-server-dropbear package-management"
```

And then build it by doing this:

```
$ bitbake custom-image
```

Of course, we can also define a new image from scratch using one of the available images as a template. An example can be found in the *Reducing the root filesystem image size* recipe in this same chapter.

There's more...

A final way to customize images is by adding shell functions that get executed once the image has been created. You do this by adding the following to your image recipe or `conf/local.conf` file:

```
ROOTFS_POSTPROCESS_COMMAND += "function1;...;functionN"
```

You can use the path to the root filesystem in your command with the `IMAGE_ROOTFS` variable.

Classes would use the `IMAGE_POSTPROCESS_COMMAND` variable instead of `ROOTFS_POSTPROCESS_COMMAND`.

Examples of usage can be found in the `debug-tweaks` feature in Poky's `rootfs-postcommands.bbclass`, when images are tweaked to allow password-less root logins. This method is also commonly used to customize the root password of a target image.

Configuring packages

As we saw in the *Configuring the Linux kernel* recipe in `Chapter 2`, *The BSP Layer*, some packages, such as the Linux kernel, provide a configuration menu and can be configured with the `menuconfig` BitBake command.

Another package worth mentioning with a configuration interface is BusyBox, well-known software for embedded systems that provides stripped down Linux tools suitable for resource-constrained devices. We will show how to configure BusyBox, for example to add `pgrep`, a tool that looks up process IDs by name.

The BusyBox recipe has support for configuration fragments, so to configure BusyBox all we need is to `bbappend` the recipe in our custom layer. To generate the configuration fragment, first we launch the configuration menu with:

```
$ bitbake -c menuconfig busybox
```

In **Process utilities**, choose **pgrep**.

Now we generate a `config` fragment with:

```
$ bitbake -c diffconfig busybox
Config fragment has been dumped into:
 /opt/yocto/fsl-community-bsp/wandboard/tmp/work/cortexa9hf-neon-poky-
linux-gnueabi/busybox/1.24.1-r0/fragment.cfg
```

And finally, we apply the change to the layer with the following append file: `recipes-core/busybox/busybox_1.24.1.bbappend`:

```
FILESEXTRAPATHS_prepend := "${THISDIR}/${PN}:"
SRC_URI += "file://fragment.cfg"
```

With the `recipes-core/busybox/busybox/fragment.cfg` file shown next:

```
CONFIG_PGREP=y
```

The creation of the `config` fragment and append file can be automated with:

```
$ recipetool appendsrcfile </path/to/layer> busybox
</path/to/config/fragment>
```

We can now copy the RPM package into the target:

```
$ bitbake -e busybox | grep ^WORKDIR=
$ scp ${WORKDIR}/deploy-rpms/cortexa9hf_neon/busybox-1.24.1-
r0.cortexa9hf_neon.rpm root@<target_ip>:/tmp
```

And install the RPM package on the target:

```
# rpm --force -U /tmp/busybox-1.24.1-r0.cortexa9hf_neon.rpm
```

Note that we are forcing the update as the package version has not increased with the configuration change.

Adding new packages

We have seen how to customize our image so that we can add supported packages to it. When we can't find an existing recipe, or we need to integrate some new software we have developed, we will need to create a new Yocto recipe.

Getting ready

There are some questions we need to ask ourselves before starting to write a new recipe:

- Where is the source code stored?
- Is it source-controlled or released as a tarball?
- What is the source code license?
- What build system is it using?

- Does it need configuration?
- Can we cross-compile it as it is, or does it need to be patched?
- What files need to be deployed to the root filesystem, and where do they go?
- Are there any system changes that need to happen, such as new users or `init` scripts?
- Are there any dependencies that need to be installed into `sysroot` beforehand?

Once we know the answers to these questions, we are ready to start writing our recipe.

How to do it...

It is best to start from a blank template such as the one that follows rather than to start from a similar recipe and modify it, as the result will be cleaner and contain only the strictly required instructions.

A good starting base for a minimal recipe addition is:

```
SUMMARY = "The package description for the package management
    system"

LICENSE = "The package's licenses typically from
    meta/files/common-licenses/"
LIC_FILES_CHKSUM = "License checksum used to track open license
    changes"
DEPENDS = "Package list of build time dependencies"

SRC_URI = "Local or remote file or repository to fetch"
SRC_URI[md5sum] = "md5 checksums for all remote fetched files (not
    for repositories)"
SRC_URI[sha256sum] = "sha256 checksum for all remote fetched files
    (not for repositories)"

S = "Location of the source in the working directory, by default
    ${WORKDIR}/${PN}-${PV}."

inherit <class needed for some functionality>

# Task overrides, like do_configure, do_compile and do_install, or
    nothing.

# Package splitting (if needed).

# Machine selection variables (if needed).
```

How it works...

We will explain each of the recipe elements in more detail in the following sections.

Package licensing

Every recipe needs to contain a LICENSE variable. The LICENSE variable allows you to specify multiple, alternative, and per-package type licenses, as seen in the following examples:

- For MIT or GPLv2 alternative licenses, we will use:

      LICENSE = "GPL-2.0 | MIT"

- For both ISC and MIT licenses, we will use:

      LICENSE = "ISC & MIT"

- For split packages, all of them GPLv2 except the documentation that is covered under the Creative Commons, we will use:

      LICENSE_${PN} = "GPLv2"
      LICENSE_${PN}-dev = "GPLv2"
      LICENSE_${PN}-dbg = "GPLv2"
      LICENSE_${PN}-doc = "CC-BY-2.0"

Open source packages usually have the license included with the source code in README, COPYING, or LICENSE files, and even the source code header files.

For open source licenses, we also need to specify LIC_FILES_CHKSUM for all licenses so that the build system can notify us when the licenses change. To add it, we locate the file or file portion that contains the license and provide its relative path from the directory containing the source and a MD5 checksum for it. For example:

    LIC_FILES_CHKSUM =
    "file://${COMMON_LICENSE_DIR}/GPL-2.0;md5=801f80980d171dd6425610833a22dbe6"

This example uses a GPL-2.0 license text from Poky's common licenses folder (meta/files/common-licenses). This can be used as an alternative when no license is included within the package source.

    LIC_FILES_CHKSUM =
        "file://COPYING;md5=f7bdc0c63080175d1667091b864cb12c"

This example points to a COPYING file included with the source.

```
LIC_FILES_CHKSUM =
    "file://usr/include/head.h;endline=7;md5=861ebad4adc7236f8d1905338
    abd7eb2"
LIC_FILES_CHKSUM =
    "file://src/file.c;beginline=5;endline=13;md5=6c7486b21a8524b1879f
    a159578da31e"
```

Both examples here point to extracts from source code files that contain the license.

Proprietary code should have the license set to CLOSED, and no LIC_FILES_CHECKSUM is needed for it.

You can use the recipetool command to create a recipe skeleton that can then be edited to completion with:

```
$ recipetool create -o helloworld.bb helloworld.c
```

Where:

- -o is the path to the file to create
- -N is the optional package name
- -V is the optional package version

Fetching package contents

The SRC_URI variable lists the files to be fetched. The build system will use different fetchers depending on the file prefix. These can be:

- Local files included with the metadata (using the prefix file://). If the local file is a patch, the SRC_URI variable can be extended with patch-specific arguments such as:
  - striplevel: The default patch strip level is 1 but it can be modified with this argument
  - patchdir: This specifies the directory location to apply the patch to, with the default being the source directory
  - apply: This argument controls whether to apply the patch or not, with the default being to apply it

- Files stored in remote servers (typically, `http(s)://`, `ftp://`, or `ssh://`).
- Files stored in remote repositories (typically, `git://`, `svn://`, `hg://`, or `bzr://`). These also need a `SRCREV` variable to specify the revision.

Files stored in remote servers (not local files or remote repositories) need to specify two checksums. If there are several files, they can be distinguished with a name argument, for example:

```
SRCREV = "04024dea2674861fcf13582a77b58130c67fccd8"
SRC_URI = "git://repo.com/git/ \
          file://fix.patch;name=patch \
          http://example.org/archive.data;name=archive"
SRC_URI[archive.md5sum] = "aaf32bde135cf3815aa3221726bad71e"
SRC_URI[archive.sha256sum] =
   "65be91591546ef6fdfec93a71979b2b108eee25edbc20c53190caafc9a92d4e7"
```

The source directory folder, `S`, specifies the location of the source files. The repository will be checked out here, or the tarball decompressed in this location. If the tarball decompresses in the standard `${BPN}-${PV}` location, it can be omitted as it is the default. For repositories, it needs to always be specified, for example:

```
S = "${WORKDIR}/git"
```

Specifying task overrides

All recipes inherit the `base.bbclass` class, which in turn inherits the `patch.bbclass` and `staging.bbclass`, and together define the following tasks:

- `do_build`: This is the default task that by default just executes all the rest.
- `do_fetch`: This method fetches the source code, selecting the fetcher using the `SRC_URI` variable. Archive formats are downloaded into `DL_DIR` while Git formats are cloned into `DL_DIR/git2` and tarballed into `DL_DIR`.
- `do_unpack`: This method creates the `WORKDIR` at `TMPDIR/work/<arch>/<PN>/<PV>`, and unpacks the code in the working directory to a location specified by the `S` variable, which is `WORKDIR/<PN>-<PV>` by default.
- `do_patch`: This method applies any specified patch using `quilt` over the unpacked source.
- `do_configure`: This method configures the source code if needed, for example if using the `autotools` or `cmake` classes, with configuration files and makefiles written to `B`, usually `WORKDIR/build`. It does nothing by default.

- `do_populate_lic`: This method populates the `TMPDIR/deploy/licenses/<PN>` directory with the licensing information.
- `do_compile`: This method compiles the source in `S` and runs the GNU make target by default to create binaries in `B`. Individual per-recipe `sysroot` directories are populated at this point.
- `do_install`: This method uses pseudo to copy the results of the build from the build directory `B` to the destination directory `D`, usually `WORKDIR/image`. It does nothing by default.
- `do_package`: This method splits the deliverables into several packages into `WORKDIR/packages-split`. It does nothing by default.
- `do_populate_sysroot`: This method populates `WORKDIR/sysroot-destdir` with header files, shared objects, and `packageconfig` files.
- `do_package_write_rpm`: This method creates the RPM packages, assuming the default RPM package class is used, in `TMPDIR/deploy/rpm`.
- `do_rootfs`: For image recipes that inherit `image.bbclass`, this method installs the RPM packages to create the final `rootfs` image in `TMPDIR/work/<machine>/<image-name>/<PV>/rootfs`, as well as copying the final images into `TMPDIR/deploy/images/<machine>`.

Tasks can be overridden, appended, or prepended. We can also add a new task with `addtask`, remove a task with `deltask`, or simply skip it as follows:

```
do_task[noexec] = "1"
```

Usually, only the configuration, compilation, and installation tasks are overridden, and this is mostly done implicitly by inheriting the `autotools` class. We will discuss different classes used for application development in Chapter 4, *Application Development*.

For a custom recipe that does not use a build system, you need to provide the required instructions for configuration (if any), compilation, and installation in their corresponding `do_configure`, `do_compile`, and `do_install` overrides. An example of this type of recipe, `meta-custom/recipes-example/helloworld/helloworld_1.0.bb`, is shown here:

```
DESCRIPTION = "Simple helloworld application"
SECTION = "examples"
LICENSE = "MIT"
LIC_FILES_CHKSUM =
    "file://${COMMON_LICENSE_DIR}/MIT;md5=0835ade698e0bcf8506ecda2f7b4
f302"
```

```
SRC_URI = "file://helloworld.c"

S = "${WORKDIR}"

do_compile() {
        ${CC} ${LDFLAGS} helloworld.c -o helloworld
}

do_install() {
        install -d ${D}${bindir}
        install -m 0755 helloworld ${D}${bindir}
}
```

The `meta-custom/recipes-example/helloworld/helloworld-1.0/helloworld.c` source file is the following:

```
#include <stdio.h>

int main(void)
{
    return printf("Hello World");
}
```

We will explore example recipes that use the most common build systems in the next chapter.

Configuring packages

The Yocto build system provides the PACKAGECONFIG variable to help in the configuration of packages by defining a number of features. Your recipe defines the individual features as follows:

```
PACKAGECONFIG ??= "feature"
PACKAGECONFIG[feature] = "--with-feature,--without-feature,build-deps-
feature,rt-deps-feature"
```

The PACKAGECONFIG variable contains a space-separated list of feature names, and it can be extended or overridden in bbappend files; have a look at the following example:

```
PACKAGECONFIG_append = " feature1 feature2"
```

To extend or override it from a distribution or local configuration file, you would use the following syntax:

```
PACKAGECONFIG_pn-<package_name> = "feature1 feature2"
PACKAGECONFIG_append_pn-<package_name> = " feature1 feature2"
```

Following that, we characterize each feature with four ordered arguments:

- Extra configuration arguments (for EXTRA_OECONF) when the feature is enabled
- Extra configuration arguments (for EXTRA_OECONF) when the feature is disabled
- Extra build dependencies (for DEPENDS) when the feature is enabled
- Extra runtime dependencies (for RDEPENDS) when the feature is enabled

The four arguments are optional, but the ordering needs to be maintained by leaving the surrounding commas.

For example, the wpa-supplicant recipe defines two features, gnutls and openssl, but only enables gnutls by default, as seen here:

```
PACKAGECONFIG ??= "gnutls"
PACKAGECONFIG[gnutls] = ",,gnutls libgcrypt"
PACKAGECONFIG[openssl] = ",,openssl"
```

Splitting into several packages

It is common to separate recipe contents into different packages that serve different needs. Typical examples are to include documentation in a doc package, and header and/or libraries in a dev package. We can do this using the FILES variable as follows:

```
FILES_${PN} += "List of files to include in the main package"
FILES_${PN}-dbg += "Optional list of files to include in the debug package"
FILES_${PN}-dev += "Optional list of files to include in the development
package"
FILES_${PN}-doc += "Optional list of files to include in the documentation
package"
```

Setting machine-specific variables

Each recipe has a PACKAGE_ARCH variable that categorizes the recipe into a package feed, as we saw in the *Exploring an image's contents* recipe. Most of the time, they are automatically sorted out by the Yocto build system. For example, if the recipe is a kernel, a kernel module recipe, or an image recipe, or even if it is cross-compiling or building native applications, the Yocto build system will set the package architecture accordingly.

BitBake will also look at the SRC_URI machine overrides and adjust the package architecture, and if your recipe is using the allarch class, it will set the package architecture to all.

So when working on a recipe that only applies to a machine or machine family, or that contains changes that are specific to a machine or machine family, we need to check whether the package is categorized in the appropriate package feed, and if not, specify the package architecture explicitly in the recipe itself by using the following line of code:

```
PACKAGE_ARCH = "${MACHINE_ARCH}"
```

Also, when a recipe is only to be parsed for specific machine types, we specify it with the COMPATIBLE_MACHINE variable. For example, to make it compatible only with the mxs, mx5, and mx6 SoC families, we would use the following:

```
COMPATIBLE_MACHINE = "(mxs|mx5|mx6)"
```

Adding data, scripts, or configuration files

All recipes inherit the base class with the default set of tasks to run. After inheriting the base class, a recipe knows how to do things such as fetching and compiling.

As most recipes are meant to install some sort of executable, the base class knows how to build it. But sometimes all we want is to install data, scripts, or configuration files into the filesystem.

If the data or configuration is related to an application, the most logical thing to do is to package it together with the application's recipe itself, and if we think it is better to be installed separately, we could even split it into its own package.

But other times, the data or configuration is unrelated to an application; maybe it applies to the whole system or we just want to provide a separate recipe for it. Or we could even want to install some interpreted language scripts that don't need to be compiled.

How to do it...

In those cases, our recipe should inherit the allarch class that is inherited by recipes that do not produce architecture-specific output.

An example of this type of recipe, meta-custom/recipes-example/example-data/example-data_1.0.bb, may be seen here:

```
DESCRIPTION = "Example of data or configuration recipe"
SECTION = "examples"
```

```
LICENSE = "GPLv2"
LIC_FILES_CHKSUM =
"file://${COMMON_LICENSE_DIR}/GPL-2.0;md5=801f80980d171dd6425610833a22dbe6"

SRCREV = "${AUTOREV}"
SRC_URI = "git://github.com/yoctocookbook2ndedition/examples.git \
           file://example.data"

S = "${WORKDIR}/git"
inherit allarch
do_compile[noexec] = "1"

do_install() {
        install -d ${D}${sysconfdir}
        install -d ${D}${sbindir}
        install -m 0755 ${WORKDIR}/example.data ${D}/${sysconfdir}/
        install -m 0755 ${S}/python-scripts/* ${D}/${sbindir}
}
```

It assumes that the fictitious `examples.git` repository contains a `python-scripts` folder, which we want to include in our root filesystem.

A working recipe example can be found in the source that accompanies the book.

There's more...

When we just want to replace a specific file from the filesystem, we can use the `recipetool` command-line utility to automatically create the `bbappend` file for us. For this to work, the package needs to have been previously built and included on a target image. The syntax to use is:

```
$ recipetool appendfile </path/to/layer> </path/to/file/in/target> <new-
file>
```

A typical file to replace is the `/etc/network/interfaces` file that contains the network settings. We can add an `append` file to `meta-custom` to replace it with a new version with:

```
$ recipetool appendfile /opt/yocto/fsl-community-bsp/sources/meta-custom/
/etc/network/interfaces interfaces-new
```

Managing users and groups

It is also common to need to add or modify users and groups to our filesystem. This recipe explains how it is done.

Getting ready

User information is stored in the `/etc/passwd` file, a text file that is used as a database for the system user's information. The `passwd` file is human-readable.

Each line in it corresponds to one user in the system, and it has the following format:

```
<username>:<password>:<uid>:<gid>:<comment>:<home directory>:<login shell>
```

Let's see each of the parameters of this format:

- `username`: A unique string that identifies the user at login
- `uid`: User ID, a number that Linux uses to identify the user
- `gid`: Group ID, a number that Linux uses to identify the user's primary group
- `comment`: Comma-separated values that describe the account, typically the user's contact details
- `home directory`: Path to the user's home directory
- `login shell`: Shell that is started for interactive logins

The default `passwd` file is stored with the `base-passwd` package and looks as follows:

```
root::0:0:root:/root:/bin/sh
daemon:*:1:1:daemon:/usr/sbin:/bin/sh
bin:*:2:2:bin:/bin:/bin/sh
sys:*:3:3:sys:/dev:/bin/sh
sync:*:4:65534:sync:/bin:/bin/sync
games:*:5:60:games:/usr/games:/bin/sh
man:*:6:12:man:/var/cache/man:/bin/sh
lp:*:7:7:lp:/var/spool/lpd:/bin/sh
mail:*:8:8:mail:/var/mail:/bin/sh
news:*:9:9:news:/var/spool/news:/bin/sh
uucp:*:10:10:uucp:/var/spool/uucp:/bin/sh
proxy:*:13:13:proxy:/bin:/bin/sh
www-data:*:33:33:www-data:/var/www:/bin/sh
backup:*:34:34:backup:/var/backups:/bin/sh
list:*:38:38:Mailing List Manager:/var/list:/bin/sh
irc:*:39:39:ircd:/var/run/ircd:/bin/sh
```

```
gnats:*:41:41:Gnats Bug-Reporting System (admin):/var/lib/gnats:/bin/sh
nobody:*:65534:65534:nobody:/nonexistent:/bin/sh
```

All accounts have disabled direct logins, indicated by an asterisk on the `password` field, except for root, which has no password. This is because, by default, the image is built with the `debug-tweaks` feature that enables password-less login for the root user, among other things. If the root password were enabled, we would see the encrypted root password.

 Do not forget to remove the `debug-tweaks` feature from production images.

There is a corresponding `/etc/group` file that is installed at the same time with the information for the system groups.

The `core-image-minimal` image does not include shadow password protection, but other images, such as `core-image-full-cmdline`, do. When enabled, all password fields contain an x, and the encrypted passwords are kept in a `/etc/shadow` file, which is only accessible to the super user.

Any user that is needed by the system, but not included in the list we saw earlier, needs to be created.

How to do it...

The standard way for a recipe to add or modify system users or groups is to use the `useradd` class, which uses the following variables:

- USERADD_PACKAGES: This variable specifies the individual packages in the recipe that require users or groups to be added. For the main package, you would use the following:

    ```
    USERADD_PACKAGES = "${PN}"
    ```

- USERADD_PARAM: This variable corresponds to the arguments passed to the Linux `useradd` command, to add new users to the system.
- GROUPADD_PARAM: This variable corresponds to the arguments passed to the Linux `groupadd` command, to add new groups to the system.

- GROUPMEMS_PARAM: This variable corresponds to the arguments passed to the Linux groupmems command, which administers members of the user's primary group.

The useradd class will add shadow passwords to the system as a dependency.

An example snippet of a recipe using the useradd class follows:

```
inherit useradd

PASSWORD ?= "9PfNy00lz0o5g"
USERADD_PACKAGES = "${PN}"
USERADD_PARAM_${PN} = "--system --create-home \
                --groups tty \
                --password ${PASSWORD} \
                --user-group <newuser>"
```

The password can be generated on your host using the mkpasswd Linux command-line utility, installed with the whois Ubuntu package:

```
$ mkpasswd password
9VuPL5UFON7lg
```

There's more...

When generating users and groups using the useradd class, the uid and gid values are assigned dynamically during package installation. If this is not desired, there is a way to assign system-wide static uid and gid values by providing your own passwd and group files.

To do this, you need to define the USERADDEXTENSION variable in your conf/local.conf file as follows:

```
USERADDEXTENSION = "useradd-staticids"
```

The build system will then search the BBPATH variable for files/passwd and files/group files to obtain the uid and gid values. The files have the standard passwd layout as defined previously, with the password field ignored.

The default filenames can be overridden by using the USERADD_UID_TABLES and USERADD_GID_TABLES variables.

You also need to define the following:

```
USERADD_ERROR_DYNAMIC = "error"
```

This is done so that the build system produces an error if the required `uid` and `gid` values are not found in the provided files.

 Note that if you use the `useradd` class in a project that is already built, you will need to remove the `tmp` directory and rebuild from the `sstate-cache` directory or you will get build errors.

There is also a way to add user and group information that is not tied to a specific recipe but to an image: by using the `extrausers` class. It is configured by the `EXTRA_USERS_PARAMS` variable in an image recipe. For example, to change the root password to `password` it is used as follows:

```
inherit extrausers

EXTRA_USERS_PARAMS = "\
  usermod -p 9PfNy001z005g root; \
  "
```

Using the sysvinit initialization manager

The initialization manager is an important part of the root filesystem. It is the first thing the kernel executes, and it has the responsibility to start the rest of the system, and manages system shutdown too.

The initialization manager is usually fixed by the Linux distribution. The Poky distribution allows you to select between initialization managers, the most used being System V init (`sysvinit`) and `systemd`. The `poky-tiny` distribution has no initialization manager and uses BusyBox init to directly read the `inittab` file and launch programs.

The UNIX System V operating system introduced an initialization system that was the basis for Linux's initialization. Several recent attempts have been made to replace it, and `systemd` has finally managed to get enough traction in between Linux distributions to be considered the successor to `sysvinit`.

This recipe will introduce the `sysvinit` initialization manager.

Getting ready

sysvinit is the default initialization manager in Yocto and it has been used in Linux since the operating system's origin. The kernel is passed an init command-line argument, typically /sbin/init, which is then launched to a default runlevel, a machine state that defines which processes to run. This init process has PID 1 and is the parent of all processes.

The init process will read an inittab file and look for a default runlevel. The default inittab file is installed with the sysvinit-inittab package and is as follows:

```
# /etc/inittab: init(8) configuration.
# $Id: inittab,v 1.91 2002/01/25 13:35:21 miquels Exp $

# The default runlevel.
id:5:initdefault:

# Boot-time system configuration/initialization script.
# This is run first except when booting in emergency (-b) mode.
si::sysinit:/etc/init.d/rcS

# What to do in single-user mode.
~~:S:wait:/sbin/sulogin

# /etc/init.d executes the S and K scripts upon change
# of runlevel.
#
# Runlevel 0 is halt.
# Runlevel 1 is single-user.
# Runlevels 2-5 are multi-user.
# Runlevel 6 is reboot.

l0:0:wait:/etc/init.d/rc 0
l1:1:wait:/etc/init.d/rc 1
l2:2:wait:/etc/init.d/rc 2
l3:3:wait:/etc/init.d/rc 3
l4:4:wait:/etc/init.d/rc 4
l5:5:wait:/etc/init.d/rc 5
l6:6:wait:/etc/init.d/rc 6
# Normally not reached, but fallthrough in case of emergency.
z6:6:respawn:/sbin/sulogin
```

Then, `init` runs all scripts starting with S (`start scripts`) in the `/etc/rcS.d` directory, followed by all the scripts starting with S in the `/etc/rcN.d` directory, where N is the runlevel value. When the system is shutting down, scripts starting with K (`kill`) are executed.

So the `init` process just performs the initialization and forgets about the processes. If something goes wrong and the processes are killed, no one will care. The system watchdog will reboot the system if it becomes unresponsive; applications built with more than one process usually need some type of process monitor that can react to the health of the system, but `sysvinit` does not offer these types of mechanism.

However, `sysvinit` is a well-understood and reliable initialization manager, and the recommendation is to keep it unless you need some extra feature.

We will now see how to make `init` launch new processes. These can be one-shot processes, daemons, that is, processes that run in the background, or applications.

How to do it...

When using `sysvinit` as the initialization manager, Yocto offers the `update-rc.d` class as a helper to install initialization scripts so that services are started and stopped when needed.

When using this class, you need to specify the `INITSCRIPT_NAME` variable with the name of the script to install and the `INITSCRIPT_PARAMS` variable with the options to pass to the `update-rc.d` utility. You can optionally use the `INITSCRIPT_PACKAGES` variable to list the packages to contain the initialization scripts. By default, this contains the main package only, and if multiple packages are provided, `INITSCRIPT_NAME` and `INITSCRIPT_PARAMS` need to be specified for each using overrides. An example snippet is:

```
INITSCRIPT_PACKAGES = "${PN}-httpd ${PN}-ftpd"
INITSCRIPT_NAME_${PN}-httpd = "httpd.sh"
INITSCRIPT_NAME_${PN}-ftpd = "ftpd.sh"
INITSCRIPT_PARAMS_${PN}-httpd = "defaults"
INITSCRIPT_PARAMS_${PN}-ftpd = "start 99 5 2 . stop 20 0 1 6 ."
```

When an initialization script is not tied to a particular recipe, we can add a specific recipe for it. For example, the following recipe will run a `mount.sh` script in the `recipes-example/sysvinit-mount/sysvinit-mount_1.0.bb` file:

```
DESCRIPTION = "Initscripts for mounting filesystems"
LICENSE = "MIT"

LIC_FILES_CHKSUM =
    "file://${COMMON_LICENSE_DIR}/MIT;md5=0835ade698e0bcf8506ecda2f7b4
    f302"

SRC_URI = "file://mount.sh"

INITSCRIPT_NAME = "mount.sh"
INITSCRIPT_PARAMS = "start 09 S ."

inherit update-rc.d

S = "${WORKDIR}"

do_install () {
    install -d ${D}${sysconfdir}/init.d/
    install -c -m 755 ${WORKDIR}/${INITSCRIPT_NAME}
${D}${sysconfdir}/init.d/${INITSCRIPT_NAME}
}
```

This recipe will install the `mount.sh` script in the `/etc/init.d/` directory and will create all the appropriate symbolic links inside the `/etc/rcN.d/` directories.

Using the systemd initialization manager

As an alternative to `sysvinit`, you can configure your project to use `systemd` as an initialization manager. `systemd` not only performs system initialization, it also manages system processes, and packs many more features than `sysvinit`.

The `systemd` initialization manager is replacing `sysvinit` and other initialization managers in most Linux distributions. However, the adoption of `systemd` in major Linux distributions has not lacked controversy. Many see `systemd` as an overly complex system with a complicated architecture that goes against the Unix philosophy of simple, short, clear, and extensible modular software, easily maintained and repurposed.

systemd is also big in size compared with sysvinit, although it can be scaled down and customized for embedded projects. Some of its features are tightly integrated with kernel features and updating it may force a kernel update, which is not always feasible for embedded devices.

It does however feature parallel service startup, which provides faster boot times, provides dependencies between services, has a better security framework, and provides software watchdogs for processes, among other features.

This recipe will introduce the systemd initialization manager.

Getting ready

systemd is based on the concepts of units, an abstraction of all elements that are relevant for system startup and maintenance, and targets, which group units and can be viewed as a runlevel equivalent. Some of the units systemd defines are:

- Services
- Sockets
- Devices
- Mount points
- Snapshots
- Timers
- Paths

The default targets and their runlevel equivalents are defined in the following table:

sysvinit	Runlevel	systemd target	Notes
0	runlevel0.target	poweroff.target	Halt the system.
1, s, single	runlevel1.target	rescue.target	Single user mode.
2, 4	runlevel2.target, runlevel4.target	multi-user.target	User-defined/site-specific runlevels. By default, identical to 3.

3	`runlevel3.target`	`multi-user.target`	Multiuser, non-graphical. Users can usually log in via multiple consoles or via the network.
5	`runlevel5.target`	`graphical.target`	Multiuser, graphical. Usually has all the services of runlevel 3 plus a graphical login.
6	`runlevel6.target`	`reboot.target`	Reboot the system.

Once `systemd` is started by the Linux kernel, it runs `default.target`, which is a link to either `multi-user.target` or `graphical.target`.

The `systemd` initialization manager is designed to be compatible with `sysvinit`, including using `sysvinit` init scripts.

Some of the features of `systemd` are:

- Parallelization capabilities that allow for faster boot times
- Service initialization via sockets and D-Bus so that services are only started when needed
- Process monitoring, which allows for process failure recovery
- System state snapshots and restoration
- Mount point management
- Transactional dependency-based unit control, where units establish dependencies between them

How to do it...

To configure your system to use `systemd`, you need to add the `systemd` distribution feature to your project by adding the following to your distribution's configuration file, under `sources/poky/meta-poky/conf/distro/poky.conf` for the default Poky distribution, or locally in your project's `conf/local.conf` file:

```
DISTRO_FEATURES_append = " systemd"
```

Note that the space is required after the starting quote.

```
VIRTUAL-RUNTIME_init_manager = "systemd"
```

This configuration example allows you to define a main image with `systemd` and a rescue image with `sysvinit`, providing it does not use the `VIRTUAL-RUNTIME_init_manager` variable. Hence, the rescue image cannot use the `packagegroup-core-boot` or `packagegroup-core-full-cmdline` recipes.

To remove `sysvinit` completely from your system, you would do the following:

```
DISTRO_FEATURES_BACKFILL_CONSIDERED = "sysvinit"
VIRTUAL-RUNTIME_initscripts = ""
```

Feature backfilling is the automatic extension of machine and distribution features to keep backward compatibility. The `sysvinit` distribution feature is automatically filled in, so to remove it we need to blacklist it by adding it to the `DISTRO_FEATURES_BACKFILL_CONSIDERED` variable as shown earlier.

If you are using an existing project and you change the `DISTRO_FEATURES` variable as explained earlier, you will need to remove the `tmp` directory and build from the `sstate-cache` or the build will fail.

There's more...

Not only does the root filesystem needs to be configured, but the Linux kernel also needs to be specifically configured with all the features required by `systemd`. There is an extensive list of kernel configuration variables in the `systemd` source `README` file. As an example, to extend the minimal kernel configuration that we will introduce in the *Reducing the Linux kernel image size* recipe later in this chapter, for the Wandboard to support `systemd`, we would need to add the following configuration changes in the `arch/arm/configs/wandboard-custom-minimal_defconfig` file:

```
+CONFIG_FHANDLE=y
+CONFIG_CGROUPS=y
+CONFIG_SECCOMP=y
+CONFIG_NET=y
+CONFIG_UNIX=y
```

```
+CONFIG_INET=y
+CONFIG_AUTOFS4_FS=y
+CONFIG_TMPFS=y
+CONFIG_TMPFS_POSIX_ACL=y
+CONFIG_SCHEDSTATS=y
-# CONFIG_PROC_SYSCTL is not set
-# CONFIG_PROC_PAGE_MONITOR is not set
-# CONFIG_SYSFS is not set
```

The default kernel configuration provided for the Wandboard will launch a `core-image-minimal` image of `systemd` just fine.

Installing systemd unit files

Yocto offers the `systemd` class as a helper to install unit files. By default, unit files are installed on the `${systemd_unitdir}/system` path on the destination directory.

When using this class, you need to specify the `SYSTEMD_SERVICE_${PN}` variable with the name of the unit file to install. You can optionally use the `SYSTEMD_PACKAGES` variable to list the packages to contain the unit files. By default, this is the main package only, and if multiple packages are provided, the `SYSTEMD_SERVICE` variable needs to be specified using overrides.

Services are configured to launch at boot by default, but this can be changed with the `SYSTEMD_AUTO_ENABLE` variable.

An example snippet is:

```
SYSTEMD_PACKAGES = "${PN}-syslog"
SYSTEMD_SERVICE_${PN}-syslog = "busybox-syslog.service"
SYSTEMD_AUTO_ENABLE = "disabled"
```

An example recipe, `recipes-example/systemd-example/systemd-example_1.0.bb`, for a simple service, is introduced next:

```
DESCRIPTION = "Example systemd service"

LICENSE = "MIT"
LIC_FILES_CHKSUM =
"file://${COMMON_LICENSE_DIR}/MIT;md5=0835ade698e0bcf8506ecda2f7b4f302"

SRC_URI = "\
    file://systemd-example.service \
    file://simple-service.c \
"
```

```
inherit systemd

S = "${WORKDIR}"

SYSTEMD_SERVICE_${PN} = "systemd-example.service"

do_compile () {
    ${CC} ${LDFLAGS} simple-service.c -o simple-service
}

do_install () {
    install -d ${D}${bindir}
    install -m 0755 ${WORKDIR}/simple-service ${D}${bindir}
    install -d ${D}${systemd_unitdir}/system
    install -m 0644 ${WORKDIR}/systemd-example.service
${D}${systemd_unitdir}/system
    sed -i -e 's,@BINDIR@,${bindir},g'
${D}${systemd_unitdir}/system/systemd-example.service
}
```

This recipe installs the following `systemd` **service unit**:

```
[Unit]
Description=Example service

[Service]
Type=forking
ExecStart=@BINDIR@/simple-service


[Install]
WantedBy=multi-user.target
```

It also runs a very simple daemon skeleton:

```
#include <unistd.h>
#include <syslog.h>

#define DAEMON_NAME "simpledaemon"

int main()
{
        setlogmask(LOG_UPTO(LOG_INFO));
        openlog(DAEMON_NAME, LOG_CONS | LOG_PERROR, LOG_USER);
        daemon(0,0);
        while (1)
        {
                syslog(LOG_INFO, "daemon running");
```

```
            sleep(10);
        }
        return 0;
    }
```

See also

- More information about `systemd` can be found at
  `http://freedesktop.org/wiki/Software/systemd/`

Installing package installation scripts

The supported package formats, `.rpm`, `.ipk`, and `.deb`, support the addition of installation scripts that can be run at different times during a package installation process. In this recipe, we will see how to install them.

Getting ready

There are different types of installation script:

- **Pre-installation scripts** (`pkg_preinst`): These are called before the package is unpacked
- **Post-installation scripts** (`pkg_postinst`): These are called after the package is unpacked, and dependencies will be configured
- **Pre-removal scripts** (`pkg_prerm`): These are called with installed or at least partially installed packages
- **Post-removal scripts** (`pkg_postrm`): These are called after the package's files have been removed or replaced

How to do it...

An example snippet showing the installation of a pre-installation script in a recipe is as follows:

```
pkg_preinst_${PN} () {
    # Shell commands
}
```

All installation scripts work in the same way, with the exception that post-installation scripts may be run either on the host at root filesystem image creation time, on the target (for those actions that cannot be performed on the host), or when a package is directly installed on the target. The following code shows a way to add a post-installation script to a recipe:

```
pkg_postinst_${PN} () {
    if [  x"$D" = "x" ]; then
        # Commands to execute on device
    else
        # Commands to execute on host
    fi
}
```

If the post-installation script succeeds, the package is marked as installed. If the script fails, the package is marked as unpacked and the script is executed when the image boots again.

How it works...

Once the recipe defines an installation script, the class for the specific package type will install it while following the packaging rules of the specific format.

For post-installation scripts, when running on the host, D is set to the destination directory, so the comparison test will fail. But D will be empty when running on the target.

Another common way to test whether a script is running on the device is:

```
if test -n "$D"; then
   # Running on host
else
   # Running on target
fi
```

> It is recommended to perform post-installation scripts on the host if possible, as we need to take into account that some root filesystems will be read-only and hence it would not be possible to perform some operations on the target.

Reducing the Linux kernel image size

Before or in parallel with the root filesystem customization, embedded projects usually require an image size optimization that will reduce the boot time and memory usage.

Smaller images mean less storage space, less transmission time, and less programming time, which saves money both in manufacturing and field updates.

By default, the compressed Linux kernel image (zImage) for the Wandboard is around 6.2 MB. This recipe will show how we can reduce that.

How to do it...

An example of a minimal kernel configuration for a Wandboard that is able to boot from a microSD card root filesystem is the arch/arm/configs/wandboard-custom-minimal_defconfig file:

```
CONFIG_KERNEL_XZ=y
# CONFIG_SWAP is not set
CONFIG_NO_HZ=y
CONFIG_HIGH_RES_TIMERS=y
CONFIG_CC_OPTIMIZE_FOR_SIZE=y
# CONFIG_KALLSYMS is not set
# CONFIG_PRINTK is not set
# CONFIG_BUG is not set
# CONFIG_ELF_CORE is not set
# CONFIG_BASE_FULL is not set
CONFIG_EMBEDDED=y
CONFIG_SLOB=y
CONFIG_ARCH_MXC=y
CONFIG_SOC_IMX6Q=y
# CONFIG_SWP_EMULATE is not set
CONFIG_ARM_ERRATA_814220=y
CONFIG_SMP=y
CONFIG_VMSPLIT_2G=y
CONFIG_AEABI=y
CONFIG_CPU_FREQ=y
# CONFIG_CPU_FREQ_STAT is not set
CONFIG_CPU_FREQ_DEFAULT_GOV_ONDEMAND=y
CONFIG_ARM_IMX6Q_CPUFREQ=y
CONFIG_CPU_IDLE=y
CONFIG_VFP=y
CONFIG_NEON=y
CONFIG_DEVTMPFS=y
```

```
CONFIG_DEVTMPFS_MOUNT=y
# CONFIG_INPUT_MOUSEDEV is not set
# CONFIG_INPUT_KEYBOARD is not set
# CONFIG_INPUT_MOUSE is not set
CONFIG_SERIAL_IMX=y
CONFIG_SERIAL_IMX_CONSOLE=y
# CONFIG_HWMON is not set
CONFIG_REGULATOR=y
CONFIG_REGULATOR_ANATOP=y
# CONFIG_USB_SUPPORT is not set
CONFIG_MMC=y
CONFIG_MMC_SDHCI=y
CONFIG_MMC_SDHCI_PLTFM=y
CONFIG_MMC_SDHCI_ESDHC_IMX=y
CONFIG_DMADEVICES=y
CONFIG_IMX_SDMA=y
CONFIG_EXT3_FS=y
# CONFIG_EXT3_FS_XATTR is not set
CONFIG_EXT4_FS=y
# CONFIG_PROC_SYSCTL is not set
# CONFIG_PROC_PAGE_MONITOR is not set
# CONFIG_SYSFS is not set
# CONFIG_ENABLE_WARN_DEPRECATED is not set
# CONFIG_ENABLE_MUST_CHECK is not set
# CONFIG_FTRACE is not set
# CONFIG_ARM_UNWIND is not set
```

This configuration builds an 867K compressed Linux kernel image (zImage) for a 3.4 MB vmlinux ELF image.

How it works...

Apart from hardware design considerations (such as running the Linux kernel from a NOR flash and **execute in place** (**XIP**) to avoid loading the image to memory), the first step in kernel size optimization is to review the kernel configuration and remove all superfluous features.

We can show a summary of kernel and module sizes by using the ksum.py script. Change to the directory of a compiled Linux kernel source, as explained previously in Chapter 2, *The BSP Layer*, and execute the script from the Linux kernel root directory:

```
$ cd /opt/yocto/linux-wandboard
$ /opt/yocto/fsl-community-bsp/sources/poky/scripts/tiny/ksum.py
Collecting object files recursively from /opt/yocto/linux-wandboard...
Collecting object files [DONE]
```

```
Totals:
vmlinux:
    text            data            bss             total
    14105252        969868          465400          15540520
modules (90):
    text            data            bss             total
    2059898         191819          20028           2271745
vmlinux + modules:
    text            data            bss             total
    16165150        1161687         485428          17812265
```

To analyze the sizes of kernel blocks, we use the `ksize.py` script, which produces user-friendly output. As before, change to the directory of a compiled Linux kernel source and execute the script from the Linux kernel root directory:

```
$ cd /opt/yocto/linux-wandboard
$ python2.7
/opt/yocto/fsl-community-bsp/sources/poky/scripts/tiny/ksize.py -d >
ksize.log
```

 Note that the script will not execute correctly with Python 3, so a Python 2.7 interpreter is used.

The report drills down to each individual driver, which makes it easy to identify savings from removing them. An edited extract from the report follows:

Linux Kernel	total	text	data
bss			
vmlinux	2158912	2021168	94736
43008			
drivers/built-in.o	656044	612008	31288
12748			
fs/built-in.o	423274	414798	2072
6404			
kernel/built-in.o	377027	353399	12572
11056			
mm/built-in.o	197932	188391	6037
3504			
block/built-in.o	120913	117081	2448
1384			
lib/built-in.o	91707	91534	112
61			
init/built-in.o	21834	7610	14160

```
64
firmware/built-in.o                     4570 |       4570           0
0
security/built-in.o                     3710 |       3694           8
8
---------------------------------------------------------------------
sum                                  1897011 |    1793085       68697
35229
delta                                 261901 |     228083       26039
7779
```

In this report, vmlinux is the Linux kernel ELF image, which can be found in the Linux build directory.

Some of the things we usually exclude are:

1. Remove IPv6 (CONFIG_IPV6) and other superfluous networking features
2. Remove block devices (CONFIG_BLOCK) if not needed
3. Remove cryptographic features (CONFIG_CRYPTO) if unused
4. Review the supported filesystem types and remove unneeded ones, such as flash filesystems on flashless devices
5. Avoid modules and remove module support (CONFIG_MODULES) from the kernel if possible

A good strategy is to start with a minimal kernel and add the essential stuff until you get a working system. Start with the allnoconfig GNU make target and review the configuration items under CONFIG_EXPERT and CONFIG_EMBEDDED as they are not included in the allnoconfig setting.

Some configuration changes that might not be obvious but reduce the image size considerably without feature removal are listed here:

- Change the default compression method from **Lempel-Ziv-Oberhumer (LZO)** to **XZ** (CONFIG_KERNEL_XZ). The decompression speed will be a bit lower though.
- Change the allocator from the **Unqueued Slab Allocator (SLUB)** to **Simple List Of Blocks (SLOB)** (CONFIG_SLOB) for small embedded systems with little memory.
- Use no high memory (CONFIG_HIGHMEM) unless you have 4 GB or more memory.

You may also want to have a different configuration for production and development systems, so you can remove the following from your production images:

- printk support (CONFIG_PRINTK)
- tracing support (CONFIG_FTRACE)

On the compilation side of things, optimize for size using CONFIG_CC_OPTIMIZE_FOR_SIZE.

Once the basics are covered, we need to analyze the kernel functions to identify further reduction areas. You can print a sorted list of kernel symbols with the following:

```
$ nm --size-sort --print-size -r vmlinux | head
8023a87c 0000485c t imx6q_clocks_init
801f3ce8 000038a8 T hidinput_connect
800cc968 00002fb8 T __blockdev_direct_IO
80111fb8 0000263c t ext4_fill_super
8025c000 00002000 D init_thread_union
8021b440 00002000 r crc32table_le
80219440 00002000 r crc32table_be
80217440 00002000 r crc32ctable_le
801a5824 00001c84 t do_con_write.part.9
80273d6c 00001740 b ipu_data
```

You then need to look into the kernel source to find optimizations.

The actual space used by the uncompressed kernel in memory can be obtained from a running Wandboard kernel log as follows:

```
$ dmesg | grep -A 3 "text"
      .text : 0x80008000 - 0x80a20538   (10338 kB)
      .init : 0x80a21000 - 0x80aae240   ( 565 kB)
      .data : 0x80ab0000 - 0x80b13644   ( 398 kB)
      .bss  : 0x80b13644 - 0x80b973fc   ( 528 kB)
```

From here, the .text section contains code and constant data, the .data section contains the initialization data for variables, and the .bss section contains all uninitialized data. The .init section contains global variables used during Linux initialization only, which are freed afterwards as can be seen from the following Linux kernel boot message:

```
Freeing unused kernel memory: 564K (80a21000 - 80aae000)
```

There are ongoing efforts to reduce the size of the Linux kernel, so it is expected that newer kernel versions will be smaller and will allow for better customization for use in embedded systems.

Reducing the root filesystem size

Images with reduced sizes are used alongside production images for tasks such as rescue systems and manufacturing test processes. They are also ideal to be built as `initramfs` images, that is, images that the Linux kernel mounts from memory, and can even be bundled into a single Linux kernel image binary.

By default, the `core-image-minimal` size for the Wandboard unpacked root filesystem tarball is around 13 MB, and `core-image-sato` is around 244 MB. This recipe will explore methods to reduce the size of the root filesystem.

How to do it...

An example of a small image that does not include the core image class and can be used as the base for a bottom-up root filesystem image with reduced size, `recipes-core/images/image-small.bb`, is shown next:

```
DESCRIPTION = "Minimal console-only image."

IMAGE_INSTALL= "\
        base-files \
        base-passwd \
        busybox \
        sysvinit \
        initscripts \
"

IMAGE_LINGUAS = " "

LICENSE = "MIT"

inherit image

IMAGE_ROOTFS_SIZE = "8192"
```

This recipe produces a root filesystem of 4.8 MB. You can go even smaller if you use the `poky-tiny` distribution by adding the following to your `conf/local.conf` file:

```
DISTRO = "poky-tiny"
```

The `poky-tiny` distribution makes a series of size optimizations that may restrict the set of packages you can include in your image. These optimizations include:

- Using the musl C library instead of `glibc`
- Removing native language support
- Streamlining distribution features
- Using the BusyBox `init` system and `mdev` device manager
- Only building a `cpio` image suitable for an `initramfsimage-small`
- Emptying `MACHINE_ESSENTIAL_EXTRA_RDEPENDS` so no machine-specific packages are installed
- Removing Perl and Python dependencies
- Blacklisting a set of core images that are not buildable with the previous restrictions

The following needs to be added to `conf/local.conf` to be able to build `image-small` with `poky-tiny`:

```
IMAGE_INSTALL_remove = "sysvinit"
```

Removing `sysvinit` is needed as `poky-tiny` uses the BusyBox `init` system and removes the `sysvinit` `DISTRO_FEATURE` by blacklisting it in `DISTRO_FEATURES_BACKFILL_CONSIDERED`, which prevents it from being automatically added.

The `poky-tiny` distribution configuration file also overrides the `virtual/kernel` provider to `linux-yocto-tiny`, which we know the Wandboard does not support, so in order to build for the Wandboard we also need to create our own `poky-tiny-custom` distribution, which is added in our `meta-custom` layer with the following `conf/distro/poky-tiny-custom.conf` file:

```
require conf/distro/poky-tiny.conf
PREFERRED_PROVIDER_virtual/kernel = "linux-wandboard"
```

We have already seen how to reduce the size of the Linux kernel in the *Reducing the Linux kernel image size* recipe.

With `poky-tiny-custom`, the size of the root filesystem is further reduced to around 2.5 MB.

Once the root filesystem size is optimized, the final size of the image depends on three factors:

- `rootfs-size`: The actual size of the root filesystem as calculated by the `du` command, multiplied by an overhead factor as defined by the `IMAGE_OVERHEAD_FACTOR` variable (which defaults to 1.3).
- `minimum-rootfs-size`: The requested minimum image size in KB specified by `IMAGE_ROOTFS_SIZE`. If the value is smaller than the requested minimum image, the latter is used.
- `extra-space`: An extra space in KB requested with the `IMAGE_ROOTFS_EXTRA_SPACE` variable, which is added to the previous value. By default, there is no extra space added.

The final image size used to generate `ext2/3/4` and `btrfs` images is calculated by adding the `extra-space` to either the `minimum-rootfs-size` or the `rootfs-size`, whichever is bigger, as expressed in the following expression:

```
size = max(rootfs-size, minimum-rootfs-size) + extra-space
```

The final image size of this `image-small` recipe is 8 MB as specified by the `IMAGE_ROOTFS_SIZE` variable.

The root filesystem needs free space on the image to cater for post-installation scripts and the package management system if any, and probably also to host application data. This can be provided either by the overhead factor or by fixing the extra space to use.

How it works...

Start with an appropriate image, such as `core-image-minimal`, analyze the dependencies as shown in the *Debugging the build system* recipe in `Chapter 1`, *The Build System*, and decide which of them are not needed. You could also use the file sizes listed in the image's build history, as seen in the *Using build history* recipe, also in `Chapter 1`, *The Build System*, to detect the biggest files in the filesystem and review them. To sort the file sizes, which appear in the fourth column of the `files-in-image.txt` file, in reverse order, we could execute:

```
$ sort -r -g  -k 4,4 files-in-image.txt -o sorted-files-in-image.txt
sorted-files-in-image.txt:
-rw-r--r-- root         root              7267688
./boot/zImage-4.1.44+g0d698de42426
-rwxr-xr-x root         root              2667248 ./usr/bin/trace
```

```
-rwxr-xr-x root        root           2667248  ./usr/bin/perf
-r-xr-xr-x root        root           1627632  ./usr/lib/libperl.so.5.24.1
-rwxr-xr-x root        root           1261024  ./usr/lib/libstdc++.so.6.0.24
-rwxr-xr-x root        root           1222352  ./lib/libc-2.26.so
-rwxr-xr-x root        root            867168  ./bin/bash.bash
-rw-r--r-- root        root            830424  ./usr/lib/libslang.so.2.3.1
-rwxr-xr-x root        root            797648
./usr/lib/libbfd-2.29.0.20170912.so
-rwxr-xr-x root        root            535396  ./bin/busybox.nosuid
-rwxr-xr-x root        root            525488  ./sbin/ldconfig
-rwxr-xr-x root        root            460144  ./lib/libm-2.26.so
-rw-r--r-- root        root            338696  ./boot/u-boot-wandboard-
v2017.09+gitAUTOINC+a6a15fedd1-r0.img
-rwxr-xr-x root        root            265796  ./usr/bin/trace-cmd
-rwxr-xr-x root        root            263592  ./usr/lib/libpcre.so.1.2.9
-rwxr-xr-x root        root            256356  ./usr/bin/udevadm
-rwxr-xr-x root        root            248212  ./sbin/udevd
```

Poky has a `dirsize.py` script that reports component sizes for the filesystem. An extract from its output (when launched from the `rootfs` directory in the `tmp` directory) is:

```
$ cd /opt/yocto/fsl-community-bsp/wandboard/tmp/work/wandboard-poky-linux-
gnueabi/core-image-minimal/1.0-r0/rootfs
$ /opt/yocto/fsl-community-bsp/sources/poky/scripts/tiny/dirsize.py
  12997690  .
   7943835  ./boot
       197  ./boot/extlinux
       197  ./boot/extlinux/extlinux.conf
   7267688  ./boot/zImage-4.1.44+g0d698de42426
    338696  ./boot/u-boot-wandboard-v2017.09+gitAUTOINC+a6a15fedd1-r0.img
     48128  ./boot/SPL-wandboard-v2017.09+gitAUTOINC+a6a15fedd1-r0
     43827  ./boot/imx6qp-wandboard-revd1.dtb
     42197  ./boot/imx6q-wandboard-revd1.dtb
     41167  ./boot/imx6q-wandboard.dtb
     41167  ./boot/imx6q-wandboard-revb1.dtb
     40956  ./boot/imx6dl-wandboard-revd1.dtb
     39906  ./boot/imx6dl-wandboard.dtb
     39906  ./boot/imx6dl-wandboard-revb1.dtb
   2958219  ./lib
```

From this, we observe that the `boot` folder, which contains `u-boot`, the kernel, the device tree, and the `extlinux.conf` used to boot the system, is the biggest contributor to filesystem size.

Some other places where some space on a console-only system can be saved are:

- Use the IPK package manager, as it is the lightest, or better yet remove the `package-management` feature from your production root filesystem altogether
- Use BusyBox's `mdev` device manager instead of `udev` by specifying it in your `conf/local.conf` file as follows:

```
VIRTUAL-RUNTIME_dev_manager = "busybox-mdev"
```

Note that this will only work with core images that include `packagegroup-core-boot`

- If we are running the root filesystem on a block device, use ext2 instead of ext3 or ext4 without the journal
- Configure BusyBox with only the essential applets by providing your own configuration file in a `bbappend` file
- Review the `glibc` configuration, which can be changed via the `DISTRO_FEATURES_LIBC` distribution configuration variable
- Compile your applications with `-Os` to optimize for size
- If using the Poky distribution, consider switching to a lighter `C` library than the default `glibc` such as `musl`, a new MIT-licensed `C` library

To enable the `musl` C library, you would add the following to your image file: `TCLIBC = "musl"`.

Memory-based root filesystems

Early user space or initial memory images, known as `initramfs` images, are typically used as early user spaces with the task of mounting complex filesystems, such as for example when an encrypted partition needs to be set up. For that use case, `initramfs` will prepare the final root filesystem and then perform a `switch_root`, effectively replacing the old filesystem with the new and running a new `init` from the new filesystem. `initramfs` needs to contain all tools needed to mount the final root filesystem.

Other uses for `initramfs` include rescue and manufacturing systems.

This recipe will show how to configure the Yocto build system to build `initramfs` images.

Getting ready

When the Linux kernel mounts a file system from physical storage, it keeps a cache for quick access. A memory filesystem is just this kernel cache without a backing store.

An `initramfs` is a compressed `cpio` format file that the kernel extracts into a memory filesystem and uses as the root filesystem. It will run the `init` program found in it. This `initramfs` can either be compiled into the kernel, so one single binary will contain both the kernel and root filesystem, or passed to the kernel as an external file. This latter use case needs the legacy `initrd` kernel support compiled in.

How to do it...

We can convert the `image-small` recipe introduced in the *Reducing the root filesystem size* recipe into an `initramfs`, as shown in `recipes-core/images/image-small-initramfs.bb` here:

```
DESCRIPTION = "Minimal console-only initramfs image."


PACKAGE_INSTALL= "\
        base-files \
        base-passwd \
        busybox \
        sysvinit \
        initscripts \
        ${ROOTFS_BOOTSTRAP_INSTALL} \
"

IMAGE_LINGUAS = " "

LICENSE = "MIT"

IMAGE_FEATURES = ""

export IMAGE_BASENAME = "image-small-initramfs"
IMAGE_FSTYPES = "${INITRAMFS_FSTYPES} ${INITRAMFS_FSTYPES}.u-boot"
inherit image

IMAGE_ROOTFS_SIZE = "8192"
```

To boot the `initramfs` as an external file, we stop the target device at the `u-boot` prompt and do the following:

1. Configure the network settings:

```
> env set ipaddr <target-ip-address>
> env set serverip <server-ip-address>
```

2. Set the Linux kernel, device tree, and `initramfs` file sources:

```
> env set image <kernel-image-name>
> env set fdtfile <device tree blob name>
> env set initrd_file <initramfs image name>
```

3. Load them into memory at the preconfigured locations:

```
> tftpboot ${loadaddr} ${image}
> tftpboot ${fdt_addr} ${fdtfile}
> tftpboot ${ramdisk_addr} ${initrd_file}
```

4. Finally, boot using the `bootz` command:

```
> bootz ${loadaddr} ${ramdiskaddr} ${fdt_addr}
```

How it works...

In order for the Yocto build system to build a `cpio` image file suitable to be used as `initramfs`, the `IMAGE_FSTYPES` variable needs to be configured to one of the following: `cpio.gz`, `cpio.tar`, `cpio.lz4`, `cpio.lzma`, or `cpio.xz`.

On the previous image, `IMAGE_FSTYPES` is set to `cpio.gz.uboot` so that the build system generates a compressed `cpio` image file with the `u-boot` header, suitable to be loaded through the `bootz` u-boot command.

`INITRAMFS_FSTYPES` defaults to `cpio.gz`, and needs to be appended to support any other format.

In this recipe, we are overriding the `PACKAGE_INSTALL` variable with the list of packages we want to install. We also add `ROOTFS_BOOTSTRAP_INSTALL`, which adds the run-postinstall package so that post installation scripts are correctly run. Standard images use the `core-image` class and the `IMAGE_INSTALL` variable to add packages and features. An `initramfs` typically wants a hardcoded list of packages so they are added setting the `PACKAGE_INSTALL` variable directly.

We also empty the `IMAGE_FEATURES` in order not to pollute the image with features.

There's more...

The Yocto build system can also be configured to bundle the `initramfs` into the Linux kernel using the kernel's build system.

For this, we need to define the image name to be used, usually on a machine configuration file, such as `conf/machine/wandboard.conf`, or in the `conf/local.conf` configuration file as follows:

```
INITRAMFS_IMAGE = "<image name>"
```

And then we can instruct Yocto to bundle the image with the kernel by adding the following to the `conf/local.conf` configuration file:

```
INITRAMFS_IMAGE_BUNDLE = "1"
```

The kernel class will then copy the `cpio` file from the deploy directory into the build directory for the Linux kernel, and the kernel build system will use it to create the Linux image and root filesystem bundle.

To boot the bundled image, we do this:

1. Configure the network settings:

    ```
    > env set ipaddr <target-ip-address>
    > env set serverip <server-ip-address>
    ```

2. Set the Linux kernel and root filesystem bundle and device tree:

    ```
    > env set image <kernel-image-name>
    > env set fdtfile <device tree blob name>
    ```

3. Load them into memory at the preconfigured locations:

    ```
    > tftpboot ${loadaddr} ${image}
    > tftpboot ${fdt_addr} ${fdtfile}
    ```

4. Finally, boot using the bootz command:

    ```
    > bootz ${loadaddr} - ${fdt_addr}
    ```

The Linux kernel will detect the bundled root filesystem and mount it at boot.

Securing the root filesystem

In the age of internet-connected devices and the Internet of Things, security in embedded devices is an important consideration in the design of an embedded system.

In this recipe, we will discuss two of the frameworks most frequently used to enhance the security of the root filesystem and show how to integrate them into your Yocto Project-based product.

Getting ready

Linux implements file-level security. Each file has a set of access attributes for user, group and others, and they can be assigned read, write, or execute permissions, as well as some special modes.

Filesystem access is hence based on the system users and groups. When you list files with the `ls -l` command, you see the file attributes with the following format:

```
-rwxr-xr-x
```

The first letter is the file type, followed by triads of user, group, and other permissions. The file can be read, written, and executed by the user that owns it, but only read and executed by a user in the same group or by a different user not in the same group. For directories, executable permissions mean the directory can be entered.

There are three other modes that can be used for certain file types:

- The setuid bit, which allows us to change the effective user ID of a process to its own user ID instead of the user that ran it. If the setuid bit is set, the `x` bit will change to `s`. If the file did not have executable permission for the user, it will use a capital `S` instead.
- The setgid bit, which is similar to setuid except it affects the effective group ID. setuid has no effect on directories, while setgid make files created inside the directory inherit the directory's group.
- The sticky bit, which affects directories so that only root or the file owner are allowed to change files inside the directory. The sticky bit is represented by a `t`, or capital `T` if the `x` permission is set.

File access modes are usually represented in octal format, for example as 0755. Each letter is a file mode bit, with the first number representing the special file mode bits where:

- 1: sticky bit
- 2: setgid
- 4: setuid

This type of file access is categorized as **Discretionary Access Control** (**DAC**) as it allows users to change access control attributes of objects they own. Processes have real (who you are) and effective (who you are acting as) user IDs that dictate whether they are able to access a file based on the file's permissions.

Mandatory Access Control (**MAC**) on the other hand implements a mechanism to constrain the ability of users (subjects) to perform operations on objects, with both subjects and objects having a set of security attributes and operating system rules controlling the access policy. Users cannot modify access permissions. In this model, subjects are usually processes or threads, and objects are operating system resources such as files and directories, but also memory, sockets, IPC, and other elements.

In Linux, MAC is implemented with the **Linux Security Module** (**LSM**) framework, over the standard DAC policies. Once access is allowed by DAC, the LSM module is called to finally allow or deny access. The number of objects that LSM controls keeps growing and includes:

- Filesystem operations
- Network operations
- IPC operations
- Task operations

LSM is used by several Linux security frameworks, including two of the most relevant: **Security Enhanced Linux** (**SELinux**) and **Simplified Mandatory Access Control Kernel** (**SMACK**). Both need to be configured in the kernel configuration.

How to do it...

SELinux is more complex and needs a carefully designed policy so as not to compromise security. Permissions are very granular over hundreds of different kernel objects. Its default policy (standard) is highly restrictive and has to be compiled and deployed. It has good tools for auditing and rule creation.

SMACK includes a permissive default policy with the kernel, which has to be extended to meet specific needs. It's easy to add new policies but the tools available are not as rich as those for SELinux. Permissions are not as granular as with SELinux either. SMACK is more suited to an embedded system than SELinux, unless higher granularity is needed.

We will show how to configure both SELinux and SMACK.

Setting up SELinux

We will first need to add Linux kernel support for our selected security framework. To enable SELinux support, we need to configure the Linux kernel as explained in the *Configuring the Linux kernel* section in Chapter 2, *The BSP Layer*. We can add the following changes to the Wandboard's defconfig in a bbappend to the Linux kernel recipe:

```
CONFIG_AUDIT=y
CONFIG_SECURITY=y
CONFIG_SECURITY_NETWORK=y
CONFIG_SECURITY_SELINUX=y
```

Refer to the source code distributed with the book for further details.

The meta-selinux layer enables SELinux support on a Yocto image. To use it, first we need to clone it into the sources directory:

```
$ cd /opt/yocto/fsl-community-bsp/sources
$ git clone git://git.yoctoproject.org/meta-selinux
```

At the time of writing, the meta-selinux layer has not been updated to support the Yocto Project 2.4 (Rocko) release. For images to build, we have to clone a patched version of meta-selinux instead of the previous, as shown here:
```
$ git clone
https://github.com/yoctocookbook2ndedition/meta-selinux.g
it -b rocko
```

Then we also need to add it to our conf/bblayers.conf, as described in the *Creating a custom BSP layer* section in Chapter 2, *The BSP Layer*. The layer also depends on meta-python, which is part of meta-oe, so we also need to add it to our conf/bblayers.conf:

```
+   ${BSPDIR}/sources/meta-selinux \
+   ${BSPDIR}/sources/meta-openembedded/meta-python \
```

We then need to explicitly change our distribution configuration file to support some extra features:

```
DISTRO_FEATURES_append = " pam selinux"
```

Finally, a reference policy to be used as a base for future customization needs to be selected. The `meta-selinux` layer supports the following:

- `minimum`, the most permissive with minimum security protection. Supports a minimal set of confined daemons.
- `standard`, which supports both confined daemons and other areas as users.
- `mls`, with support for multilevel security protection.
- `targeted`, supporting a greater number of daemons, as well as other areas as users.
- `mcs`, a standard for multicategory security protection systems.

To choose, for example, the minimum policy, we add the following to the `conf/local.conf` configuration file:

```
PREFERRED_PROVIDER_virtual/refpolicy ?= "refpolicy-minimum"
```

The `meta-selinux` layer incorporates two SELinux enabled images, `core-image-selinux-minimal` and `core-image-selinux`. In order to add SELinux functionality to an existing image, you can add the following to `conf/local.conf`:

```
IMAGE_INSTALL_append = " packagegroup-core-selinux"
```

To build `core-image-selinux`, change to the `fsl-community-bsp` directory and type:

```
$ source setup-environment wandboard
$ bitbake core-image-selinux
```

You may see the following error when building this with the Poky distribution:
```
ERROR: cairo-1.14.10-r0 do_prepare_recipe_sysroot: The
file /usr/lib/pkgconfig/wayland-egl.pc is installed by
both mesa and imx-gpu-viv, aborting
```
To work around it, remove the `wayland` distribution feature in your `conf/local.conf` as follows:
```
DISTRO_FEATURES_remove = "wayland"
```

Remember that, if you change the `DISTRO_FEATURES` variable as explained earlier, you need to remove the `tmp` directory and build with `sstate-cache` or the build will fail.

We will learn how to choose between the different graphical backends available in the FSL community BSP in Chapter 4, *Application Development*.

The `core-image-selinux` image will relabel the filesystem to the new policy on boot as it includes the `selinux-autorelabel` recipe; we should see the following messages on boot:

```
Checking SELinux security contexts:
  * First booting, filesystem will be relabeled...
  * Relabel done, rebooting the system.
```

With `core-image-selinux-minimal`, the relabeling needs to be manually triggered after booting into an SELinux-enabled system with:

```
# fixfiles -f -F relabel
```

After booting, we can verify SELinux is enabled and enforcing by doing this:

```
$ sestatus
SELinux status:                 enabled
SELinuxfs mount:                /sys/fs/selinux
SELinux root directory:         /etc/selinux
Loaded policy name:             minimum
Current mode:                   permissive
Mode from config file:          permissive
Policy MLS status:              enabled
Policy deny_unknown status:     allowed
Memory protection checking:     requested (insecure)
Max kernel policy version:      29
```

The `meta-selinux` minimum policy will currently only boot in permissive mode and would need to be tweaked in order to switch it to enforcing mode.

Setting up SMACK

To enable SMACK support, we need to configure the Linux kernel as explained in the *Configuring the Linux kernel* section in `Chapter 2`, *The BSP Layer*. We can add the following changes to the Wandboard's `defconfig` in a `bbappend` to the Linux kernel recipe:

```
+CONFIG_SECURITY=y
+CONFIG_SECURITY_SMACK=y
+CONFIG_AUDIT=y
```

Refer to the source code distributed with the book for further details.

The `meta-security-smack` layer, part of `meta-intel-iot-security`, enables SMACK support on a Yocto image. To use it, first we need to clone it into the `sources` directory:

```
$ cd /opt/yocto/fsl-community-bsp/sources
$ git clone git://github.com/01org/meta-intel-iot-security
```

Then we also need to add it to our `conf/bblayers.conf`, as described in the *Creating a custom BSP layer* section in `Chapter 2`, *The BSP Layer* by adding the following:

```
+    ${BSPDIR}/sources/meta-intel-iot-security/meta-security-smack \
```

We then need to configure our `conf/local.conf` file to use it as follows:

```
OVERRIDES .= ":smack"
DISTRO_FEATURES_append = " smack"
```

We will also install some extra user space applications to work with SMACK:

```
CORE_IMAGE_EXTRA_INSTALL += "coreutils smack-userspace"
```

Finally, we can build our core image of choice.

How it works...

Let's see how both security frameworks work in more detail.

Looking into SELinux

Once SELinux is configured it can be in three modes:

- **Disabled**: SELinux is not policing access
- **Permissive**: SELinux allows all access but logs access violations
- **Enforcing**: SELinux is actively policing access

The mode can be set either in the kernel command-line, in the SELinux configuration file, or with the `getenforce`/`setenforce` command-line tools.

The Linux kernel command-line accepts the following SELinux-related parameters:

- `selinux=0` or `selinux=1`: This disables or enables SELinux respectively
- `enforcing=0` or `enforcing=1`: This boots into permissive mode (the kernel's default) or into enforcing mode

The root filesystem contains a configuration file in `/etc/selinux/config` with a `SELINUX` variable that controls the security mode:

- `SELINUX=disabled`
- `SELINUX=permissive`
- `SELINUX=enforcing`

When enforcing, SELinux allows no access by default, and rules must be created and loaded to allow specific actions. A set of rules is called an SELinux policy. SELinux policies are usually formed of thousands of rules, and writing them is challenging.

Every object contains a security context stored in the inodes extended attribute fields, formed by:

- A user associated with a subject or object (`root`, `user_u`, or `system_u`).
- A role that defines a set of permissions granted to a user (`object_r` or `system_r`).
- A domain (for processes) or types (for objects) is a combination of subjects and objects that may interact with each other. They use the `_t` suffix.

On an SELinux-enabled system `ls -Z` lists the contexts as `:<role>:<type>`, for example:

```
-rw-r--r-- root root root:object_r:user_home_t file.txt
```

Allow rules have four elements:

- source-type
- target-type
- object-class
- permissions

For example, a process with domain type `user_t` is able to read, execute, and stat (`getattr`) a file object of type `bin_t` with the following rule:

```
allow user_t bin_t : file {read execute getattr};
```

These policy files need to be compiled from source into a binary module format (using the `checkmodule` tool) and are loaded at boot time into the kernel early in the boot process from `/etc/selinux`. The first SELinux boot is a deployment boot that relabels the entire root filesystem according to the policy and then reboots itself. Policies can be managed with the `semodule` command-line tool.

Looking into SMACK

SMACK uses the term label to describe what SELinux calls the security context. These are unstructured case-sensitive strings up to 23 characters in length. All subjects and objects are assigned a label. Labels are stored as extended attributes on filesystem objects, and as **Commercial Internet Protocol Security Option (CIPSO)** tags in the header of IP packets. The mapping of labels to CIPSO values is done by the `smackcipso` utility, which formats data and writes it to `/sys/fs/smack/cipso`.

The `chsmack` utility allows us to display or set extended attribute values. For example, you can show the smack label for a file with:

```
# chsmack /bin/cat
cat access="_"
```

Processes can read their SMACK label from `/proc/<pid>/attr/current`.

Some predefined labels are:

- _: A single underscore character
- ^: A single circumflex character
- ?: A single question mark character
- @: A single at character

All tasks are assigned a label, with _ being used for system tasks.

SMACK configuration is done via the `smackfs` filesystem. The `meta-security-smack` layer does not mount it by default, but we can add the following `recipes-core/base-files/base-files_%.bbappend` to our custom layer to do so:

```
do_install_append () {
    cat >> ${D}${sysconfdir}/fstab <<EOF
  # Mount smackfs
  smackfs /sys/fs/smackfs smackfs defaults 0 0
  EOF
}
```

As opposed to SELinux, Linux kernel SMACK support already has a default policy in place.

SMACK uses the kernel's audit support (`CONFIG_AUDIT`) to log access violations, logging all denied accessed by default. This can be changed in `/sys/fs/smackfs/logging` where:

- 0 is no logging
- 1 logs denied events (default)
- 2 logs accepted events
- 3 logs both denied and accepted events

SMACK rules are as follows:

1. Subjects labeled * are denied all access to objects
2. Subjects labeled ^ are allowed rx access to objects
3. Objects labeled _ are allowed rx access
4. Objects labeled * are allowed all access
5. Any access by subjects on objects with the same label is allowed
6. Any access explicitly allowed in the loaded rule set is allowed
7. Other access is denied

Rules are stored under `/etc/smack/accesses` and look like this:

```
<subject-label> <object-label> <accesses>
```

Rules are loaded using the `smackload` utility, which formats the data and writes it to `/sys/fs/smack/load`.

Access can be:

- Read (`r`)
- Write (`w`)
- Execute (`x`)
- Append (`a`)
- Transmute (`t`) (allows for applications with different labels to share data in a directory, allowing files to inherit labels from directories instead of processes)
- No access (`-`)

Rules can either be added using the `chsmack` utility or to `/etc/smack/accesses.d/`.

See also

- More information about SELinux can be found at the project's webpage: `http://selinuxproject.org/`.
- Kernel documentation regarding SMACK is available in the kernel source documentation. For new kernel versions, it can be accessed online at `https://www.kernel.org/doc/html/latest/admin-guide/LSM/Smack.html`.
- Generic security-related packages that could be useful when hardening a Linux system can be found in the meta-security layer. Its contents are described in `http://git.yoctoproject.org/cgit/cgit.cgi/meta-security/tree/README`.

Releasing software

When releasing a product based on the Yocto project, we have to consider that we are building on top of a multitude of different open source projects, each with different licensing requirements.

At the minimum, your embedded product will contain a bootloader (probably u-boot), the Linux kernel, and a root filesystem with one or more applications. Both u-boot and the Linux kernel are licensed under the **General Public License version 2** (**GPLv2**), and the root filesystem could contain a variety of programs with different licenses.

All open source licenses allow you to sell a commercial product with a mixture of proprietary and open licenses as long as they are independent and the product complies with all the open source licenses. We will discuss open source and proprietary cohabiting in the *Working with open source and proprietary code* recipe later on.

When developing open source applications, it's important to give careful thought to the license the software will be released under. It is very common to take sections of code from other open source projects, or to use an existing open source library. By doing that you might need to inherit the license from the other project, as outlined in the table at:

```
https://www.gnu.org/licenses/gpl-faq.html#AllCompatibility
```

As a general rule, software under the GPLv3 license will only be reusable by the free software community. A LGPLv3 license will allow you to include code from permissive licenses such as MIT or Apache 2.0, but LGPLv2.1 will allow the code to be used by most free software. For the code to be reused even by commercial projects, choose a permissive license such as MIT.

It is important to understand all the licensing implications before releasing your product to the public. The Yocto Project provides tools to make handling licensing requirements an easier job.

Getting ready

We first need to specify what requirements we need to comply with to distribute a product built with the Yocto Project. For the most restrictive open source licenses, this usually means:

- Source code distribution, including modifications
- License text distributions
- Distribution of the tools used to build and run the software

How to do it...

We can use the `archiver` and `license` classes to provide the deliverables that need to be distributed to comply with the licenses. We can configure our build to:

- Provide the original unpatched source as tarballs
- Provide patches to apply to the original source
- Provide recipes used to build the source
- Provide the license text that must sometimes accompany the binary (according to some licenses)

To use the `archiver` class to provide source, patches, and recipes as specified earlier, we add the following to our `conf/local.conf` file:

```
INHERIT += "archiver"
ARCHIVER_MODE[src] = "original"
ARCHIVER_MODE[diff] = "1"
ARCHIVER_MODE[recipe] = "1"
```

To configure the `license` class to provide licensing information, we do this:

```
COPY_LIC_MANIFEST = "1"
COPY_LIC_DIRS = "1"
```

The sources will be provided in the `tmp/deploy/sources` directory under a package subdirectory hierarchy.

For the Wandboard, we find the following directories under `tmp/deploy/sources`:

- `allarch-poky-linux`
- `arm-poky-linux-gnueabi`
- `x86_64-linux`

And looking for what's distributed for the Linux kernel source, a GPLv2 package, we find it under `tmp/deploy/sources/arm-poky-linux-gnueabi/linux-wandboard-4.1-2.0.x-r0`:

- `defconfig`
- `linux-wandboard-4.1-2.0.x-r0.tar.gz`
- The patches applied to the source by the different layers, both as individual patches and a single unified diff
- `linux-wandboard-4.1-2.0.x-r0-recipe.tar.gz`

So we have the kernel configuration, the source tarball, the patches applied with the order, and the recipes used to build it, which include:

- `linux-wandboard_4.1-2.0.x.bb`
- `linux-wandboard_4.1-2.0.x.bbappend`
- `linux-wandboard.inc`

And the license text for the packages will be included under `tmp/deploy/licenses`, under a package subdirectory hierarchy. For `linux-wandboard`, for example, we find:

- The `COPYING` file included in the Linux kernel source
- `generic_GPLv2`, a copy of the GPLv2 license
- `recipeinfo`, a text file containing recipe versioning information

License information will also be included in the root filesystem under `/usr/share/common-licenses`, and in a package directory hierarchy. A consideration for license text is that it is added when the image is built. If we need to add a new package with its license without rebuilding the image, for example by installing a new RPM package, we will need to do the following:

```
LICENSE_CREATE_PACKAGE = "1"
```

This creates a new `${PN}-lic` package for all recipes that installs license text under `/usr/share/licenses`. This allows us to install both the package and its license in standalone mode.

This configuration will provide deliverables for all build packages, but what we really want to do is provide them only for those whose licenses require us to.

For sure, we don't want to blindly distribute all the contents of the sources directory as-is, as it will also contain our proprietary source, which we most likely don't want to distribute.

We can configure the `archiver` class only to provide the source for `GPL` and `LGPL` packages with the following:

```
COPYLEFT_LICENSE_INCLUDE = "GPL* LGPL*"
COPYLEFT_LICENSE_EXCLUDE = "CLOSED Proprietary"
```

And also, for an embedded product, we are usually only concerned with the software that ships in the product itself, so we can limit the recipe type so it is only to be archived to target images with the following:

```
COPYLEFT_RECIPE_TYPES = "target"
```

We should obtain legal advice to decide which packages have licenses that make source distribution a requirement.

Other configuration options exist, such as providing the patched or configured source instead of the separated original source and patches, or source RPMs instead of source tarballs. See the `archiver` class for more details.

There's more...

We can also choose to distribute the whole of our build environment. The best way to do this is usually to publish our BSP and software layers on a public Git repository. Our software layer can then provide `bblayers.conf.sample` and `local.conf.sample`, which can be used to set up ready-to-use build directories.

See also

- There are other requirements that haven't been discussed here, such as the mechanism chosen for distribution. It is recommended you get legal advice before releasing a product to ensure all the license obligations have been met.

Analyzing your system for compliance

The Yocto build system makes it easy to provide auditing information to our legal advisers. This recipe will explain how.

How to do it...

Under `tmp/deploy/licenses`, we find a directory list of packages (including their corresponding licenses) and an `image` folder with a package and license manifest.

For the example reduced image provided before, `image-small`, we have the following:

```
tmp/deploy/licenses/image-small-initramfs-wandboard-
<timestamp>/package.manifest
base-files
base-passwd
busybox
```

```
busybox-syslog
busybox-udhcpc
initscripts
initscripts-functions
libc6
run-postinsts
sysvinit
sysvinit-inittab
sysvinit-pidof
update-alternatives-opkg
update-rc.d
```

And the corresponding `tmp/deploy/licenses/image-small-initramfs-wandboard-<timestamp>/license.manifest` file excerpt is as follows:

```
PACKAGE NAME: base-files
PACKAGE VERSION: 3.0.14
RECIPE NAME: base-files
LICENSE: GPLv2
PACKAGE NAME: base-files-lic
PACKAGE VERSION: 3.0.14
RECIPE NAME: base-files
LICENSE: GPLv2
```

These files can be used to analyze all the different packages that form our root filesystem. We can also audit them to make sure we comply with the licenses when releasing our product to the public.

There's more...

You can instruct the Yocto build system to specifically avoid certain licenses by using the `INCOMPATIBLE_LICENSE` configuration variable. The usual way to use it is to avoid GPLv3-type licenses by adding the following to your `conf/local.conf` file:

```
INCOMPATIBLE_LICENSE = "GPL-3.0 LGPL-3.0 AGPL-3.0"
```

This will build `core-image-minimal` and `core-image-base` images as long as no extra image features are included.

Working with open source and proprietary code

It is common for an embedded product to be built upon an open source system like the one built by Yocto, and to include proprietary software that adds value and specializes the product. This proprietary part usually contains intellectual property and needs to be protected, and it's important to understand how it can coexist with open source code.

This recipe will discuss some examples of open source packages commonly found on embedded products and will briefly explain how to use proprietary software with them.

How to do it...

Open source licenses can be broadly divided into two categories based on whether they are:

- **Permissive**: These are similar to **Internet Software Consortium** (**ISC**), MIT, and BSD licenses. They have few requirements attached to them and they just require us to preserve copyright and limited warranty notices.
- **Restrictive**: These are similar to the GPL, and bind us to not only distribute the source code and modifications, either with the binary itself or at a later date, but also to distribute tools to build, install, and run the source.

However, some licenses might pollute modifications and derivative work with their own conditions, commonly referred to as *viral licenses*, while others will not. For example, if you link your application to GPL-licensed code, your application will be bound by the GPL too.

The virulent nature of GPL has made some people wary of using GPL-licensed software, but it's important to note that proprietary software can run alongside GPL software as long as the license terms are understood and respected.

For example, violating the GPLv2 license would mean losing the right to distribute GPLv2 code in the future, even if further distribution is GPLv2-compliant. In this case, the only way to be able to distribute the code again would be to ask the copyright holders for permission.

How it works...

Next, we will provide guidance regarding licensing requirements for some open source packages commonly used in embedded products. It does not constitute legal advice, and as stated before, proper legal auditing of your product should be done before public release.

The U-Boot bootloader

U-Boot is licensed under the GPLv2, but any program launched by it does not inherit its license. So you are free to use U-Boot to launch a proprietary operating system, for example. However, your final product must comply with the GPLv2 with regard to U-Boot, so U-Boot source code and modifications must be provided.

The Linux kernel

The Linux kernel is also licensed under the GPLv2. Any application that runs in the Linux kernel user space does not inherit its license, so you can run your proprietary software in Linux freely. However, Linux kernel modules are part of the Linux kernel and as such must comply with the GPLv2. Also, your final product must release the Linux kernel source and modifications, including external modules that run in your product.

glibc

The GNU C library version 2.26 included in Yocto Project 2.4 is licensed under the **Lesser General Public License v2.1 (LGPLv2.1)**, which allows dynamic linking without license inheritance. So your proprietary code can dynamically link with glibc, but of course you still have to comply with the LGPL with regard to glibc. Note, however, that statically linking your application would pollute it with the LGPL.

musl

The musl C library is licensed under an MIT license, a permissive software license that has very limited restrictions on reuse as long as MIT license terms and copyright notices are included. Your proprietary code would therefore be able to link with musl without license pollution.

BusyBox

BusyBox is also licensed under the GPLv2. The license allows for non-related software to run alongside it, so your proprietary software can run alongside BusyBox freely. As before, you have to comply with the GPLv2 with regard to BusyBox and distribute its source and modifications.

The Qt framework

Qt is licensed under three different licenses. You can choose whether you want a commercial license (in which case, your proprietary application is protected in exchange for a per-developer license plus royalties), an LGPL license (which, as discussed before, would also protect your proprietary software by allowing the dynamic linking of your application as long as you complied with the LGPL for the Qt framework itself), or the GPLv3 (which would be inherited by your application).

The LGPL version of Qt library versioning has changed with each software release:

- In Qt5.3 most modules were under LGPLv2.1, with a few commercial-only modules
- From Qt5.4, new modules were published under LGPLv3, which was also added as an option for older modules
- Qt5.7 dropped LGPLv2.1 support, with the only option being commercial, GPLv3, or LGPLv3
- The licensing model for Qt5.9, which is the version in Yocto 2.4, has not changed so it allows commercial, GPLv3, or LGPLv3

LGPLv3 is an extended version of LGPLv2.1 that basically adds what is called an anti-tivoization clause that requires us to allow for modified source code to run on the device as well as to provide instructions for it. When using Yocto Project, this could be done by providing the SDK to build the Qt library source with, as well as a way to deploy it, which could be via a package update. Note that this only refers to the Qt library, not the application that links with it dynamically, so the system should be designed in such a way that the Qt application that uses the library has no access to critical parts of the system, for example, by a well-designed SELinux policy as explained in the *Securing the root filesystem* recipe in this chapter.

Details about Qt's current licensing models can be found at
`https://www1.qt.io/licensing-comparison/`.

The X Windows system

The x.Org source is licensed under permissive MIT-style licenses. As such, your proprietary software is free to make any use of it as long as its use is stated and copyright notices are preserved.

There's more...

Let's see how to integrate our proprietary-licensed code into the Yocto build system. When preparing the recipe for our application, we can take several approaches to licensing:

- Mark LICENSE as closed. This is the usual case for a proprietary application. We use the following:

  ```
  LICENSE = "CLOSED"
  ```

- Mark LICENSE as proprietary and include some type of license agreement. This is commonly done when releasing binaries with some sort of end user agreement that is referenced in the recipe. For example, the meta-freescale layer uses this type of license to comply with Freescale's End User License Agreement. An example is:

  ```
  LICENSE = "Proprietary"
  LIC_FILES_CHKSUM =
  "file://EULA.txt;md5=93b784b1c11b3fffb1638498a8dde3f6"
  ```

- Provide multiple licensing options, such as an open source license and a commercial license. In this case, the LICENSE variable is used to specify the open licenses, and the LICENSE_FLAGS variable is used for commercial licenses. A typical example is the gstreamer1.0-plugins-ugly package in Poky:

  ```
  LICENSE = "GPLv2+ & LGPLv2.1+ & LGPLv2+"
  LICENSE_FLAGS = "commercial"
  LIC_FILES_CHKSUM =
  "file://COPYING;md5=a6f89e2100d9b6cdffcea4f398e37343 \
  file://tests/check/elements/xingmux.c;beginline=1;endline=21;md5=4c
  771b8af188724855cb99cadd390068"
  ```

When the LICENSE_FLAGS variable is set on a recipe, the package will not be built unless the license appears on the LICENSE_FLAGS_WHITELIST variable too, typically defined in your conf/local.conf file. For the earlier example, we would add this:

```
LICENSE_FLAGS_WHITELIST = "commercial"
```

The LICENSE and LICENSE_FLAGS_WHITELIST variables can match exactly for a very narrow match or broadly, as in the preceding example, which matches all licenses that begin with the word commercial. For narrow matches, the package name must be appended to the license name; for instance, if we only wanted to whitelist the gstreamer1.0-plugins-ugly package from the earlier example but nothing else, we could use the following:

```
LICENSE_FLAGS_WHITELIST = "commercial_gstreamer1.0-plugins-ugly"
```

See also

- You should refer to specific licenses for a complete understanding of the requirements imposed by them. You can find a complete list of open source licenses and their documentation at http://spdx.org/licenses/.

4
Application Development

In this chapter, we will cover the following recipes:

- Introducing toolchains
- Preparing an SDK
- Using the extensible SDK
- Using the Eclipse IDE
- Developing GTK+ applications
- Using the Qt Creator IDE
- Developing Qt applications
- Describing workflows for application development
- Working with GNU make
- Working with the GNU build system
- Working with the CMake build system
- Working with the SCons builder
- Developing with libraries
- Working with the Linux framebuffer
- Using the X Windows system
- Using Wayland
- Adding a web browser application
- Adding Python applications
- Integrating the Open Java Development Kit
- Integrating Java applications
- Integrating Node.js applications
- Running Docker application containers

Introduction

Dedicated applications are what define an embedded product and Yocto offers helpful application development tools, as well as the functionality to integrate with popular **Integrated Development Environments** (**IDE**) such as Eclipse and Qt Creator. It also provides a wide range of utility classes to help in the integration of finished applications into the build system and target images. A normal embedded Linux software development team is logically divided into the following roles:

- **BSP developers** in charge of the Board Support Package, which is the bootloader and Linux kernel. This team has the greatest exposure to the hardware. As we have seen in `Chapter 2`, *The BSP layer*, BSP development uses primarily the Yocto SDK.
- **Application developers** will work on the Linux user space applications that define the product, including user interfaces. Developing applications for embedded Linux is not that different from developing applications for a Linux server or desktop, as the kernel abstracts most of the embedded device particularities. Application developers will also use the Yocto SDK to develop their applications.
- **System integrators** who release an SDK for the other teams to use and integrate both the applications and BSP changes into the Yocto build system. They also create the final product images.

In summary, the Yocto SDK is the interface between the Yocto Project, BSP and application developers and allows the work of the different developers to be shared and developed simultaneously. Some teams have the same engineers covering all roles, while some others prefer to specialize. This chapter will introduce the Yocto SDK, an important component on the application development workflow when using the Yocto Project. The SDK contains the cross-compilation toolchain, but also the header files and libraries used to cross-compile root filesystem applications. We will also introduce IDEs and show how they are used to build and debug C and C++ applications on real hardware and will explore application development, including graphical frameworks and Yocto integration, not only for C and C++ but also other languages.

Introducing toolchains

A toolchain is a set of tools, binaries, and libraries used to build applications to run on a computer platform. In Yocto, the default toolchains are based on GNU components with GPL licenses.

Getting ready

A GNU toolchain contains the following components:

- **Assembler (GNU as)**: This is part of the binutils package
- **Linker (GNU ld)**: This is also part of the binutils package
- **Compiler (GNU gcc)**: Latest versions have support for C, C++, Java, Ada, Fortran, Go, and Objective C/C++
- **Debugger (GNU gdb)**: This is the GNU debugger
- **Binary file tools** (`objdump`, `nm`, `objcopy`, `readelf`, `strip`, and so on): These are part of the binutils package.

These components are enough to build bare-metal applications, bootloaders like U-Boot, or operating systems like the Linux kernel, as they don't need a C library and they implement the C library functions they need. However, for Linux user space applications, a POSIX-compliant C library is needed. The GNU C library, `glibc`, is the default C library used in the Yocto Project, and `musl`, a smaller C library, is a supported alternative popular for resource-constrained devices. On embedded systems, it is not just a toolchain we need, but a cross-compilation toolchain. This is because we build in a host computer but run the resulting binaries on the target, which is usually a different architecture. In reality, there are several types of toolchain, based on the architecture of the machine building the toolchain (build machine), running the toolchain (host machine), and running the binaries built by the toolchain (target machine). The most common combinations are:

- **Native**: An example of this is an x86 machine running a toolchain that has also been built on an x86 machine producing binaries to run on an x86 machine. This is common in desktop computers.
- **Cross-compilation**: This is the most common on embedded systems; for example, an x86 machine running a toolchain that has also been built on an x86 machine but producing binaries to run on a different architecture, like ARM.
- **Cross-native**: This is typically the toolchain running on targets. An example of this is where a toolchain has been built on an x86 machine but runs on ARM and produces binaries for ARM.
- **Canadian**: This is rarely seen and is where the build, host, and target machines are all different.

The process of building a cross-compilation toolchain is complex and fault-prone, so automated tools for toolchain building have emerged, like **crosstool-NG**. The Yocto build system also compiles its own toolchain on every build and, as we will see, you can use this toolchain for application development too. However, the cross-compilation toolchain and C library are not the only things we need in order to build applications; we also need a `sysroot`; that is, a root filesystem on the host with the libraries and header files that can be found on the target root filesystem. The combination of the cross-compilation toolchain, the `sysroot`, and sometimes other development tools such as an IDE is referred to as an SDK.

How to do it...

There are several ways to obtain an SDK with the Yocto project:

1. Downloading a precompiled SDK:

   The easiest way to obtain an SDK with a cross-compilation toolchain for a supported platform is to download a precompiled one; for example, from the Yocto Project downloads site:
   `http://downloads.yoctoproject.org/releases/yocto/yocto-2.4/toolchain/`.

   Installation scripts are named as follows:

   ```
   <distro>-<c library>-<host>-<image name>-<architecture>-toolchain-
   <version>.sh
   ```

   Where:

   - `distro` is the configured distribution, usually Poky
   - The `c` library is usually `glibc` but could be `musl`
   - `host` is the machine the toolchain is intended to run on; usually it is either i686 or x86_64
   - `image name` is `core-image-minimal` or `core-image-sato` for precompiled toolchains, but will match the image name used to build the toolchain against
   - `architecture` will be a combination of CPU and in the case of ARM, also ABI (hard or soft floating point)
   - `version` will be the Yocto Project release

- The Yocto Project provides prebuilt toolchains for both 32- and 64-bit x86 host machines, and prebuilt ARM toolchains both for **ARMv5E** and **Cortex-A8** (**ARMv7A**) architectures. These contain sysroots that match the `core-image-minimal` and `core-image-sato` target images. To install the prebuilt ARMv7A toolchain for an x86_64 host, run the following:

```
$ wget
http://downloads.yoctoproject.org/releases/yocto/yocto-2.4/toolchai
n/x86_64/poky-glibc-x86_64-core-image-sato-cortexa8hf-neon-
toolchain-2.4.sh
$ chmod a+x poky-glibc-x86_64-core-image-sato-cortexa8hf-neon-
toolchain-2.4.sh
$ ./poky-glibc-x86_64-core-image-sato-cortexa8hf-neon-
toolchain-2.4.sh
```

2. Building your own toolchain installer:

   On most embedded Linux projects, your machine will be supported by an external layer and you will have a customized root filesystem that your `sysroot` will need to match. So, building your own toolchain installer is recommended when you have a customized root filesystem. For example, the ideal toolchain to work with the Wandboard would be Cortex-A9-specific and targeted to produce hard floating point binaries.

3. Using the Yocto Project build system:

   Finally, if you already have a Yocto build system installation on your host, you can also use it for application development. Usually, application developers do not need the complexity of a Yocto build system installation, so a toolchain installer for the target system will be enough.

Preparing an SDK

The Yocto build system can be used to generate a cross-compilation toolchain with a matching `sysroot` for a target system, as well as a `sysroot` with native applications. This is referred to as a standard Yocto Project SDK. The Yocto Project can also build an extensible SDK that extends the standard SDK by adding tools to facilitate adding new applications and libraries. This recipe will show how to build both types of SDK.

Getting ready

The standard SDK contains the cross-compilation toolchain, including the debugger as well as target and host sysroots. Its size depends on the image it is built to match, but is usually hundreds of MB. The extensible SDK comes in two flavors, full (the default) and minimal, and it allows for a certain degree of customization as well as being updatable.

- The full extensible SDK includes the following:
  - Toolchain
  - Complete shared state cache artifacts and everything needed to recreate the images it is built against
  - The `devtool` command-line application
  - Its size depends on the image it is built against, but can be several GB
- The minimal extensible SDK produces a small SDK, around 35 MB in size, which does not include the toolchain or libraries. The minimal SDK needs to be updated using `devtool`, so it also needs to include package information, which will increase the size of the SDK significantly, or be configured with a shared state mirror it can use.

We will use the previously used `wandboard` build directory and source the `setup-environment` script as follows:

```
$ cd /opt/yocto/fsl-community-bsp/
$ source setup-environment wandboard
```

How to do it...

There are several ways to build an SDK with the Yocto build system:

- The `meta-toolchain` target:

  This method will build a standard SDK toolchain that matches your target platform and a basic `sysroot` that will not match your target root filesystem. However, this toolchain can be used to build bare metal software like the U-Boot bootloader or the Linux kernel, which do not need a `sysroot`. The Yocto Project offers downloadable `toolchains` for supported hardware platforms. You can also build this toolchain yourself with the following command:

  ```
  $ bitbake meta-toolchain
  ```

Once built, it can be installed with the following instructions:

```
$ cd tmp/deploy/sdk
$ ./poky-glibc-x86_64-meta-toolchain-cortexa9hf-neon-
  toolchain-2.4.sh
```

- The `populate_sdk` or `populate_sdk_ext` tasks:

This is the recommended way to build a toolchain matching your target platform with a `sysroot` matching your target root filesystem. You build a standard SDK with the following:

```
$ bitbake core-image-sato -c populate_sdk
```

You can also build an extensible SDK with the following:

```
$ bitbake core-image-sato -c populate_sdk_ext
```

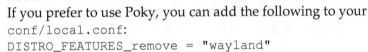

In order to build `core-image-sato` we need to remove the Wayland distro feature. The recommended way to do this is to use one of the available FSL community distributions like `fslc-x11`. To use the `fslc-x11` distribution, add the following to the `conf/local.conf` configuration file:
`DISTRO = "fslc-x11"`
If you prefer to use Poky, you can add the following to your `conf/local.conf`:
`DISTRO_FEATURES_remove = "wayland"`

You should replace `core-image-sato` for the target root filesystem image you want the `sysroot` to match. The resulting toolchain can be installed with the following:

```
$ cd tmp/deploy/sdk
$ ./poky-glibc-x86_64-core-image-sato-cortexa9hf-neon-
toolchain-2.4.sh
```

Alternatively, for the extensible SDK, use the following:

```
$ ./poky-glibc-x86_64-core-image-sato-cortexa9hf-neon-toolchain-
ext-2.4.sh
```

The extensible SDK installs on the `poky_sdk` directory on the `home` folder by default.

The location chosen to install the extensible SDK needs to be writable by its users.

Also, if you want your toolchain to be able to build static applications, you need to add static libraries to it. You can do this by adding specific static libraries to your target image, which could also be used for native compilation. For example, to add static `glibc` libraries, add the following to your `conf/local.conf` file:

```
IMAGE_INSTALL_append = " libc-staticdev"
```

Then, build the toolchain to match your root filesystem as explained previously.

However, toolchains can be customized to add static libraries without having to add them to the image too, as we will see later.

- The `meta-toolchain-qt` target:

This method will extend `meta-toolchain` to build Qt applications. We will see how to build Qt applications in the *Developing Qt applications* recipe. To build this toolchain, execute the following command:

```
$ bitbake meta-toolchain-qt
```

Once built, it can be installed with the following code:

```
$ cd tmp/deploy/sdk
$ ./poky-glibc-x86_64-meta-toolchain-qt-cortexa9hf-vfp-neon-
toolchain-qt-2.4.sh
```

The resulting toolchain installers will be located under `tmp/deploy/sdk` for all cases mentioned here.

- The `meta-ide-support` target:

This method does not generate a toolchain installer, but it prepares the current build project to use its own toolchain. It will generate an `environment-setup` script inside the `tmp` directory. To use it, run the following:

```
$ bitbake meta-ide-support
```

To use the bundled toolchain, you can now source that script as follows:

```
$ source tmp/environment-setup-cortexa9hf-vfp-neon-poky-linux-
  gnueabi
```

How it works...

As described before, the SDK is a central piece on software development workflows using the Yocto Project. The existence of both a standard and an extensible SDK should be seen as a transitional period and it is likely that in future the standard SDK will be deprecated in favor of a single configurable SDK. However, the standard SDK still offers advantages due to its size and simplicity for early project stages and small teams. The standard SDK is prepared by the `populate_sdk_base` class, which in turn is inherited by `populate_sdk_ext`, which prepares the extensible SDK in Poky.

Customizing standard and extensible SDKs

Even though the default SDK settings will be appropriate for the majority of users, the SDKs can be customized using the following variables:

- `SDKMACHINE`: Specifies the architecture of the host machine for the SDK. It defaults to the architecture of the host machine, for example x86_64.
- `SDKIMAGE_FEATURES`: A list of image features to include in the target `sysroot`; for example, you usually won't want the static libraries added to your image, but you do want to be able to cross-compile static applications, so you can add all the static libraries to the toolchain by adding the following SDK feature:

```
SDKIMAGE_FEATURES_append = " staticdev-pkgs"
```

- `SDKPATH`: Allows us to customize the default installation path offered by the installer.
- `SDK_TITLE`: The title printed when running the installer, which defaults to <distro> SDK or the <distro> extensible SDK.
- `SDK_VENDOR`: The vendor of the SDK. The Poky distro sets this to "-pokysdk".

- `SDK_POSTPROCESS_COMMAND`: Contains a list of functions called after the SDK is built. The `SDK_DIR` variable is available for functions to locate the SDK path. Hooks also exist that run after the host or target parts of the SDK have been created with `POPULATE_SDK_POST_HOST_COMMAND` and `POPULATE_SDK_POST_TARGET_COMMAND`.

Adding packages to the SDKs

The Yocto build system will automatically include in the target `sysroot` all the libraries and header files that are needed to build the applications running in the target. Extra packages can be added to the target `sysroot` by appending them to the `TOOLCHAIN_TARGET_TASK` variable. For example, you can selectively add only the static libraries you need to the toolchain by adding them as follows in your image recipe or `conf/local.conf` file:

```
TOOLCHAIN_TARGET_TASK_append = " libc-staticdev"
```

To add a native package to the host `sysroot` in the SDK, two things are needed:

1. The package needs to inherit the `nativesdk` class, and usually the `native` class too, by doing the following:

   ```
   BBCLASSEXTEND = "native nativesdk"
   ```

2. The package needs to be added to the `TOOLCHAIN_HOST_TASK` variable, for example, by appending the `nativesdk-packagegroup-sdk-host` recipe, which is added to it by default, as follows:

   ```
   RDEPENDS_${PN} += " \
       nativesdk-<packagename> \
   "
   ```

Using the extensible SDK

In previous chapters, we have already been using the standard SDK to build the U-Boot bootloader and the Linux kernel, so in this recipe we will focus on the extensible SDK and in particular in using `devtool`, a command-line tool that helps in the development of packages. The `devtool` utility supports a wide range of recipe types and build systems, including:

- Autotools
- CMake
- SCons
- qmake
- GNU Make (Makefile)
- Out-of-tree kernel module
- Binary package
- Node.js
- Python `setuptools` or `distutils`

We will see examples of some of the above in the rest of this chapter.

Getting ready

We will need to build and install the extensible SDK as we have seen in the previous recipe so that the `devtool` command-line application is available. To build the full extensible SDK we do the following:

```
$ bitbake -c populate_sdk_ext <image name>
```

Depending on the chosen image, it may happen that the size of the full SDK is too big to manage. In that case, we can configure our build to use the minimal extensible SDK as follows:

```
SDK_EXT_TYPE = "minimal"
SDK_INCLUDE_TOOLCHAIN = "1"
SDK_INCLUDE_PKGDATA = "1"
```

Here, the following applies:

- `SDK_EXT_TYPE` can be either `full`, the default, or `minimal`.
- `SDK_INCLUDE_TOOLCHAIN` controls whether the toolchain is included or not in the SDK. As mentioned previously, the full SDK will by default include the toolchain, and the minimal SDK will not, unless configured to do so.
- `SDK_INCLUDE_PKGDATA` includes the package data for all world target recipes in the extensible SDK. This allows `devtool` to find these recipes and map dependencies effectively, but increases significantly the build time. This is used in conjunction with the minimal extensible SDK, and the `EXCLUDE_FROM_WORLD_pn-<recipename>` variable can be used to limit the built queue. For example, to exclude the `ffmpeg` recipe you would add the following to `conf/local.conf`:

```
EXCLUDE_FROM_WORLD_pn-ffmpeg = "1"
```

Most layers are not prepared to build for the world target, so it is likely that a lot of recipes will need to be excluded. The minimal SDK does not include a toolchain or libraries by default. In the previous configuration, we configure it to include the toolchain and we add the package data for all world target recipes so that `devtool` knows about them. With the configuration above, `devtool` will need to build the items it needs from source. To avoid that, we can configure a shared state cache it can use as we saw in Chapter 1, *The Build System* in the *Sharing the shared state cache* recipe. We then need to share this `SSTATE_MIRROR` variable with the SDK. This can be done in a `conf/sdk-extra.conf` file, either in your build directory or any of the layers. If the `SSTATE_MIRRORS` are common between the build system and the SDK, it can also be passed to the SDK with:

```
SDK_LOCAL_CONF_WHITELIST = "SSTATE_MIRRORS"
```

The extensible SDK build environment can be customized by the following variables:

- `SDK_LOCAL_CONF_WHITELIST`, which contains a list of variables from the build system available in the SDK configuration
- `SDK_LOCAL_CONF_BLACKLIST`, a list of build system variables not allowed into the SDK
- `SDK_INHERIT_BLACKLIST` lists all the classes removed from the `INHERIT` variable in the SDK configuration

Once the SDK build finishes, the toolchain can be found under `tmp/deploy/sdk`. To install it, we copy it to the destination machine and do the following:

```
$ ./poky-glibc-x86_64-core-image-minimal-cortexa9hf-neon-toolchain-
ext-2.4.sh
Poky (Yocto Project Reference Distro) Extensible SDK installer version
2.4======================================================================
===========
Enter target directory for SDK (default: ~/poky_sdk):
You are about to install the SDK to " ~/poky_sdk". Proceed[Y/n]?Extracting
SDK........................done
Setting it up...
Extracting buildtools...
Preparing build system...
Parsing recipes: 100%
|######################################################################
#####################| Time: 0:00:5$
Initialising tasks: 100%
|######################################################################
###################| Time: 0:00:0$
Checking sstate mirror object availability: 100%
|######################################################################
Time: 0:00:0$
Parsing recipes: 100%
|######################################################################
#####################| Time: 0:00:4$
Initialising tasks: 100%
|######################################################################
###################| Time: 0:00:02
done
SDK has been successfully set up and is ready to be used.
Each time you wish to use the SDK in a new shell session, you need to
source the environment setup script e.g.
$ . / ~/poky_sdk/environment-setup-cortexa9hf-neon-poky-linux-gnueabi
```

Exploring the extensible SDK contents

Comparing the full extensible SDK and the standard SDK, they both contain a toolchain, that is, the environment setup script and both host (`x86_64-pokysdk-linux`) and target (`cortexa9hf-neon-poky-linux-gnueabi`) sysroots:

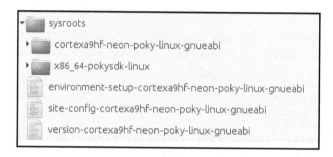

Yocto SDK common structure

However, the extensible SDK has some extra directories:

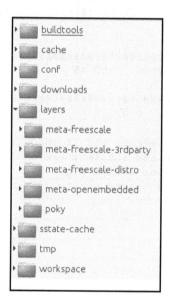

Extensible SDK directory hierarchy

These extra directories include:

- `buildtools`, a collection of distribution independent tools used by the Yocto build system. The `buildtools` package was discussed on *Setting up the host system* in `Chapter 1`, *The Build System* and is used to remove dependencies on the host distribution.
- `cache`, where the local file checksum cache, an SQLite persistent storage database, and the BitBake code parser cache, are stored.
- `conf`, with all the configurations files for the SDK, including `bblayers.conf`, `local.conf`, `devtool.conf`, and `templateconf.cfg`.
- `downloads`, which contains the uninative artifact, that is, a pre-built C library used to isolate the build system from the C library in the host.
- `layers`, with all the layers meta data.
- `sstate-cache`, a copy of the shared state cache to speed up build times.
- `tmp`, a copy of the `tmp` folder from the build project without the build objects.
- `workspace`, the workspace area prepared by the `devtool` command-line tool.

How to do it...

The first step in order to use the extensible SDK is to source the environment setup script, as follows:

```
$ . environment-setup-cortexa9hf-neon-poky-linux-gnueabi
```

The `source` Bash built-in command we have been using can also be substituted by a single `.`, as shown previously, which is a portable POSIX-compliant syntax.

The SDK environment is now set up; additionally, you may now run `devtool` to perform development tasks. Run `devtool --help` for further details.

The `devtool` command-line application can also be used within a Yocto Project build directory, as we will see in *Describing workflows for application development* in this chapter.

Let's now add a new `helloworld` package. This is a Makefile-based C `hello world` example. We start by using `devtool` to add the new package by specifying the package name and the GitHub URL that contains the source code:

```
$ devtool add helloworld
https://github.com/yoctocookbook2ndedition/helloworld.git
NOTE: Starting bitbake server...
NOTE: Starting bitbake server...
NOTE: Fetching
git://github.com/yoctocookbook2ndedition/helloworld.git;protocol=https...
Loading cache: 100%
|###################################################################
#####################| Time: 0:00:02
Loaded 2269 entries from dependency cache.Parsing recipes: 100%
|###################################################################
#####################| Time: 0:00:01
Parsing of 1658 .bb files complete (1656 cached, 2 parsed). 2271 targets,
192 skipped, 0 masked, 0 errors.
NOTE: Resolving any missing task queue dependencies
Initialising tasks: 100%
|###################################################################
###################| Time: 0:00:00
NOTE: Executing RunQueue Tasks
NOTE: Tasks Summary: Attempted 2 tasks of which 0 didn't need to be rerun
and all succeeded.
NOTE: Using default source tree path
/home/alex/poky_sdk/workspace/sources/helloworldNOTE: Starting bitbake
server...
NOTE: Using source tree as build directory since that would be the default
for this recipe
NOTE: Recipe
/home/alex/poky_sdk/workspace/recipes/helloworld/helloworld_git.bb has been
automatically created; further editing may be required to make it fully
functional
```

The `devtool` utility has cloned the repository and placed it under the `~/poky_sdk/workspace/sources/helloworld/` directory. We are now ready to edit the template recipe that was prepared for us:

```
$ devtool edit-recipe helloworld
# Recipe created by recipetool
# This is the basis of a recipe and may need further editing in order to be
fully functional.
# (Feel free to remove these comments when editing.)

# Unable to find any files that looked like license statements. Check the
accompanying
```

```
# documentation and source headers and set LICENSE and LIC_FILES_CHKSUM
accordingly.
#
# NOTE: LICENSE is being set to "CLOSED" to allow you to at least start
building - if
# this is not accurate with respect to the licensing of the software being
built (it
# will not be in most cases) you must specify the correct value before
using this
# recipe for anything other than initial testing/development!
LICENSE = "CLOSED"
LIC_FILES_CHKSUM = ""

SRC_URI =
"git://github.com/yoctocookbook2ndedition/helloworld.git;protocol=https"

# Modify these as desired
PV = "1.0+git${SRCPV}"
SRCREV = "34d80d900550333d23c1b9193d6569298fb0e968"

S = "${WORKDIR}/git"

# NOTE: this is a Makefile-only piece of software, so we cannot generate
much of the
# recipe automatically - you will need to examine the Makefile yourself and
ensure
# that the appropriate arguments are passed in.

do_configure () {
        # Specify any needed configure commands here
        :
}

do_compile () {

        # You will almost certainly need to add additional arguments here
        oe_runmake
}

do_install () {
        # NOTE: unable to determine what to put here - there is a Makefile
but no
        # target named "install", so you will need to define this yourself
        :
}
```

We edit the recipe to review it and add some basic information that could not be extracted from the source code, like the following:

- **Licensing information**: By default, a CLOSED license is set when no specific license can be identified. We will change this to a MIT license.
- **Install task**: If the Makefile used had contained an install rule, it would have been called from the install task. As we don't have one, we need to manually provide the installation instructions.

The final recipe is shown next:

```
DESCRIPTION = "Simple helloworld application"
SECTION = "examples"
LICENSE = "MIT"
LIC_FILES_CHKSUM =
"file://${COMMON_LICENSE_DIR}/MIT;md5=0835ade698e0bcf8506ecda2f7b4f302"

SRC_URI =
"git://github.com/yoctocookbook2ndedition/helloworld.git;protocol=https"

PV = "1.0+git${SRCPV}"
SRCREV = "34d80d900550333d23c1b9193d6569298fb0e968"

S = "${WORKDIR}/git"

do_compile () {
        oe_runmake
}

do_install () {
    install -d ${D}${bindir}
    install -m 0755 helloworld ${D}${bindir}
}
```

We can now build the package with the following command:

```
$ devtool build helloworld
NOTE: Starting bitbake server...Loading cache: 100%
|#######################################################################
########################| Time: 0:00:02
Loaded 2269 entries from dependency cache.
Parsing recipes: 100%
|#######################################################################
#######################| Time: 0:00:06
Parsing of 1658 .bb files complete (1656 cached, 2 parsed). 2271 targets,
192 skipped, 0 masked, 0 errors.
```

```
NOTE: Resolving any missing task queue dependencies
Initialising tasks: 100%
|##################################################################
###################| Time: 0:00:00
Checking sstate mirror object availability: 100%
|##################################################################|
Time: 0:00:00
NOTE: Executing SetScene Tasks
NOTE: Executing RunQueue Tasks
NOTE: helloworld: compiling from external source tree
/home/alex/poky_sdk/workspace/sources/helloworld
NOTE: Tasks Summary: Attempted 443 tasks of which 436 didn't need to be
rerun and all succeeded.
```

Next, we will deploy it into the target to test. Assuming we have an SSH server running on the target, we can do the following:

```
$ devtool deploy-target helloworld root@<ipaddress>:/bin
```

The preceding line will only deploy the new package. If it has dependencies on other packages in the devtool workspace, we can also build a whole image and program it into the target with the following command:

```
$ devtool build-image core-image-base
```

Once it is tested, we finish working on the package with the final recipe being copied to its final location on the ~/poky_sdk/layers/meta-custom layer:

```
$ devtool finish helloworld meta-custom
NOTE: Starting bitbake server...Loading cache: 100%
|##################################################################
########################| Time: 0:00:00
Loaded 2269 entries from dependency cache.Parsing recipes: 100%
|##################################################################
######################| Time: 0:00:04
Parsing of 1658 .bb files complete (1656 cached, 2 parsed). 2271 targets,
192 skipped, 0 masked, 0 errors.
NOTE: Updating SRCREV in recipe helloworld_git.bb
NOTE: Moving recipe file to /home/alex/poky_sdk/layers/meta-custom/recipes-
example/helloworld
NOTE: Leaving source tree /home/alex/poky_sdk/workspace/sources/helloworld
as-is; if you no longer need it then please delete it manually
```

How it works...

The most common syntax for `devtool` is the following:

```
$ devtool <subcommad>
```

Each subcommand's `help` syntax can be displayed with the following command:

```
$ devtool <subcommand> --help
```

The workspace layer

`Devtool` uses a workspace layer where all the new or edited recipes are added. This workspace layer can either be explicitly created, or it will be automatically created when needed. The following command will create a workspace layer:

```
$ devtool create-workspace <dest-path>
```

If no destination path is provided, `devtool` will create it under the build project with the default `workspace` name as shown in the next image:

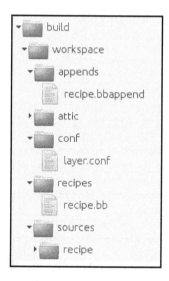

Workspace layer directory hierarchy

Recipe development workflow

The most common workflow when developing recipes is shown next:

1. `add`/`modify`/`upgrade`, these commands will either add a new recipe, modify an existing one, or upgrade an existing one to a newer version
2. `edit-recipe`, this command will edit a recipe after it has been added to the workspace layer by the `devtool` sub-commands shown previously
3. `build`/`build-image`, these commands will build the recipe or a full image containing the recipe
4. `deploy-target`, we will use this command to deploy the built package into the target so we can test it
5. `finish`, with this command we finish work on the recipe

Adding a recipe to the workspace layer

To create a new recipe we use the following syntax:

```
$ devtool add <recipe-name> <source path> <fetch-uri>
```

Here,

- `recipe-name` is the name of the recipe
- `source path` is the local path to the source code
- `fetch-uri` is the URI to fetch the source from if it does not exist locally

New recipes are added to the `recipes` folder on the workspace layer. When creating a new recipe, the source code can either be fetched from a URI and placed on the `source path` or must already exist locally in the `source path`. If the `source path` is not provided, `devtool` will store it in the `source` folder on the workspace layer.

 The `devtool add` sub-command is a wrapper around the `recipetool create` command-line utility.

Existing recipes can also be added to the workspace layer. Find the recipe you are interested in by providing a regular expression pattern with the following command:

```
$ devtool search <pattern>
```

`Devtool` can then extract the source of an existing recipe, set it up as a Git repository with a specified branch name or a `devtool` branch by default, and apply the patches from the existing recipe. We do all of those steps with the `modify` sub-command, as follows:

```
$ devtool modify <recipe-name>
```

Finally, instead of modifying an existing recipe, it can be upgraded to a new upstream version with the following command:

```
$ devtool upgrade <recipe-name> <source path>
```

Again, if no source code path is specified the `sources` folder inside the workspace layer will be used. Alternatively, if the source for the recipe is fetched from Git the following command is used:

```
$ devtool upgrade <recipe-name> --srcrev <git-sha1> --srcbranch <git-branch> <source path>
```

Here,

- `recipe-name` is the name of the recipe
- `git-sha1` is the git revision to check out
- `git-branch` is the git branch to use
- `source path` is the local path to store the source code into

Recipes added to the workspace layer can be listed, along with their respective source code paths, with the following command:

```
$ devtool status
```

Removing a recipe from the workspace layer

A recipe can be erased from the workspace layer with the following command:

```
$ devtool reset <recipe-name>
```

Unless told otherwise, it will also remove the recipe files from the sysroot. Recipes must have been copied out of the workspace layer and into their final location layer before running this command, otherwise changes could be lost. `Devtool` is smart enough to make a backup copy inside the `attic` directory if it detects that the recipe or `append` files have been modified.

Modifying a recipe in the workspace layer

To edit a recipe after it has been added to the workspace layer you do the following:

```
$ devtool edit-recipe <recipe-name>
```

The previous code uses the default editor as defined in the EDITOR environmental variable.

Building and testing your recipe

During development, devtool can build the recipe in the working directory with the following syntax:

```
$ devtool build <recipe-name>
```

It can then be copied to the target via SSH with the following command:

```
$ devtool deploy-target <recipe-name> <user>@<target-ip>[:<destdir>]
```

Here,

- recipe-name is the name of the recipe
- user is the SSH username to log in with
- target-ip is the IP address of the target device that is running the SSH server
- destdir is the destination path in the target device

This is the equivalent to performing a do_install over SSH, so no dependencies are managed as this process does not use the package manager. Once the testing is finished, the deployed files can be removed with the following syntax:

```
$ devtool undeploy-target <recipe-name> <user>@<target-ip>[:<destdir>]
```

Alternatively, devtool can also add the recipe to an image with the following command:

```
$ devtool build-image -p <packages> <target-image-name>
```

Here,

- packages is a list of packages to add to the image. If no specific packages are provided, all recipes available in the workspace layer are added.
- target-image-name is the name of the output image.

Updating a recipe with your changes

Once all modifications have been tested and committed to the source Git repository in the workspace layer, `devtool` can be instructed to create patches for the modifications and update the original recipe with them by running:

```
$ devtool update-recipe <recipe-name>
```

It can also be instructed to create or modify a bbappend on a specific layer instead of modifying the original layer with:

```
$ devtool update-recipe --append <dest-layer-path> <recipe-name>
```

Here,

- `dest-layer-path` is the path to the layer to modify
- `recipe-name` is the name of the recipe

Finishing work on a recipe

The `finish` command will perform the equivalent action to `update-recipe` followed by a `reset`:

```
$ devtool finish <recipe-name> <dest-layer-path>
```

There's more...

One interesting feature of the extensible SDK is that it can be updated. This is especially useful when sharing the SDK between a group of application developers. All we need is a web server to serve the SDK, and to configure the SDK with its URL, for example:

```
SDK_UPDATE_URL = "http://example.com/sdk"
```

When new or modified meta-data or configuration changes are introduced in an SDK and it is rebuilt, we can easily distribute it to all users of the SDK. First, we need to publish the SDK to a location where it is served by a HTTP(S) web server with the following syntax:

```
$ oe-publish-sdk tmp/deploy/sdk/poky-glibc-x86_64-core-image-sato-
cortexa9hf-neon-toolchain-ext-2.4.sh /path/to/web/root
```

Then, we instruct SDK users to update it as follows:

```
$ devtool sdk-update <server>
```

Here, `server` defaults to the `SDK_UPDATE_URL` configured in the SDK. If it was not configured, a remote server could still be specified.

Using the Eclipse IDE

Eclipse is an open source IDE that is written mostly in Java and released under the **Eclipse Public License** (**EPL**). It can be extended using plugins and the Yocto Project releases a Yocto plugin that allows to use Eclipse for Yocto application development.

Getting ready

Yocto 2.4 provides Eclipse Yocto plugins for three different Eclipse versions: Mars, Neon and Oxygen. They can be downloaded at `http://downloads.yoctoproject.org/releases/yocto/yocto-2.4/eclipse-plugin/`. We will use Oxygen, but the instructions are compatible with all versions. We will start with the Eclipse IDE for C/C++ developers and install all the required plugins we need.

It is recommended to run Eclipse under Oracle Java 1.8, although other Java providers are supported. You can install Oracle Java 1.8 from Oracle's web site, `https://www.java.com/en/`, or using a Ubuntu Java Installer PPA, `https://launchpad.net/~webupd8team/+archive/ubuntu/java`. The latter will integrate Java with your package management system, so it's preferred. To install it, follow these steps:

```
$ sudo add-apt-repository ppa:webupd8team/java
$ sudo apt-get update
$ sudo apt-get install oracle-java8-installer
```

You can verify Java is correctly installed by doing the following:

```
$ java -version
java version "1.8.0_144"
Java(TM) SE Runtime Environment (build 1.8.0_144-b01)
Java HotSpot(TM) 64-Bit Server VM (build 25.144-b01, mixed mode)
```

To download and install the Eclipse Oxygen IDE for C/C++ developers for an x86_64 Linux host, follow these steps:

1. Fetch the tarball from the Eclipse download site, `http://www.eclipse.org/downloads/packages/release/Oxygen/1A`. For example:

```
$ wget -O eclipse-cpp-oxygen-1a-linux-gtk-x86_64.tar.gz
"http://mirror.kumi.systems/eclipse/technology/epp/downloads/releas
e/oxygen/1a/eclipse-cpp-oxygen-1a-linux-gtk-x86_64.tar.gz"
```

2. Unpack it to a location of your choice, as follows:

```
$ tar xvf  eclipse-cpp-neon-3-linux-gtk-x86_64.tar.gz
```

3. Start the Eclipse IDE with the following:

```
$ nohup eclipse/eclipse &
```

4. Close the **Welcome** tab and select **Install New Software** from the **Help** pull-down menu. Then, select the **Oxygen** `http://download.eclipse.org/releases/oxygen` source.

5. Install the following Eclipse components:

- Mobile and device development:
  - C/C++ Remote (Over TCF/TE) Run/Debug Launcher
  - Remote System Explorer User Actions
  - TM Terminal via Remote System Explorer add-in
  - TCF Remote System Explorer add-in
  - TCF Target Explorer

- Programming languages:
  - C/C++ Development Tools SDK

6. Install the Eclipse Yocto plugin by adding this repository source: `http://downloads.yoctoproject.org/releases/eclipse-plugin/2.4/oxygen`, as shown in the following screenshot:

| Name: | Eclipse Yocto plugin | Local... |
| Location: | http://downloads.yoctoproject.org/releases/eclips | Archive... |

Add Repository window

7. Choose the **Yocto Project SDK plug-in** option.

Finally, make sure all the components are up-to-date by checking the **Help** | **Check for Updates** menu option.

How to do it...

To configure Eclipse to use a Yocto toolchain, go to **Window** | **Preferences** | **Yocto Project SDK**. The SDK configuration offers two cross-compiler options:

1. **Standalone pre-built toolchain**: Choose this when you have installed a Yocto SDK including a toolchain
2. **Build system derived toolchain**: Choose this when using a Yocto build directory prepared with `meta-ide-support` as explained previously

It also offers two target options:

1. **QEMU**: Choose this if you are using Poky with a virtualized machine like `qemuarm`.
2. **External HW**: Choose this if you are using real hardware like the Wandboard hardware. This option is the most useful for embedded development.

An example configuration when using a downloaded Yocto SDK installer would be to choose the **Standalone pre-built toolchain** option along with the **QEMU** emulator as follows:

- **Cross Compiler Options**:
  - **Standalone pre-built toolchain**:
    - **Toolchain Root Location**: `/opt/poky/2.4`
    - **Sysroot Location**: `/opt/poky/2.4/sysroots/armv5e-poky-linux-gnueabi`
    - **Target Architecture**: `armv5e-poky-linux-gnueabi`
  - **Target Options**:
    - **QEMU Kernel**: `/opt/poky/2.4/sysroots/armv5e-poky-linux-gnueabi/zImage-qemuarm.bin`

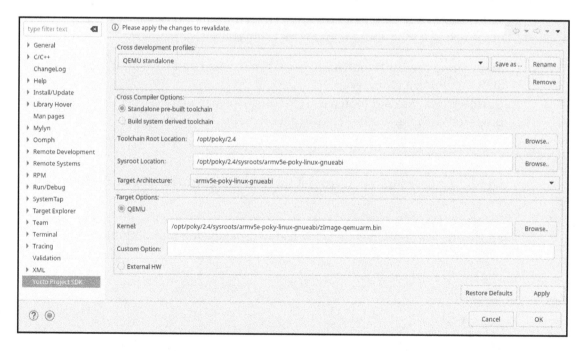

Yocto Project SDK plugin Standalone pre-built toolchain QEMU configuration

To use the **QEMU** emulator with the **Standalone pre-built toolchain**, we need to download the following into the configured `sysroot` directory:

- **The qemuboot configuration file**:
  `http://downloads.yoctoproject.org/releases/yocto/yocto-2.4/machines/qemu/qemuarm/core-image-sato-sdk-qemuarm.qemuboot.conf`

  The `runqemu` application will look for this file in the configured `sysroot` directory root and will use it to configure some QEMU defaults. Apart from other defaults, it sets the `qemuarm` machine to `versatilepb` and specifies a device tree to use, as well as setting the default file system type to `ext4`:

  ```
  qb_machine = -machine versatilepb
  qb_dtb = zImage-versatile-pb.dtb
  qb_default_fstype = ext4
  ```

- **A QEMU kernel image**: For example,
  `http://downloads.yoctoproject.org/releases/yocto/yocto-2.4/machines/qemu/qemuarm/zImage-qemuarm.bin`

- **A QEMU ARM versatilepb machine device tree**:
  `http://downloads.yoctoproject.org/releases/yocto/yocto-2.4/machines/qemu/qemuarm/zImage-versatile-pb.dtb`

- **An ext4 root filesystem SDK image**: For example, `core-image-sato-sdk`:
  `http://downloads.yoctoproject.org/releases/yocto/yocto-2.4/machines/qemu/qemuarm/core-image-sato-sdk-qemuarm.ext4`

 Make sure the file permissions are set so that Eclipse has read/write access to them.

You will then be able to run QEMU using the **Run** I **External Tools** I **External Tools Configurations** I **Run** menu:

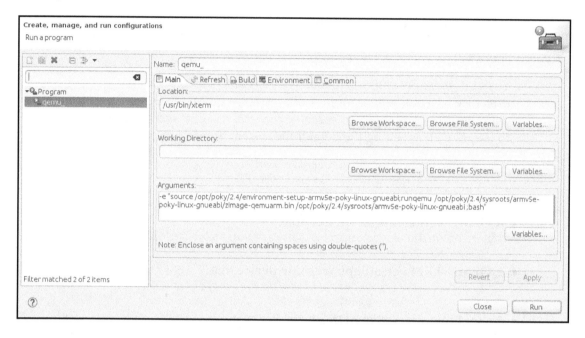

Create, manage, and run configurations
Run a program

Name: qemu_

☐ Main ⟳ Refresh 🔨 Build 🖥 Environment ☐ Common

Location:
/usr/bin/xterm

[Browse Workspace...] [Browse File System...] [Variables...]

Working Directory:

[Browse Workspace...] [Browse File System...] [Variables...]

Arguments:
-e "source /opt/poky/2.4/environment-setup-armv5e-poky-linux-gnueabi;runqemu /opt/poky/2.4/sysroots/armv5e-poky-linux-gnueabi/zImage-qemuarm.bin /opt/poky/2.4/sysroots/armv5e-poky-linux-gnueabi ;bash"

[Variables...]

Note: Enclose an argument containing spaces using double-quotes (").

Filter matched 2 of 2 items   [Revert] [Apply]

⊙   [Close] [Run]

External tool configuration window

For a build system derived toolchain using the `wandboard` reference board, we first need to configure the project as follows:

```
$ cd /opt/yocto/fsl-community-bsp
$ source setup-environment wandboard
$ bitbake meta-ide-support
```

Then, we can configure the Eclipse Yocto plugin as shown next:

- **Cross Compiler Options**:
    - **Build system derived toolchain**:
        - **Toolchain Root Location**: /opt/yocto/fsl-community-bsp/wandboard
        - **Sysroot Location**: /opt/yocto/fsl-community-bsp/wandboard/tmp/sysroots/wandboard

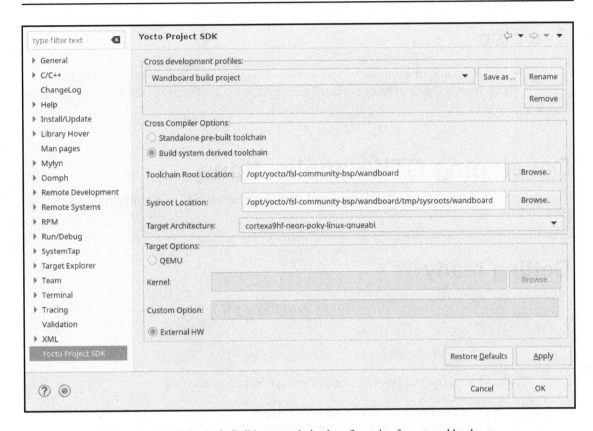

Yocto Project SDK plugin Build system-derived configuration for external hardware

Finally, we can configure to a **Standalone pre-built toolchain** for the Wandboard that we have previously compiled and installed too. We will see an example of this configuration in the next sections.

There's more...

In order to perform debugging on a remote target, it needs to be running the `tcf-agent` daemon. It is included by default on the `-sdk` images, but you can also include it in any other image by adding the following to your `conf/local.conf` file:

```
EXTRA_IMAGE_FEATURES += "eclipse-debug"
```

See also

- For more information, refer to the *Yocto Project Software Development Kit (SDK) Developer's Guide* at `http://www.yoctoproject.org/docs/2.4/sdk-manual/sdk-manual.html`

Developing GTK+ applications

This recipe will show how to build, run, and debug a graphical GTK+ application using the Eclipse IDE.

Getting ready

1. Add the `eclipse-debug` feature to your project's `conf/local.conf` file, as follows:

   ```
   EXTRA_IMAGE_FEATURES += "eclipse-debug"
   ```

2. Build a `core-image-sato` target image, as follows:

   ```
   $ cd /opt/yocto/fsl-community-bsp/
   $ source setup-environment wandboard
   $ bitbake core-image-sato
   ```

3. Build a `core-image-sato` toolchain with the following command:

   ```
   $ bitbake -c populate_sdk core-image-sato
   ```

4. Install the toolchain by running the installer, as follows:

   ```
   $ cd tmp/deploy/sdk
   $ ./poky-glibc-x86_64-core-image-sato-cortexa9hf-neon-toolchain-2.4.sh
   ```

Before launching the Eclipse IDE, we can check whether we are able to build and launch a GTK application manually. We will build the following GTK+ `hello world` application source. The following is the code in `gtk_hello_world.c`:

```
#include <gtk/gtk.h>

int main(int argc, char *argv[])
{
  GtkWidget *window;
  gtk_init (&argc, &argv);
  window = gtk_window_new (GTK_WINDOW_TOPLEVEL);
  gtk_widget_show (window);
  gtk_main ();
  return 0;
}
```

To build it, we use the `core-image-sato` toolchain installed as described previously:

```
$ source /opt/poky/2.4/environment-setup-cortexa9hf-neon-poky-linux-gnueabi
$ ${CC} gtk_hello_world.c -o helloworld `pkg-config --cflags --libs
  gtk+-3.0`
```

This command uses the `pkg-config` helper tool to read the `.pc` files that are installed with the GTK libraries in the `sysroot` to determine which compiler switches (`--cflags` for `include` directories and `--libs` for libraries to link with) are needed to compile programs that use GTK. We can manually copy the resulting binary to our Wandboard, while booting `core-image-sato` over NFS, and run it from the target's console with the following command:

```
# DISPLAY=:0 helloworld
```

This will open a GTK+ window over the SATO desktop.

How to do it...

We can now configure the Eclipse SDK plugin using the standalone toolchain as described before, or we could decide to use the **Build system derived toolchain** instead:

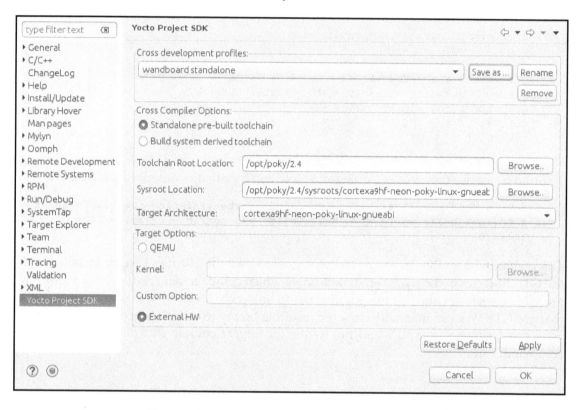

Yocto Project SDK standalone configuration for Wandboard

Follow the next steps to build and run an example `hello world` application:

1. Create a new hello world GTK autotools project. Accept all the defaults in the Project creation wizard. Browse to **File | New | C/C++ Project | C Managed Build | Yocto Project SDK Autotools Project | Hello World GTK C Autotools Project**:

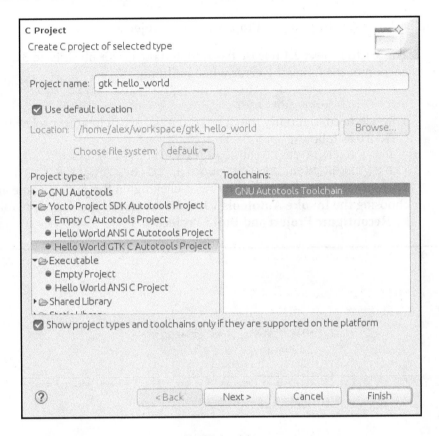

C Project
Create C project of selected type

Project name: [gtk_hello_world]

☑ Use default location

Location: [/home/alex/workspace/gtk_hello_world]   [Browse...]

Choose file system: [default ▾]

Project type: Toolchains:

▸ 🗁 GNU Autotools   [GNU Autotools Toolchain]
▾ 🗁 Yocto Project SDK Autotools Project
   ● Empty C Autotools Project
   ● Hello World ANSI C Autotools Project
   ● Hello World GTK C Autotools Project
▾ 🗁 Executable
   ● Empty Project
   ● Hello World ANSI C Project
▸ 🗁 Shared Library

☑ Show project types and toolchains only if they are supported on the platform

[?]   [< Back] [Next >] [Cancel]   [Finish]

New C Project window

When choosing a name for your project, avoid using special characters like dashes or spaces, as they could cause problems with the build tools.

Build the project by going to **Project** | **Build Project**.

The Yocto Project 2.4 release has updated the GTK+ libraries to 3.0. If you encounter the following error while building:

```
configure: error: Package requirements (glib-2.0
gtk+-2.0) were not met
```

You will need to modify the `configure.ac` script in your project to use GTK+3.0 as follows:

```
- PKG_CHECK_MODULES(helloworld, glib-2.0 gtk+-2.0)
+ PKG_CHECK_MODULES(helloworld, glib-2.0 gtk+-3.0)
```

Then, reconfigure the project by right-clicking on the project name and choosing the **Invoke Autotools** | **Invoke Autoconf** menu option, followed by **Reconfigure Project** and **Build Project**.

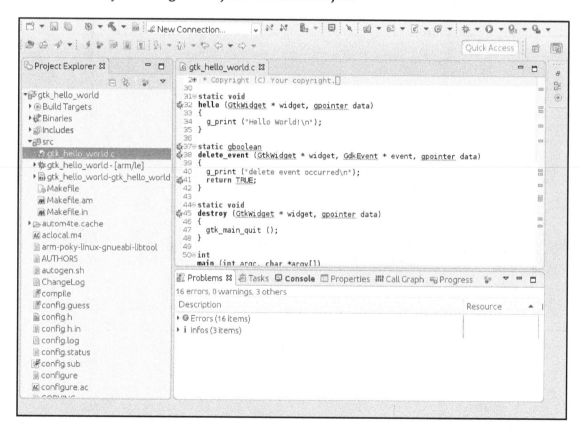

Eclipse displaying symbol resolution errors

2. Even though the project builds successfully, you may see errors both marked in the source and in the **Problems** tab. This is because Eclipse's code analysis feature cannot resolve all the project's symbols. To resolve it, add the needed `include` header files to your project's properties by going to **Project | Properties | C/C++ General | Paths and Symbols | Includes**:

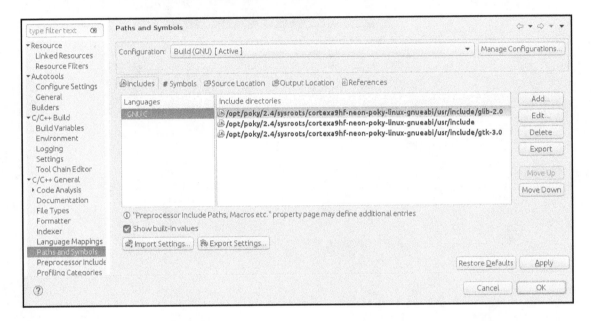

Paths and Symbols configuration window with the new filesystem paths added

 If the index is not automatically rebuilt, you can trigger it with **Project | C/C++ Index | Rebuild**.

3. We will now create a new connection to the target. Click on the **New Connection** menu on the top bar and choose **Generic Connection**:

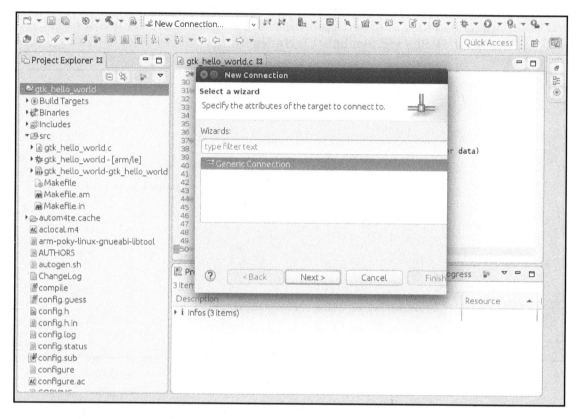

New Connection window

4. In the next window, press the **Browse** button to the right of the **Connection Name** field. This will autodetect the TCF target running on the device and list it along with its IP address as in the next screenshot:

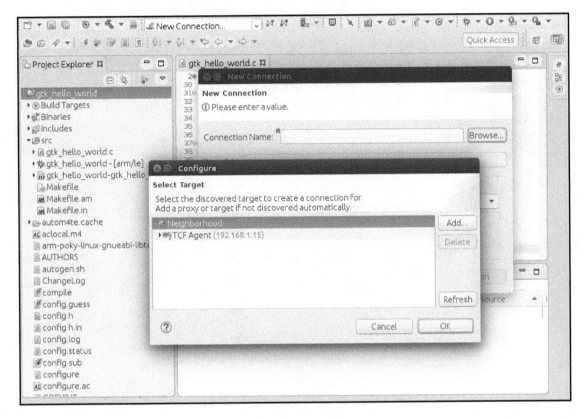

Autodetected TCF agent on the 192.168.1.15 Wandboard device

5. Under **Run | Run Configurations**, you should have **C/C++ Remote Application** with a target called `<project_name>_gdb_arm-poky-linux-gnueabi`. If you don't, create one:

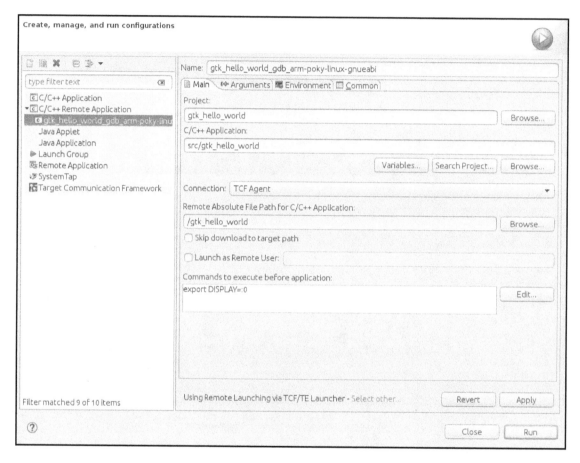

C/C++ Remote Application run configuration window

6. At the bottom of the window, click on **Select other** to select one of the multiple launchers available:

- **Remote Launching via TCF/TE Launcher**
- **Legacy Remote Create Process Launcher**

The first will use the TCF connection previously configured, but the second one, which will use an SSH connection to the target can also be used.

7. To configure an SSH connection, click on the **New** button to the right of the **Connection** drop-down menu.

> If you have problems logging into the device and you have built a target image using the `debug-tweaks` feature for password-less logins, try setting a root password and using it as the tool may not be able to log in with an empty password.

8. Locate the C/C++ application to launch by clicking on the **Search Project** button.
9. Next, modify the **Remote Absolute File Path for C/C++ Application** to an existing remote path on the target device, for example `/gtk_hello_world`.
10. In the **Commands to execute before application** field, enter the following:

```
export DISPLAY=:0
```

> At the time of writing, the TCF launcher did not allow us to add a command to execute before launching the application, failing instead with the following error:
> ```
> Failed to create script with the Commands before launch
> in
> '/home/alex/workspace/.metadata/.plugins/org.eclipse.tcf.
> te.tcf.launch.cdt/prerun_commands_scripts/00-03-59-716_gt
> k_hello_world.sh'. Possibly caused by: Failed to read the
> Commands before launch script template 'null'.
> ```
> The TCF launcher patch that fixes it has not yet made it to the Oxygen update channel:
> ```
> http://git.eclipse.org/c/gerrit/tcf/org.eclipse.tcf.git/commit/?
> h=1.4_neon_bugfixid=c54f26b7e07319b7ad309aab8c02b72be6d1afff
> ```
> As a workaround, the `DISPLAY` variable can be added to the **Environment** tab instead.

11. Run the application and, if you are using SSH, log in as `root` with an empty password. You should see the GTK application on your SATO desktop and the following output in the **Console** tab:

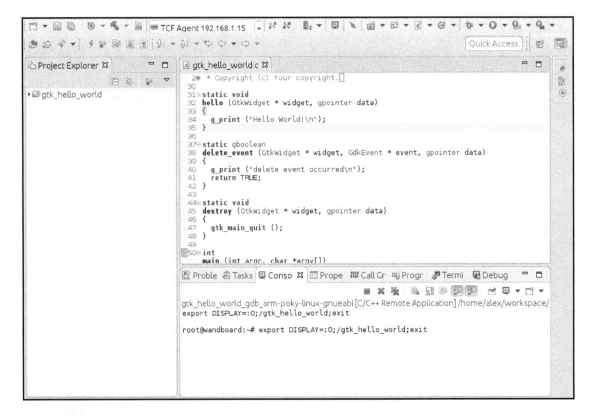

Console output showing the remote application being executed

If you have problems connecting to the target, verify that it is running `tcf-agent` by typing in the following on the target's console:

```
# ps w | grep tcf
735 root    11428S    /usr/sbin/tcf-agent -d -L- -10
```

If you have login problems, you can use Eclipse's **Remote System Explorer** (**RSE**) perspective to clear passwords and debug the connection to the target. Once the connection can be established and you are able to browse the target's filesystem through RSE, you can come back to the run configuration.

There's more...

To debug the application, follow these steps:

1. Double-click on the `main` function in the source file to add a breakpoint. A blue dot will appear on the side-bar.
2. Go to **Run | Debug Configuration**.
3. Under the **Debugger** tab, verify the GDB debugger path is the correct toolchain debugger location:

```
/opt/poky/2.4/sysroots/x86_64-pokysdk-linux/usr/bin/arm-poky-
linux-gnueabi/arm-poky-linux-gnueabi-gdb
```

If it isn't, point it to the correct location:

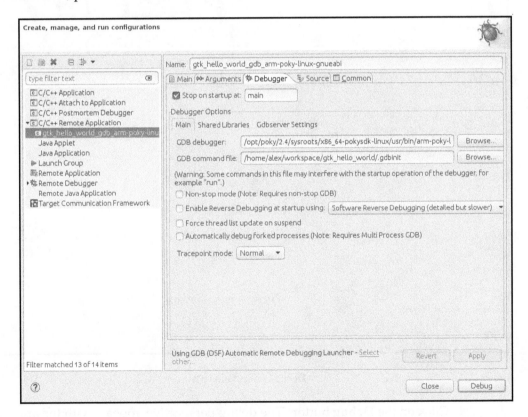

Debug Configuration window

On the **Main** tab, you can also choose between multiple launchers:

- **GDB (DSF) Automatic Remote Debugging Launcher**
- **GDB (DSF) Automatic Remote Debugger Launcher via TCF/TE Launcher**

Again, the first will use an SSH connection and the second will use the TCF connection:

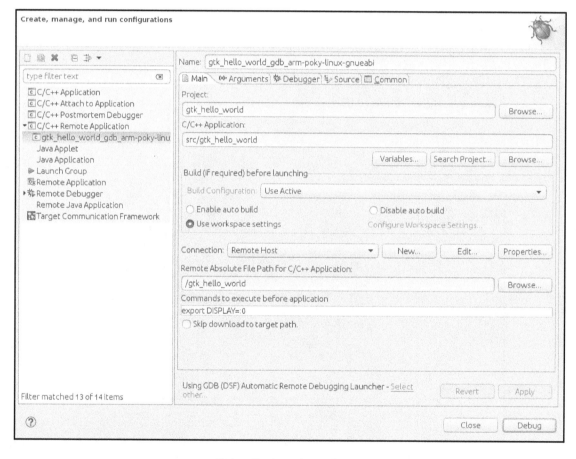

Debug Configuration Main tab

4. Click on the **Debug** button. The debug perspective appears with the application executing on the remote Wandboard hardware:

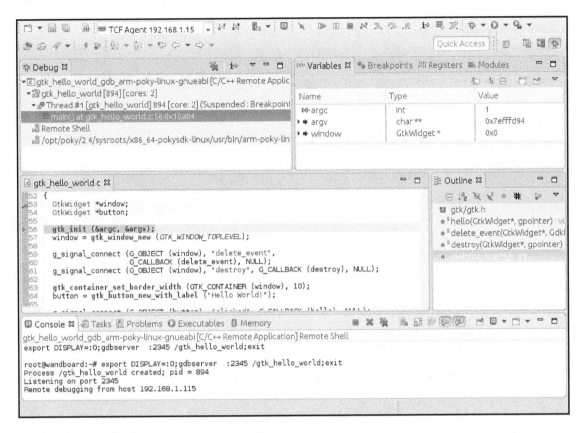

Debug Perspective window

If you get **Text file busy** error, remember to close the application we ran in the previous step.

Using the Qt Creator IDE

Qt is a cross-platform application framework written in C++ and developed both by Digia, under the Qt company name, and by the open source Qt project community. Qt Creator is a multiplatform IDE and part of the Qt application development framework SDK. It is the IDE of choice for Qt application development in C++ and QML and is available with multiple licenses, including (L)GPLv3, and commercial licenses as well.

Getting ready

Download and install the Qt Creator 4.5.0 for your host from the Qt project downloads website. To download and install into your x86_64 Linux host, you can use the following commands:

```
$ wget
http://download.qt.io/official_releases/qtcreator/4.5/4.5.0/qt-creator-open
source-linux-x86_64-4.5.0.run
$ chmod u+x qt-creator-opensource-linux-x86_64-4.5.0.run
$ ./qt-creator-opensource-linux-x86_64-4.5.0.run
```

Qt support in Yocto 2.4 has been moved to the external `meta-qt4` and `meta-qt5` layers:

- `http://git.yoctoproject.org/cgit/cgit.cgi/meta-qt4`
- `https://github.com/meta-qt5/meta-qt5`

In order to work with Qt, we first need to clone the corresponding layer into our `sources` directory. We will install the `meta-qt5` layer, as follows:

```
$ cd /opt/yocto/fsl-community-bsp/sources/
$ git clone https://github.com/meta-qt5/meta-qt5 -b rocko
```

Then, we will add it to our `conf/bblayers.conf` file in our build directory:

```
+ ${BSPDIR}/sources/meta-qt5 \
```

The `meta-qt5` layer includes a `meta-toolchain-qt5` recipe that can be used to build a Qt5-ready SDK including a target sysroot with the corresponding Qt5 libraries, headers, and a toolchain with Qt tools. However, as with the `meta-toolchain` target introduced before, this toolchain will not match the root filesystem of your target image. To build `meta-toolchain-qt5` you do the following:

```
$ cd /opt/yocto/fsl-community-bsp/
$ source setup-environment wandboard
$ bitbake meta-toolchain-qt5
```

However, the recommended way to create a Qt5 SDK is to add the following to your image recipe:

```
inherit populate_sdk_qt5
```

For example, we could extend the `core-image-sato` image from Poky with a `recipes-sato/images/core-image-sato.bbappend` in our `meta-custom` layer that included the preceding line. Then, we could build the SDK with:

```
$ bitbake -c populate_sdk core-image-sato
```

> If you see the build fail with the following error when building:
> `ERROR: custom-image-1.0-r0 do_populate_sdk: Could not invoke dnf.`
> Swap to using the IPK package format by adding the following to your `conf/local.conf`:
> `PACKAGE_CLASSES = "package_ipk"`
> A different workaround for this problem is to remove the `nativesdk-cmake` package from your toolchain by adding the following to your `conf/local.conf` configuration file:
> `RDEPENDS_nativesdk-packagegroup-sdk-host_remove = "nativesdk-cmake"`

Finally, to install it we do the following:

```
$ cd tmp/deploy/sdk
$ ./poky-glibc-x86_64-core-image-sato-cortexa9hf-neon-toolchain-2.4.sh
```

How to do it...

Before launching Qt Creator, we need to set up the development environment by sourcing the environment setup script:

```
$ . /opt/poky/2.4/environment-setup-cortexa9hf-neon-poky-linux-gnueabi
```

Now, we can run Qt Creator from the same Terminal as follows:

```
$ ./bin/qtcreator.sh &
```

Then, we can configure it by going to **Tools | Options** and using the following steps:

1. First, we configure a new device for our Wandboard. Under **Devices | Add**, we select **Generic Linux Device**:

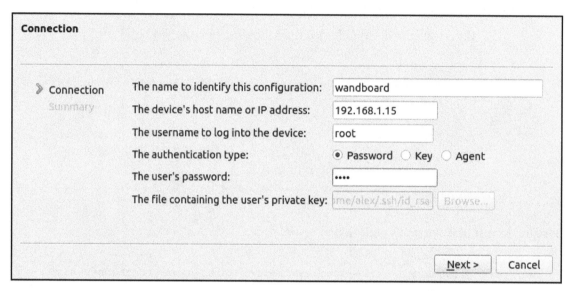

Wandboard device connection settings

The wizard will test the configured connection with your device so it should be running Linux.

If your target images were created with the debug-tweaks image feature, you will be able to log in to the system with an empty password. Otherwise, set the root password in the target by using the passwd command from the target's root console and type it in the password field.

2. Under **Build & Run**, we configure new C and C++ compilers pointing to the Yocto compiler path we just installed by doing **Add | GCC.**

3. Here's the path for the C compiler, as shown in the following screenshot:

```
/opt/poky/2.4/sysroots/x86_64-pokysdk-linux/usr/bin/arm-poky-
linux-gnueabi/arm-poky-linux-gnueabi-gcc
```

If the **ABI** is not auto-selected, choose `arm-linux-generic-elf-32bit` and click **Apply**.

4. For the C++ compiler, use the following:

```
/opt/poky/2.4/sysroots/x86_64-pokysdk-linux/usr/bin/arm-poky-
linux-gnueabi/arm-poky-linux-gnueabi-g++
```

If the **ABI** is not auto-selected, choose `arm-linux-generic-elf-32bit`, and click **Apply**:

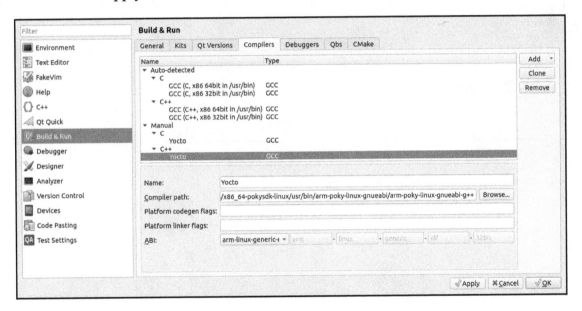

Device Compiler Configuration window

5. Similarly for a cross-debugger, the following is the path which is also mentioned in the following screenshot:

```
/opt/poky/2.4/sysroots/x86_64-pokysdk-linux/usr/bin/arm-poky-
linux-gnueabi/arm-poky-linux-gnueabi-gdb
```

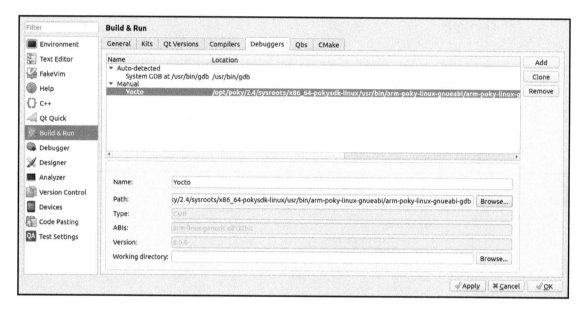

Device Debugger Configuration window

6. Then, we configure **Qt Versions** by selecting the `qmake` builder from the toolchain. Here's the path, which is also mentioned in the following screenshot:

```
/opt/poky/2.4/sysroots/x86_64-pokysdk-linux/usr/bin/qt5/qmake
```

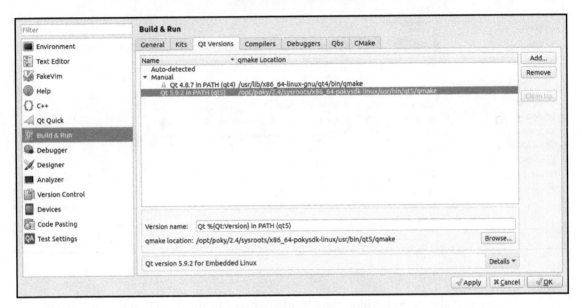

Qmake builder selection screen

Finally, we configure a new kit, as follows:

1. Select Generic Linux Device and configure its Sysroot to:

```
/opt/poky/2.4/sysroots/cortexa9hf-neon-poky-linux-gnueabi
```

2. Select the Compiler, Debugger, and Qt version we just defined:

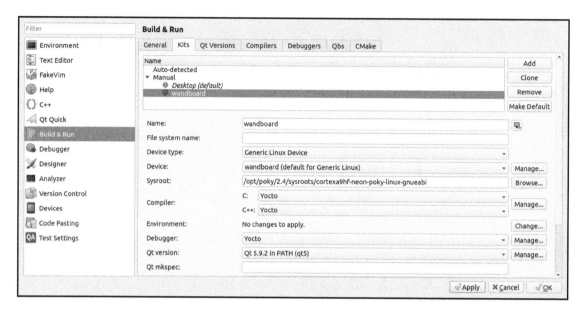

Kit configuration window

3. You will also need to fill in the **Qt mkspec** (configurations that define a build environment) line with `linux-oe-g++`. This is the name of the OpenEmbedded cross-compilation platform in `meta-qt5`.

> In Ubuntu, Qt Creator stores its configuration on the user's `home` directory under `.config/QtProject/`. Removing this directory will remove all the Qt Creator configuration

Developing Qt applications

This recipe will show how to build, run, and debug a graphical Qt application using Qt Creator.

Getting ready

Before launching Qt Creator, we check whether we are able to build and launch a Qt application manually. We will build a Qt hello world application. Here is the code for qt_hello_world.cpp:

```
#include <QApplication>
#include <QPushButton>

int main(int argc, char *argv[])
{
    QApplication app(argc, argv);

    QPushButton hello("Hello world!");

    hello.show();
    return app.exec();
}
```

To build it, we use the SDK installed, as described previously:

```
$ . /opt/poky/2.4/environment-setup-cortexa9hf-neon-poky-linux-gnueabi
$ qmake -project
$ qmake
```

This uses qmake to create a project file and a Makefile file with all the relevant code files in the directory. We can now build with the following command:

```
$ make
```

The previous build will fail with the following error:
`qt_hello_world.cpp:1:10: fatal error: QApplication: No such file or directory`
To fix it, we need to add the following to the auto-generated `qt_hello_world.pro` file:
`QT += widgets`

To run it, we first need to build a filesystem with Qt support. When compiling a Qt application with a Yocto recipe, the build system will automatically install the needed libraries in the target image. On this occasion we will add some Qt example applications to `core-image-base` so the Qt libraries are also installed. We first prepare the environment as follows:

```
$ cd /opt/yocto/fsl-community-bsp/
$ source setup-environment wandboard
```

Then, we configure our project so that the `qtbase-examples` package is built and included in the image by adding the following to the `conf/local.conf` file:

```
PACKAGECONFIG_append_pn-qtbase = " fontconfig examples"
IMAGE_INSTALL_append = " qtbase-examples"
```

We can then build it with the following command:

```
$ bitbake core-image-sato
```

Once finished, we can program the microSD card image and boot the Wandboard. Copy the `qt_hello_world` binary to the target and run the following:

```
# DISPLAY=:0 qt_hello_world
```

You should see the Qt hello world window on the X11 desktop.

How to do it...

Follow these steps to build and run an example hello world application using Qt Creator:

1. Create a new empty project by going to **File** | **New File or Project** | **Other project** | **Empty qmake project**.

2. Select only the **wandboard** kit we just created:

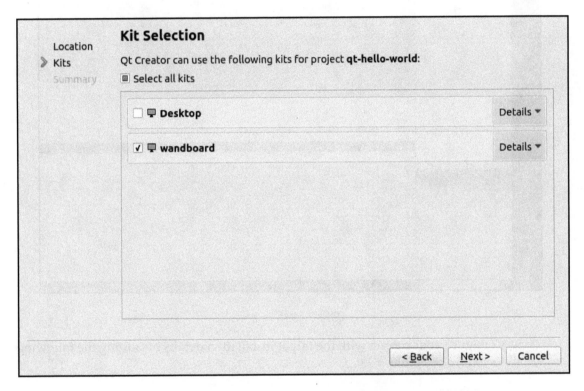

Kit Selection

Location
Kits
Summary

Qt Creator can use the following kits for project **qt-hello-world**:

☒ Select all kits

☐ 🖥 **Desktop**   Details ▾

☑ 🖥 **wandboard**   Details ▾

                                          < _B_ack   _N_ext >   Cancel

Qt Creator Kit Selection window

3. Add a new C++ file, `qt_hello_world.cpp`, by going to **File** | **New File or Project** | **C++** | **C++ Source File**.

4. Paste the contents of the `qt_hello_world.cpp` file into **Qt Creator**, as shown in the following screenshot:

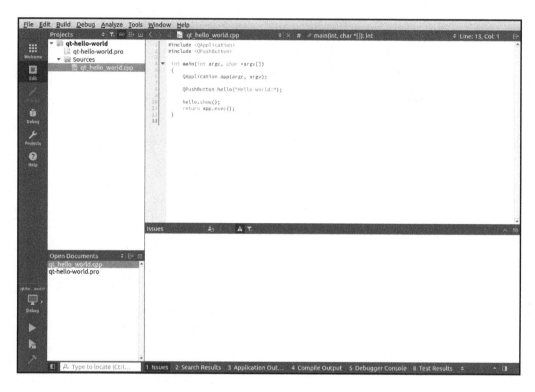

Qt Creator source editing view

5. Configure your project with the target installation details by adding the following to your `hw.pro` file:

```
SOURCES += \
    qt_hello_world.cpp

TARGET =  qt_hello_world
    target.files =  qt_hello_world
    target.path = /

INSTALLS += target
QT += widgets
```

Replace `qt_hello_world` with the name of your project.

6. Build the project. If you have build errors, verify that the Yocto build environment has been correctly set up.

7. Go to **Projects** | **Run** and check your **Project Settings**:

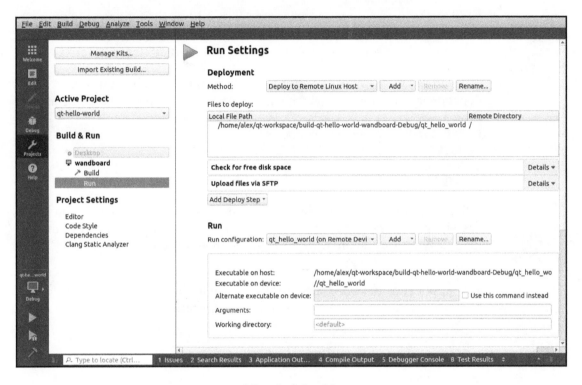

Qt Creator Run Settings window

8. As can be seen in this screenshot, Qt Creator will use the SFTP protocol to transfer the files to the target. By default, the dropbear SSH server running on `core-image-sato` does not have SFTP support. We need to add it to our image to allow Qt Creator to work by adding the `openssh-sftp-server` package to the project's `conf/local.conf` file:

```
IMAGE_INSTALL_append = " openssh-sftp-server"
```

However, there are other tools we will need, like **gdbserver** if we want to debug our application, so it's easier to add the `qtcreator-debug` feature, which will add all of the needed applications to the target image:

```
EXTRA_IMAGE_FEATURES += "qtcreator-debug"
```

You may encounter the following error:

```
Problem: package openssh-sshd-7.5p1-r0.cortexa9hf_neon
conflicts with dropbear provided by dropbear-2017.75-
r0.cortexa9hf_neon
```

Until this is fixed, you can workaround it by adding the following to your `conf/local.conf` configuration file:

```
EXTRA_IMAGE_FEATURES += "qtcreator-debug ssh-server-
openssh "
```

This forces the removal of the `dropbear` package by adding a runtime dependency on `openssh`, which has a defined conflict with `dropbear` as shown next:

```
RCONFLICTS_${PN} = "dropbear"
RCONFLICTS_${PN}-sshd = "dropbear"
```

9. You can now run the project:

If the application fails to be deployed with a login error, verify that you have built with the `debug-tweaks` image feature, set a root password in the target or that you are using SSH key authentication.

Once the application has been successfully copied to the device and launched, you will see the following output in the **Application Output** tab:

```
Starting //qt_hello_world...

QStandardPaths: XDG_RUNTIME_DIR not set, defaulting to
'/tmp/runtime-root'
qt.qpa.screen: QXcbConnection: Could not connect to display
Could not connect to any X display.

Application finished with exit code 1.
```

We are missing the code needed to export the `DISPLAY` variable. We can add it to the **Run Environment** configuration under **Projects | Run**:

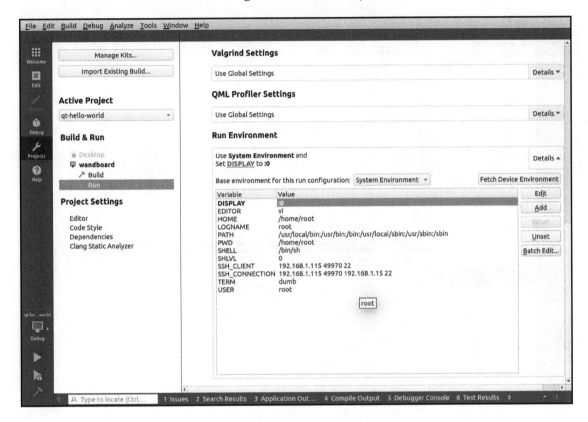

Run Environment settings window

Re-run the application; it is now launched correctly. You should now see the example Qt hello world application running on your SATO desktop:

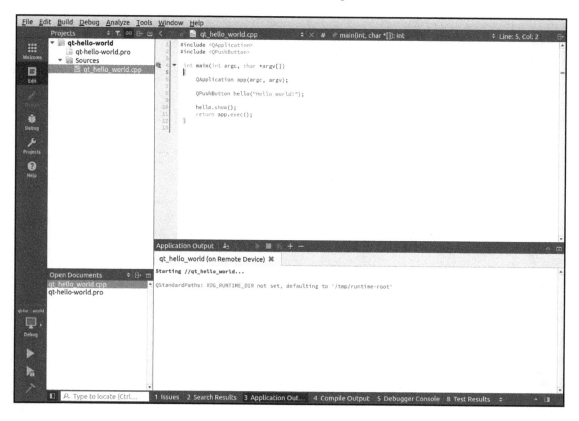

Application Output tab

There's more...

To debug the application, toggle a breakpoint on the source and click on the **Debug** button. A debug session screenshot is shown next:

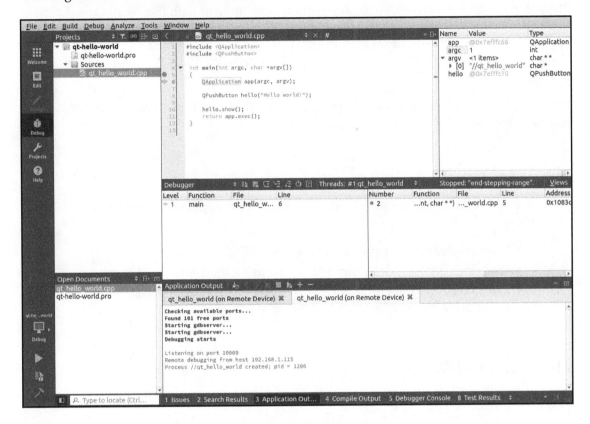

Qt Creator debug view

Describing workflows for application development

The recommended way to approach application development with the Yocto Project is to use either the standard or the extensible Yocto SDK as an iterative interface between the application developers and the system integrators. The latter feed the new software into the Yocto build system to produce and share new SDKs between the application and BSP developers.

However, there are other application development workflows that are useful and these will be introduced next.

How to do it...

We will see how the following development workflows are applied to application development:

- **External development**: When using Yocto SDKs
- **Working directory development**: When using the Yocto build directory
- **External source development**: When using the Yocto build system but configuring an external directory for the source

How it works...

Let's see how the different development workflows work in more detail.

External development

This workflow uses either the standard or the extensible SDKs generated by the Yocto Project. This is what we have been using on the recipes we saw before when building from the command line and also when using both the Eclipse and Qt Creator IDEs. This workflow produces binaries that have to be individually copied to the hardware to be run and debugged. It can be used in conjunction with the other workflows.

This is the recommended workflow for application development especially when using all the features of the full extensible Yocto SDK. Refer to the *Using the extensible SDK* for a detailed explanation.

However, sometimes we are not the main developers of the package and we only want to introduce some fixes or modifications. The two workflows explained in the following sections use the Yocto build system.

Working directory development

When the application is being built by the Yocto build system, we use this workflow to debug sporadic problems. However, this is not the recommended workflow for long developments. We will use the helloworld_1.0.bb custom recipe we saw back in the *Adding new packages* recipe in Chapter 3, *The Software Layer,* meta-custom/recipes-example/helloworld/helloworld_1.0.bb, as an example. The following recipe should already be in your meta-custom layer:

```
DESCRIPTION = "Simple helloworld application"
SECTION = "examples"
LICENSE = "MIT"
LIC_FILES_CHKSUM =
    "file://${COMMON_LICENSE_DIR}/MIT;md5=0835ade698e0bcf8506ecda2f7b4
    f302"

SRC_URI = "file://helloworld.c"

S = "${WORKDIR}"

do_compile() {
            ${CC} ${LDFLAGS} helloworld.c -o helloworld
}

do_install() {
            install -d ${D}${bindir}
            install -m 0755 helloworld ${D}${bindir}
}
```

Here, the helloworld.c source file is the following:

```
#include <stdio.h>

int main(void)
{
    return printf("Hello World");
}
```

The workflow steps are as follows:

1. Start the package compilation from scratch:

   ```
   $ cd /opt/yocto/fsl-community-bsp/
   $ source setup-environment wandboard
   $ bitbake -c cleanall helloworld
   ```

   This will erase the package's build folder, shared state cache, and downloaded package source.

2. Start a development shell:

   ```
   $ bitbake -c devshell helloworld
   ```

   This will fetch, unpack, and patch the helloworld sources and spawn a new shell with the environment ready for compilation. The new shell will change to the package's build directory.

3. Depending on the SRC_URI variable, the package's build directory might be revision-controlled already. If not, as is the case in this example, we will create a local Git repository, as follows:

   ```
   $ git init
   $ git add helloworld.c
   $ git commit -s -m "Original revision"
   ```

4. Perform the modifications we need; for example, change helloworld.c to print Howdy World as follows:

   ```
   #include <stdio.h>

   int main(void)
   {
       return printf("Howdy World");
   }
   ```

5. Exit devshell and build the package without erasing our modifications:

   ```
   $ bitbake -C compile helloworld
   ```

Note the capital C (which invokes the compile task) and also all the tasks that follow it.

6. Test your changes on the hardware by copying the generated package and installing it. Because you have only modified one package, the rest of the dependencies should be already installed in the running root filesystem. Run the following:

```
$ bitbake -e helloworld | grep ^WORKDIR=
WORKDIR="/usr/local/ssd/fsl-community-
bsp/wandboard/tmp/work/cortexa9hf-neon-poky-linux-
gnueabi/helloworld/1.0-r0"
$ scp ${WORKDIR_PATH}/deploy-rpms/cortexa9hf_neon/helloworld-1.0-
r0.cortexa9hf_neon.rpm root@<target_ip_address>:/
```

7. In the target, we install the new package with the following:

```
$ dnf install /helloworld-1.0-r0.cortexa9hf_neon.rpm
```

This assumes the target's root filesystem has been built with the package-management feature and the helloworld package is added to the RM_WORK_EXCLUDE variable when using the rm_work class.

8. Go back to the devshell and commit your change to the local Git repository, as follows:

```
$ bitbake -c devshell helloworld
$ git add helloworld.c
$ git commit -s -m "Change greeting message"
```

9. Generate a patch into the recipe's patch directory:

```
$ git format-patch -1 -o /opt/yocto/fsl-community-
  bsp/sources/meta-custom/recipes-
  example/helloworld/helloworld-1.0
```

10. Finally, add the patch to the recipe's SRC_URI variable, as shown here:

```
-SRC_URI = "file://helloworld.c"
+SRC_URI = "file://helloworld.c \
+           file://0001-Change-greeting-message.patch
+"
```

External source development

This workflow is recommended for development work once the application has been integrated into the Yocto build system. It can be used in conjunction with external development using an IDE, for example. In the sample recipe we saw earlier, the source file was placed on the meta-custom layer along with the metadata. It is more common to have the recipe fetched directly from a revision control system like Git, so we will change the meta-custom/recipes-example/helloworld/helloworld_1.0.bb file to be sourced from a Git directory as follows:

```
DESCRIPTION = "Simple helloworld application"
SECTION = "examples"
LICENSE = "MIT"
LIC_FILES_CHKSUM =
"file://${COMMON_LICENSE_DIR}/MIT;md5=0835ade698e0bcf8506ecda2f7b4f302"

SRCREV = "${AUTOREV}"
SRC_URI = "git://github.com/yoctocookbook2ndedition/helloworld.git"

S = "${WORKDIR}/git"

do_compile() {
          ${CC} ${LDFLAGS} helloworld.c -o helloworld
}

do_install() {
          install -d ${D}${bindir}
          install -m 0755 helloworld ${D}${bindir}
}
```

We can then clone it into a local directory, as follows:

```
$ cd /opt/yocto/
$ git clone git://github.com/yoctocookbook2ndedition/helloworld.git
```

An alternative to using a remote revision-controlled repository it to use a local one. To do so, follow these steps:

1. Create a local Git repository that will hold the source:

   ```
   $ mkdir -p /opt/yocto/helloworld
   $ cd /opt/yocto/helloworld
   $ git init
   ```

2. Copy our `helloworld.c` file over here and add it to the repository:

   ```
   $ git add helloworld.c
   ```

3. Then, commit it with a signature and a message, as follows:

   ```
   $ git commit -s -m "Original revision"
   ```

In any case, we have the version-controlled source in a local directory. We will then configure our `conf/local.conf` file to work from it, as follows:

```
INHERIT += "externalsrc"
EXTERNALSRC_pn-helloworld = "/opt/yocto/helloworld"
EXTERNALSRC_BUILD_pn-helloworld = "/opt/yocto/helloworld"
```

Then, we build it with the following:

```
$ cd /opt/yocto/fsl-community-bsp/
$ source setup-environment wandboard
$ bitbake helloworld
```

We can then work directly in the local folder without the risk of accidentally having BitBake erase our code. Once development is complete, the modifications to `conf/local.conf` are removed and the recipe will fetch the source from its original `SRC_URI` location.

Working with GNU make

GNU make is a make implementation for Linux systems. It is used by a wide variety of open source projects, including the Linux kernel. The build is managed by a `Makefile`, which tells `make` how to build the source code.

How to do it...

Yocto recipes inherit `base.bbclass` and hence their default behavior is to look for a
`Makefile`, `makefile`, or `GNUmakefile` and use GNU make to build the package. If your
package already contains a `Makefile`, then all you need to worry about are the arguments
that need to be passed to `make`. `make` arguments can be passed using the `EXTRA_OEMAKE`
variable, and a `do_install` override that calls the `oe_runmake` install needs to be
provided, otherwise an empty install is run. For example, the `mingetty` recipe is based on a
`Makefile` and looks as follows:

```
SUMMARY = "Compact getty terminal handler for virtual consoles only"
SECTION = "console/utils"
HOMEPAGE = "http://sourceforge.net/projects/mingetty/"
LICENSE = "GPLv2"
PR = "r3"

LIC_FILES_CHKSUM = "file://COPYING;md5=0c56db0143f4f80c369ee3af7425af6e"
SRC_URI = "${SOURCEFORGE_MIRROR}/${BPN}/${BP}.tar.gz"

SRC_URI[md5sum] = "2a75ad6487ff271424ffc00a64420990"
SRC_URI[sha256sum] =
"0f55c90ba4faa913d91ef99cbf5cb2eb4dbe2780314c3bb17953f849c8cddd17"

# substitute our CFLAGS for "-O2 -Wall -W -pipe"
#
EXTRA_OEMAKE = "CC='${CC}' \
                CFLAGS='${CFLAGS} -D_GNU_SOURCE'"

do_install(){
    install -d ${D}${mandir}/man8 ${D}/${base_sbindir}
    oe_runmake install DESTDIR=${D}
}

inherit update-alternatives
ALTERNATIVE_${PN} = "getty"
ALTERNATIVE_LINK_NAME[getty] = "${base_sbindir}/getty"
ALTERNATIVE_TARGET[getty] = "${base_sbindir}/mingetty"
ALTERNATIVE_PRIORITY = "10"
```

The `update-alternatives` class used in the previous recipe is a helper class that manages the alternative system for multiple providers for the same command. To use it the following variables need to be provided:

`ALTERNATIVE_{PN}`: A list of all the commands in the package that need alternative providers.
`ALTERNATIVE_LINK_NAME[<command>]`: Path for the alternative command, defaults to `${bindir}/<command>`
`ALTERNATIVE_TARGET`: Sets a default link for all commands. Individual default links can be specified with `ALTERNATIVE_TARGET[<command>]`.
`ALTERNATIVE_PRIORITY`: Sets a default priority for all commands. Individual priorities can be specified by `ALTERNATIVE_PRIORITY[<command>]`.

See also

- For more information about GNU Make, visit
  `https://www.gnu.org/software/make/manual/`

Working with the GNU build system

A `Makefile` is a good solution when you are always going to build and run your software on the same system and things like `glibc` and `gcc` versions and the available library versions are known. However, most software needs to be built and run in a variety of systems.

Getting ready

The GNU build system, or autotools, is a set of tools whose aim is to create a `Makefile` for your software in a variety of systems. It's made up of three main tools:

- **Autoconf**: This parses the contents of a `configure.ac` file that describes the source code to be built and creates a `configure` script. This script will then be used to generate the final `Makefile`.
- **Automake**: This parses the contents of a `Makefile.am` file and converts it into a `Makefile.in` file. This is then used by the `configure` script generated earlier to obtain a `config.status` script that gets automatically executed to obtain the final `Makefile`.
- **Libtools**: This manages the creation of both static and dynamic libraries.

Before looking into autotools-based recipes, let's see how to use the Yocto SDK to build an autotools-based package, for example, the GNU hello sample. Let's fetch and extract the code:

```
$ wget http://ftp.gnu.org/gnu/hello/hello-2.10.tar.gz
$ tar xvf hello-2.10.tar.gz
```

Once the code has been prepared, we need to set up the compilation environment as usual:

```
$ source /opt/poky/2.4/environment-setup-cortexa9hf-neon-poky-linuxgnueabi
```

Next, we can launch the `configure` script:

```
$ ./configure ${CONFIGURE_FLAGS}
```

The `CONFIGURE_FLAGS` environment variable is already set up with all that configure needs:

```
$ echo $CONFIGURE_FLAGS
--target=arm-poky-linux-gnueabi --host=arm-poky-linux-gnueabi --
build=x86_64-linux -with-libtool-sysroot=/opt/poky/2.4/sysroots/cortexa8hf-
neon-poky-linux-gnueabi
```

We can now build and install, using the following command:

```
$ make
$ make install DESTDIR=</path/to/destination/directory>
```

How to do it...

The Yocto build system contains classes with the required knowledge to build `autotools` packages. All your recipe needs to do is inherit the `autotools` class and configure the arguments to be passed to the `configure` script in the `EXTRA_OECONF` variable. Usually, the `autotools` system understands how to install the software, so you do not need a `do_install` override. There is a wide variety of open source projects that use `autotools` as the build system. An example, `meta-custom/recipes-example/hello/hello_2.10.bb`, which does not need any extra configure options, follows:

```
DESCRIPTION = "GNU helloworld autotools recipe"
SECTION = "examples"
LICENSE = "GPLv3"
LIC_FILES_CHKSUM = "file://${COREBASE}/meta/files/common-
licenses/GPL-3.0;md5=c79ff39f19dfec6d293b95dea7b07891"

SRC_URI = "${GNU_MIRROR}/hello/hello-${PV}.tar.gz"
SRC_URI[md5sum] = "6cd0ffea3884a4e79330338dcc2987d6"
SRC_URI[sha256sum] =
"31e066137a962676e89f69d1b65382de95a7ef7d914b8cb956f41ea72e0f516b"

inherit autotools gettext
```

If extra configuration options need to be passed to the `configure` script, the `EXTRA_OECONF` and `PACKAGECONFIG_CONFARGS` variables can be used.

See also

- For more information about the GNU build system, visit
  `http://www.gnu.org/software/automake/manual/html_node/GNU-Build-System.html`

Working with the CMake build system

The GNU make system is a great tool when you build exclusively for Linux systems. However, some packages are multiplatform and need a way to manage `Makefile` files on different operating systems. **CMake** is a cross-platform build system that can work not only with GNU make, but also Microsoft Visual Studio and Apple's Xcode.

Getting ready

The CMake tool parses `CMakeLists.txt` files in every directory to control the build process. An example `CMakeLists.txt` file, to compile the `helloworld` example, follows:

```
cmake_minimum_required(VERSION 2.8.10)
project(helloworld)
add_executable(helloworld helloworld.c)
install(TARGETS helloworld RUNTIME DESTINATION bin)
```

How to do it...

The Yocto build system also contains classes with the required knowledge to build CMake packages. All your recipe needs to do is inherit the `cmake` class and configure the arguments to be passed to the `configure` script in the `EXTRA_OECMAKE` variable. Usually, the CMake system understands how to install the software, so you do not need a `do_install` override. A recipe to build the `helloworld.c` example application, `meta-custom/recipes-example/helloworld-cmake/helloworld-cmake_1.0.bb`, follows:

```
DESCRIPTION = "Simple helloworld cmake application"
SECTION = "examples"
LICENSE = "MIT"
LIC_FILES_CHKSUM =
"file://${COMMON_LICENSE_DIR}/MIT;md5=0835ade698e0bcf8506ecda2f7b4f302"

SRC_URI = "file://CMakeLists.txt \
           file://helloworld.c"

S = "${WORKDIR}"

inherit cmake

EXTRA_OECMAKE = ""
```

If extra configuration options need to be passed to cmake, the EXTRA_OECMAKE and PACKAGECONFIG_CONFARGS variables can be used.

See also

- For more information about CMake, visit http://www.cmake.org/documentation/

Working with the SCons builder

SCons is also a multiplatform build system written in Python, with its configuration files also written in the same language. It also includes support for Microsoft Visual Studio, among other features.

Getting ready

SCons parses SConstruct files, and by default it does not propagate the environment into the build system. This is to avoid build issues caused by environment differences. This is a complication for Yocto, as it configures the environment with cross-compilation toolchain settings. SCons does not define a standard way to support cross-compilation, so every project will implement it differently. For a simple example as the helloworld program, we can just initialize the CC, LINKFLAGS and PATH variables in our SConstruct file from the external environment as follows:

```
import os
env = Environment(CC = os.environ['CC'], LINKFLAGS = os.environ['LDFLAGS'],
ENV = {'PATH': os.environ['PATH']})
env.Program("helloworld", "helloworld.c")
```

How to do it...

The Yocto build system also contains classes with the required knowledge to build SCons packages. All your recipe needs to do is to inherit the `scons` class and configure the arguments to be passed to the `configure` script in the `EXTRA_OESCONS` variable. Although some packages using SCons might deal with installation through an install alias as required by the `scons` class, your recipe will mostly need to provide a `do_install` task override. An example recipe to build the `helloworld.c` example application, `meta-custom/recipes-example/helloworld-scons/helloworld-scons_1.0.bb`, follows:

```
DESCRIPTION = "Simple helloworld scons application"
SECTION = "examples"
LICENSE = "MIT"
LIC_FILES_CHKSUM =
"file://${COMMON_LICENSE_DIR}/MIT;md5=0835ade698e0bcf8506ecda2f7b4f302"

SRC_URI = "file://SConstruct \
           file://helloworld.c"

S = "${WORKDIR}"

inherit scons

EXTRA_OESCONS = ""

do_install() {
    install -d ${D}/${bindir}
    install -m 0755 helloworld ${D}${bindir}
}
```

See also

- For more information about SCons, visit
  http://www.scons.org/doc/HTML/scons-user/

Developing with libraries

Most applications make use of shared libraries, which saves system memory and disk space, as they are shared between different applications. Modularizing code into libraries also allows for easier versioning and code management, as well as independent updates from the applications that use them. This recipe will explain how to work with both static and shared libraries.

Getting ready

By convention, library files start with the lib prefix. All libraries need to be explicitly passed to the linker so that they are used, except libc which will be automatically linked. There are basically two library types:

- **Static libraries** (.a): When the object code is linked and becomes part of the application.
- **Dynamic libraries** (.so): These are linked at compile time but not included in the application, so they need to be available at runtime. Multiple applications can share a dynamic library so they need less disk space.

Libraries are typically placed in the following standard root filesystem locations:

- /lib: Libraries required for startup
- /usr/lib: Most system libraries
- /usr/local/lib: Non-system libraries

Dynamic libraries follow certain naming conventions on running systems so that multiple versions can co-exist; thus a library can be referenced by different names. Some of them are explained next:

- The linker name with the .so suffix; for example, libexample.so.
- The fully qualified name or soname, a symbolic link to the library name. For example, libexample.so.x, where x is the version number. Increasing the version number means the library is not compatible with previous versions.
- The real name. For example, libexample.so.x.y[.z], where x is the major version number, y is the minor version number, and the optional z is a release number. Increasing minor or release numbers retains compatibility.

So, for a given `libexample` library, we find the following:

- `libexample.so.x.y[.z]`, the actual shared library that needs to be present in both host and target
- `libexample.so.x`, a symbolic link to the preceding file used in the target when loading the library at runtime
- `libexample.so`, also a symbolic link as before used in the host when linking

In GNU `glibc`, starting an ELF binary calls a program loader, `/lib/ld-linux-X`. Here, X contains both an architecture string and the version number. The program loader finds all the needed shared libraries. This process uses a couple of interesting files:

- `/etc/ld.so.conf`: This stores the directories searched by the loader
- `/etc/ld.so.preload`: This is used to override libraries

The `ldconfig` tool reads the `ld.so.conf` file and creates a cache file (`/etc/ld.so.cache`) to increase access speed. The following environment variables can also be helpful:

- `LD_LIBRARY_PATH`: This is a colon-separated directory list to search libraries in. It is used when debugging or using non-standard library locations.
- `LD_PRELOAD`: This is used to override shared libraries.

Building a static library

We will build a static library, `libhelloworld`, from two source files, `hello.c` and `world.c`, and use it to build a hello world application. The source files for the library are presented here. The following is the code for the `hello.c` file:

```
char * hello (void)
{
  return "Hello";
}
```

This is the code for the `world.c` file:

```
char * world (void)
{
  return "World";
}
```

To build the library, follow these steps:

1. Configure the build environment:

   ```
   $ source /opt/poky/2.4/environment-setup-cortexa9hf-neon-poky-
   linux-gnueabi
   ```

2. Compile and link the library:

   ```
   $ ${CC} -c hello.c world.c
   $ ${AR} -cvq libhelloworld.a hello.o world.o
   ```

3. Verify the contents of the library:

   ```
   $ ${AR} -t libhelloworld.a
   ```

The application source code is presented next:

- For the `helloworld.c` file, the following is the code:

  ```
  #include <stdio.h>
  #include "helloworld.h"

  int main (void)
  {
     return printf("%s %s\n",hello(),world());
  }
  ```

  With the `helloworld.h` header file being the following:

  ```
  #ifndef HELLOWORLD_H
  #define HELLOWORLD_H
  char * hello (void);
  char * world (void);
  #endif
  ```

- We now build it indicating where to find the static library (inside `libs/`) and the include file (inside `inc/`) to the compiler:

  ```
  $ ${CC} -o helloworld helloworld.c -l helloworld -L libs/ -I inc/
  ```

- We can check which libraries it links with using `readelf`:

```
$ readelf -d helloworld
Dynamic section at offset 0x534 contains 24 entries:
 Tag         Type                     Name/Value
0x00000001 (NEEDED)                   Shared library:
    [libc.so.6]
```

Building a shared dynamic library

Dynamic libraries must be compiled in a position-independent way, so that the linker can locate them in any memory location at runtime. To do this, we use the `-fPIC` parameter to the compiler. To build a dynamic library from the same sources, we run the following:

```
$ ${CC} -fPIC -g -c hello.c world.c
$ ${CC} -shared -Wl,-soname,libhelloworld.so.1 -o libhelloworld.so hello.o
world.o
```

We now build it indicating where to find the dynamic library (inside `libs/`) and the include file (inside `inc/`) to the compiler:

```
$ ${CC} -o helloworld helloworld.c -l helloworld  -L libs/ -I inc/
```

Again, we can check the dynamic libraries using `readelf`, as follows:

```
$ readelf -d helloworld
Dynamic section at offset 0x6ec contains 25 entries:
 Tag         Type                     Name/Value
0x00000001 (NEEDED)                   Shared library:
    [libhelloworld.so.1]
0x00000001 (NEEDED)                   Shared library: [libc.so.6]
```

How to do it...

A sample recipe for the static library example we just saw follows, `meta-custom/recipes-example/libhelloworld-static/libhelloworldstatic_1.0.bb`:

```
DESCRIPTION = "Simple helloworld example static library"
SECTION = "libs"
LICENSE = "MIT"
LIC_FILES_CHKSUM =
"file://${COMMON_LICENSE_DIR}/MIT;md5=0835ade698e0bcf8506ecda2f7b4f302"

SRC_URI = "file://hello.c \
```

```
                file://world.c \
                file://helloworld.h \
                file://helloworld.pc"

S = "${WORKDIR}"

do_compile() {
        ${CC} -c hello.c world.c
        ${AR} -cvq libhelloworld.a hello.o world.o
}

do_install() {
        install -d ${D}${includedir}
        install -d ${D}${libdir}
        install -m 0755 helloworld.h ${D}${includedir}
        install -m 0755 libhelloworld.a ${D}${libdir}
}
```

By default, the configuration in `meta/conf/bitbake.conf` places all static libraries in a `-staticdev` package. It is also placed in the `sysroot` so that it can be used, as well as the `helloworld.h` header file. For a dynamic library, we would use the following recipe, `meta-custom/recipes-example/libhelloworld-dyn/libhelloworld-dyn_1.0.bb`:

```
DESCRIPTION = "Simple helloworld example dynamic library"
SECTION = "libs"
LICENSE = "MIT"
LIC_FILES_CHKSUM =
"file://${COMMON_LICENSE_DIR}/MIT;md5=0835ade698e0bcf8506ecda2f7b4f302"

SRC_URI = "file://hello.c \
            file://world.c \
            file://helloworld.h \
            file://helloworld.pc"

S = "${WORKDIR}"

do_compile() {
        ${CC} ${LDFLAGS} -fPIC -g -c hello.c world.c
        ${CC} ${LDFLAGS} -shared -Wl,-soname,libhelloworld.so.1 -o
libhelloworld.so.1.0 hello.o world.o
}

do_install() {
        install -d ${D}${includedir}
        install -d ${D}${libdir}
        install -m 0755 helloworld.h ${D}${includedir}
        install -m 0755 libhelloworld.so.1.0 ${D}${libdir}
```

```
        ln -s libhelloworld.so.1.0 ${D}/${libdir}/libhelloworld.so.1
        ln -s libhelloworld.so.1 ${D}/${libdir}/libhelloworld.so
}
```

Usually, we would list the library dependencies (if any) in the RDEPENDS variable, but this is not always needed as the build system performs some automatic dependency checking by inspecting both the library file and the pkg-config file, and adding the dependencies it finds to RDEPENDS automatically. Multiple versions of the same library can co-exist on the running system. For that, you need to provide different recipes with the same package name but a different package revision. For example, we would have libhelloworld-1.0.bb and libhelloworld-1.1.bb. To build an application using the static library, we would create a recipe in meta-custom/recipes-example/helloworld-static/helloworldstatic_1.0.bb, as follows:

```
DESCRIPTION = "Simple helloworld example"
SECTION = "examples"
LICENSE = "MIT"
LIC_FILES_CHKSUM =
"file://${COMMON_LICENSE_DIR}/MIT;md5=0835ade698e0bcf8506ecda2f7b4f302"

DEPENDS = "libhelloworld-static"

SRC_URI = "file://helloworld.c"

S = "${WORKDIR}"

do_compile() {
        ${CC} ${LDFLAGS} -o helloworld helloworld.c -l helloworld
}

do_install() {
        install -d ${D}${bindir}
        install -m 0755 helloworld ${D}${bindir}
}
```

To build using the dynamic library, we use the following meta-custom/recipes-example/helloworld-dyn/helloworld-dyn_1.0.bb:

```
DESCRIPTION = "Simple helloworld example"
SECTION = "examples"
LICENSE = "MIT"
LIC_FILES_CHKSUM =
"file://${COMMON_LICENSE_DIR}/MIT;md5=0835ade698e0bcf8506ecda2f7b4f302"

DEPENDS = "libhelloworld-dyn"
```

```
SRC_URI = "file://helloworld.c"

S = "${WORKDIR}"

do_compile() {
        ${CC} ${LDFLAGS} -o helloworld helloworld.c -lhelloworld
}

do_install() {
        install -d ${D}${bindir}
        install -m 0755 helloworld ${D}${bindir}
}
```

How it works...

Libraries should provide the information required to use them, such as include headers and library dependencies. The Yocto Project provides two ways for libraries to provide build settings:

- The `binconfig` class is a legacy class used for libraries that supply a `-config` script to provide build settings
- The `pkgconfig` class is the recommended method for libraries to provide build settings

A `pkg-config` build settings file has the `.pc` suffix, is distributed with the library, and is installed in a common location known to the `pkg-config` tool. The `helloworld.pc` file for the dynamic library looks as follows:

```
prefix=/usr/local
exec_prefix=${prefix}
includedir=${prefix}/include
libdir=${exec_prefix}/lib

Name: helloworld
Description: The helloworld library
Version: 1.0.0
Cflags: -I${includedir}/helloworld
Libs: -L${libdir} -lhelloworld
```

However, for the static library, we would change the last line to:

```
Libs: -L${libdir} libhelloworld.a
```

A package wanting to use this `.pc` file would inherit the `pkgconfig` class.

There's more...

There's a provision for packages that build both a library and an executable but do not want both of them installed together. By inheriting the `lib_package` class, the package will create a separate `-bin` package with the executables.

See also

- More details regarding `pkg-config` can be found at
  `http://www.freedesktop.org/wiki/Software/pkg-config/`

Working with the Linux framebuffer

The Linux kernel provides an abstraction for the graphical hardware in the form of framebuffer devices. These allow applications to access graphics hardware through a well-defined API. The framebuffer is also used to provide a graphical console to the Linux kernel, so that it can, for example, display colors and a logo. In this recipe, we will explore how applications can use the Linux framebuffer to display graphics and video.

Getting ready

Some applications, especially in embedded devices, are able to access the framebuffer by mapping memory and accessing it directly. For example, the `gstreamer` framework is able to work directly over the framebuffer, as is the Qt graphical framework. Some applications, like the Qt framework, also include support for hardware acceleration-not only video but also 2D and 3D graphical acceleration provided through the OpenGL and OpenVG APIs.

How to do it...

The FSL community BSP layer provides a `fsl-image-multimedia` target image that includes the `gstreamer` framework, including plugins that make use of the hardware acceleration features within the i.MX6 SoC. A `fsl-image-multimedia-full` image is also provided, which extends the supported `gstreamer` plugins. To build the `fsl-image-multimedia` image with framebuffer support, you need to remove the graphical distribution features by adding the following to your `conf/local.conf` file:

```
DISTRO_FEATURES_remove = "x11 directfb wayland vulkan"
```

Alternatively, the FSL BSP community offers a `fslc-framebuffer` distribution as part of `meta-freescale-distro` with a reference configuration for framebuffer images. To use it, change your `DISTRO` in `conf/local.conf` to `fslc-framebuffer`.

> You will need to build from scratch by removing both the `tmp` and `sstate-cache` directories when changing the `DISTRO_FEATURES` variable.

Build the image with the following:

```
$ cd /opt/yocto/fsl-community-bsp/
$ source setup-environment wandboard
$ bitbake fsl-image-multimedia
```

We are using the `fsl-image-multimedia` image as an example, but any image where the afore mentioned graphical distribution features are removed will build packages with framebuffer support for packages that support it. The resulting `fsl-image-multimedia-wandboard.wic.gz` image at `tmp/deploy/images` can be programmed into a microSD card and booted. The default Wandboard device tree defines an `mxcfb1` node, as follows:

```
mxcfb1: fb@0 {
        compatible = "fsl,mxc_sdc_fb";
        disp_dev = "hdmi";
        interface_pix_fmt = "RGB24";
        mode_str ="1920x1080M@60";
        default_bpp = <24>;
        int_clk = <0>;
        late_init = <0>;
};
```

So, connecting a 1920x1080 HDMI monitor should show a virtual Terminal with the Poky login prompt. We can then use the `gstreamer` command-line tool, `gst-launch-1.0`, to construct `gstreamer` pipelines. For example, to view a hardware-accelerated video over the framebuffer, you can download the *Big Buck Bunny* teaser full HD video file and play it over the framebuffer using the `gstreamer` framework's `gst-launch-1.0` command-line tool, as follows:

```
# cd /home/root
# wget
 http://mirror.cessen.com/blender.org/peach/trailer/trailer_1080p.mov
# gst-launch-1.0 playbin uri=file:///home/root/trailer_1080p.mov
```

The `playbin` gstreamer plugin will automatically create a pipeline with the correct elements. In this case the video will use the `h.264` video decoder plugin, `imxvpu`, which makes use of the hardware video processing unit inside the i.MX6 SoC to decode the `h.264` video.

You can see a list of the available i.MX6-specific plugins by running the following:

```
# gst-inspect-1.0 | grep imx
imxpxp:    imxpxpvideosink: Freescale PxP video sink
imxpxp:    imxpxpvideotransform: Freescale PxP video transform
imxvpu:    imxvpudec: Freescale VPU video decoder
imxvpu:    imxvpuenc_h263: Freescale VPU h.263 video encoder
imxvpu:    imxvpuenc_h264: Freescale VPU h.264 video encoder
imxvpu:    imxvpuenc_mpeg4: Freescale VPU MPEG-4 video encoder
imxvpu:    imxvpuenc_mjpeg: Freescale VPU motion JPEG video encoder
imxg2d:    imxg2dvideosink: Freescale G2D video sink
imxg2d:    imxg2dvideotransform: Freescale G2D video transform
imxg2d:    imxg2dcompositor: Freescale G2D video compositor
imxaudio:  imxuniaudiodec: Freescale i.MX uniaudio decoder
imxaudio:  imxmp3audioenc: Freescale i.MX MP3 encoder
imxeglvivsink:  imxeglvivsink: Freescale EGL video sink
imxipu:    imxipuvideotransform: Freescale IPU video transform
imxipu:    imxipuvideosink: Freescale IPU video sink
imxipu:    imxipucompositor: Freescale IPU video compositor
imxv4l2videosrc:  imxv4l2videosrc: V4L2 CSI Video Source
```

How it works...

Framebuffer devices are located under /dev. The default framebuffer device is /dev/fb0 and, if the graphics hardware provides more than one, they will be sequentially numbered. By default, the Wandboard boots with three framebuffer devices, fb0, fb1, and fb2. The first is the default video display, the second one is an overlay plane that can be used to combine content on the display, and the third is a secondary display. However, the i.MX6 SoC supports up to four displays, so it could have up to four framebuffer devices in addition to two overlay framebuffers. You can change the default framebuffer used by applications with the FRAMEBUFFER environment variable. For example, if your hardware supports several framebuffers, you could use the second one by running:

```
# export FRAMEBUFFER=/dev/fb1
```

Framebuffer devices are memory-mapped and you can perform file operations on them. For example, you can clear the contents of the screen by running the following:

```
# cat /dev/zero > /dev/fb0
```

Alternatively, you can copy it with the following:

```
# cat /dev/fb0 > fb.raw
```

You may even restore the contents with the following:

```
# cat fb.raw > /dev/fb0
```

User space programs can also interrogate framebuffers or modify their configuration programmatically using ioctls or from the console by using the fbset application, which is included in Yocto's core images as a BusyBox applet.

```
# fbset -fb /dev/fb0
mode "1920x1080-60"
        # D: 148.500 MHz, H: 67.500 kHz, V: 60.000 Hz
        geometry 1920 1080 1920 1080 24
        timings 6734 148 88 36 4 44 5
        accel false
        rgba 5/11,6/5,5/0,0/0
endmode
```

You can configure the framebuffer HDMI device with a specific resolution, bits per pixel, and refresh rate by passing the `video` command-line option from the U-Boot bootloader to the Linux kernel. The specific format depends on the device framebuffer driver and for the Wandboard it is as follows:

```
video=mxcfb<n>:dev=hdmi,<xres>x<yres><M>[@<rate>]
```

Here, the following applies:

- `n` is the framebuffer number
- `xres` is the horizontal resolution
- `yres` is the vertical resolution
- `M` specifies that timings are to be calculated using the **Video Electronics Standards Association** (**VESA**) coordinated video timings instead of from a look-up table
- `rate` is the refresh rate

For example, for the `fb0` framebuffer, you could add the following to your `conf/local.conf`:

```
UBOOT_EXTLINUX_KERNEL_ARGS = "video=mxcfb0:dev=hdmi,1920x1080M@60"
```

This line will add the video kernel command-line argument specified to the `extlinux.conf` boot script.

 Note that, after a period of inactivity, the virtual console will blank out. To unblank the display, use the following:
```
# echo 0 > /sys/class/graphics/fb0/blank
```

There's more...

We can now complement our framebuffer image with Qt5 applications. Prior to the Qt5 release, Qt had its own window system implementation (QWS). Qt5 uses Qt platform plugins instead:

- For **single-process applications** with one main window, Qt5 recommends the EGLFS plugin, which uses the underlying graphical hardware acceleration, but can use others such as LinuxFB or DirectFB
- For **multiple graphical processes** the Wayland plugin must be used

EGL is an interface between OpenGL ES and the native windowing system (like X11 or Wayland) and EGLFS is the platform plugin that runs Qt5 applications over EGL and OpenGL ES 2.0 without a windowing system. EGLFS will force the first window to become full screen and become the root widget window. EGLFS supports only one native full-screen GL window.

The LinuxFB plugin writes directly to the framebuffer using the `fbdev` Linux subsystem. As such it only supports software rendering and has a limited performance. To compile the Qt hello world application we saw in the *Developing Qt applications* recipe earlier in this same chapter, we could use the following `meta-custom/recipes-qt/qt-helloworld/qt-helloworld_1.0.bb` Yocto recipe:

```
DESCRIPTION = "Simple QT helloworld example"
SECTION = "examples"
LICENSE = "MIT"
LIC_FILES_CHKSUM =
"file://${COMMON_LICENSE_DIR}/MIT;md5=0835ade698e0bcf8506ecda2f7b4f302"

SRC_URI = "file://qt_hello_world.cpp \
            file://qt_hello_world.pro"

DEPENDS += "qtbase fontconfig"

S = "${WORKDIR}"

inherit qmake5

do_install() {
        install -d ${D}${bindir}
        install -m 0755 qt_hello_world ${D}${bindir}
}
```

Here, the `meta-custom/recipes-qt/qt-helloworld/qt-helloworld-1.0/qt_hello_world.cpp` source file is as follows:

```
#include <QApplication>
#include <QPushButton>

int main(int argc, char *argv[])
{
    QApplication app(argc, argv);

    QPushButton hello("Hello world!");

    hello.show();
    return app.exec();
```

```
    }
```

The `meta-custom/recipes-qt/qt-helloworld/qt-helloworld-1.0/qt_hello_world.pro` project file is as follows:

```
SOURCES += \
    qt_hello_world.cpp
QT += widgets
```

The previous recipe just inherits the `qmake5` class with the tools needed for the compilation and a couple of dependencies, the `qtbase` package and `fontconfig`, which is the Qt preferred way to access system fonts. If space is a concern, `fontconfig` may be omitted and Qt will use both pre-rendered and TrueType fonts available at its `lib/fonts` directory.

Qt5 is very modular so the `DEPENDS` variable will need to be extended to include all the relevant Qt5 modules. The `meta-qt5` layer has examples that can be used as a reference.

Then, we add the `qt-helloworld` package to the image by using the following in your project's `conf/local.conf` file:

```
IMAGE_INSTALL_append = " qt-helloworld"
```

Next, we build the image with the following:

```
$ bitbake fsl-image-multimedia
```

We can then program the microSD card image, boot it, log in to the Wandboard, and launch the application by running:

```
# export QT_QPA_PLATFORM="eglfs"
# /usr/bin/qt_hello_world
```

The `QT_QPA_PLATFORM` environment variable mentioned previously is used to select the EGLFS plugin. It can also be passed to the application on the command line using the `-platform` argument.

When exploring the capabilities of Qt5 it is useful to take a look at the available examples. The `recipes-qt/packagegroups/packagegroup-qt5-examples.bb` packagegroup recipe shown next can be used to add some examples to an image:

```
SUMMARY = "QT5 examples packagegroup"

inherit packagegroup

RDEPENDS_${PN} = " \
    liberation-fonts \
```

```
    icu \
    qtbase-examples \
    qt3d-examples \
    qtconnectivity-examples \
    qtdeclarative-examples \
    qtdeclarative-tools \
    qtmultimedia-examples \
    qtsvg-examples \
    cinematicexperience \
    qt5-demo-extrafiles \
    qt5everywheredemo \
    qtsmarthome \
    "
```

To build the preceding code, we also need to configure qtbase and qtmultimedia by adding the following PACKAGECONFIG switches to the conf/local.conf file in our build directory:

```
PACKAGECONFIG_append_pn-qtbase = " accessibility examples fontconfig sql-
sqlite icu"
PACKAGECONFIG_append_pn-qtmultimedia = " gstreamer"
```

These could also be added as bbappends to the corresponding recipes.

The different examples are installed on the target root filesytem under /usr/share.

> You may encounter the following error while building:
> /opt/yocto/fsl-community-
> bsp/wandboard/tmp/work/cortexa9hf-neon-poky-linux-
> gnueabi/qtdeclarative/5.9.2+gitAUTOINC+7c45b035b9-
> r0/git/tests/benchmarks/qml/binding/tst_binding.cpp:175:1
> 0: fatal error:tst_binding.moc: No such file or
> directory| #include "tst_binding.moc"
> If this is the case, you may need to remove the tests pkgconfig configuration item from the qtbase package as done in the following patch:
> https://github.com/yoctocookbook2ndedition/meta-qt5/commit/331f0
> e8e0428927594c4b8a2790df2f881fd4663

See also

- The framebuffer API is documented in the Linux kernel documentation at `https://www.kernel.org/doc/Documentation/fb/api.txt`
- For more information regarding Qt for Embedded Linux, refer to `https://doc.qt.io/qt-5/embedded-linux.html`
- Documentation for the GStreamer 1.0 framework can be found at `https://gstreamer.freedesktop.org/data/doc/gstreamer/head/gstreamer-libs/html/`

Using the X Windows system

The X Windows system provides the framework for a GUI environment-things like drawing and moving windows on the display and interacting with input devices like the mouse, the keyboard, and touchscreens. The protocol version has been v11 for over two decades, so it also known as X11.

Getting ready

The reference implementation for the X Windows system is the **X.Org** server, which is released under permissive licenses such as MIT. It uses a client/server model, with the server communicating with several client programs, serving user input, and accepting graphical output. The X11 protocol is network-transparent, so that clients and server may run on different machines with different architectures and operating systems. However, mostly they both run on the same machine and communicate using local sockets. User interface specifications, such as buttons or menu styles, are not defined in X11, which leaves it to other window manager applications that are usually part of desktop environments, such as Gnome or **K Desktop Environment** (**KDE**). X11 has input and video drivers to handle the hardware. For example, it has `fbdev`, a framebuffer driver that can output to a non-accelerated Linux framebuffer, and `evdev`, a generic Linux input device driver with support for mice, keyboards, tablets, and touchscreens.

The design of the X11 Windows systems makes it heavy for embedded devices, and although a powerful device like the quad-core i.MX6 has no trouble using it, many embedded devices choose other graphical alternatives. However, there are many graphical applications, mostly from the desktop environment, that run over the X11 Windows system.

The FSL community BSP layer provides a hardware-accelerated X video driver for the i.MX6 SoC, `xf86-video-imxfb-vivante`, which is included in the X11-based `core-image-sato` target image and other graphical images.

The X server is configured by an `/etc/X11/xorg.conf` file that configures the accelerated device, as follows:

```
Section "Device"
    Identifier  "i.MX Accelerated Framebuffer Device"
    Driver      "vivante"
    Option      "fbdev"       "/dev/fb0"
    Option      "vivante_fbdev" "/dev/fb0"
    Option      "HWcursor"  "false"
EndSection
```

The graphical acceleration is provided by the Vivante GPUs included in the i.MX6 SoC. Low-level X11 development is not recommended and toolkits such as GTK+ and Qt are preferred. We will see how to integrate both types of graphical applications into our Yocto target image.

How to do it...

SATO is the default visual style for the Poky distribution, based on **Gnome Mobile and Embedded** (**GMAE**). It is a desktop environment based on GTK+ that uses the matchbox window manager. It has the peculiarity of showing one single fullscreen window at a time. To build the `core-image-sato` image with X11 support, you need to remove other graphical distribution features by adding the following to your `conf/local.conf` file:

```
DISTRO_FEATURES_remove = "wayland"
```

Alternatively, the FSL BSP community offers a `fslc-x11` distribution as part of `meta-freescale-distro` with a reference configuration for X11-based images. To use it, change your `DISTRO` in `conf/local.conf` to `fslc-x11`.

To build the GTK hello world application, `meta-custom/recipes-graphics/gtk-helloworld/gtk-helloworld-1.0/gtk_hello_world.c`, that we introduced earlier, uses the following code:

```
#include <gtk/gtk.h>

int main(int argc, char *argv[])
{
    GtkWidget *window;
    gtk_init (&argc, &argv);
    window = gtk_window_new (GTK_WINDOW_TOPLEVEL);
    gtk_widget_show (window);
    gtk_main ();
    return 0;
}
```

We can use the following `meta-custom/recipes-graphics/gtk-helloworld/gtk-helloworld_1.0.bb` recipe:

```
DESCRIPTION = "Simple GTK helloworld application"
SECTION = "examples"
LICENSE = "MIT"
LIC_FILES_CHKSUM =
"file://${COMMON_LICENSE_DIR}/MIT;md5=0835ade698e0bcf8506ecda2f7b4f302"

SRC_URI = "file://gtk_hello_world.c"

S = "${WORKDIR}"

DEPENDS = "gtk+3"

inherit pkgconfig

do_compile() {
    ${CC} ${LDFLAGS} gtk_hello_world.c -o helloworld `pkg-config --cflags -
-libs gtk+-3.0`
}

do_install() {
    install -d ${D}${bindir}
    install -m 0755 helloworld ${D}${bindir}
}
```

We can then add the package to the `core-image-sato` image by using the following:

```
IMAGE_INSTALL_append = " gtk-helloworld"
```

Next, we can build it with the following:

```
$ cd /opt/yocto/fsl-community-bsp/
$ source setup-environment wandboard
$ bitbake core-image-sato
```

After the build completes, we will find the image under `tmp/deploy/images/wandboard`. We can then program it and run the application from the serial Terminal with the following:

```
# export DISPLAY=:0
# /usr/bin/helloworld
```

There's more...

Accelerated graphical output is also supported on the Qt framework, either directly on the framebuffer through EGLFS as we saw before, or using the X11 server available in `core-image-sato`. To build the Qt hello world source we introduced in the previous recipe but over X11, we only need to add the application to the target image with the following:

```
IMAGE_INSTALL_append = " qt-helloworld"
```

We can then build `core-image-sato` using the following command:

```
$ bitbake core-image-sato
```

Program and boot our target. Then, run the application with the following:

```
# export DISPLAY=:0
# /usr/bin/qt_hello_world
```

By default, Qt5 uses the xcb Qt platform abstraction to run against X11.

See also

- More information on the X.Org server can be found at `http://www.x.org`
- The Qt application framework documentation can be found at `https://www.qt.io/developers/`
- More information and documentation about GTK+ can be found at `http://www.gtk.org/`

Using Wayland

Wayland is a display server protocol that is intended to replace the X Window system and it is licensed under the MIT license. This recipe will provide an overview of Wayland, including some key differences with the X Window system, and will show how to make use of it in Yocto.

Getting ready

The Wayland protocol follows a client/server model in which clients are the graphical applications requesting the display of pixel buffers on the screen, and the server, or compositor, is the service provider that controls the display of these buffers.

The Wayland compositor can be a Linux display server, an X application, or a special Wayland client. Weston is the reference Wayland compositor in the Wayland project. It is written in C and works with the Linux kernel APIs. It relies on `evdev` for the handling of input events.

Wayland uses **Direct Rendering Manager** (DRM) in the Linux kernel and does not need something like an X server. The client renders the window contents to a buffer shared with the compositor by itself, using a rendering library, or an engine like Qt or GTK+.

Wayland lacks the network transparency features of X, but it is likely that similar functionality will be added in the future. It also has better security features than X and is designed to provide confidentiality and integrity. Wayland does not allow applications to look at the input of other programs, capture other input events, or generate fake input events. It also makes a better job of protecting Window outputs. However, this also means that it currently offers no way to provide some of the features we are used to in desktop X systems like screen capturing, or features common in accessibility programs.

Being lighter and more secure than X.Org, Wayland is better suited to use with embedded systems. If needed, X.Org can run as a client of Wayland for backwards compatibility. However, Wayland is not as established as X11 and Wayland-based images in Poky do not receive as much community attention as the X11-based ones.

How to do it...

Poky offers a `core-image-weston` image that includes the Weston compositor. To build the `core-image-weston` image, you need to remove other graphical distribution features by adding the following to your `conf/local.conf` file:

```
DISTRO_FEATURES_remove = "x11 directfb"
```

Alternatively, the FSL BSP community offers an `fslc-wayland` distribution as part of `meta-freescale-distro` with a reference configuration for Wayland images. To use it, change your `DISTRO` in `conf/local.conf` to `fslc-wayland`.

> You will need to build from scratch by removing both the `tmp` and `sstate-cache` directories when changing the `DISTRO_FEATURES` variable.

Wayland is supported in the Qt5 toolkit by the **Qt Platform Abstraction** (**QPA**) Wayland plugin. We can use the same Qt hello world example from the *Using the X Windows system* recipe and run it with Weston just by adding the application and the Wayland plugin to the image by adding the next line to the `conf/local.conf` file:

```
IMAGE_INSTALL_append = " qtwayland qt-helloworld"
```

Then, we build the image with the following:

```
$ cd /opt/yocto/fsl-community-bsp/
$ source setup-environment wandboard
$ bitbake core-image-weston
```

Once the build finishes, you will find the WIC image ready to be programmed under `tmp/deploy/images/wandboard`.

> At the time of writing, the `meta-freescale` layer needed to be patched for this build to succeed. The `meta-freescale` layer used can be found at:
> https://github.com/yoctocookbook2ndedition/meta-freescale.

On boot, we see a single application, the Wayland Terminal, which we can launch and use to start other applications. To do that, we need to connect a USB mouse and keyboard, and click on the Terminal icon to launch it. You can then launch the helloworld application from the Wayland graphical Terminal by running the following:

```
# qt_hello_world -platform wayland
```

Wayland can also run an X11 server for backwards compatibility in a mode known as XWayland. To build XWayland, we can either use Poky's default distribution features or configure our `conf/local.conf` configuration file with the `fslc-xwayland` distro as follows:

```
DISTRO = "fslc-xwayland"
```

We will then be able to launch our application just by doing:

```
# qt_hello_world
```

As the default QPA is already xcb.

There's more...

Running GTK applications under Wayland is also possible. However the current Weston version in Yocto 2.4 Rocko is 1.11.1, and GTK is version 3.22.17. Unfortunately only Weston 1.12 includes support for the `xdg-shell-v6` protocol, which is required to run GTK 3.22 applications using Wayland compositor.

If we try to run a GTK 3.22 application on Weston 1.11.1, we see this error on launch:
```
Gdk-WARNING **: wayland compositor does not support
xdg_shell interface, not using Wayland display.
```
This is a known bug; see
`https://bugs.debian.org/cgi-bin/bugreport.cgi?bug=842001`.

Building XWayland instead, as explained before, we can use the same GTK hello world example from the *Using the X Windows system* recipe and run it just by adding the application to the image with the following line added to the `conf/local.conf` file:

```
IMAGE_INSTALL_append = " gtk-helloworld"
```

Then, we can build and program the `core-image-weston` image as explained before. We can then launch the application by running:

```
# export XDG_RUNTIME_DIR=/var/run/user/root
# helloworld
```

See also

- You can find more information about Wayland on the project's web page at `http://wayland.freedesktop.org/`

Adding a web browser application

A web browser may not seem like the typical package to run on an embedded device; however, the i.MX6 is a high-end application processor and its powerful graphical and video capabilities make it fully capable of running one. In this recipe, we will explore the different web browser options available.

Getting ready

The web browser choice will depend on the specific task the browser will be used for and what the hardware acceleration needs are. The following browsers are currently available:

- Epiphany (known as Gnome Web in recent versions)
- Firefox
- Chromium, and Qt WebEngine for Qt5 integration

How to do it...

The **Epiphany web browser** is included with Poky. Epiphany started as a fork of the Mozilla Suite intended to make a lean, fast browser. Epiphany started off as Galeon and it needed a second fork to become the current Epiphany project. It moved away from Mozilla's Gecko layout engine in favor of using Webkit, a layout engine with origins in the KDE project. It is the default browser for the GNOME project and it complies with the GNOME Human Interface Guidelines. It is released under the GPLv3 license. To include Epiphany, we only need to add it to our image by modifying `conf/local.conf`, as follows:

```
IMAGE_INSTALL_append = " epiphany"
```

The Epiphany browser can make use of graphical acceleration if run under a hardware-accelerated X11 or Wayland back-end, but it does not currently make use of the video acceleration features on the i.MX6 CPU.

The **Firefox web browser** also originated from the Mozilla Suite. Firefox is developed by the Mozilla Foundation under a MPL-2.0 license. To include the Firefox web browser, we need to add the `meta-browser` layer to our Yocto installation as follows:

```
$ cd /opt/yocto/fsl-community-bsp/sources
$ git clone https://github.com/OSSystems/meta-browser.git
$ cd /opt/yocto/fsl-community-bsp/
$ source setup-environment wandboard
$ bitbake-layers add-layer /opt/yocto/fsl-community-bsp/sources/meta-browser
```

We can then add the `firefox` package to our image using the next line in our `conf/local.conf` file:

```
IMAGE_INSTALL_append = " firefox"
```

The Firefox browser can make use of graphical acceleration if run under a hardware-accelerated X11 or Wayland back-end, but it does not currently make use of the video acceleration features on the i.MX6 CPU.

Chromium is an open source browser started by Google and maintained by the Chromium project. It has a mixture of open source licenses that include BSD, MIT, LGPL, and MPL. It is also available on the `meta-browser` layer installed previously. It has a dependency on the `meta-gnome` layer, which in turn depends on `meta-networking` and `meta-python`, so we also have to add them to our `conf/bblayers.conf` with:

```
$ bitbake-layers add-layer /opt/yocto/fsl-community-bsp/sources/meta-openembedded/meta-python
$ bitbake-layers add-layer /opt/yocto/fsl-community-bsp/sources/meta-openembedded/meta-networking
$ bitbake-layers add-layer /opt/yocto/fsl-community-bsp/sources/meta-openembedded/meta-gnome
```

We can add the `chromium` package to our image using the next line in our `conf/local.conf` file:

```
IMAGE_INSTALL_append = " chromium"
```

Chromium can use the graphical acceleration on the i.MX6 CPU if it runs over a hardware-accelerated X11 or Wayland backend. It can also run over the framebuffer using the EGLFS Qt5 platform plugin.

There's more...

Video acceleration for Chromium is made possible with the patches available at `https://github.com/Freescale/chromium-imx`. Video acceleration works over X11 and Wayland, although reports on usability vary. However, Qt5 WebEngine video acceleration is only commercially available.

These patches are already applied by the `meta-freescale` layer. At the time of writing, the patches apply only to a specific version of Chromium and they would need to be reviewed for newer versions.

In order to be able to build Chromium on the Yocto 2.4 release, the bbappends that applies these patches need to be omitted by adding the following to your `conf/local.conf`:

```
BBMASK .= "dynamic-layers/browser-layer/recipes-browser"
```

The preceding line instructs Bitbake to ignore the recipes and bbappends on the specified path.

See also

- To learn more about Gnome Web visit `https://wiki.gnome.org/Apps/Web/`
- The home page for the Chromium browser is `https://www.chromium.org/Home`
- The Mozilla Firefox web page is `https://www.mozilla.org/en-US/firefox/`

Adding Python applications

Python is a widely-used, interpreted high-level programming language. Poky has support for building both Python 2 and Python 3 applications, and includes a small set of Python development tools in the `meta/recipes-devtools/python` directory. A wider variety of Python applications are available in the `meta-python` layer included as part of `meta-openembedded`, which you can optionally add to your `conf/bblayers.conf`.

Getting ready

The standard tool for packaging Python modules is Distutils, which is included for both Python 2 and Python 3. Poky includes the `distutils` class (`distutils3` in Python 3), which is used to build Python packages that use `distutils`. An example recipe in `meta-python` that uses the `distutils` class is `meta-python/recipes-devtools/python/python-numeric_24.2.bb`, shown next:

```
SUMMARY = "A sophisticated Numeric Processing Package for Python"
SECTION = "devel/python"
LICENSE = "PSF & LLNL"
LIC_FILES_CHKSUM = "file://Legal.htm;md5=e3ce75dedd4043918d15979ae43e312e"

PR = "ml3"
SRC_URI = "${SOURCEFORGE_MIRROR}/numpy/Numeric-${PV}.tar.gz
           file://0001-it-tries-to-define-this-function-differently-than-it.patch \
"

S = "${WORKDIR}/Numeric-${PV}"

inherit distutils

SRC_URI[md5sum] = "2ae672656e06716a149acb048cca3093"
SRC_URI[sha256sum] =
"5f72e729eb6ff57442f2a38bfc9931738b59e5077928e2e70d22b4610ff15258"
```

Distutils is useful for simple Python applications but it lacks features. For example, `distutils` does not install package dependencies, allows package uninstallation, or allows us to install several versions of the same package, so it is only recommended for simple requirements. Hence, `setuptools` was developed to expand on `distutils`. It is not included in the standard Python libraries, but it is available in Poky. There is also a `setuptools` class in Poky (`setuptools3` for Python 3) that is used to build Python packages distributed with `setuptools`.

How to do it...

To build a Python hello world example application with `setuptools`, we would use a `meta-custom/recipes-python/python-helloworld/python-helloworld_1.0.bb` recipe, as follows:

```
DESCRIPTION = "Simple Python setuptools hello world application"
SECTION = "examples"
LICENSE = "MIT"
LIC_FILES_CHKSUM =
    "file://${COMMON_LICENSE_DIR}/MIT;md5=0835ade698e0bcf8506ecda2f7b4
    f302"

SRC_URI = "file://setup.py \
        file://python-helloworld.py \
        file://helloworld/__init__.py \
        file://helloworld/main.py"

S = "${WORKDIR}"

inherit setuptools

do_install_append () {
    install -d ${D}${bindir}
    install -m 0755 python-helloworld.py ${D}${bindir}
}
```

To create an example hello world package, we create the directory structure shown in the following screenshot:

Directory structure

Here is the code for the same directory structure:

```
$ mkdir -p meta-custom/recipes-python/python-helloworld/python-
    helloworld-1.0/helloworld/
$ touch meta-custom/recipes-python/python-helloworld/python-
    helloworld-1.0/helloworld/__init__.py
```

You will also need to create the following `meta-custom/recipes-python/python-helloworld/python-helloworld-1.0/setup.py` Python setup file:

```
import sys
from setuptools import setup

setup(
    name = "helloworld",
    version = "0.1",
    packages=["helloworld"],
    author="Alex Gonzalez",
    author_email = "alex@example.com",
    description = "Hello World packaging example",
    license = "MIT",
    keywords= "example",
    url = "",
)
```

You will also need the `meta-custom/recipes-python/python-helloworld/python-helloworld-1.0/helloworld/main.py` python file:

```
import sys

def main(argv=None):
    if argv is None:
        argv = sys.argv
    print "Hello world!"
    return 0
```

And finally a `meta-custom/recipes-python/python-helloworld/python-helloworld-1.0/python-helloworld.py` test script that makes use of the module:

```
#!/usr/bin/env python
import sys
import helloworld.main

if __name__ == '__main__':
        sys.exit(helloworld.main.main())
```

We can then add it to our image with the following addition to the `conf/local.conf` or image file:

```
IMAGE_INSTALL_append = " python-helloworld"
```

Then, we can build it using the following:

```
$ cd /opt/yocto/fsl-community-bsp/
$ source setup-environment wandboard
$ bitbake core-image-minimal
```

Once programmed and booted, we can test the module by running the example script:

```
# /usr/bin/python-helloworld.py
Hello world!
```

There's more...

In `meta-python`, you can also find the `python-pip` (`python3-pip` for Python 3) recipe that will add the `pip` utility to your target image. It can be used to install packages from the **Python Package Index (PyPI)**. You can add it to your image with the following:

```
IMAGE_INSTALL_append  = " python3-pip"
```

You will need to add the `meta-openembedded/meta-python` layer to your `conf/bblayers.conf` file in order to build your image. Then, you can build for the `core-image-minimal` image with the following:

```
$ cd /opt/yocto/fsl-community-bsp/
$ source setup-environment wandboard
$ bitbake core-image-minimal
```

Once installed, you can use it from the target, as follows:

```
# pip search <package_name>
# pip install <package_name>
```

Integrating the Open Java Development Kit

Up until Java SE version 8, Oracle offered a commercially-licensed and royalties-based Java SE embedded edition. However, Java SE Embedded 8 was the last embedded specific Java SE release that Oracle will offer.

The open source alternative to Oracle Java SE embedded is the **Open Java Development Kit (OpenJDK)**, an open source implementation of Java SE licensed under the GPLv2, with the classpath exception, which means that applications are allowed to link without being bound by the GPL license. This recipe will show how to build OpenJDK with Yocto and integrate the **Java Runtime Environment (JRE)** into our target images.

Getting ready

The main components of OpenJDK are:

- The **HotSpot Java Virtual Machine (JVM)**
- The **Java Class Library (JCL)**
- The Java compiler, **javac**

Initially, OpenJDK needed to be built using a proprietary JDK. However, the **IcedTea** project allowed us to build OpenJDK using the GNU classpath, the **GNU Compiler for Java (GCJ)**, and bootstrap a JDK to build OpenJDK. It also complements OpenJDK with some missing components available on Java SE like a web browser plugin and web start implementations.

Yocto can build OpenJDK using the `meta-java` layer, which includes recipes for cross-compiling OpenJDK using IcedTea. Development discussions can be followed and contributed to by visiting the development mailing list at `http://lists.openembedded.org/mailman/listinfo/openembedded-devel`.

The `meta-java` layer also includes recipes for a wide variety of Java libraries and VMs, as well as tools for application development like **ant** and **fastjar**.

How to do it...

To build OpenJDK 8, you need to clone the `meta-java` layer, as follows:

```
$ cd /opt/yocto/fsl-community-bsp/sources/
$ git clone git://git.yoctoproject.org/meta-java
```

At the time of writing, there is no Rocko branch yet, so we will work directly from the master branch. Add the layer to your `conf/bblayers.conf` file:

```
$ bitbake-layers add-layer /opt/yocto/fsl-community-bsp/sources/meta-java
```

Then, configure the project by adding the following to your `conf/local.conf` file:

```
PREFERRED_PROVIDER_virtual/java-initial-native = "cacao-initial-native"
PREFERRED_PROVIDER_virtual/java-native = "jamvm-native"
PREFERRED_PROVIDER_virtual/javac-native = "ecj-bootstrap-native"
```

You can then add the OpenJDK package to your image with the following:

```
IMAGE_INSTALL_append = " openjre-8"
```

Finally, you can build the image of your choice:

```
$ cd /opt/yocto/fsl-community-bsp/
$ source setup-environment wandboard
$ bitbake core-image-minimal
```

 If you have installed the dependencies listed in *Setting up the host system* on `Chapter 1`, *The Build System* you should be ready to go. Otherwise, you may need to install the `libx11-dev` package to your host for the build to succeed.

When you run the target image, you will get the following Java version:

```
# java -version
openjdk version "1.8.0_102-internal"
OpenJDK Runtime Environment (build 1.8.0_102-internal-b14)
OpenJDK Zero VM (build 25.102-b14, interpreted mode)
```

How it works...

To test the JVM, we can byte-compile a Java class on our host and copy it to the target to execute it. For instance, we can use the following simple `HelloWorld.java` example:

```
class HelloWorld {
  public static void main(String[] args) {
    System.out.println("Hello World!");
  }
}
```

To byte-compile it in the host, we need to have a Java SDK installed. To install a Java SDK in Ubuntu, just run the following:

```
$ sudo apt-get install openjdk-8-jdk
```

To byte-compile the example, we execute the following:

```
$ javac HelloWorld.java
```

To run it, we copy the `HelloWorld.class` to the target and from the same folder we run the following:

```
# java HelloWorld
```

There's more...

When using OpenJDK on a production system, it is recommended to always use the latest available release, which contains bug and security fixes. At the time of writing, the latest OpenJDK 8 release is update 112, so `meta-java` recipes should be updated.

See also

- Up-to-date information regarding OpenJDK can be obtained at `http://openjdk.java.net/`

Integrating Java applications

The `meta-java` layer also offers helper classes to ease the integration of Java libraries and applications into Yocto. In this recipe, we will see an example of building a Java library using the provided classes.

Getting ready

The meta-java layer provides two main classes to help with the integration of Java applications and libraries:

- **The Java bbclass**: This provides the default target directories and some auxiliary functions, namely:
    - oe_jarinstall: This installs and symlinks a JAR file
    - oe_makeclasspath: This generates a classpath string from JAR filenames
    - oe_java_simple_wrapper: This wraps your Java application in a shell script
- **The Java-library bbclass**: This inherits the Java bbclass and extends it to create and install JAR files

How to do it...

We will use the following meta-custom/recipes-java/java-helloworld/java-helloworld-1.0/HelloWorldSwing.java graphical Swing hello world example:

```
import javax.swing.JFrame;
import javax.swing.JLabel;

public class HelloWorldSwing {
    private static void createAndShowGUI() {
        JFrame frame = new JFrame("Hello World!");
        frame.setDefaultCloseOperation(JFrame.EXIT_ON_CLOSE);

        JLabel label = new JLabel("Hello World!");
        frame.getContentPane().add(label);

        frame.pack();
        frame.setVisible(true);
    }

    public static void main(String[] args) {
        javax.swing.SwingUtilities.invokeLater(new Runnable() {
            public void run() {
                createAndShowGUI();
            }
        });
    }
```

```
}
```

To integrate this `HelloWorldSwing` application, we can use a Yocto `meta-custom/recipes-java/java-helloworld/java-helloworld_1.0.bb` recipe, as follows:

```
DESCRIPTION = "Simple Java Swing hello world application"
SECTION = "examples"
LICENSE = "MIT"
LIC_FILES_CHKSUM =
"file://${COMMON_LICENSE_DIR}/MIT;md5=0835ade698e0bcf8506ecda2f7b4
    f302"

RDEPENDS_${PN} = "java2-runtime"

SRC_URI = "file://HelloWorldSwing.java"

S = "${WORKDIR}"

inherit java-library

do_compile() {
        mkdir -p build
        javac -d build `find . -name "*.java"`
        fastjar cf ${JARFILENAME} -C build .
}

BBCLASSEXTEND = "native"
```

The recipe is also buildable for the host native architecture. We can do this either by providing a separate `java-helloworld-native` recipe that inherits the `native` class or by using the `BBCLASSEXTEND` variable as we did earlier. In both cases, we could then use the `_class-native` and `_class-target` overrides to differentiate between native and target functionality. Even though Java is byte-compiled and the compiled class will be the same for both, it still makes sense to add the native support explicitly.

How it works...

The `java-library` class will create a library package with the name `lib<package>-java`. To add it to a target image, we would use the following:

```
IMAGE_INSTALL_append = " libjava-helloworld-java"
```

The recipe above adds the `java2-runtime` as a runtime dependency. To select which of the available providers, like OpenJRE 7 or 8, to use, we add the following to either our distro configuration or `conf/local.conf`:

```
PREFERRED_PROVIDER_java2-runtime = "openjre-8"
```

However, the `RPROVIDES` in the library recipe will not install OpenJRE into the filesystem; so, we need to add it ourselves to our image recipe or `conf/local.conf` file with the following:

```
IMAGE_INSTALL_append = " openjre-8"
```

The available JREs do not currently run over the framebuffer or Wayland, so we will use an X11-based graphical image like `core-image-sato`:

```
$ cd /opt/yocto/fsl-community-bsp/
$ source setup-environment wandboard-quad
$ bitbake core-image-sato
```

We can then boot it, log in to the target, and execute the example with OpenJDK by running:

```
# export DISPLAY=:0
# java -cp /usr/share/java/java-helloworld.jar HelloWorldSwing
```

There's more...

JavaFX support for OpenJDK, OpenJFX, reportedly works for i.MX6 platforms, including graphical acceleration, but there is currently no layer to build it. Pre-built OpenJFX builds for ARMv6 platforms are available, but the author has not verified it that they work.

See also

- More information about running OpenJFX on i.MX6 platforms can be found on the OpenJDK wiki
  https://wiki.openjdk.java.net/display/OpenJFX/OpenJFX+on+Freescale+i.MX6

Integrating Node.js applications

Node.js is a MIT-licensed open source JavaScript runtime environment. Built on Chrome's JavaScript Runtime (v8), it is an event-driven, non-blocking, and lightweight framework, initially mostly used to produce dynamic web content but currently used in a wide variety of applications, from scripting to HTML5 user interfaces. This recipe will show how to add Node.js applications to a target image.

Getting ready

Node.js has its own package manager, **Node Packaged Modules** (npm), which allows you to install third party modules and their dependencies. Modules are either installed locally, inside a directory, or globally, that is, on a location typically available as part of your path so they can be globally accessed.

Most Node.js applications make extensive use of modules. A module is basically application code described by a `package.json` file. The code and `packages.json` files can be in a directory, a Git repository, a compressed tarball, or a URI to a compressed tarball.

A package or module can be published to the `npm` registry. Once published, it can be referred to by a `<name>@<version>` string, where `<version>` can also be a tag or defaults to the latest tag if omitted. A module can be installed by doing the following:

```
$ npm install [-g] <module reference>
```

In this case, `<module reference>` is one of the following:

- A directory containing the `packages.json` file and the code itself
- A compressed tarball of the above, or a URI to it
- A Git repository with the `packages.json` file and the code itself
- A `<name>@<version>` string that represents a module published in the `npm` registry

In the previous command, the optional `-g` is specifying a global install.

To create a package we can, for example, use the following `helloworld.js` code:

```
var http = require('http');
http.createServer(function (request, response) {
    response.writeHead(200, {'Content-Type': 'text/plain'});
    response.end('Hello World\n');
}).listen(8080);
console.log('Server started');
```

You will also need to use its corresponding `packages.json` description file:

```
{
  "name": "nodejs-helloworld",
  "version": "1.0.0",
  "description": "An example node.js hello world server",
  "main": "helloworld.js",
  "author": "Alex Gonzalez <alex@lindusembedded.com>",
  "license": "ISC"
}
```

The creation of a `packages.json` file can be automated with the npm tool by doing the following from the same directory:

```
$ npm init
```

To try the module out, we can install it globally with the following:

```
$ npm install -g .
```

The . in the previous command specifies the current directory. It can be executed with the following:

```
$ nodejs helloworld.js
```

Directing a browser to `localhost:8080` displays the `Hello World` message.

Once it works, we can publish it to the npm registry with the following:

```
$ npm adduser
$ npm publish
```

Assuming your package name is unique, you should be able to see your package at `https://npmjs.com/package/<package>`. It can also be published to GitHub, so that it can be directly installed.

How to do it...

The Node.js package is available in the `meta-openembedded` layer. To add it to our image we just have to modify either the image recipe or our `conf/local.conf` with the following:

```
IMAGE_INSTALL_append = " nodejs"
```

After building our image of choice, for example `core-image-minimal`, we can check that Node.js is correctly installed with the following command:

```
# node --version
v8.4.0
```

We are also able to open the Node.js **Read Eval Print Loop** (**REPL**) interactive JavaScript prompt with the following command:

```
# node
```

To exit, press *Ctrl + D*.

To install `npm` to the target image, add the following to either your image file or `conf/local.conf` file:

```
IMAGE_INSTALL_append = " nodejs-npm"
```

After building and programming the image, we are now able to search for packages with the following:

```
# npm search <package>
```

We can install them locally with the following command:

```
# npm install <package>
```

Alternatively, we can install them globally with the following command:

```
# npm install -g <package>
```

How it works...

The preceding code will install the Node.js package into your image. However, most times we only need to add our Node.js application and add Node.js as a dependency.

We can add simple Node.js scripts, as we explained in *Adding data, scripts or configuration files*, in Chapter 3, *The Software Layer*, with a recipe that just installs the JavaScript scripts in the root filesystem.

However, Node.js applications are usually built on modules, each one of them with its own license. We could create a Yocto recipe that uses the npm tool to install dependencies, but we would also need to manually trace all their different licenses.

The devtool command-line utility can do this for us automatically either installing from the npm registry or from a Git repository. For example, to install the nodejs-helloworld package we can do the following:

```
$ devtool add "npm://registry.npmjs.org;name=nodejs-
helloworld;version=1.0.1"
```

Here, both the name and version are mandatory. The devtool command-line tool creates a skeleton recipe for us that looks as follows:

```
SUMMARY = "An example node.js hello world server"
LICENSE = "MIT"
LIC_FILES_CHKSUM = "file://LICENSE;md5=2459e4101d5fabab9d291bde6cdc5a56"

SRC_URI = "npm://registry.npmjs.org;name=nodejs-helloworld;version=${PV}"

NPM_SHRINKWRAP := "${THISDIR}/${PN}/npm-shrinkwrap.json"
NPM_LOCKDOWN := "${THISDIR}/${PN}/lockdown.json"

inherit npm

# Must be set after inherit npm since that itself sets S
S = "${WORKDIR}/npmpkg"
LICENSE_${PN} = "MIT"
```

As we can see in the previous code, shrinkwrap and lockdown JSON files are generated so the versions are frozen to ensure build integrity.

Alternatively, it can be generated from the Git repository:

```
$ devtool add
https://github.com/yoctocookbook2ndedition/nodejs-helloworld.git
```

In this case, the devtool command-line tool creates a skeleton recipe for us that looks as follows:

```
SUMMARY = "An example node.js hello world server"
LICENSE = "MIT"
LIC_FILES_CHKSUM = "file://LICENSE;md5=2459e4101d5fabab9d291bde6cdc5a56"
SRC_URI = "git://github.com/yoctocookbook2ndedition/nodejs-
helloworld.git;protocol=https"

PV = "1.0.1+git${SRCPV}"
SRCREV = "41c359a25365880ef880c10c2d405314439d6666"

NPM_SHRINKWRAP := "${THISDIR}/${PN}/npm-shrinkwrap.json"
NPM_LOCKDOWN := "${THISDIR}/${PN}/lockdown.json"

inherit npm

# Must be set after inherit npm since that itself sets S
S = "${WORKDIR}/git"
LICENSE_${PN} = "MIT"
```

It would also have listed all license dependencies, if there were any, and added all the module dependencies as different packages under the same recipe.

We can now follow the usual devtool workflow as explained in the *Using the extensible SDK* section, to build, test, and integrate them into our final images.

The package can then be added to our target image by adding the following to either its recipe or `conf/local.conf`:

```
IMAGE_INSTALL_append = " nodejs-helloworld"
```

Note that the `meta-openembedded` Yocto 2.4 Rocko branch has been updated to Node.js 8.4.0. Unfortunately, this newer version does not work well with the `npm` class and `devtool` command-line utility in Poky. The previous 4.8.3 Node.js version from `meta-openembedded` was working correctly. However, even when using 4.8.3, there are open issues like the following:
`https://bugzilla.yoctoproject.org/show_bug.cgi?id=11728`
Until this is fixed in the Yocto 2.4 Rocko branch, the following revert in Poky will leave a working revision:
`git revert ebe531b38bea54bd29ed7b3d2ea6c533b9331953`

There's more...

There is also a `meta-nodejs` layer with alternative versions of Node.js, for example **Long Term Suport** (**LTS**) and maintenance versions. If we want to use it, we first need to clone it into our Yocto installation:

```
$ cd /opt/yocto/fsl-community-bsp/sources
$ git clone https://github.com/imyller/meta-nodejs.git
```

Then, add it to our `conf/bblayers.conf` by doing the following:

```
$ bitbake-layers add-layer /opt/yocto/fsl-community-bsp/sources/meta-nodejs
```

The cross-compilation of some Node.js versions will need `multilibs` installed if building on an x86_64 host. On Ubuntu 16.04 you can add them by doing the following:

```
$ sudo dpkg --add-architecture i386
$ sudo apt-get update
$ sudo apt-get install g++-multilib libssl-dev:i386 libcrypto++-dev:i386
zlib1g-dev:i386
```

To add it to our chosen image, we add the following into either an image recipe or `conf/local.conf`:

```
IMAGE_INSTALL_append = " nodejs"
```

At the time of writing, 6.10.3 is the LTS version and, to select it, we add the following to our `distro.conf` configuration file or `conf/local.conf`:

```
PREFERRED_VERSION_nodejs = "6.10.3"
```

After building our image of choice, for example `core-image-minimal`, we can check Node.js is installed with the following syntax:

```
# node --version
v6.10.3
```

 Note that the v6.10.3 version needed to be patched in order to build with Yocto 2.4. The bbappend with the patch can be found on the `meta-custom` layer of the source that accompanies the book.

See also

- Recipes for community-contributed packages can be found on the companion `meta-nodejs-contrib` layer found at `https://github.com/imyller/meta-nodejs-contrib`
- More information about Node.js can be found on the project's webpage: `https://nodejs.org/en/`
- The NPM package manager and software registry can be accessed at the following URL: `https://www.npmjs.com/`

Running Docker application containers

Back in `Chapter 1`, *The Build System,* we saw how **Docker CE (community edition)** could be used to run an embedded Yocto development environment, and also how to run a Toaster Docker instance. Its use can be extended to test environment replication and chroots environments.

However, this type of lightweight container isolation is not only useful in the host but can also be leveraged on an embedded target. The performance of a container is virtually equivalent to a native application, and they are also light and quick to start and stop.

Docker is Apache 2.0-licensed and provides self-contained applications that can be moved between different machines, so, although it is not yet common, I expect to see Docker used more extensively in embedded systems as it facilitates the deployment and update of embedded applications by separating the core system software from the application layer that runs under Docker. Imagine being able to deploy and manage your software across a range of embedded devices in similar ways as you currently do for cloud applications.

Containers also provide the extra security of knowing that your application is isolated from the operating system and that even if compromised the danger is constrained. You could, for example, isolate a database in a container and a network application in another, having them communicate between them while securely separated, or even have them running on different devices.

This recipe will explain how to install and run Docker on your target.

Getting ready

For Docker to run properly, it needs a recent Linux kernel configured with specific support. The v4.1 kernel in the Wandboard is able to run Docker. However, the default configuration needs to be configured for Docker, for example enabling `OverlayFS` support, among other items.

The following useful script can be used to check whether a running kernel is correctly configured to run Docker: `https://raw.githubusercontent.com/moby/moby/master/contrib/check-config.sh`.

Using it over the standard Wandboard kernel, we find out that the following items need to be added for a minimum Docker configuration:

```
CONFIG_POSIX_MQUEUE=y
CONFIG_CGROUP_FREEZER=y
CONFIG_CGROUP_DEVICE=y
CONFIG_CPUSETS=y
CONFIG_CGROUP_CPUACCT=y
CONFIG_MEMCG=y
CONFIG_CGROUP_SCHED=y
CONFIG_NAMESPACES=y
CONFIG_BRIDGE_NETFILTER=y
CONFIG_NETFILTER_XT_MATCH_ADDRTYPE=y
CONFIG_NETFILTER_XT_MATCH_IPVS=m
CONFIG_BRIDGE=y
CONFIG_VETH=y
CONFIG_DEVPTS_MULTIPLE_INSTANCES=y
CONFIG_OVERLAY_FS=y
```

There are a lot of optional features that have been left out. Check the source code that accompanies the book for this working minimal configuration example.

How to do it...

1. The Docker application is provided by the `meta-virtualization` layer, so we first need to clone it into our FSL community BSP installation with the following code:

```
$ cd /opt/yocto/fsl-community-bsp/sources/
$ git clone git://git.yoctoproject.org/meta-virtualization
```

2. Then, we need to add it to our `conf/bblayers.conf` file with the following:

```
$ bitbake-layers add-layer /opt/yocto/fsl-community-
bsp/sources/meta-virtualization
```

3. We can then checkout the 2.4 branch with the following:

```
$ git checkout -b rocko origin/rocko
```

4. In the same way, we need to add the `meta-networking`, `meta-filesystems` and `meta-python` layers from `meta-openembedded` as dependencies, also on the Rocko branch.

5. The next step is to configure our `distro.conf` or `conf/local.conf` configuration file, as follows:

```
DISTRO_FEATURES_append = " virtualization"
```

6. We can then add some extra space to our image to download containers:

```
IMAGE_ROOTFS_EXTRA_SPACE = "10000"
```

7. Finally, add Docker to the image by adding the following to either the image recipe or `conf/local.conf` files:

```
IMAGE_INSTALL_append = " docker"
```

8. We can then build the image of our choice, for example:

```
$ bitbake core-image-minimal
```

9. Once the build is finished and the images are programmed, we can test Docker by running a `hello-world` container, as follows:

```
$ docker run hello-world
```

10. Alternatively, we can also launch a Busybox container and run the ash shell with the following command:

```
$ docker run -it --rm busybox sh
```

How it works...

Lightweight process virtualizations, or containers, make use of Linux kernel cgroups and namespace support. A namespace abstracts a global system resource so that a process in that namespace appears to have its own isolated instance of a resource. Namespaces include filesystems, processes, network, and user IDs, among other things. In basic terms, cgroups allow us to allocate resources among user defined process groups.

Containers can orchestrate via network sockets and can mount data volumes on the host system. It is common to use Docker volumes to write data from the container to the host, so little data needs to be written to the container itself. However, keeping data inside the container is also possible using Docker storage drivers. From the different storage drivers available to Docker, overlay2, which uses the kernel's `OverlayFS` support, is the default storage as it is the one that provides the best performance and stability.

Docker also provides the following features:

- Application portability
- Automated builds using Dockerfiles
- Git-style versioning
- Reusable containers and a public registry (`https://hub.docker.com/`) for third party containers

Let's see some common Docker commands. To query the Docker daemon, use the following:

```
$ docker info
```

To run a new container, do the following:

```
$ docker run [-d] [--rm] [-i] [-t] <image> <command> <arguments>
```

In the previous example:

- `image` is the name of the container image to run
- `command` is the command to be passed to the container
- `arguments` are the command's arguments

The options shown have the following meaning:

- -d detaches from the container and leaves it running on the background

When running on the foreground,

- -i keeps stdin open even when not attached
- -t allocates a pseudo-tty

  Both (-it) are needed when running an interactive process like a shell.

- --rm cleans up the container and removes the file system on exit. Otherwise they are kept

To list Docker containers, use the following command:

```
$ docker ps -a
```

To attach to a running container, use the following command:

```
$ docker attach <container_name>
```

To stop and remove containers, use the following commands:

```
$ docker stop <container_id>
$ docker rm <container_id>
```

Both container_name and container_id can be obtained from the preceding docker ps command.

See also

- Docker documentation can be found at
  https://docs.docker.com/engine/reference/commandline/docker/

5

Debugging, Tracing, and Profiling

In this chapter, we will cover the following recipes:

- Analyzing core dumps
- Native GDB debugging
- Cross GDB debugging
- Using strace for application debugging
- Using the kernel's performance counters
- Using static kernel tracing
- Using dynamic kernel tracing
- Using dynamic kernel events
- Exploring Yocto's tracing and profiling tools
- Tracing and profiling with perf
- Using SystemTap
- Using LTTng
- Using blktrace

Introduction

Debugging an embedded Linux product is a common task not only during development, but also in deployed production systems.

Application debugging in embedded Linux is different from debugging in a traditional embedded device in that we don't have a flat memory model with an operating system and applications sharing the same address space. Instead, we have a virtual memory model with the Linux operating system sharing the address space, and assigning virtual memory areas to running processes.

With this model, the mechanisms used for kernel and user space debugging differ. For example, the traditional model of using a JTAG-based hardware debugger is useful for kernel debugging, but unless it knows about the user space process' memory mapping, it will not be able to debug user space applications.

Application debugging is approached with the use of a user space debugger service. We have seen an example of this methodology in action with the TCF agent used in the Eclipse GDB. The other commonly used agent is **gdbserver**, which we will use in this chapter.

Finally, we will explore the area of tracing and profiling. Tracing is a low-level logging of frequent system events, and the statistical analysis of these captured traces is called profiling.

We will use some of the tools embedded Linux and Yocto offer, to trace and profile our systems so that they run to their maximum potential.

Analyzing core dumps

Even after extensive quality assurance testing, embedded systems in-field also fail and need to be debugged. Moreover, often the failure is not something that can be easily reproduced in a laboratory environment, so we are left with production, often hardened, systems to debug.

Assuming we have designed our system with the aforementioned scenario in mind, our first debugging choice is usually to extract as much information about the failing system, for example, by obtaining and analyzing a core dump of the misbehaving processes.

Getting ready

In the process of debugging embedded Linux systems, we can use the same toolbox as standard Linux systems. One of these tools enables applications to generate a memory core dump upon crashing. This assumes that we have enough disk space to store the application's entire memory map, and that writing to disk is quick enough that it will not drag the system to a halt.

Once the memory core dump is generated, we use the host's GDB to analyze the core dump. GDB needs to have debug information available. To install debug information, we use the `dbg-pkgs` feature. By default, this installs the debug information of a package in a `.debug` directory in the same location as the executable itself. To add debug information for all packages in a target image, we add the following to our `conf/local.conf` configuration file:

```
EXTRA_IMAGE_FEATURES += "dbg-pkgs"
```

Debug packages can also be added only for those packages we are interested in by adding the debug version of the package to our image with:

```
IMAGE_INSTALL_append = " <packagename>-dbg"
```

We can then build an appropriate toolchain generated to match our filesystem, as we saw in the *Preparing and using an SDK* recipe in `Chapter 4`, *Application Development*. The core dump contains build IDs for the executables and libraries in use at the time of the crash, so it's important to match the toolchain and the target image.

How to do it...

We can display the limits of the system-wide resources with the `ulimit` tool, a command built-in to shells like Bash and BusyBox's ash. We are interested in the core file size, which by default is set to zero to avoid the creation of application core dumps. In our failing system, preferably in a test environment, make your application dump a memory core upon crashing with:

```
$ ulimit -c unlimited
```

The Wandboard's root filesystem will use BusyBox's ash `ulimit` by default. Its output will be different from other shells such as Bash.

You can then verify the change with:

```
$ ulimit -a
-f: file size (blocks)          unlimited
-t: cpu time (seconds)          unlimited
-d: data seg size (kb)          unlimited
-s: stack size (kb)             8192
-c: core file size (blocks)     unlimited
-m: resident set size (kb)      unlimited
-l: locked memory (kb)          64
-p: processes                   5489
-n: file descriptors            1024
-v: address space (kb)          unlimited
-w: locks                       unlimited
-e: scheduling priority         0
-r: real-time priority          0
```

For this example, we will be using the `wvdial` application and forcing a segmentation fault scenario. The purpose is not to debug the application itself but to showcase the methodology used for core dump analysis; so, details regarding the application-specific configuration and system setup are not provided.

To run `wvdial` on the target, use the following code:

```
# wvdial -c
--> WvDial: Internet dialer version 1.61
--> Warning: section [Dialer Defaults] does not exist in wvdial.conf.
--> Initializing modem.
--> Sending: ATZ
--> Sending: ATQ0
--> Re-Sending: ATZ
Segmentation fault (core dumped)
```

The segmentation fault is caused by killing the process with a `SIGSEGV` signal from a different shell as follows:

```
# kill -SEGV <wvdial-pid>
```

The application will create a core file in the same folder, which you can then copy to your host system to analyze. We can control the file name pattern for the core file via the `/proc/sys/kernel/core_pattern` file. A common pattern is as follows:

```
/coredumps/core.<process-name>.<timestamp>
```

We can obtain that with the following:

```
$ echo /coredumps/core.%e.%t > /proc/sys/kernel/core_pattern
```

 The /coredumps directory must exist and be writable by the process for the core dump to be generated.

How it works...

Once in possession of the core dump file, use the cross GDB in the host to load it and get some useful information, such as the backtrace, using the following steps:

First set up the environment in the host:

```
$ source /opt/poky/2.4/environment-setup-cortexa9hf-neon-poky-linux-gnueabi
```

This is using the toolchain we have previously prepared with debug information for all packages.

You can then start the cross GDB debugger, passing it a debug version of the application. Debug versions are stored in the sysroot in the same location as the unstripped binary, but under a .debug directory.

The whole GDB banner looks as follows but will be omitted in future examples:

```
$ ${GDB} /opt/poky/2.4/sysroots/cortexa
9hf-neon-poky-linux-gnueabi/usr/bin/.debug/wvdial core
GNU gdb (GDB) 8.0
Copyright (C) 2017 Free Software Foundation, Inc.
License GPLv3+: GNU GPL version 3 or later
<http://gnu.org/licenses/gpl.html>
This is free software: you are free to change and redistribute it.
There is NO WARRANTY, to the extent permitted by law.  Type "show copying"
and "show warranty" for details.
This GDB was configured as "--host=x86_64-pokysdk-linux --target=arm-poky-
linux-gnueabi".
Type "show configuration" for configuration details.
For bug reporting instructions, please see:
<http://www.gnu.org/software/gdb/bugs/>.
Find the GDB manual and other documentation resources online at:
<http://www.gnu.org/software/gdb/documentation/>.
For help, type "help".
Type "apropos word" to search for commands related to "word"...
```

```
Reading symbols from /opt/poky/2.4/sysroots/cortexa9hf-neon-poky-linux-
gnueabi/usr/bin/.debug/wvdial...done.
[New LWP 560]

warning: Could not load shared library symbols for 14 libraries, e.g.
/usr/lib/libwvstreams.so.4.6.
Use the "info sharedlibrary" command to see the complete listing.
Do you need "set solib-search-path" or "set sysroot"?
Core was generated by `wvdial -c'.
Program terminated with signal SIGSEGV, Segmentation fault.
#0  0x76b43c7c in ?? ()
```

Now point GDB to the location of the toolchain's `sysroot`:

```
(gdb) set sysroot /opt/poky/2.4/sysroots/cortexa9hf-neon-poky-linux-
gnueabi/
Reading symbols from /opt/poky/2.4/sysroots/cortexa9hf-neon-poky-linux-
gnueabi/usr/lib/libwvstreams.so.4.6...(no debugging symbols foun
d)...done.
Reading symbols from /opt/poky/2.4/sysroots/cortexa9hf-neon-poky-linux-
gnueabi/usr/lib/libwvutils.so.4.6...(no debugging symbols found)
...done.
Reading symbols from /opt/poky/2.4/sysroots/cortexa9hf-neon-poky-linux-
gnueabi/usr/lib/libwvbase.so.4.6...(no debugging symbols found).
..done.
Reading symbols from /opt/poky/2.4/sysroots/cortexa9hf-neon-poky-linux-
gnueabi/usr/lib/libuniconf.so.4.6...(no debugging symbols found)
...done.
Reading symbols from /opt/poky/2.4/sysroots/cortexa9hf-neon-poky-linux-
gnueabi/usr/lib/libstdc++.so.6...Reading symbols from /opt/poky/
2.4/sysroots/cortexa9hf-neon-poky-linux-
gnueabi/usr/lib/.debug/libstdc++.so.6.0.24...done.
done.
warning: File "/opt/poky/2.4/sysroots/cortexa9hf-neon-poky-linux-
gnueabi/usr/lib/libstdc++.so.6.0.24-gdb.py" auto-loading has been decl
ined by your `auto-load safe-path' set to "$debugdir:$datadir/auto-load".
To enable execution of this file add
        add-auto-load-safe-path /opt/poky/2.4/sysroots/cortexa9hf-neon-poky-
linux-gnueabi/usr/lib/libstdc++.so.6.0.24-gdb.py
line to your configuration file "/home/alex/.gdbinit".
To completely disable this security protection add
        set auto-load safe-path /
line to your configuration file "/home/alex/.gdbinit".
For more information about this security protection see the
"Auto-loading safe path" section in the GDB manual.  E.g., run from the
shell:
    info "(gdb)Auto-loading safe path"
[...]
```

```
Reading symbols from /opt/poky/2.4/sysroots/cortexa9hf-neon-poky-linux-
gnueabi/lib/libdl.so.2...Reading symbols from
/opt/poky/2.4/sysroots/cortexa9hf-neon-poky-linux-
gnueabi/lib/.debug/libdl-2.26.so...done.
```

You can now inquire GDB for the application's backtrace as follows:

```
(gdb) bt
    #0  0x76b43c7c in __GI___select (nfds=1, readfds=0x7ee58018,
    writefds=0x7ee58098, exceptfds=0x7ee58118, timeout=0x7ee57fe8)
        at /usr/src/debug/glibc/2.26-
    r0/git/sysdeps/unix/sysv/linux/select.c:41
    #1  0x76db3cd8 in WvStream::_do_select(IWvStream::SelectInfo&) ()
        from /opt/poky/2.4/sysroots/cortexa9hf-neon-poky-linux-
    gnueabi/usr/lib/libwvbase.so.4.6
    #2  0x76db3ea4 in WvStream::_select(long, bool, bool, bool, bool)
        ()
        from /opt/poky/2.4/sysroots/cortexa9hf-neon-poky-linux-
    gnueabi/usr/lib/libwvbase.so.4.6
    #3  0x000191bc in WvStream::select (isex=false, writable=false,
        readable=true, msec_timeout=1, this=<optimized out>)
        at /usr/include/wvstreams/wvstream.h:417
    #4  WvDialer::wait_for_modem (this=this@entry=0x7ee58cb0,
    strs=0x0, strs@entry=0x76df4c00 <WvFastString::nullbuf>,
    timeout=1,
        timeout@entry=5000, neednewline=neednewline@entry=true,
    verbose=verbose@entry=true)
        at /usr/src/debug/wvdial/1.61-r0/wvdial-1.61/wvdialer.cc:1357
    #5  0x00019b60 in WvDialer::init_modem
    (this=this@entry=0x7ee58cb0) at /usr/src/debug/wvdial/1.61-
    r0/wvdial-1.61/wvdialer.cc:768
    #6  0x0001c9c0 in WvDialer::WvDialer (this=0x7ee58cb0, _cfg=...,
    _sect_list=<optimized out>, _chat_mode=<optimized out>)
        at /usr/src/debug/wvdial/1.61-r0/wvdial-1.61/wvdialer.cc:119
    #7  0x00014d74 in main (argc=<optimized out>, argv=<optimized
    out>) at /usr/src/debug/wvdial/1.61-r0/wvdial-1.61/wvdial.cc:212
```

Even though the core dump came from a production system with no debug information, by creating a matching `sysroot` with the debug symbols we have been able to show a complete backtrace.

See also

- More details about core dumps can be found on the *core(5)* man page
- The usage documentation for GDB found
  at: `http://www.gnu.org/software/gdb/documentation/`

Native GDB debugging

On devices as powerful as the Wandboard, native debugging is also an option for debugging sporadic failures. This recipe will explore the native debugging method.

Getting ready

For native development, Yocto offers the `-dev` and `-sdk` target images. We can create `-dev` and `-sdk` versions of any image recipe by adding the following image features:

- `tools-sdk`: Adds developing tools to the target image. This is already included in the available `-sdk` images but not on `-dev` images.
- `tools-debug`: Adds debugging tools to the target image. This is already included in the available `-sdk` images but not on `-dev` images.
- `dev-pkgs`: Adds development packages with headers and libraries to the target image. This is included in both `-sdk` and `-dev` image types available.
- `dbg-pkgs`: Adds debug information to all packages in our image.

To just add native GDB debugging capabilities to an image such as `core-image-minimal`, we only need the `dbg-pkgs` and `tools-debug` features, which we can add with the following line in our `conf/local.conf` file:

```
EXTRA_IMAGE_FEATURES += "dbg-pkgs tools-debug"
```

To add complete native development capabilities to `core-image-minimal-dev` for example, we would add the following to our `conf/local.conf` file:

```
EXTRA_IMAGE_FEATURES += "tools-sdk dbg-pkgs tools-debug"
```

To keep the image sizes small we might want to remove the source that is installed alongside the debug package with the following:

```
PACKAGE_DEBUG_SPLIT_STYLE = "debug-without-src"
```

To prepare a development-ready version of the `core-image-minimal-dev` target image, we would execute the following commands:

```
$ cd /opt/yocto/fsl-community-bsp/
$ source setup-environment wandboard
$ bitbake core-image-minimal-dev
```

We will then program the development image to our target.

These images can be quite big and on occasions they exceed the actual size available. Network booting, as explained in *Configuring network booting for a development setup* in `Chapter 2`, *The BSP Layer*, is recommended in those cases.

How to do it...

Once the target has booted, you can start the `wvdial` application through the native GDB using the following steps:

1. In the target Command Prompt, start the GDB debugger with the application as argument:

   ```
   # gdb --args wvdial -c
   ```

2. Now instruct GDB to run the application:

   ```
   (gdb) run
   Starting program: /usr/bin/wvdial -c
   Program received signal SIGILL, Illegal instruction.
   _armv7_tick () at armv4cpuid.S:94
   94              mrrc    p15,1,r0,r1,c14             @ CNTVCT
   ```

3. To obtain the PID of the process being debugged from the GDB console (which we will use later on when we send a signal to it), type the following:

   ```
   (gdb) info inferiors
   ```

4. Then request to print a backtrace:

```
(gdb) bt
#0  _armv7_tick () at armv4cpuid.S:94
#1  0x768c782c in OPENSSL_cpuid_setup () at
/usr/src/debug/openssl/1.0.21-r0/openssl-1.0.21/crypto/armcap.c:157
#2  0x76fde148 in call_init (l=<optimized out>, argc=argc@entry=2,
argv=argv@entry=0x7efffdf4, env=env@entry=0x7efffe00)
at /usr/src/debug/glibc/2.26-r0/git/elf/dl-init.c:72
#3  0x76fde254 in call_init (env=<optimized out>, argv=<optimized
out>, argc=<optimized out>, l=<optimized out>)
at /usr/src/debug/glibc/2.26-r0/git/elf/dl-init.c:30
#4  _dl_init (main_map=0x76fff908, argc=2, argv=0x7efffdf4,
env=0x7efffe00) at /usr/src/debug/glibc/2.26-r0/git/elf/dl-
init.c:120
#5  0x76fceac4 in _dl_start_user () from /lib/ld-linux-armhf.so.3
Backtrace stopped: previous frame identical to this frame (corrupt
stack?)
```

This is not the same backtrace you got when analyzing the core dump. What is going on here? The clue is on `libcrypto`, part of the OpenSSL library. OpenSSL probes the capabilities of the system by trying each capability and trapping the illegal instruction errors. So the `SIGILL` signal you are seeing during startup is normal and you should instruct GDB to continue as follows:

```
(gdb) c
Continuing.
--> WvDial: Internet dialer version 1.61
--> Warning: section [Dialer Defaults] does not exist in
wvdial.conf.
--> Initializing modem.
--> Sending: ATZ
```

5. We will now send the `SIGSEGV` signal from a different shell with the following:

```
# kill -SEGV <wvdial-pid>
Program received signal SIGSEGV, Segmentation fault.
0x76b45c7c in __GI___select (nfds=1, readfds=0x7effdfe8,
writefds=0x7effe068, exceptfds=0x7effe0e8, timeout=0x7effdfb8)
 at /usr/src/debug/glibc/2.26-
r0/git/sysdeps/unix/sysv/linux/select.c:41
41          return SYSCALL_CANCEL (select, nfds, readfds, writefds,
exceptfds,
```

6. And then request the backtrace:

```
(gdb) bt
#0  0x76b45c7c in __GI___select (nfds=1, readfds=0x7effdfe8,
writefds=0x7effe068, exceptfds=0x7effe0e8, timeout=0x7effdfb8)
   at /usr/src/debug/glibc/2.26-
   r0/git/sysdeps/unix/sysv/linux/select.c:41
#1  0x76db5cd8 in WvStream::_do_select(IWvStream::SelectInfo&) ()
from /usr/lib/libwvbase.so.4.6
#2  0x76db5ea4 in WvStream::_select(long, bool, bool, bool, bool)
() from /usr/lib/libwvbase.so.4.6
#3  0x000191bc in WvStream::select (isex=false, writable=false,
readable=true, msec_timeout=1, this=<optimized out>)
   at /usr/include/wvstreams/wvstream.h:417
#4  WvDialer::wait_for_modem (this=this@entry=0x7effec80, strs=0x0,
strs@entry=0x76df6c00 <WvFastString::nullbuf>, timeout=1,
   timeout@entry=5000, neednewline=neednewline@entry=true,
   verbose=verbose@entry=true)
   at /usr/src/debug/wvdial/1.61-r0/wvdial-1.61/wvdialer.cc:1357
#5  0x00019b60 in WvDialer::init_modem (this=this@entry=0x7effec80)
at /usr/src/debug/wvdial/1.61-r0/wvdial-1.61/wvdialer.cc:768
#6  0x0001c9c0 in WvDialer::WvDialer (this=0x7effec80, _cfg=...,
_sect_list=<optimized out>, _chat_mode=<optimized out>)
   at /usr/src/debug/wvdial/1.61-r0/wvdial-1.61/wvdialer.cc:119
#7  0x00014d74 in main (argc=<optimized out>, argv=<optimized out>)
at /usr/src/debug/wvdial/1.61-r0/wvdial-1.61/wvdial.cc:212
```

This result is now compatible with the core dump we saw in the previous recipe.

There's more...

When debugging applications, it is sometimes useful to reduce the level of optimization used by the compiler. This will reduce the application's performance but will facilitate debugging by improving the accuracy of the debug information. You can configure the build system to reduce optimization and add extra debug information by adding the following line of code to your `conf/local.conf` file:

```
DEBUG_BUILD = "1"
```

By using this configuration, the optimization is reduced from FULL_OPTIMIZATION (-O2) to DEBUG_OPTIMIZATION (-O -fno-omit-frame-pointer). But sometimes this is not enough, and you may like to build with no optimization. You can achieve this by overriding the DEBUG_OPTIMIZATION variable either globally or for a specific recipe.

Cross GDB debugging

When we run a cross compiled GDB in the host that connects to a native gdbserver running on the target, it is referred to as cross debugging. This is the same scenario we saw in the *Using the Eclipse IDE* recipe in `Chapter 4`, *Application Development*, except that Eclipse was using the **Target Communications Framework** (**TCF**). Cross debugging has the advantage of not needing debug information on target images, as they are already available in the host.

This recipe will show how to use a cross GDB and gdbserver.

Getting ready

To include gdbserver in your target image, you can use an `-sdk` image if there is one, or you can add the `tools-debug` feature to your image by adding the following to your `conf/local.conf` configuration file:

```
EXTRA_IMAGE_FEATURES += "tools-debug"
```

We will now build our images and program them in the target.

The images running on the target and the toolchain's `sysroot` need to match, and the `sysroot` needs to contain debug information on shared libraries and executables. Before building the SDK we need to configure our `conf/local.conf` file to add debug information as follows:

```
EXTRA_IMAGE_FEATURES += "dbg-pkgs"
```

For example, if you are using `core-image-minimal` images, the SDK needs to have been generated in the same project as follows:

```
$ bitbake -c populate_sdk core-image-minimal
```

This will generate a `sysroot` containing debug information for binaries and libraries.

How to do it...

Once the SDK is installed, you can run the application to be debugged on the target, in this case `wvdial`, using gdbserver.

1. Launch gdbserver with the application to run as argument:

    ```
    # gdbserver localhost:1234 /usr/bin/wvdial -c
    Process /usr/bin/wvdial created; pid = 549
    Listening on port 1234
    ```

    The `gdbserver` is launched listening on localhost on a random `1234` port and is waiting for a connection from the remote GDB.

2. In the host, you can now set up the environment using the recently installed SDK:

    ```
    $ cd /opt/poky/2.4/
    $ source environment-setup-cortexa9hf-neon-poky-linux-gnueabi
    ```

3. You can then launch the cross GDB, passing to it the absolute path to the debug version of the application to debug, which is located in a `.debug` directory on the `sysroot`:

    ```
    $ ${GDB} /opt/poky/2.4/sysroots/cortexa9hf-neon-poky-linux-
    gnueabi/usr/bin/.debug/wvdial
    Reading symbols from /opt/poky/2.4/sysroots/cortexa9hf-neon-poky-
    linux-gnueabi/usr/bin/.debug/wvdial...done.
    ```

4. Next, configure GDB to consider all files as trusted so that it auto loads whatever it needs:

    ```
    (gdb) set auto-load safe-path /
    ```

5. Also, as you know, `wvdial` will generate a `SIGILL` signal that will interrupt our debugging session, so let's instruct GDB not to stop when that signal is seen:

    ```
    (gdb) handle SIGILL nostop
    ```

6. You can then connect to the remote target on the `1234` port with the following:

```
(gdb) target remote <target_ip>:1234
Remote debugging using 192.168.1.105:1234
warning: Unable to find dynamic linker breakpoint function.
GDB will be unable to debug shared library initializers
and track explicitly loaded dynamic code.
0x76fcea80 in ?? ()
```

7. The first thing to do is to set the `sysroot` so that GDB is able to find dynamically loaded libraries:

```
(gdb) set sysroot /opt/poky/2.4/sysroots/cortexa9hf-neon-poky-
linux-gnueabi/
```

8. Type `c` to continue with the program's execution. You will see `wvdial` continuing on the target:

```
--> WvDial: Internet dialer version 1.61
--> Warning: section [Dialer Defaults] does not exist in
wvdial.conf.
--> Initializing modem.
--> Sending: ATZ
```

9. You will then see GDB intercepting a `SIGILL` signal on the host:

```
Program received signal SIGILL, Illegal instruction.
```

10. We will now send the `SIGSEGV` signal to the application from a different shell with the following:

```
$ kill -SEGV <wvdial-pid>
Program received signal SIGSEGV, Segmentation fault.
0x76b45c7c in __GI___select (nfds=1, readfds=0x7effe008,
writefds=0x7effe088,
   exceptfds=0x7effe108, timeout=0x7effdfd8)
   at /usr/src/debug/glibc/2.26-
r0/git/sysdeps/unix/sysv/linux/select.c:41
41                     /usr/src/debug/glibc/2.26-
r0/git/sysdeps/unix/sysv/linux/select.c: No such file or directory.
```

11. You can now ask to see a backtrace:

```
(gdb) bt
#0   0x76b45c7c in __GI___select (nfds=1, readfds=0x7effe008,
      writefds=0x7effe088, exceptfds=0x7effe108, timeout=0x7effdfd8)
      at /usr/src/debug/glibc/2.26-
r0/git/sysdeps/unix/sysv/linux/select.c:41
#1   0x76db5cd8 in WvStream::_do_select(IWvStream::SelectInfo&) ()
      from /opt/poky/2.4/sysroots/cortexa9hf-neon-poky-linux-
gnueabi/usr/lib/libwvbase.so.4.6
#2   0x76db5ea4 in WvStream::_select(long, bool, bool, bool, bool)
()
      from /opt/poky/2.4/sysroots/cortexa9hf-neon-poky-linux-
gnueabi/usr/lib/libwvbase.so.4.6
#3   0x000191bc in WvStream::select (isex=false, writable=false,
readable=true,
   msec_timeout=1, this=<optimized out>)
      at /usr/include/wvstreams/wvstream.h:417
#4   WvDialer::wait_for_modem (this=this@entry=0x7effeca0, strs=0x0,
      strs@entry=0x76df6c00 <WvFastString::nullbuf>, timeout=1,
      timeout@entry=5000, neednewline=neednewline@entry=true,
      verbose=verbose@entry=true)
      at /usr/src/debug/wvdial/1.61-r0/wvdial-1.61/wvdialer.cc:1357
#5   0x00019b60 in WvDialer::init_modem (this=this@entry=0x7effeca0)
      at /usr/src/debug/wvdial/1.61-r0/wvdial-1.61/wvdialer.cc:768
#6   0x0001c9c0 in WvDialer::WvDialer (this=0x7effeca0, _cfg=...,
      _sect_list=<optimized out>, _chat_mode=<optimized out>)
      at /usr/src/debug/wvdial/1.61-r0/wvdial-1.61/wvdialer.cc:119
#7   0x00014d74 in main (argc=<optimized out>, argv=<optimized out>)
---Type <return> to continue, or q <return> to quit---
```

There's more...

To build packages with debug compilation flags, add the following to the conf/local.conf configuration file:

```
DEBUG_BUILD = "1"
```

This changes the compilation flags to debug optimization as follows:

```
DEBUG_OPTIMIZATION = "-O -fno-omit-frame-pointer ${DEBUG_FLAGS} -
   pipe"
```

The -fno-omit-frame-pointer flag will tell gcc to keep stack frames. The compiler will also reduce the optimization level to provide a better debugging experience.

After building and installing the target images and SDK again, you can now follow the same process.

Using strace for application debugging

Debugging does not always involve working with source code. Sometimes it is a change in an external factor that is causing the problem.

Strace is a tool that is useful for scenarios where we are looking for problems outside of the binary itself; for example, configuration files, input data, and kernel interfaces. This recipe will explain how to use it.

Getting ready

To include strace in your system, add the following to your conf/local.conf file:

```
IMAGE_INSTALL_append = " strace"
```

Strace is also part of the tools-debug image feature, so you can also add it with:

```
EXTRA_IMAGE_FEATURES += "tools-debug"
```

Strace is also included in the -sdk images.

Before starting, we will also include pgrep, a process utility that will make our debugging easier by looking up process IDs by name. To do so, add the following to your conf/local.conf configuration file:

```
IMAGE_INSTALL_append = " procps"
```

How to do it...

When printing a system call, strace prints the values passed to the kernel or returned from the kernel. The verbose option prints more details for some system calls.

For example, filtering just the sendto() system calls from a single ping looks as follows:

```
# strace -f -t -e sendto /bin/sh -c "ping -c 1 127.0.0.1"
[pid   430] 21:40:25 sendto(0,
"10\0\2543\256\1\0\0\360\310\255\1\0\0\0\0\0\0\0\0\0\0\0\0\0\0\0\0\0\0"
..., 64, 0, {sa_family=AF_I4
```

How it works...

Strace allows the monitoring of system calls of running processes into the Linux kernel. It uses the ptrace() system call to do so. This means that other programs that use ptrace(), such as gdb, will not run simultaneously.

Strace is a disruptive monitoring tool, and the process being monitored will slow down and create many more context switches. A generic way of running strace on a given program is:

```
strace -f -e <filter> -t -s<num> -o <log file>.strace <program>
```

The arguments are as follows:

- f: Tells strace to trace all child processes.
- e: Filters the output to a selection of comma separated system calls.
- t: Prints absolute timestamps. Use r for timestamps relative to the last syscall, and T to add the time spent in the syscall.
- s: Increases the maximum length of strings from the default of 32.
- o: Redirects the output to a file that can then be analyzed offline.

It can also attach to running processes using the following command:

```
$ strace -p $( pgrep <program> )
```

Or several instances of a process using the following command:

```
$ strace $( pgrep <program> | sed 's/^/-p' )
```

To detach, just press *Ctrl + C*.

See also

- The corresponding man pages for more information about strace at: http://man7.org/linux/man-pages/man1/strace.1.html

Using the kernel's performance counters

Hardware performance counters are perfect for code optimization, especially in embedded systems with a single workload. They are actively used by a wide range of tracing and profiling tools. This recipe will introduce the Linux performance counters subsystem and show how to use it.

Getting ready

The **Linux Kernel Performance Counters Subsystem** (**LPC**), commonly known as `linux_perf`, is an abstraction interface for different CPU-specific performance measurements. The `perf_events` subsystem not only exposes hardware performance counters from the CPU, but also kernel software events using the same API. It also allows the mapping of events to processes, although this has a performance overhead. Furthermore, it provides generalized events that are common across architectures.

Events can be categorized into three main groups:

- **Software events**: Based on kernel counters, these events are used for things such as context switches and minor faults tracking.
- **Hardware events**: These come from the processor's CPU **Performance Monitoring Unit** (**PMU**) and are used to track architecture-specific items, such as the number of cycles, cache misses, and so on. They vary with each processor type.
- **Hardware cache events**: These are common hardware events that will only be available if they actually map to a CPU hardware event.

To know whether `perf_event` support is available for your platform, you can check for the existence of the `/proc/sys/kernel/perf_event_paranoid` file. This file is also used to restrict access to the performance counters, which by default are set to allow both user and kernel measurement. It can have the following values:

- 2: Only allows user-space measurements
- 1: Allows both kernel and user measurements (default)
- 0: Allows access to CPU-specific data but not raw tracepoint samples
- -1: No restrictions

The i.MX6 SoC has a Cortex-A9 CPU, which includes a PMU, providing six counters to gather statistics on the operation of the processor and memory, each one of them able to monitor any of 58 available events.

You can find a description of the available events in the *Cortex-A9 Technical Reference Manual*.

The i.MX6 performance counters do not only allow exclusive access to user or kernel measurements. Also, i.MX6 SoC designers have joined the PMU interrupts from all CPU cores, when ideally they should only be handled by the same CPU that raises them. You can start the i.MX6 with just one core, using the `maxcpus=1` kernel command-line argument, so that you can still use the `perf_events` interface.

To configure the Linux kernel to boot with one core, we set the `UBOOT_EXTLINUX_KERNEL_ARGS` configuration variable to the following and build new images:

```
UBOOT_EXTLINUX_KERNEL_ARGS += "maxcpus=1"
```

The preceding line will change the `extlinux.conf` file included in the filesystem to pass the specified command-line argument to the Linux kernel.

How to do it...

The interface introduces a `sys_perf_event_open()` syscall, with the counters being started and stopped using `ioctls`, and read either with `read()` calls or `mmapping` samples into circular buffers. The `perf_event_open()` syscall is defined as follows:

```
#include <linux/perf_event.h>
#include <linux/hw_breakpoint.h>

int perf_event_open(struct perf_event_attr *attr,
                    pid_t pid, int cpu, int group_fd,
                    unsigned long flags);
```

There is no C library wrapper for it, so it needs to be called using `syscall()`.

How it works...

Following is an example. `perf_example.c` is a program modified from the `perf_event_open` man page to measure instruction count for a `printf()` call:

```c
#include <stdlib.h>
#include <stdio.h>
#include <unistd.h>
#include <string.h>
#include <sys/ioctl.h>
#include <linux/perf_event.h>
#include <asm/unistd.h>
static long
perf_event_open(struct perf_event_attr *hw_event, pid_t pid,
                int cpu, int group_fd, unsigned long flags)
{
    int ret;

    ret = syscall(__NR_perf_event_open, hw_event, pid, cpu,
                  group_fd, flags);
    return ret;
}

int
main(int argc, char **argv)
{
    struct perf_event_attr pe;
    long long count;
    int fd;

    memset(&pe, 0, sizeof(struct perf_event_attr));
    pe.type = PERF_TYPE_HARDWARE;
    pe.size = sizeof(struct perf_event_attr);
    pe.config = PERF_COUNT_HW_INSTRUCTIONS;
    pe.disabled = 1;
    fd = perf_event_open(&pe, 0, -1, -1, 0);
    if (fd == -1) {
        fprintf(stderr, "Error opening leader %llx\n", pe.config);
        exit(EXIT_FAILURE);
    }

    ioctl(fd, PERF_EVENT_IOC_RESET, 0);
    ioctl(fd, PERF_EVENT_IOC_ENABLE, 0);

    printf("Measuring instruction count for this printf\n");

    ioctl(fd, PERF_EVENT_IOC_DISABLE, 0);
```

```
read(fd, &count, sizeof(long long));

printf("Used %lld instructions\n", count);

close(fd);

return 0;
}
```

For compiling this program externally, we can use the following commands:

```
$ source /opt/poky/2.4/environment-setup-cortexa9hf-neon-poky-linux-gnueabi
$ ${CC} ${CFLAGS} ${LDFLAGS} perf_example.c -o perf_example
```

After copying the binary to your target, you can then execute it with the help of the following steps:

```
# chmod a+x perf_example
# ./perf_example
Measuring instruction count for this printf
Used 0 instructions
```

Obviously, using zero instructions for the `printf()` call can't be correct. Looking into possible causes, we find a documented erratum (*ERR006259*) on i.MX6 processors that states that in order for the PMU to be used, the SoC needs to receive at least 4 JTAG clock cycles after power on reset.

Rerunning the example with the JTAG connected and running:

```
# ./perf_example
Measuring instruction count for this printf
Used 3977 instructions
```

 You will need to solder a JTAG connector to the Wandboard as it is not populated by default. Refer to the Wandboard SoM schematics for a pinout of the JTAG1 connector.

Signal name	Wandboard JTAG1 connector Pin number
3.3V	1
nTRST	2
TMS	3
TDI	4

TDO	5
nSRST	6
TCK	7
GND	8

 Alternatively, a free running clock on the JTAG TCK pin can also be used.

There's more...

Even though you can access the `perf_events` interface directly as in the preceding example, the recommended way to use it is through a user space application, such as perf, which we will see in the *Tracing and profiling with perf* recipe in this chapter.

See also

- The *Technical Reference Manual* at
  `http://infocenter.arm.com/help/index.jsp?topic=/com.arm.doc.ddi0388f/B EHGGDJC.html` for more information about the Cortex-A9 PMU

Using static kernel tracing

The Linux kernel is continuously being instrumented with static probe points called **tracepoints**, which when disabled have a negligible overhead. They allow us to record more information than the function tracer we saw in Chapter 2, *The BSP Layer*. Tracepoints are used by multiple tracing and profiling tools in Yocto.

This recipe will explain how to use and define static tracepoints independently of user space tools.

Getting ready

Static tracepoints can be instrumented using custom kernel modules, and also through the event tracing infrastructure. Enabling any of the tracing features in the kernel will create a `/sys/kernel/debug/tracing/` directory; for example, the function tracing feature as explained in the *Using the kernel function tracing system* in `Chapter 2`, *The BSP Layer*.

So before continuing with this recipe, you need to configure the function tracing feature in the Linux kernel as explained before.

How to do it...

The static tracing functionality is exposed via the `debugfs` filesystem. The functionality offered by the interface includes:

Listing events

You can see a list of available tracepoints exposed via `sysfs` and ordered in subsystem directories with the following:

```
# ls /sys/kernel/debug/tracing/events/
asoc                  ipi            regmap
block                 irq            regulator
cfg80211              jbd            rpm
clk                   jbd2           sched
cma                   kmem           scsi
coda                  libata         signal
compaction            mac80211       skb
cpufreq_interactive   migrate        sock
drm                   module         spi
enable                napi           sunrpc
ext3                  net            swiotlb
ext4                  nfs            task
fence                 nfs4           thermal
filelock              oom            timer
filemap               pagemap        udp
ftrace                power          v4l2
gpio                  printk         vmscan
header_event          random         workqueue
header_page           raw_syscalls   writeback
i2c                   rcu
```

Or in the `available_events` file with the `<subsystem>:<event>` format using the following commands:

```
# grep 'net' /sys/kernel/debug/tracing/available_events
net:netif_rx_ni_entry
net:netif_rx_entry
net:netif_receive_skb_entry
net:napi_gro_receive_entry
net:napi_gro_frags_entry
net:netif_rx
net:netif_receive_skb
net:net_dev_queue
net:net_dev_xmit
net:net_dev_start_xmit
```

Describing events

Each event has a specific printing format that describes the information included in the log event, as follows:

```
# cat /sys/kernel/debug/tracing/events/net/netif_receive_skb/format
name: netif_receive_skb
ID: 579
format:
    field:unsigned short common_type;        offset:0;        size:2;
signed:0;
    field:unsigned char common_flags;        offset:2;        size:1;
signed:0;
    field:unsigned char common_preempt_count;        offset:3;
size:1; signed:0;
    field:int common_pid;     offset:4;        size:4; signed:1;
    field:void * skbaddr;     offset:8;        size:4; signed:0;
    field:unsigned int len; offset:12;        size:4; signed:0;
    field:__data_loc char[] name;    offset:16;        size:4; signed:0;
print fmt: "dev=%s skbaddr=%p len=%u", __get_str(name), REC->skbaddr,
REC->len
```

Enabling and disabling events

You can enable or disable events in the following ways:

- By echoing 0 or 1 to the event `enable` file:

```
# echo 1 >
/sys/kernel/debug/tracing/events/net/netif_receive_skb/enable
```

- By subsystem directory, which will enable or disable all the tracepoints in the directory/subsystem:

    ```
    # echo 1 > /sys/kernel/debug/tracing/events/net/enable
    ```

- By echoing the unique tracepoint name into the `set_event` file:

    ```
    # echo netif_receive_skb >>
    /sys/kernel/debug/tracing/set_event
    ```

    Note the append operation >> is used not to clear events.

- Events can be disabled by appending an exclamation mark to their names:

    ```
    # echo '!netif_receive_skb' >>
    /sys/kernel/debug/tracing/set_event
    ```

- Events can also be enabled/disabled by subsystem:

    ```
    # echo 'net:*' > /sys/kernel/debug/tracing/set_event
    ```

- To disable all events:

    ```
    # echo > /sys/kernel/debug/tracing/set_event
    ```

- You can also enable tracepoints from boot by passing a `trace_event=<comma separated event list>` kernel command line-argument.

Adding events to the tracing buffer

To see the tracepoints appear on the tracing buffer, turn tracing on:

```
# echo 1 > /sys/kernel/debug/tracing/tracing_on
```

Tracepoint events are integrated into the `ftrace` subsystem so that if you enable a tracepoint when a tracer is running, it will show up in the trace. This behavior is shown in the following commands:

```
# cd /sys/kernel/debug/tracing
# echo 1 > events/net/netif_receive_skb/enable
# echo netif_receive_* > set_ftrace_filter
# echo function > current_tracer
# cat trace
          <idle>-0      [000] ..s2    66.498472: netif_receive_skb_internal
<-napi_gro_receive
          <idle>-0      [000] ..s2    66.498483: netif_receive_skb: dev=eth0
```

```
skbaddr=d86c2600 len=328
```

How it works...

A tracepoint is inserted using the TRACE_EVENT macro. It inserts a callback in the kernel source that gets called with the tracepoint parameters as arguments. Tracepoints added with the TRACE_EVENT macro allow ftrace or any other tracer to use them. The callback inserts the trace at the calling tracer's ring buffer.

To insert a new tracepoint into the Linux kernel, define a new header file with a special format. By default, tracepoint kernel files are located in include/trace/events, but the kernel has functionality so that the header files can be located in a different path. This is useful when defining a tracepoint in a kernel module.

To use the tracepoint, the header file must be included in any file that inserts the tracepoint, and a single C file must define CREATE_TRACE_POINT. For example, to extend the hello world Linux kernel module we saw in a previous chapter with a tracepoint, add the following code to meta-bsp-custom/recipes-kernel/hello-world-tracepoint/files/hello_world.c:

```c
#include <linux/module.h>
#include "linux/timer.h"
#define CREATE_TRACE_POINTS
#include "trace.h"

static struct timer_list hello_timer;

void hello_timer_callback(unsigned long data)
{
        char a[] = "Hello";
        char b[] = "World";
        printk("%s %s\n",a,b);
    /* Insert the static tracepoint */
        trace_log_dbg(a, b);
    /* Trigger the timer again in 8 seconds */
        mod_timer(&hello_timer, jiffies + msecs_to_jiffies(8000));
}

static int hello_world_init(void)
{
    /* Setup a timer to fire in 2 seconds */
        setup_timer(&hello_timer, hello_timer_callback, 0);
        mod_timer(&hello_timer, jiffies + msecs_to_jiffies(2000));
        return 0;
```

```
}

static void hello_world_exit(void)
{
      /* Delete the timer */
        del_timer(&hello_timer);
}

module_init(hello_world_init);
module_exit(hello_world_exit);

MODULE_LICENSE("GPL v2");
```

The tracepoint header file in `meta-bsp-custom/recipes-kernel/hello-world-tracepoint/files/trace.h` would be as follows:

```
#undef TRACE_SYSTEM
#define TRACE_SYSTEM log_dbg

#if !defined(_HELLOWORLD_TRACE) || defined(TRACE_HEADER_MULTI_READ)
#define _HELLOWORLD_TRACE

#include <linux/tracepoint.h>

TRACE_EVENT(log_dbg,
            TP_PROTO(char *a, char *b),
            TP_ARGS(a, b),
            TP_STRUCT__entry(
                    __string(a, a)
                    __string(b, b)),
            TP_fast_assign(
                    __assign_str(a, a);
                    __assign_str(b, b);),
            TP_printk("log_dbg: a %s b %s",
                    __get_str(a), __get_str(b))
        );
#endif

/* This part must be outside protection */
#undef TRACE_INCLUDE_PATH
#undef TRACE_INCLUDE_FILE
#define TRACE_INCLUDE_PATH .
#define TRACE_INCLUDE_FILE trace
#include <trace/define_trace.h>
```

And the module's `Makefile` file in `meta-bsp-custom/recipes-kernel/hello-world-tracepoint/files/Makefile` would look as follows:

```
obj-m    := hello_world.o
CFLAGS_hello_world.o    += -I$(src)

SRC := $(shell pwd)

all:
        $(MAKE) -C "$(KERNEL_SRC)" M="$(SRC)"

modules_install:
        $(MAKE) -C "$(KERNEL_SRC)" M="$(SRC)" modules_install

clean:
        rm -f *.o *~ core .depend .*.cmd *.ko *.mod.c
        rm -f Module.markers Module.symvers modules.order
        rm -rf .tmp_versions Modules.symvers
```

Note the highlighted line that includes the current folder in the search path for `include` files.

We can now build the module externally, as we saw in the *Building external kernel modules* recipe in `Chapter 2`, *The BSP Layer:*

```
$ cd /opt/yocto/fsl-community-bsp/sources/meta-bsp-custom/recipes-
kernel/hello-world-tracepoint/files/
$ source /opt/poky/2.4/environment-setup-cortexa9hf-neon-poky-linux-
gnueabi
$ KERNEL_SRC=/opt/yocto/linux-wandboard make
```

If you have an existing Yocto build, you can also use it to build the kernel by doing the following:

```
$ KERNEL_SRC=/opt/yocto/fsl-community-bsp/wandboard/tmp/work-
shared/wandboard/kernel-build-artifacts/ make
```

The corresponding Yocto recipe is included in the source that accompanies the book.

After copying the resulting `hello_world.ko` module to the Wandboard's root filesystem, you can load it with the following:

```
# insmod hello_world.ko
Hello World
```

You can now see a new `log_dbg` directory inside `/sys/kernel/debug/tracing/events`, which contains a `log_dbg` event tracepoint with the following format:

```
# cat /sys/kernel/debug/tracing/events/log_dbg/log_dbg/format
name: log_dbg
ID: 864
format:
        field:unsigned short common_type;        offset:0;        size:2;
signed:0;
        field:unsigned char common_flags;        offset:2;        size:1;
signed:0;
        field:unsigned char common_preempt_count;        offset:3;
size:1; signed:0;
        field:int common_pid;    offset:4;        size:4; signed:1;
        field:__data_loc char[] a;        offset:8;        size:4; signed:0;
        field:__data_loc char[] b;        offset:12;        size:4; signed:0;
print fmt: "log_dbg: a %s b %s", __get_str(a), __get_str(b)
```

You can then enable the function tracer on the `hello_timer_callback` function:

```
# cd /sys/kernel/debug/tracing
# echo 1 > events/log_dbg/log_dbg/enable
# echo 1 > /sys/kernel/debug/tracing/tracing_on
# cat trace
<idle>-0        [000] .ns2        64.306483: log_dbg: log_dbg: a Hello b World
```

There's more...

Static tracepoints can also be filtered. When an event matches a filter set, it is kept, otherwise it is discarded. Events without filters are always kept.

For example, to set a matching filter for the `log_dbg` event inserted in the preceding code, you could match either the a or b variables:

```
# echo "a == \"Hello\"" >
/sys/kernel/debug/tracing/events/log_dbg/log_dbg/filter
```

See also

- The Linux kernel documentation at
  `https://git.kernel.org/cgit/linux/kernel/git/torvalds/linux.git/plain/`
  `Documentation/trace/events.txt` for more information regarding static
  tracepoints events
- The *Using the TRACE_EVENT() macro* article series by *Steven Rostedt* at:
  `http://lwn.net/Articles/379903/`

Using dynamic kernel tracing

Kprobes is a kernel debugging facility that allows us to dynamically break into almost any kernel function (except kprobe itself) to collect debugging and profiling information non-disruptively. Architectures can keep an array of blacklisted functions, which cannot be probed using Kprobes.

Because kprobes can be used to change a function's data and registers, it should only be used in development environments.

There are three types of probes:

- `kprobes`: This is the kernel probe, which can be inserted into any location with more than one kprobe added at a single location, if needed.
- `jprobe`: This is the jumper probe inserted at the entry point of a kernel function to provide access to its arguments. Only one `jprobe` may be added at a given location.
- `kretprobe`: This is the return probe and triggers on a function return. Also, only one `kretprobe` may be added to the same location.

They are packaged into a kernel module, with the `init` function registering the probes and the `exit` function unregistering them.

This recipe will explain how to use all types of dynamic probes.

Getting ready

To configure the Linux kernel with `kprobes` support, you need to:

- Define the `CONFIG_KPROBES` configuration variable.
- Define `CONFIG_MODULES` and `CONFIG_MODULE_UNLOAD` so that modules can be used to register probes.
- Define `CONFIG_KALLSYMS` and `CONFIG_KALLSYMS_ALL` so that kernel symbols can be looked up.
- Optionally, define the `CONFIG_DEBUG_INFO` configuration variable so that probes can be inserted in the middle of functions as offsets from the entry point. To find the insertion point, you can use `objdump`, as seen in the following excerpt for the `do_sys_open` function:

```
$ arm-poky-linux-gnueabi-objdump -d -l vmlinux | grep
   do_sys_open
8010bfa8 <do_sys_open>:
do_sys_open():
8010c034:        0a000036        beq        8010c114
   <do_sys_open+0x16c>
8010c044:        1a000031        bne        8010c110
   <do_sys_open+0x168>
```

The `kprobes` API is defined in the `kprobes.h` file and includes registration/unregistration and enabling/disabling functions for the three types of probes as follows:

```
#include <linux/kprobes.h>
int register_kprobe(struct kprobe *kp);
int register_jprobe(struct jprobe *jp)
int register_kretprobe(struct kretprobe *rp);

void unregister_kprobe(struct kprobe *kp);
void unregister_jprobe(struct jprobe *jp);
void unregister_kretprobe(struct kretprobe *rp);
```

By default, a `kprobe` probe is enabled when registering, except when the `KPROBE_FLAG_DISABLED` flag is passed. The following function definitions enable or disable the probe:

```
int disable_kprobe(struct kprobe *kp);
int disable_kretprobe(struct kretprobe *rp);
int disable_jprobe(struct jprobe *jp);

int enable_kprobe(struct kprobe *kp);
```

```
int enable_kretprobe(struct kretprobe *rp);
int enable_jprobe(struct jprobe *jp);
```

The registered `kprobe` probes can be listed through the `debugfs` filesystem:

```
$ cat /sys/kernel/debug/kprobes/list
```

They can be globally enabled or disabled with the following:

```
$ echo 0/1 > /sys/kernel/debug/kprobes/enabled
```

How to do it...

On registration, the `kprobe` probe places a breakpoint (or jump, if optimized) instruction at the start of the probed instruction. When the breakpoint is hit, a trap occurs, the registers are saved, and control passes to `kprobes`, which calls the pre-handler. It then single steps the breakpoint and calls the post-handler. If a fault occurs, the fault handler is called. Handlers can be null if desired.

A `kprobe` probe can be inserted either in a function symbol or into an address, using the offset field, but not in both.

 On occasions, `kprobe` will still be too intrusive to debug certain problems, as it slows the functions and may affect scheduling and be problematic when called from interrupt context.

For example, to place a `kprobe` probe in the `open` syscall, we would use the `meta-bsp-custom/recipes-kernel/open-kprobe/files/kprobe_open.c` custom module as follows:

```
#include <linux/kernel.h>
#include <linux/module.h>
#include <linux/kprobes.h>

static struct kprobe kp = {
  .symbol_name  = "do_sys_open",
};

static int handler_pre(struct kprobe *p, struct pt_regs *regs)
{
  pr_info("pre_handler: p->addr = 0x%p, lr = 0x%lx,"
    " sp = 0x%lx\n",
  p->addr, regs->ARM_lr, regs->ARM_sp);
```

```
  /* A dump_stack() here will give a stack backtrace */
  return 0;
}

static void handler_post(struct kprobe *p, struct pt_regs *regs,
      unsigned long flags)
{
  pr_info("post_handler: p->addr = 0x%p, status = 0x%lx\n",
    p->addr, regs->ARM_cpsr);
}

static int handler_fault(struct kprobe *p, struct pt_regs *regs,
   int trapnr)
{
  pr_info("fault_handler: p->addr = 0x%p, trap #%dn",
    p->addr, trapnr);
  /* Return 0 because we don't handle the fault. */
  return 0;
}

static int kprobe_init(void)
{
  int ret;
  kp.pre_handler = handler_pre;
  kp.post_handler = handler_post;
  kp.fault_handler = handler_fault;

  ret = register_kprobe(&kp);
  if (ret < 0) {
    pr_err("register_kprobe failed, returned %d\n", ret);
    return ret;
  }
  pr_info("Planted kprobe at %p\n", kp.addr);
  return 0;
}

static void kprobe_exit(void)
{
  unregister_kprobe(&kp);
  pr_info("kprobe at %p unregistered\n", kp.addr);
}
module_init(kprobe_init)
module_exit(kprobe_exit)
MODULE_LICENSE("GPL");
```

We compile it with a Yocto recipe, as explained in the *Building external kernel modules* recipe in Chapter 2, *The BSP Layer*. Here is the code for the meta-bsp-custom/recipes-kernel/open-kprobe/open-kprobe.bb Yocto recipe file:

```
SUMMARY = "kprobe on do_sys_open kernel module."
LICENSE = "GPLv2"
LIC_FILES_CHKSUM = "file://${COMMON_LICENSE_DIR}/GPL-
    2.0;md5=801f80980d171dd6425610833a22dbe6"

inherit module

PV = "0.1"

SRC_URI = " \
    file://kprobe_open.c \
    file://Makefile \
"

S = "${WORKDIR}"
```

With the Makefile file in meta-bsp-custom/recipes-kernel/open-kprobe/files/Makefile being as follows:

```
obj-m  := kprobe_open.o

SRC := $(shell pwd)

all:
  $(MAKE) -C "$(KERNEL_SRC)" M="$(SRC)"

modules_install:
  $(MAKE) -C "$(KERNEL_SRC)" M="$(SRC)" modules_install

clean:
  rm -f *.o *~ core .depend .*.cmd *.ko *.mod.c
  rm -f Module.markers Module.symvers modules.order
  rm -rf .tmp_versions Modules.symvers
```

Copy it to a target running the same kernel it has been linked against, and load it with the following:

```
$ insmod kprobe_open.ko
Planted kprobe at 8010da84
```

We can now see the handlers printing in the console when a file is opened:

```
pre_handler: p->addr = 0x8014d608, lr = 0x8014d858, sp = 0xd8b99f98
pre_handler: p->addr = 0x8014d608, lr = 0x8014d858, sp = 0xd89abf98
post_handler: p->addr = 0x8014d608, status = 0x800e0013
post_handler: p->addr = 0x8014d608, status = 0x80070013
```

There's more...

A `jprobe` probe is implemented with a `kprobe`. It sets a breakpoint at the given symbol or address (but it must be the first instruction of a function), and makes a copy of a portion of the stack. When hit, it then jumps to the handler with the same registers and stack as the probed function. The handler must have the same argument list and return type as the probed function, and call the `jprobe_return()` function before returning to pass the control back to `kprobes`. Then the original stack and CPU state are restored and the probed function is called.

Following is an example of a `jprobe` in the open syscall in the `meta-bsp-custom/recipes-kernel/open-jprobe/files/jprobe_open.c` file:

```c
#include <linux/kernel.h>
#include <linux/module.h>
#include <linux/kprobes.h>
static long jdo_sys_open(int dfd, const char __user *filename, int
    flags, umode_t mode)
{
  pr_info("jprobe: dfd = 0x%x, filename = 0xs "
    "flags = 0x%x mode umode %x\n", dfd, filename, flags, mode);

  /* Always end with a call to jprobe_return(). */
  jprobe_return();
  return 0;
}

static struct jprobe my_jprobe = {
  .entry         = jdo_sys_open,
  .kp = {
    .symbol_name  = "do_sys_open",
  },
};

static int jprobe_init(void)
{
  int ret;
```

```
    ret = register_jprobe(&my_jprobe);
    if (ret < 0) {
      pr_err("register_jprobe failed, returned %d\n", ret);
      return -1;
    }
    pr_info("Planted jprobe at %p, handler addr %p\n",
          my_jprobe.kp.addr, my_jprobe.entry);
    return 0;
  }

  static void jprobe_exit(void)
  {
    unregister_jprobe(&my_jprobe);
    pr_info("jprobe at %p unregistered\n", my_jprobe.kp.addr);
  }

  module_init(jprobe_init)
  module_exit(jprobe_exit)
  MODULE_LICENSE("GPL");
```

A `kretprobe` probe sets a `kprobe` at the given symbol or function address which when hit, replaces the return address with a trampoline, usually a nop instruction, where `kprobe` is registered. When the probed function returns, the `kprobe` probe on the trampoline is hit, calling the return handler and setting back the original return address before resuming execution.

Following is an example of a `kretprobe` probe in the open syscall in the `meta-bsp-custom/recipes-kernel/open-kretprobe/files/kretprobe_open.c` file:

```
#include <linux/kernel.h>
#include <linux/module.h>
#include <linux/kprobes.h>
#include <linux/ktime.h>
#include <linux/limits.h>
#include <linux/sched.h>

/* per-instance private data */
struct my_data {
  ktime_t entry_stamp;
};

static int entry_handler(struct kretprobe_instance *ri, struct
  pt_regs *regs)
{
  struct my_data *data;

  if (!current->mm)
```

```
      return 1;   /* Skip kernel threads */

  data = (struct my_data *)ri->data;
  data->entry_stamp = ktime_get();
  return 0;
}

static int ret_handler(struct kretprobe_instance *ri, struct
    pt_regs *regs)
{
  int retval = regs_return_value(regs);
  struct my_data *data = (struct my_data *)ri->data;
  s64 delta;
  ktime_t now;

  now = ktime_get();
  delta = ktime_to_ns(ktime_sub(now, data->entry_stamp));
  pr_info("returned %d and took %lld ns to execute\n",
        retval, (long long)delta);
  return 0;
}

static struct kretprobe my_kretprobe = {
  .handler     = ret_handler,
  .entry_handler    = entry_handler,
  .data_size    = sizeof(struct my_data),
  .maxactive     = 20,
};

static int kretprobe_init(void)
{
  int ret;

  my_kretprobe.kp.symbol_name = "do_sys_open";
  ret = register_kretprobe(&my_kretprobe);
  if (ret < 0) {
    pr_err("register_kretprobe failed, returned %d\n",
        ret);
    return -1;
}
  pr_info("Planted return probe at %s: %p\n",
  my_kretprobe.kp.symbol_name,               my_kretprobe.kp.addr);
  return 0;
}

static void kretprobe_exit(void)
{
  unregister_kretprobe(&my_kretprobe);
```

```
    pr_info("kretprobe at %p unregistered\n",
        my_kretprobe.kp.addr);

    /* nmissed > 0 suggests that maxactive was set too low. */
    pr_info("Missed probing %d instances of %s\n",
      my_kretprobe.nmissed, my_kretprobe.kp.symbol_name);
}

module_init(kretprobe_init)
module_exit(kretprobe_exit)
MODULE_LICENSE("GPL");
```

The highlighted `maxactive` variable is the number of reserved stores for return addresses in the `kretprobe` probe, and by default, it is the number of CPUs (or twice the number of CPUs in preemptive systems with a maximum of 10). If `maxactive` is too low, some probes will be missed.

The complete examples, including Yocto recipes, can be found in the source that accompanies the book.

See also

- The kprobes documentation on the Linux kernel at:
  https://git.kernel.org/cgit/linux/kernel/git/torvalds/linux.git/tree/Documentation/kprobes.txt

Using dynamic kernel events

Although dynamic tracing is a very useful feature, custom kernel modules do not have a user-friendly interface. Fortunately, the Linux kernel has been extended with the support of `kprobe` events, which allow us to set `kprobes` probes using a `debugfs` interface.

Getting ready

To make use of this feature, we need to configure our kernel with the `CONFIG_KPROBE_EVENT` configuration variable.

How to do it...

The debugfs interface adds probes via the
/sys/kernel/debug/tracing/kprobe_events file.

For example, to add a kprobe called example_probe to the do_sys_open function, you
can execute the following command:

```
# echo 'p:example_probe do_sys_open dfd=%r0 filename=%r1 flags=%r2
mode=%r3' > /sys/kernel/debug/tracing/kprobe_events
```

The probe will print the function's argument list, according to the function's declaration
arguments as seen in the function's definition as follows:

```
long do_sys_open(int dfd, const char __user *filename, int flags,
umode_t mode);
```

You can then manage kprobes through the sysfs as follows:

- To see all the registered probes:

```
# cat /sys/kernel/debug/tracing/kprobe_events
p:kprobes/example_probe do_sys_open dfd=%r0 filename=%r1
flags=%r2 mode=%r3
```

- To print the probe format:

```
# cat
/sys/kernel/debug/tracing/events/kprobes/example_probe/format
name: example_probe
ID: 1235
  format:
          field:unsigned short common_type;        offset:0;
     size:2; signed:0;
          field:unsigned char common_flags;        offset:2;
     size:1; signed:0;
          field:unsigned char common_preempt_count;
     offset:3;         size:1; signed:0;
          field:int common_pid;      offset:4;        size:4;
     signed:1;
          field:unsigned long __probe_ip; offset:8;
     size:4; signed:0;
          field:u32 dfd;  offset:12;        size:4; signed:0;
          field:u32 filename;      offset:16;        size:4;
     signed:0;
          field:u32 flags;         offset:20;        size:4;
     signed:0;
```

```
                field:u32 mode; offset:24;        size:4; signed:0;
            print fmt: "(%lx) dfd=%lx filename=%lx flags=%lx mode=%lx",
        REC->__probe_ip, REC->dfd, REC->filename, REC->flags, REC-
        >mode
```

- To enable the probe use the following command:

```
# echo 1 >
/sys/kernel/debug/tracing/events/kprobes/example_probe/enable
```

- To see the probe output on either the trace or trace_pipe files:

```
# cat /sys/kernel/debug/tracing/trace
# tracer: nop
#
# entries-in-buffer/entries-written: 59/59    #P:4
#
#                                  _-----=> irqs-off
#                                 / _----=> need-resched
#                                | / _---=> hardirq/softirq
#                                || / _--=> preempt-depth
#                                ||| /     delay
#           TASK-PID   CPU#  ||||     TIMESTAMP  FUNCTION
#              | |       |   ||||        |          |
              sh-737   [000] d...  1610.378856: example_probe:
   (do_sys_open+0x0/0x184) dfd=ffffff9c filename=f88488
      flags=20241 mode=16
              sh-737   [000] d...  1660.888921: example_probe:
   (do_sys_open+0x0/0x184) dfd=ffffff9c filename=f88a88
      flags=20241 mode=16
```

- To clear the probe (after disabling it):

```
# echo '-:example_probe' >>
/sys/kernel/debug/tracing/kprobe_events
```

- To clear all probes:

```
# echo > /sys/kernel/debug/tracing/kprobe_events
```

- To check the number of hit and missed events (before disabling):

```
# cat /sys/kernel/debug/tracing/kprobe_profile
example_probe                          78              0
```

- With the format being as follows:

```
<event name> <hits> <miss-hits>
```

How it works...

To set a probe we use the following syntax:

```
<type>:<event name> <symbol> <fetch arguments>
```

Let's explain each of the mentioned parameters:

- `type`: This is either `p` for `kprobe` or `r` for a `return` probe.
- `event name`: This is optional and has the format `<group/event>`. If the group name is omitted, it defaults to `kprobes`, and if the event name is omitted, it is autogenerated based on the symbol. When an event name is given, it adds a directory under `/sys/kernel/debug/tracing/events/kprobes/` with the following content:
    - `id`: This is the ID of the probe event
    - `filter`: This specifies user filtering rules
    - `format`: This is the format of the probe event
    - `enabled`: This is used to enable or disable the probe event
- `symbol`: This is either the symbol name plus an optional offset or the memory address where the probe is to be inserted.
- `fetch arguments`: These are optional and represent the information to extract with a maximum of 128 arguments. They have the following format:

```
<name>=<offset>(<argument>):<type>
```

Lets explain each of the mentioned parameters:

- `name`: This sets the argument name
- `offset`: This adds an offset to the address argument
- `argument`: This can be of the following format:
    - `%<register>`: This fetches the specified register. For ARM these are:
        - `r0` to `r10`
        - `fp`
        - `ip`

- sp
- lr
- pc
- cpsr
- ORIG_r0
- @<address>: This fetches the memory at the specified kernel address
- @<symbol><offset>: This fetches the memory at the specified symbol and optional offset
- $stack: This fetches the stack address
- $stack<N>: This fetches the *nth* entry of the stack

And for return probes we have:

- $retval: This fetches the return value

- type: This one sets the argument type used by kprobe to access the memory from the following options:
    - u8, u16, u32, u64, for unsigned types
    - s8, s16, s32, s64, for signed types
    - string, for null terminated strings
    - bitfield, with the following format:

    b<bit-width>@<bit-offset>/<container-size>

There's more...

Current versions of the Linux kernel (from v3.14 onwards) also have support for user space probe events (uprobes), with a similar interface to the one for the kprobes events.

To configure the Linux kernel with user space probes support you need to add the CONFIG_UPROBE_EVENT configuration variable to the kernel configuration file.

Exploring Yocto's tracing and profiling tools

Tracing and profiling tools are used to increase the performance, efficiency, and quality of both, applications and systems. User space tracing and profiling tools make use of performance counters and static and dynamic tracing functionality that the Linux kernel offers, as we have seen in the previous recipes.

Getting ready

Tracing enables us to log an application's activity so that its behavior can be analyzed, optimized, and corrected.

Yocto offers several tracing tools including:

- **trace-cmd**: This is a command-line interface to the `ftrace` kernel subsystem, and `kernelshark`, a graphical interface to `trace-cmd`.
- **perf**: This is a tool that originated in the Linux kernel as a command-line interface to its performance counter events subsystem. It has since then expanded and added several other tracing mechanisms.
- **blktrace**: This is a tool that provides information about the block layer input/output.
- **Linux Trace Toolkit Next Generation** (**LTTng**): This is a tool that allows for correlated tracing of the Linux kernel, applications, and libraries. Yocto also includes babeltrace, a tool to translate the traces into human readable logs.
- **SystemTap**: This is a tool to dynamically instrument the Linux kernel.

Profiling refers to a group of techniques used to measure an application's consumed resources and the time taken to execute an application. The data is then used to improve the application's performance and optimize it. Some of the aforementioned tools such as perf and SystemTap have evolved to become powerful tracing and profiling tools.

Apart from the enlisted tracing tools, which can also be used for profiling, Yocto offers several other profiling tools:

- **OProfile**: This is a statistical profiler for Linux that profiles all running code with low overhead. Although the `oprofile` package is still available, it is not provided as part of the `tools-profile` image feature. Perf is recommended over OProfile as it's easier to use and provides the same, and more, functionality.
- **PowerTOP**: This is a tool used to analyze the system's power consumption and power management.

- **LatencyTOP**: This is a tool used to analyze system latencies.
- **Sysprof**: This tool is included for Intel architectures on X11 graphical images. It does not work on ARM architectures.
- **Valgrind:** An instrumentation framework for dynamic application analysis that detects mostly memory management related errors.

How to do it...

These tools can be added to your target image either individually or with the `tools-profile` feature. To use the tools, we also need to include debug information in our applications. To this extent we should use the `-dbg` version of the packages, or better, configure Yocto so that debug information is generated with the `dbg-pkgs` image feature. To add both features to your images, add the following to your project's `conf/local.conf` file:

```
EXTRA_IMAGE_FEATURES += "tools-profile dbg-pkgs"
```

The `-sdk` version of target images already adds these features.

There's more...

Apart from these tools, Yocto also offers the standard monitoring tools available on a Linux system. Some examples are:

- **htop**: This tool is available in the `meta-oe` layer and provides process monitoring
- **iotop**: This tool is also included in the `meta-oe` layer and provides block device I/O statistics by process
- **procps**: This one is available in Poky and includes the following tools:
  - `ps`: This tool is used to list and provide process statuses.
  - `vmstat`: This is used for virtual memory statistics.
  - `uptime`: This is useful for load averages monitoring.
  - `free`: This is used for memory usage monitoring. Remember to take kernel caches into account.
  - `slabtop`: This one provides memory usage statistics for the kernel slab allocator.

- **sysstat**: This is available in Poky and contains, among others, the following tools:
  - `pidstat`: This is another option for process statistics
  - `iostat`: This one provides block I/O statistics
  - `mpstat`: This tool provides multi-processor statistics

And Yocto also offers the following network tools:

- `tcpdump`: This networking tool is included in the `meta-networking` layer in `meta-openembedded`. It captures and analyzes network traffic.
- `netstat`: This is part of the `net-tools` package in Poky. It provides network protocol statistics.
- `ss`: This tool is included in the `iproute2` package in Poky. It provides sockets statistics.

Tracing and profiling with perf

The perf Linux tool can instrument the Linux kernel with both hardware and software performance counter events as well as static and dynamic kernel trace points. For this, it uses the kernel functionality we have seen in previous recipes, providing a common interface to all of them.

This tool can be used to debug, troubleshoot, optimize, and measure applications, workloads, or the full system, and covers the processor, kernel, and applications. Perf is probably the most complete of the tracing and profiling tools available for a Linux system.

Getting ready

The perf source is part of the Linux kernel. To include perf in your system, add the following to your `conf/local.conf` file:

```
IMAGE_INSTALL_append = " perf"
```

Perf is also part of the `tools-profile` image feature, so you can also add it with the following:

```
EXTRA_IMAGE_FEATURES += "tools-profile"
```

Perf is also included in the `-sdk` images.

To take the maximum advantage of this tool, we need to have symbols both in user space applications and libraries, as well as the Linux kernel. For this, we need to avoid stripping binaries by adding the following to the `conf/local.conf` configuration file:

```
INHIBIT_PACKAGE_STRIP = "1"
```

Also, adding debug information for the applications by adding the following is recommended:

```
EXTRA_IMAGE_FEATURES += "dbg-pkgs"
```

By default, the debug information is placed in a `.debug` directory in the same location as the binary it corresponds to. But perf needs a central location to look for all debug information. So, to configure our debug information with a structure that perf understands, we also need the following in our `conf/local.conf` configuration file:

```
PACKAGE_DEBUG_SPLIT_STYLE = 'debug-file-directory'
```

The debug information will decode symbols, but in order for perf to provide stack traces for user space applications we need to compile them with frame pointers information. As we have already mentioned, this is achieved by adding the following to the `conf/local.conf` configuration file:

```
DEBUG_INFO = "1"
```

By default, perf will use frame pointers to construct a stack trace. However, if frame pointers are not available, recent versions of perf allow to use dwarf debug information and the `libunwind` library instead.

Finally, configure the Linux kernel with the `CONFIG_DEBUG_INFO` configuration variable to include debug information, `CONFIG_KALLSYMS` to add debug symbols into the kernel, and `CONFIG_FRAME_POINTER` to be able to see complete stack traces.

As we saw in the *Using the kernel's performance counters* recipe, we will also need to pass `maxcpus=1` (or `maxcpus=0` to disable SMP) to the Linux kernel in order to use the i.MX6 PMU, due to the sharing of the PMU interrupt between all cores. Also, in order to use the PMU on i.MX6 processors, the SoC needs to receive at least four JTAG clock cycles after power on reset. This is documented in the erratum number *ERR006259*.

How to do it...

Perf can be used to provide a default set of event statistics for a particular workload with:

```
# perf stat <command>
```

For example, a single ping will provide the following output:

```
# perf stat ping -c 1 192.168.1.1
PING 192.168.1.1 (192.168.1.1): 56 data bytes
64 bytes from 192.168.1.1: seq=0 ttl=64 time=6.489 ms
--- 192.168.1.1 ping statistics ---
1 packets transmitted, 1 packets received, 0% packet loss
round-trip min/avg/max = 6.489/6.489/6.489 ms
Performance counter stats for 'ping -c 1 192.168.1.1':
         3.447000      task-clock (msec)         #     0.518 CPUs utilized
                2      context-switches          #   0.580 K/sec
                0      cpu-migrations            #   0.000 K/sec
               40      page-faults               #   0.012 M/sec
          2705987      cycles                    #   0.785 GHz
           682239      stalled-cycles-frontend   #  25.21% frontend cycles
idle
          2162693      stalled-cycles-backend    #  79.92% backend  cycles
idle
           836593      instructions              #   0.31  insns per cycle
                                                 #   2.59  stalled
cycles per insn
            76777      branches                  #  22.274 M/sec
            40112      branch-misses             #  52.24% of all branches
      0.006651333 seconds time elapsed
```

If we are only interested in a particular set of events, we can specify the events we want to output information from using the -e option.

We can also sample data and store it so that it can be later analyzed:

```
# perf record <command>
```

Better still, we can add stack backtraces with the -g option:

```
# perf record -g -- ping -c 5 <ip address>
```

The result will be stored in a `perf.data` file, which we would then analyze with the following:

```
# perf report
```

Its output can be seen in the following screenshot:

```
Samples  24  of event 'cycles', Event count (approx.) 3141263
   Children       Self  Command  Shared Object          Symbol
+  41.90%       0.00%  ping     [kernel.kallsyms]     [k] ret_fast_syscall
+  28.90%       0.00%  ping     [kernel.kallsyms]     [k] ret_from_exception
+  28.90%       0.00%  ping     [kernel.kallsyms]     [k] do_PrefetchAbort
+  28.90%       0.00%  ping     [kernel.kallsyms]     [k] do_page_fault
+  28.90%       0.00%  ping     [kernel.kallsyms]     [k] handle_mm_fault
+  28.90%       7.58%  ping     [kernel.kallsyms]     [k] filemap_map_pages
+  17.54%       0.00%  ping     [unknown]             [.] 0x7ec9971c
+  17.54%       0.00%  ping     ld-2.24.so            [.] open
+  17.54%       0.00%  ping     [kernel.kallsyms]     [k] sys_open
+  17.54%       8.64%  ping     [kernel.kallsyms]     [k] do_sys_open
+  13.94%       0.00%  ping     [kernel.kallsyms]     [k] do_set_pte
+  11.57%       0.00%  ping     [kernel.kallsyms]     [k] __wake_up_parent
+  11.57%       0.00%  ping     [kernel.kallsyms]     [k] do_group_exit
+  11.57%       0.00%  ping     [kernel.kallsyms]     [k] do_exit
+   8.90%       0.00%  ping     [kernel.kallsyms]     [k] putname
+   8.90%       8.90%  ping     [kernel.kallsyms]     [k] kmem_cache_free
+   8.56%       0.00%  ping     [unknown]             [.] 0x7ec99c9c
+   8.56%       8.56%  ping     ld-2.24.so            [.] _dl_map_object_deps
+   8.05%       0.00%  ping     [unknown]             [.] 0x7ec99cdc
+   8.05%       8.05%  ping     ld-2.24.so            [.] dl_main
+   7.58%       0.00%  ping     [unknown]             [.] 00000000
+   7.58%       0.00%  ping     [unknown]             [.] 0x7ec99d04
+   7.58%       0.00%  ping     libc-2.24.so          [.] __ctype_init
+   7.38%       0.00%  ping     [unknown]             [.] 0x7ec99d34
+   7.38%       0.00%  ping     [unknown]             [.] 0x7ec99bd4
+   7.38%       0.00%  ping     libc-2.24.so          [.] malloc_consolidate
+   7.38%       0.00%  ping     [kernel.kallsyms]     [k] unlock_page
+   7.38%       7.38%  ping     [kernel.kallsyms]     [k] __wake_up_bit
+   7.22%       0.00%  ping     [unknown]             [.] 0x7ec9992c
+   7.22%       0.00%  ping     libc-2.24.so          [.] __sbrk
+   7.22%       0.00%  ping     [kernel.kallsyms]     [k] page_add_file_rmap
+   7.22%       7.22%  ping     [kernel.kallsyms]     [k] mem_cgroup_begin_page_stat
+   6.72%       0.00%  ping     [unknown]             [.] 0x7ec999ac
+   6.72%       0.00%  ping     libc-2.24.so          [.] memcpy
+   6.72%       6.72%  ping     [kernel.kallsyms]     [k] v7_flush_icache_all
+   6.61%       0.00%  ping     [unknown]             [.] 0x7ec99a4c
+   6.61%       0.00%  ping     libc-2.24.so          [.] __GI___libc_sendto
```

Perf report TUI interface output

The functions order may be customized with the `--sort` option.

Perf will read kernel symbols from the Linux kernel ELF file under /boot. If it is stored in a non-standard location, we can optionally pass its location with a -k option. If it does not find it, it will fall back to using /proc/kallsyms, where the Linux kernel exports the kernel symbols to the user space when built with the CONFIG_KALLSYMS configuration variable.

If a perf report is not showing kernel symbols, it may be because the ELF file does not match the running kernel. You can try to rename it and see if using /proc/kallsyms works.

By default, perf will try to print user space backtraces by using the frame pointer information if available. If this is not available, we can ask perf to use dwarf debug information instead by doing the following:

```
# perf record --call-graph dwarf -- ping -c 5 <ip address>
```

```
Samples: 38  of event 'cycles', Event count (approx.): 4419691
  Children      Self  Command  Shared Object       Symbol
+  51.66%     0.00%  ping     busybox.suid        [.] _start
+  51.66%     0.00%  ping     libc-2.26.so        [.] __libc_start_main
+  49.01%     0.00%  ping     [kernel.kallsyms]   [k] ret_fast_syscall
+  47.81%     0.00%  ping     busybox.suid        [.] main
+  39.85%     0.00%  ping     busybox.suid        [.] run_applet_and_exit
+  39.85%     0.00%  ping     busybox.suid        [.] run_applet_no_and_exit
-  39.85%     0.00%  ping     busybox.suid        [.] ping6_main
     ping6_main
     run_applet_no_and_exit
     run_applet_and_exit
     main
     __libc_start_main
     _start
-  39.85%     0.00%  ping     busybox.suid        [.] common_ping_main
     common_ping_main
     ping6_main
     run_applet_no_and_exit
     run_applet_and_exit
     main
     __libc_start_main
     _start
+  34.74%     0.00%  ping     ld-2.26.so          [.] _dl_start_user
+  27.38%     0.00%  ping     ld-2.26.so          [.] _dl_start
+  27.38%     0.00%  ping     ld-2.26.so          [.] _dl_sysdep_start
+  23.63%     3.74%  ping     [kernel.kallsyms]   [k] do_page_fault
+  23.12%     0.00%  ping     ld-2.26.so          [.] dl_main
+  19.89%     0.00%  ping     [kernel.kallsyms]   [k] handle_mm_fault
+  19.89%     0.00%  ping     [kernel.kallsyms]   [k] filemap_map_pages
+  15.94%     0.00%  ping     [kernel.kallsyms]   [k] ret_from_exception
+  15.94%     0.00%  ping     [kernel.kallsyms]   [k] do_PrefetchAbort
+  14.02%     0.00%  ping     busybox.suid        [.] sendping4
+  14.02%     0.00%  ping     busybox.suid        [.] sendping_tail
+  13.36%    13.36%  ping     [kernel.kallsyms]   [k] _raw_spin_unlock_irqrestore
+  11.72%     0.00%  ping     ld-2.26.so          [.] _dl_map_object_deps
+  11.72%     0.00%  ping     ld-2.26.so          [.] _dl_catch_error
+  11.72%     0.00%  ping     ld-2.26.so          [.] openaux
```

Perf report TUI interface output with dwarf backtraces

By default, Perf uses a **text-based graphical interface** (TUI). Still, you can ask for a text-only output with the following:

```
# perf report --stdio
```

After executing the preceding command we get the following output:

```
# To display the perf.data header info, please use --header/--header-only options.
#
# Samples: 38  of event 'cycles'
# Event count (approx.): 4419691
#
# Children      Self  Command  Shared Object      Symbol
#
#
  [31m 51.66%[m    0.00%  ping    busybox.suid      [.] _start
            |
            ---_start

  [31m 51.66%[m    0.00%  ping    libc-2.26.so      [.] __libc_start_main
            |
            ---__libc_start_main
               _start

  [31m 49.01%[m    0.00%  ping    [kernel.kallsyms] [k] ret_fast_syscall
            |
            ---ret_fast_syscall
               |
               |[31m--14.56%-- [m__libc_sendto
               |         xsendto
               |         sendping_tail
               |         sendping4
               |         |
               |         |[31m--52.44%-- [mcommon_ping_main
               |         |         ping6_main
               |         |         run_applet_no_and_exit
               |         |         run_applet_and_exit
               |         |         main
               |         |         __libc_start_main
               |         |         _start
               |         |
               |         |[31m--47.56%-- [m__default_sa_restorer
               |                   __libc_recvfrom
               |                   common_ping_main
               |                   ping6_main
               |                   run_applet_no_and_exit
               |                   run_applet_and_exit
               |                   main
               |                   __libc_start_main
               |                   _start
```

Perf report text format output

We can see all the functions called with the following columns:

- `Children`: This represents the percentage of the sampling data (overhead) corresponding to the child processes. They accumulate on the parent process above them.
- `Self`: This represents the percentage of the sampling data (overhead) corresponding to that specific function.
- `Command`: This refers to the name of the command passed to `perf record`.
- `Shared Object`: This represents the ELF image name (`kernel.kallsyms` will appear for the kernel).
- `Privilege Level`: This has the following modes:
    - `.` for user mode
    - `k` for kernel mode
    - `g` for virtualized guest kernel
    - `u` for virtualized host user space
    - `H` for hypervisor
- `Symbol`: This is the resolved symbol name.

In the TUI interface, we can press *Enter* on a function name to access a sub-menu, which will give us the following output:

```
Annotate strcmp
Zoom into ping(1020) thread
Zoom into libc-2.19.so DSO
Browse map details
Run scripts for samples of thread [ping]
Run scripts for samples of symbol [do_page_fault]
Run scripts for all samples
Switch to another data file in PWD
Exit
```

Perf TUI interface function sub-menu

From this we can, for example, annotate the code as shown in the following screenshot:

```
do_page_fault
                        Disassembly of section .text:

                        80018be4 <do_page_fault>:
                            mov    ip,
                            push   {r4, r5, r6, r7, r8, r9, sl, fp, ip, lr, pc}
                            sub    fp, ip, #4
                            sub    sp, sp, #116    ; 0x74
                            mov    r3,
                            bic    r5, r3, #8128   ; 0x1fc0
                            bic    r3, r5, #63     ; 0x3f
                            mov    r6,
                            mov    r4,
                            ldr    r2, [r2, #64]   ; 0x40
                            ands   r1, r1, #2048   ; 0x800
                            ldr    r9, [r3, #12]
                            str    r1, [fp, #-128] ; 0x80
                            mov    r8,
                            moveq  r3, #40 ; 0x28
                            movne  r3, #41 ; 0x29
                            tst    r2, #128        ; 0x80
                            str    r3, [fp, #-124] ; 0x7c
                            ldr    r7, [r9, #196]  ; 0xc4
                            bne    80018c38 <do_page_fault+0x54>
                            cpsie  i
50.00                       bic    r3, r5, #63     ; 0x3f
                            ldr    r3, [r3, #4]
                            bics   r1, r3, #1073741824      ; 0x40000000
                            bne    80018d4c <do_page_fault+0x168>
```

Perf TUI interface function disassembly

If using text mode, we can also get annotated output with the following:

```
# perf annotate -d <command>
```

The annotate command drills down into the function providing disassembled code and interleaved source code using objdump, and also a hit count per instruction.

Perf can also do system-wide profiling instead of focusing on a specific workload. For example, to monitor the system for five seconds, we would execute the following command:

```
# perf stat -a sleep 5
Performance counter stats for 'system wide':
    5006.232669      task-clock (msec)          #    1.000 CPUs utilized
(100.00%)
            415      context-switches           #    0.083 K/sec
(100.00%)
              0      cpu-migrations             #    0.000 K/sec
```

```
(100.00%)
          178        page-faults          #    0.036 K/sec
       58189623      cycles               #    0.012 GHz
(100.00%)
        3954881      stalled-cycles-frontend  #  6.80% frontend cycles
idle      (100.00%)
       49777199      stalled-cycles-backend   #  85.54% backend  cycles
idle      (100.00%)
       11125213      instructions         #    0.19  insns per cycle
                                          #    4.47    stalled

cycles per insn  (100.00%)
        1570462      branches             #    0.314 M/sec
(100.00%)
         304949      branch-misses        #    19.42% of all
branches
         5.005881334 seconds time elapsed
```

Or to sample the system for five seconds, we will execute the following command:

```
# perf record -a -g -- sleep 5
```

When using system-wide measurements the command is only used as measurement duration. For this, the `sleep` command will not consume extra cycles.

How it works...

The perf tool provides statistics for both user and kernel events occurring in the system. It can function in two modes:

- **Event counting** (`perf stat`): This counts events in kernel context and prints statistics at the end. It has the least overhead.
- **Event sampling** (`perf record`): This writes the gathered data to a file at a given sampling period. The data can then be read as profiling (`perf report`) or trace data (`perf script`). Gathering data to a file can be resource intensive and the file can quickly grow in size.

By default, perf counts events for all the threads in the given command, including child processes, until the command finishes or is interrupted.

A generic way to run perf is as follows:

```
perf stat|record [-e <comma separated event list> --filter '<expr>']
    [-o <filename>] [--] <command> [<arguments>]
```

Let's explain the preceding arguments in more detail:

- e: This specifies an event list to use instead of the default set of events. An event filter can also be specified, with its syntax explained in the Linux kernel source documentation at: `Documentation/trace/events.txt`.
- o: This specifies the output file name, by default `perf.data`.
- --: This is used as a separator when the command needs arguments.

It can also start sampling a running process by passing the `-p <pid>` option.

We can obtain a list of all available events by executing the following command:

```
# perf list
```

Or on a specific subsystem with the following command:

```
# perf list '<subsystem>:*'
```

You can also access raw PMU events directly by using the `r<event>` event, for example, to read the data cache misses on an ARM core:

```
# perf stat -e r3 sleep 5
Performance counter stats for 'sleep 5':
        12791        r3
    5.006582001 seconds time elapsed
```

Unless specified, `perf record` will sample hardware events at an average rate of 1000 Hz, but the rate can be modified with the `-F <freq>` argument. Tracepoints will be counted on each occurrence.

Reading tracing data

Perf records samples and stores tracing data in a file. The raw timestamped trace data can be seen with the following:

```
# perf script
```

After executing the command we get the following output:

```
ping  579  224.991897:       29611 cycles:
           80911b10 down_write ([kernel.kallsyms])
           80197b44 load_elf_binary ([kernel.kallsyms])
           8014e60c search_binary_handler.part.4 ([kernel.kallsyms])
           8014f248 do_execveat_common ([kernel.kallsyms])
           8014f6e0 sys_execve ([kernel.kallsyms])
           8000fe40 ret_fast_syscall ([kernel.kallsyms])

ping  579  224.991978:       64466 cycles:
           80361ed0 memcpy ([kernel.kallsyms])
           800e9c60 perf_event_mmap_output ([kernel.kallsyms])
           800e7bc4 perf_event_aux_ctx ([kernel.kallsyms])
           800e9138 perf_event_aux ([kernel.kallsyms])
           800f0dd0 perf_event_mmap ([kernel.kallsyms])
           801284d8 mmap_region ([kernel.kallsyms])
           80128b38 do_mmap_pgoff ([kernel.kallsyms])
           80112c10 vm_mmap_pgoff ([kernel.kallsyms])
           80112c90 vm_mmap ([kernel.kallsyms])
           8019651c elf_map ([kernel.kallsyms])
           80197e18 load_elf_binary ([kernel.kallsyms])
           8014e60c search_binary_handler.part.4 ([kernel.kallsyms])
           8014f248 do_execveat_common ([kernel.kallsyms])
           8014f6e0 sys_execve ([kernel.kallsyms])
           8000fe40 ret_fast_syscall ([kernel.kallsyms])

ping  579  225.000839:      188236 cycles:
           80913550 _raw_spin_unlock_irqrestore ([kernel.kallsyms])
           80420310 extract_buf ([kernel.kallsyms])
           80421374 extract_entropy ([kernel.kallsyms])
           804217cc get_random_bytes ([kernel.kallsyms])
           8019823c load_elf_binary ([kernel.kallsyms])
           8014e60c search_binary_handler.part.4 ([kernel.kallsyms])
           8014f248 do_execveat_common ([kernel.kallsyms])
           8014f6e0 sys_execve ([kernel.kallsyms])
           8000fe40 ret_fast_syscall ([kernel.kallsyms])
```

Perf script output

As we have seen, we can use `perf report` to look at the sampled data formatted for profiling analysis, but we can also generate Python scripts that we can then modify to change the way the data is presented, by running the following line of code:

```
# perf script -g python
```

This will generate a `perf-script.py` script that looks as follows:

```python
import os
import sys

sys.path.append(os.environ['PERF_EXEC_PATH'] + \
        '/scripts/python/Perf-Trace-Util/lib/Perf/Trace')

from perf_trace_context import *
from Core import *

def trace_begin():
        print "in trace_begin"

def trace_end():
        print "in trace_end"

def trace_unhandled(event_name, context, event_fields_dict):
                print ' '.join(['%s=%s'%(k,str(v))for k,v in sorted(event_fields_dict.items())])

def print_header(event_name, cpu, secs, nsecs, pid, comm):
        print "%-20s %5u %05u.%09u %8u %-20s " % \
        (event_name, cpu, secs, nsecs, pid, comm),
```

Generated perf script

To run the script, use the following command:

```
# perf script -s perf-script.py
```

For the previous command to work, you need to install the `perf-python` package in our target image. You can add this to your image with the following line in the `conf/local.conf` file:

```
IMAGE_INSTALL_append = " perf-python"
```

Now you will get a similar output as with the `perf` script earlier, but now you can modify the print statements in the Python code to post-process the sampled data to your specific needs.

There's more...

Perf can use dynamic events to extend the event list to any location where `kprobe` can be placed. For this, configure the kernel for `kprobe` and `uprobe` support (if available), as seen in the *Using dynamic kernel events* recipe earlier.

1. To add a probe point in a specific function execute the following command:

```
# perf probe --add "tcp_sendmsg"
Added new event:
probe:tcp_sendmsg      (on tcp_sendmsg)
```

2. You can now use it in all perf tools, such as profiling the download of a file:

```
# perf record -e probe:tcp_sendmsg -a -g -- wget
http://downloads.yoctoproject.org/releases/yocto/yocto-
2.4/RELEASENOTES
Connecting to downloads.yoctoproject.org (198.145.29.10:80)
RELEASENOTES           100%
|***********************************************************
*******************| 11924    0:00:00 ETA
[ perf record: Woken up 1 times to write data ]
[ perf record: Captured and wrote 0.025 MB perf.data (~1074
samples) ]
```

3. You can view the profiling data by executing the following command:

```
# perf report
```

Then you get the following output:

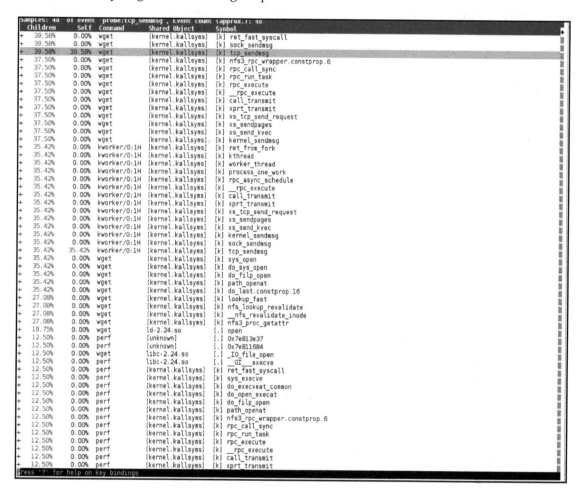

Perf report probe output

You may need to configure DNS servers in your target for the `wget` command, as seen in the preceding example, to work. To use Google's public DNS servers, you can add the following to your `/etc/resolv.conf` file:

```
nameserver 8.8.8.8
nameserver 8.8.4.4
```

5. You can then delete the probe with:

```
# perf probe --del tcp_sendmsg
Removed event: probe:tcp_sendmsg
```

Profile charts

System behavior can be visualized using a perf timechart. To gather data, run the following:

```
# perf timechart record -- <command> <arguments>
```

To turn it into an `svg` file use the following command:

```
# perf timechart
```

Using perf as a strace substitute

Perf can be used as an alternative to `strace` but with much less overhead with the following syntax:

```
# perf trace record <command>
```

However, the Yocto recipe for perf does not currently build this support. We can see the missing library in the compilation log:

```
Makefile:681: No libaudit.h found, disables 'trace' tool, please
install audit-libs-devel or libaudit-dev
```

In order to build perf with trace support we need to add the `audit` package to the `DEPENDS` package list in its recipe, which is available, for example, in the `meta-selinux` layer.

See also

- A list of the available ARM i.MX6 PMU events at:
  http://infocenter.arm.com/help/index.jsp?topic=/com.arm.doc.ddi0388f/B
  EHGGDJC.html
- An extended tutorial in the use of perf at:
  https://perf.wiki.kernel.org/index.php/Tutorial
- Some advanced examples at Brendan Gregg's perf site:
  http://www.brendangregg.com/perf.html

Using SystemTap

SystemTap is a GPLv2 licensed system-wide tool that allows you to gather tracing and profiling data from a running Linux system. The user writes a `systemtap` script, which is then compiled into a Linux kernel module linked against the same kernel source it is going to run under.

The script sets events and handlers, which are called by the kernel module on the specified events triggering. For this, it uses the `kprobes` and `uprobes` (if available) interfaces in the kernel, as we saw in the *Using dynamic kernel events* recipe before.

Getting ready

To use SystemTap, we need to add it to our target image by adding it specifically, as follows:

```
IMAGE_INSTALL_append = " systemtap"
```

Or we can also add it by using the `tools-profile` image feature, or an `-sdk` image.

We will also need an SSH server running on the target. This is already available on the `-sdk` image; otherwise we can add one to our image with the following:

```
EXTRA_IMAGE_FEATURES += "ssh-server-openssh"
```

We will also need to compile the kernel with the `CONFIG_DEBUG_INFO` configuration variable to include debug information, but not the `CONFIG_DEBUG_INFO_SPLIT` as this is not handled well by SystemTap, as well as performance events counters and kprobes (`CONFIG_KPROBES`, `CONFIG_UPROBES`) as explained in previous recipes.

Other kernel configuration parameters needed are `CONFIG_RELAY`, `CONFIG_ARM_UNWIND`, `CONFIG_DEBUG_FS`, `CONFIG_MODULES`, and `CONFIG_MODULE_UNLOAD`, but these are usually part of the default kernel configurations and they are already defined on the default Wandboard's `defconfig`.

How to do it...

To use SystemTap on a Yocto system, we need to run the `crosstap` utility in the host, passing it the `systemtap` script to run. For example, to run the `sys_open.stp` sample script, we can use the following code:

```
probe begin
{
        print("Monitoring starts\n")
        printf("%6s %6s %16s\n", "UID", "PID", "NAME");
}

probe kernel.function("sys_open")
{
        printf("%6d %6d %16s\n", uid(), pid(), execname());
}

probe timer.s(60)
{
        print("Monitoring ends\n")
        exit()
}
```

We would run the following commands:

```
$ source setup-environment wandboard
$ cd </path/to/systemtap_script/folder>
$ crosstap root@<target_ip> sys_open.stp
```

If you get the following error:
`Error: Native (host) systemtap not found.`
It means the host does not have SystemTap installed, which is needed by CrossTap. You can just ask BitBake to build it by doing:
`$ bitbake systemtap-native`

Yocto does not support running scripts on the target, as that would require building modules on the target, and that is untested.

Once the module loads on the target, the host will report all the open syscalls in a 60-second period.

```
Monitoring starts
UID     PID             NAME
  0     622               ls
  0     622               ls
  0     622               ls
```

```
0    622              ls
0    622              ls
0    622              ls
0    622              ls
0    622              ls
0    622              ls
0    622              ls
0    622              ls
0    622              ls
0    622              ls
0    622              ls
0    622              ls
0    622              ls
0    622              ls
Monitoring ends
```

How it works...

SystemTap scripts are written with its own C/awk-like language. They enable us to trace events by using the kernel code at different locations, such as:

- Beginning and end of SystemTap sessions
- Entry, return, or specific offset of kernel and user space functions
- Timer events
- Performance hardware counter events

They also enable us to extract data, such as:

- Thread, process, or user ID
- Current CPU
- Process name
- Time
- Local variables
- Kernel and user space backtraces

Additionally, SystemTap also offers the ability to analyze the gathered data, and allows different probes to work together. SystemTap includes a wide selection of example scripts and a framework for creating script libraries that can be shared. These tapsets are installed by default and can be extended by the user's own scripts. When a symbol is not defined in a script, SystemTap will search the tapset library for it.

See also

- The tapset reference at: `https://sourceware.org/systemtap/tapsets/`
- All examples included in the source at:
  `https://sourceware.org/systemtap/examples/`
- A reference to the SystemTap scripting language at:
  `https://sourceware.org/systemtap/langref/`

Using LTTng

LTTng is a set of dual licensed GPLv2 and LGPL tracing and profiling tools for both applications and kernels. It produces binary trace files in the production optimized **Compact Trace Format** (**CTF**), which can then be analyzed by tools such as **babeltrace**.

Getting ready

To include the different LTTng tools in your system, add the following to your `conf/local.conf` file:

```
IMAGE_INSTALL_append = " lttng-tools lttng-modules lttng-ust"
```

They are also part of the `tools-profile` image feature, so you can also add them with the following:

```
EXTRA_IMAGE_FEATURES += "tools-profile"
```

These are also included in the `-sdk` images.

The default Wandboard Linux kernel is already configured to use LTTng, but other platforms might need to enable `CONFIG_TRACEPOINTS`.

The LTTng command-line tool is the main user interface to LTTng. It can be used to trace both the Linux kernel-using the kernel tracing interfaces we have seen in previous recipes—as well as instrumented user space applications.

How to do it...

A kernel profiling session workflow is as follows:

1. Create a profiling session with the following:

   ```
   # lttng create test-session
   Spawning a session daemon
   Session test-session created.
   Traces will be written in /home/root/lttng-traces/test-
   session-20171213-201520
   ```

2. Enable the events you want to trace with the following:

   ```
   # lttng enable-event --kernel sched_switch,sched_process_fork
   Kernel event sched_switch created in channel channel0
   Kernel event sched_process_fork created in channel channel0
   ```

3. You can get a list of the available kernel events with the following:

   ```
   # lttng list --kernel
   ```

   This corresponds to the static tracepoint events available in the Linux kernel.

4. Now, you are ready to start sampling profiling data:

   ```
   # lttng start
   Tracing started for session test-session
   ```

6. Run the workload you want to profile:

   ```
   # ping -c 1 192.168.1.1
   ```

7. When the command finishes or is interrupted, stop the gathering of profiling data:

   ```
   # lttng stop
   Waiting for data availability.
   Tracing stopped for session test-session
   ```

8. Finally, destroy the profiling session using the following command. Note that this keeps the tracing data and only destroys the session:

```
# lttng destroy
Session test-session destroyed
```

9. To view the profiling data so that it is readable by humans, start babeltrace with:

```
# babeltrace /home/root/lttng-traces/test-session-20171213-201520
```

The profiling data can also be copied to the host to be analyzed.

User space applications and libraries need to be instrumented so that they can be profiled. This is done by linking them with the liblttng-ust and the libdl libraries.

Applications can then make use of the tracef() function call, which has the same format as printf(), to output traces. For example, to instrument the example helloworld.c application we saw in previous chapters, modify the source in meta-custom/recipes-example/helloworld/helloworld-1.0/helloworld.c as follows:

```
#include <stdio.h>
#include <lttng/tracef.h>
int main(void)
{
        printf("Hello World");
        tracef("I said: %s", "Hello World");
        return 0;
}
```

Modify its Yocto recipe in meta-custom/recipes-example/helloworld/helloworld_1.0.bb as follows:

```
DESCRIPTION = "Simple helloworld application"
SECTION = "examples"
LICENSE = "MIT"
LIC_FILES_CHKSUM =
    "file://${COMMON_LICENSE_DIR}/MIT;md5=0835ade698e0bcf8506ecda2f7b4f302"

SRC_URI = "file://helloworld.c"
DEPENDS = "lttng-ust"

S = "${WORKDIR}"
do_compile() {
        ${CC} ${LDFLAGS} helloworld.c -o helloworld -llttng-ust -ldl
}
```

```
do_install() {
        install -d ${D}${bindir}
        install -m 0755 helloworld ${D}${bindir}
}
```

Then build the package, copy it to the target, and start a profiling session as follows:

1. Create a profiling session by executing the following command:

   ```
   # lttng create test-user-session
   Spawning a session daemon
   Session test-user-session created.
   Traces will be written in /home/root/lttng-traces/test-user-
   session-20171214-213957
   ```

2. Enable the events you want to profile—in this case, all the user space events:

   ```
   # lttng enable-event -u -a
   All UST events are enabled in channel channel0
   ```

3. Start to gather profiling data:

   ```
   # lttng start
   Tracing started for session test-user-session
   ```

4. Run the workload—in this case, the instrumented `hello world` example program:

   ```
   # helloworld
   Hello World
   ```

5. Once it finishes, stop gathering data:

   ```
   # lttng stop
   Waiting for data availability.
   Tracing stopped for session test-user-session
   ```

6. Without destroying the session, you can inspect the recorded events by executing:

   ```
   # lttng view
   [21:40:38.250606174] (+0.004467000) wandboard
   lttng_ust_tracef:event: { cpu_id = 1 }, { _msg_length = 19, msg =
   "I said: Hello World" }
   ```

7. Finally, you can destroy the profiling session:

```
# lttng destroy test-user-session
Session test-user-session destroyed
```

How it works...

Kernel tracing is done using the tracing functionalities available in the Linux kernel, as we have seen in previous recipes. For the examples to work, the Linux kernel must be configured appropriately as seen in the corresponding recipes earlier.

LTTng provides a common user interface to control some of the kernel tracing features we saw previously, such as the following:

- **Static tracepoint events**:
    - You can enable specific static tracepoint events with the following:

    ```
    # lttng enable-event <comma separated event list> -k
    ```

    - You can enable all tracepoints with the following:

    ```
    # lttng enable-event -a -k --tracepoint
    ```

    - You can also enable all syscalls as follows:

    ```
    # lttng enable-event -a -k --syscall
    ```

    - You can enable all tracepoints and syscalls as follows:

    ```
    # lttng enable-event -a -k
    ```

- **Dynamic tracepoint events**:
    - You can also add dynamic tracepoints by symbol with the following:

    ```
    # lttng enable-event <probe_name> -k --probe
    <symbol>+<offset>
    ```

    - You can also add them by specifying an address as follows:

    ```
    # lttng enable-event <probe_name> -k --probe <address>
    ```

- **Function tracing**:
    - You can also use the function tracing kernel functionality as follows:

    ```
    # lttng enable-event <probe_name> -k --function <symbol>
    ```

- **Performance counter events:**
    - The hardware performance counters, for example for the CPU cycles, can be used with the following command:

    ```
    # lttng add-context -t perf:cpu:cpu-cycles -k
    ```

    Use the `add-context --help` option to list further context options and perf counters.

Extending application profiling

Further applications tracing flexibility can be achieved with the `tracepoint()` call by writing a template file (`.tp`), and using the `lttng-gen-tp` script along with the source file. This generates an object file that can then be linked to your application.

At the time of writing, Yocto has no standard way to cross-instrument user space applications, but it can be done natively using an `-sdk` image, or adding the following image features to the `conf/local.conf` file:

```
EXTRA_IMAGE_FEATURES += "tools-sdk dev-pkgs"
```

For example, define a tracepoint `hw.tp` file as follows:

```
TRACEPOINT_EVENT(
    hello_world_trace_provider,
    hw_tracepoint,
    TP_ARGS(
        int, my_integer_arg,
        char*, my_string_arg
    ),
    TP_FIELDS(
        ctf_string(my_string_field, my_string_arg)
        ctf_integer(int, my_integer_field, my_integer_arg)
    )
)
```

[412]

Pass this through the `lttng-gen-tp` tool to obtain `hw.c`, `hw.h`, and `hw.o` files:

```
# lttng-gen-tp hw.tp
```

Note that the `lttng-gen-tp` tool is not installed with the `lttng-ust` package, but with the `lttng-ust-bin` package. This, as well as its `python3-subprocess` dependency, has to be added to be the target image, for example, by adding the following in your `conf/local.conf` file:
`IMAGE_INSTALL_append = " lttng-ust-bin python3-subprocess"`

You can now add the `hw.h` header file to your helloworld application that is in the `helloworld.c` file and use the `tracepoint()` call as follows:

```
#include <stdio.h>
#include "hw.h"
int main(void)
{
    printf("Hello World");
    tracepoint(hello_world_trace_provider,  hw_tracepoint, 1, "I said:
Hello World");
    return 0;
}
```

Now link your application with the native `gcc` as follows:

```
# gcc -o hw helloworld.c hw.o -llttng-ust -ldl
```

Note that in order to use `gcc` on the target, we need to build one of the -sdk images, or add some extra features to our image, such as:
`EXTRA_IMAGE_FEATURES = "tools-sdk dev-pkgs"`

To profile your application, do the following:

1. Create a profiling session:

```
# lttng create test-session
Spawning a session daemon
Session test-session created.
Traces will be written in /home/root/lttng-traces/test-
session-20171215-203431
```

2. Enable the specific event you want to profile:

```
# lttng enable-event --userspace
hello_world_trace_provider:hw_tracepoint
UST event hello_world_trace_provider:hw_tracepoint created in
channel channel0
```

3. Start gathering profiling data:

```
# lttng start
Tracing started for session test-session
```

4. Run the workload to profile—in this case the helloworld application:

```
# ./hw
Hello World
```

5. Stop gathering data:

```
# lttng stop
```

6. Now inspect the recorded events with:

```
# lttng view
[20:35:55.477038948] (+?.?????????) wandboard
hello_world_trace_provider:hw_tracepoint: { cpu_id = 2 }, {
my_string_field = "I said: Hello World", my_integer_field = 1 }
```

7. Finally, destroy the profiling session:

```
# lttng destroy test-session
```

There's more...

You can also use the Trace Compass application or Eclipse plugin to analyze the traces in the host by visiting
http://projects.eclipse.org/projects/tools.tracecompass/downloads. Trace Compass supports not only the LTTng output format, but a wide variety of other formats including the **Common Trace Format** (**CFT**) that can be exported from recent versions of the perf tool. It is now included as part of the Eclipse IDE for C/C++ Developers.

See also

- Details on using LTTng at: `http://lttng.org/docs/`
- Details about the instrumenting of C applications at: `http://lttng.org/docs/#doc-c-application`
- A `tracepoint()` example in the `lttng-ust` source at: `http://git.lttng.org/?p=lttng-ust.git;a=blob;f=tests/hello/hello.c;h=058f7fae10abaa2c7c5a957c1bdc80fe40f8f8f1;hb=HEAD#198`

Using blktrace

There are a few tools available to perform block devices I/O monitoring and profiling.

`iotop`, which we mentioned in the *Exploring Yocto's tracing and profiling tools* recipe, gives a general idea of the throughput on a system and a particular process. `iostat` provides many more statistics regarding CPU usage and device utilization, but does not provide per process details. Finally, `blktrace`, a GPLv2 licensed tool that monitors specific block devices' I/O at a low level, and can also compute **I/O operations per second** (**IOPS**).

This recipe will explain how to use `blktrace` to trace block devices and `blkparse`, to convert the traces into human readable format.

Flash filesystems, even if they are presented to the user space as block devices, cannot be profiled with `blktrace`.

Getting ready

To use `blktrace` and `blkparse`, you can add them to the target image by adding them specifically to your `conf/local.conf` file as in the following:

```
IMAGE_INSTALL_append = " blktrace"
```

Alternatively, you can also use the `tools-profile` image feature, or an `-sdk` image.

You will also need to configure the Linux kernel with `CONFIG_FTRACE` and `CONFIG_BLK_DEV_IO_TRACE` to be able to trace block I/O actions.

When profiling a block device, it is important to minimize the effect of the tracing on the results; for example, not storing the tracing data on the block device being profiled.

There are several ways to achieve this:

- Running the trace from a different block device.
- Running the trace from a RAM-based `tmpfs` device (such as `/var/volatile`). However, running from a memory-based device will limit the amount of tracing data that can be stored.
- Running the trace from a network-mounted filesystem.
- Running the trace over the network.

Also, the filesystem being used in the block device to profile is an important factor, as filesystem features, such as journaling, will distort the I/O statistics. In order to disable the journal on an ext4 filesystem we will need the `tune2fs` utility, and we will also need the `e2fsck` filesystem check utility, both of which can be added to the filesystem with the following line in our `conf/local.conf`:

```
IMAGE_INSTALL_append = " e2fsprogs-tune2fs e2fsprogs-e2fsck"
```

How to do it...

Let's imagine you want to profile the I/O for the microSD card device on the Wandboard. By booting the system from the network, as seen in the *Configuring network booting for a development setup* recipe from Chapter 1, *The Build System*, you can avoid unnecessary access to the device by the system.

For this example, we will disable the journal from the ext4 partition by doing the following:

```
# e2fsck /dev/mmcblk2p1
# tune2fs -O ^has_journal /dev/mmcblk2p1
```

Check that `/dev/mmcblk2p1` is the correct partition for your device by checking into the boot log messages with the `dmesg` command. You should see something like the following:

```
[ 0.000000] mmc2: SDHCI controller on 2198000.usdhc
[2198000.usdhc] using ADMA
[ 0.000000] mmc2: host does not support reading read-only
switch, assuming write-enable
[ 0.000000] mmc2: new high speed SDHC card at address
1234
[ 0.000000] mmcblk2: mmc2:1234 SA04G 3.68 GiB
[ 0.000000] mmcblk2: p1
```

And then mount it with the following:

```
# mount /dev/mmcblk2p1 /mnt
EXT4-fs (mmcblk2p1): mounted filesystem without journal. Opts: (null)
```

Other tweaks may be needed for effective profiling of a specific workload.

The workflow to profile a specific workload is as follows:

1. Start `blktrace` to gather tracing data on the `/dev/mmcblk2` device with the following:

    ```
    # blktrace /dev/mmcblk2
    ```

2. Start the workload to profile, for example, the creation of a 10 KB file. Open an SSH connection to the target and execute the following:

    ```
    # dd if=/dev/urandom of=/mnt/home/root/random-10k-file bs=1k
    count=10 conv=fsync
    10+0 records in
    10+0 records out
    10240 bytes (10 kB, 10 KiB) copied, 2.1445 s, 4.8 kB/s
    ```

3. Stop the profiling on the console with *Ctrl* + *C*. This will create a file in the same directory called `mmcblk2.blktrace.0`. You will see the following output:

    ```
    === mmcblk2 ===
      CPU  0:          32 events,        2 KiB data
      CPU  1:           1 events,        1 KiB data
      CPU  2:          22 events,        2 KiB data
      CPU  3:           0 events,        0 KiB data
      Total:          55 events (dropped 0),       3 KiB
    data
    ```

Some useful options for `blktrace` are:

- `-w`: This is used to run only for the specified number of seconds
- `-a`: This adds a mask to the current file, where the masks can be:
  - `barrier`: This refers to the barrier attribute
  - `complete`: This refers to an operation completed by the driver
  - `fs`: These are the FS requests
  - `issue`: This option refers to operations issued to the driver
  - `pc`: This refers to packet command events
  - `queue`: This option represents queue operations
  - `read`: This refers to read traces
  - `requeue`: This is used for requeue operations
  - `sync`: This represents synchronous attributes
  - `write`: This refers to write traces

How it works...

Once you have gathered the tracing data, you can process it with `blkparse` as follows:

```
# blkparse mmcblk2
```

This provides an `stdout` output for all the gathered data, and a final summary, as follows:

```
Input file mmcblk2.blktrace.0 added
Input file mmcblk2.blktrace.1 added
Input file mmcblk2.blktrace.2 added
179,0    0         1    0.000000000    645  A  WS 1056768 + 24 <- (179,1)
1048576
179,0    0         2    0.000005667    645  Q  WS 1056768 + 24 [dd]
179,0    0         3    0.000021667    645  G  WS 1056768 + 24 [dd]
179,0    0         4    0.000029000    645  P   N [dd]
179,0    0         5    0.000047334    645  I  WS 1056768 + 24 [dd]
179,0    0         6    0.000054667    645  U   N [dd] 1
179,0    0         7    0.000104667     95  D  WS 1056768 + 24 [mmcqd/2]
179,0    0         8    0.711890667     95  C  WS 1056768 + 24 [0]
179,0    0         9    0.712024667    645  A  WSM 25184 + 8 <- (179,1) 16992
179,0    0        10    0.712027334    645  Q  WSM 25184 + 8 [dd]
179,0    0        11    0.712036334    645  G  WSM 25184 + 8 [dd]
179,0    0        12    0.712044667    645  I  WSM 25184 + 8 [dd]
179,0    0        13    0.712073667     95  D  WSM 25184 + 8 [mmcqd/2]
179,0    0        14    1.428851001     95  C  WSM 25184 + 8 [0]
```

```
179,0    0         15     1.428936334   645   A WSM 170024 + 8 <- (179,1)
161832
179,0    0         16     1.428938667   645   Q WSM 170024 + 8 [dd]
179,0    0         17     1.428946001   645   G WSM 170024 + 8 [dd]
179,0    0         18     1.428950667   645   P   N [dd]
179,0    0         19     1.428959001   645   I WSM 170024 + 8 [dd]
179,0    0         20     1.428964667   645   U   N [dd] 1
179,0    0         21     1.428993667    95   D WSM 170024 + 8 [mmcqd/2]
179,0    0         22     2.135076667    95   C WSM 170024 + 8 [0]
.........
CPU0 (mmcblk2):
Reads Queued:         0,        0KiB    Writes Queued:         3,
20KiB
Read Dispatches:      0,        0KiB    Write Dispatches:      5,
28KiB
Reads Requeued:       0             Writes Requeued:      0
Reads Completed:      0,        0KiB    Writes Completed:      7,
36KiB
Read Merges:          0,        0KiB    Write Merges:          0,
0KiB
Read depth:           0             Write depth:          2
IO unplugs:           2             Timer unplugs:        0
CPU2 (mmcblk2):
Reads Queued:         0,        0KiB    Writes Queued:         4,
16KiB
Read Dispatches:      0,        0KiB    Write Dispatches:      2,
8KiB
Reads Requeued:       0             Writes Requeued:      0
Reads Completed:      0,        0KiB    Writes Completed:      0,
0KiB
Read Merges:          0,        0KiB    Write Merges:          0,
0KiB
Read depth:           0             Write depth:          2
IO unplugs:           1             Timer unplugs:        0
Total (mmcblk2):
Reads Queued:         0,        0KiB    Writes Queued:         7,
36KiB
Read Dispatches:      0,        0KiB    Write Dispatches:      7,
36KiB
Reads Requeued:       0             Writes Requeued:      0
Reads Completed:      0,        0KiB    Writes Completed:      7,
36KiB
Read Merges:          0,        0KiB    Write Merges:          0,
0KiB
IO unplugs:           3             Timer unplugs:        0
Throughput (R/W): 0KiB/s / 1KiB/s
Events (mmcblk2): 48 entries
Skips: 0 forward (0 -   0.0%)
```

The output format from `blkparse` is as follows:

```
179,0    0       7     0.000181333     83  D   W 1138688 + 8    [mmcqd/2]
```

This corresponds to the following:

```
<mayor,minor> <cpu> <seq_nr> <timestamp> <pid> <actions> <rwbs>
<start block> + <nr of blocks> <command>
```

The actions column corresponds to:

- A: I/O remapped to a different device
- B: I/O bounced
- C: I/O completed
- D: I/O issued to driver
- F: I/O front merged with request on queue
- G: Get request
- I: I/O inserted into request queue
- M: I/O back merged with request on queue
- P: Plug request
- Q: I/O handled by request queue code
- S: Sleep request
- T: Unplug due to timeout
- U: Unplug request
- X: Split

The RWBS field corresponds to:

- R: Read
- W: Write
- B: Barrier
- S: Synchronous

Another way of tracing non-disruptively is using live monitoring, that is, piping the output of `blktrace` to `blkparse` directly without writing anything to disk, as follows:

```
# blktrace /dev/mmcblk2 -o - | blkparse -i -
```

This can also be done in just one line:

```
# btrace /dev/mmcblk2
```

There's more...

The `blktrace` command can also send the tracing data over the network so that it is stored on a different device.

For this, start `blktrace` on the host system that is going to hold the data as follows:

```
$ sudo blktrace -l
```

And on the target device, run another instance as follows:

```
# blktrace -d /dev/mmcblk2 -h <host_ip>
```

Also on the target, but on a different SSH connection, you can now execute the specific workload you want to trace:

```
# dd if=/dev/urandom of=/mnt/home/root/random-10k-file bs=1k count=10
  conv=fsync
10+0 records in
10+0 records out
10240 bytes (10 kB) copied, 0.00585167 s, 1.7 MB/s
```

Once it finishes, interrupt the `blktrace` on the target with *Ctrl + C*. A summary will be printed at both the target and the host. On the host, a new directory with the tracing data has been created with the format:

```
<ipaddress>-<date>-<time>
```

You can now run `blkparse` on the host to process the gathered data by providing the directory path and the device name:

```
$ blkparse -D <directory-name> mmcblk2
```

Other Books You May Enjoy

If you enjoyed this book, you may be interested in these other books by Packt:

Embedded Linux Development using Yocto Projects
Otavio Salvador, Daiane Angolini

ISBN: 978-1-78847-046-9

- Understand the basic concepts involved in Poky workflows along with configuring and preparing the Poky build environment.
- Configure a build server and customize images using Toaster.
- Generate images and fit packages into created images using BitBake.
- Support the development process by setting up and using Package feeds.
- Debug Yocto Project by configuring Poky.
- Build an image for the BeagleBone Black, RaspberryPi 3, and Wandboard, and boot it from an SD card.

Linux Device Drivers Development
John Madieu

ISBN: 978-1-78528-000-9

- Use kernel facilities to develop powerful drivers
- Develop drivers for widely used I2C and SPI devices and use the regmap API
- Write and support devicetree from within your drivers
- Program advanced drivers for network and frame buffer devices
- Delve into the Linux irqdomain API and write interrupt controller drivers
- Enhance your skills with regulator and PWM frameworks
- Develop measurement system drivers with IIO framework
- Get the best from memory management and the DMA subsystem
- Access and manage GPIO subsystems and develop GPIO controller drivers

Leave a review - let other readers know what you think

Please share your thoughts on this book with others by leaving a review on the site that you bought it from. If you purchased the book from Amazon, please leave us an honest review on this book's Amazon page. This is vital so that other potential readers can see and use your unbiased opinion to make purchasing decisions, we can understand what our customers think about our products, and our authors can see your feedback on the title that they have worked with Packt to create. It will only take a few minutes of your time, but is valuable to other potential customers, our authors, and Packt. Thank you!

Index